The *Deutschlandbilc*

Diane Milburn

The *Deutschlandbild* of A. R. Orage and the *New Age* Circle

PETER LANG

Frankfurt am Main · Berlin · Bern · New York · Paris · Wien

Die Deutsche Bibliothek - CIP-Einheitsaufnahme

Milburn, Diane:

The Deutschlandbild of A. R. Orage and the New Age circle /
Diane Milburn. - Frankfurt am Main ; Berlin ; Bern ; New
York ; Paris ; Wien : Lang, 1996
   Zugl.: Leeds, Univ., Diss., 1994
   ISBN 3-631-49558-7

ISBN 3-631-49558-7
US-ISBN 0-8204-2957-0

© Peter Lang GmbH
Europäischer Verlag der Wissenschaften
Frankfurt am Main 1996
All rights reserved.

Printed in Germany 1 2 3 4   6 7

Contents

List of Illustrations   11

List of Abbreviations   13

Acknowledgements   15

Introduction   17

Alfred Richard Orage: 'a desperado of genius'   17
Early Life and Development of the 'swordsman of the mind'   19
Holbrook Jackson: 'My dear Jackson...'   20
Plans for the *New Age*: 'I like the idea of a magazine'   21
Bernard Shaw: 'The Philosopher'   22

1. Germany and the *New Age*: May 1907-October 1908   25

Reducing 'Leeds to Nietzscheism'   25
The Leeds Arts Club: developing 'supermania'   26
Bernard Shaw and Germany: 'I can neither claim knowledge of the
German language nor plead ignorance of it'   28
The *New Age*: 'An Independent Socialist Review of Politics,
Literature and Art'   30
Orage's 'Socialist *Spectator*'   31
Armament: the need to resist 'the wanton aggression of other nations'   32
Cecil Chesterton: 'Artistically it would be an anti-climax to assassinate
the German Emperor'   34
Concern about 'the fear of sudden attack which now animates the pens
of English sensational journalism'   35
Book Reviews: *Die sexuelle Frage* 'a book for cultured persons'   37
Nietzsche 'will always appeal to the Latin more than the Teutonic
temperament'   38
A. R. Orage: 'the difficulties of Nietzsche in England'   39
Nietzsche in Translation   41
Max Nordau and 'his gospel of *Entartung*'   41

German Drama in London: 'Anyone who has ever been through a
German reading primer should catch on at once'   43
Music: 'Oh! for an English Nietzsche'   44

2. Germany and the *New Age*: November 1908-October 1910   47

'Scare' Novels: The Coming War with Germany   48
S. Verdad: Germany seeks 'a war with England'   52
Nietzsche in English   53
Nietzsche: 'A Lyrical Bismarck'   56
Book Reviews: 'to most Englishmen modern German poetry is virgin
soil'   58
Katherine Mansfield: *In a German Pension*   60
Ashley Dukes: 'the German-speaking public takes its theatre seriously' 62
Bernard Shaw in German: 'every German book seems to have a new
vocabulary of its own'   64
August Strindberg: 'there is hardly a repertory theatre in the smallest
German town where some of his plays at least have not been performed' 66
Ludwig Thoma: 'a decatholicised, altogether unmoral, Rabelaisian
Chesterton'   67
Recent German Drama: Gerhart Hauptmann, Hermann Sudermann,
Frank Wedekind   67
Arthur Schnitzler: 'nothing to do with moralists or morality'   70
Music: The Hallé Orchestra is so 'intensely German' that 'English
composers need not apply'   70

3. Germany and the *New Age*: November 1910-August 1914   73

The *New Statesman*: 'as dull as a privet hedge in Leeds'   73
J. M. Kennedy: in the grip of the 'German eagle's talons'   76
Nostalgia for the old Germany: 'a land where the inhabitants were lost
in the clouds of abstract, idealistic, romantic thought'   78
French Civilisation versus German Culture   80
General Friedrich von Bernhardi: *Germany and the Next War*   84
Orage and Foreign Affairs: 'The brute Bismarck'   86
Book Reviews   88
Paul Selver: guilty of a 'wholly romantic' attitude towards Germany 89
R.H.C.: 'Readers and Writers'   91
The Nietzscheans: J. M. Kennedy and A. M. Ludovici   93
A. E. Randall: August Bebel is 'the enemy of democracy'   94
Orage: Nietzsche 'never really transcended his negative doctrine at all' 96

Orage and the Nietzscheans: 'parasites on the weakness of Nietzsche,
parasites on his defects and mistakes'   100
Henri Bergson: 'the intellectual has no energy, no élan vital, no "go"
in him'   101
F. T. Marinetti: 'We wish to glorify war'   103
Orage and France: 'Down with the Tricolour'   105
Katherine Mansfield: the English as a nation 'are dying for war'   105
Ashley Dukes: the 'Art of Theatre'   107
Huntley Carter: theatre-goers are tired of 'hyper-modern perversities
and mortuary atrocities'   108
Music: Strauss and Schönberg   111

4. Germany and the *New Age*: August 1914-December 1916   113

English writers on the Germans: 'a people who had suddenly
become incredible'   114
Bernard Shaw: 'both armies should shoot their officers and go home'   117
J. M. Kennedy: the war as 'racial conflict between Slav and Teuton'   119
Ramiro de Maeztu: war as 'the organisation of adventure'   124
T. E. Hulme: 'the German army offers a career...'   127
Conscription: 'the essential feature of the Prussian system'   128
Pacifism: an outrage to 'the proprieties of language'   130
Beatrice Hastings: 'no possibility of suddenly hating my German
friends'   132
A. R. Orage: confronting 'the nakedness of the Teuton'   134
Oscar Levy: 'I am an "Alien" of yours'   139
Nietzsche and Treitschke: 'Nitch and Tritch'   142
Bernhardi: war as 'a condition of civilisation'   146
J. A. Cramb: 'an embracing of Bernhardi's big boots'   148
Nietzsche or Carlyle?   151
Books for Wartime: 'Huns and Hohenzollerns'   153
Werner Sombart: 'Faust and Zarathustra and Beethoven in the rifle-pit'   155
R.H.C.: German Literature 'in the period before the Fall'   156
Paul Selver: 'heartily sick of the yelp, yelp, yelp about Huns'   158
'Russian versus German Culture'   159

5. Germany and the *New Age*: January 1917-October 1919   161

Search for new values after the war: Shaw - hailing the Russian
revolution and Lenin   162

The *New Age*: in need of money 'to be frittered away in salaries to
the clerical and editorial staff'   163

A. R. Orage: 'the jackboot we have taken off the German people is
now on the other leg'   164

Germans 'are men even if they are possessed by a collective madness'   167

Prince Lichnowsky: 'the man who first broke the evil spell that has
been cast on Germany'   167

Allied war aims: to defeat 'the attempt of Militarism to strangle
Democracy in the cradle'   168

Prussia at war: 'with *kultur* in one hand and a bomb in the other'   169

Any man expecting a revolution in Germany 'should have his mind
inquired into'   172

Germany facing 'the choice between revolution and perpetual war'   172

German Social Democrats: the only 'section that has not yet been
hopelessly ingrained with Prussian theories'   173

Looking forward to 'the democratisation of Germany'   173

Armistice: exchanging 'the black flag of militarism for the white flag
of surrender'   175

Europe in 1919: 'the cessation of war has not brought peace'   177

J. M. Kennedy: 'a bit of a mystery-monger, if not a downright
mystery-man'   178

G. K. Chesterton: 'Prussia is like prussic acid; its poisonous
essence is a fact'   179

Chesterton and the *New Witness*: seeking 'to merely vilify the
Prussians'   180

Ramiro de Maeztu: 'an outsider, who culturally at least was a
Germanophile'   182

George D. Herron: 'the world cannot continue in flames and so big
a house as the United States escape conflagration'   185

Ezra Pound: 'the Hun must get the word "Macht" out of his occiput'   188

Beatrice Hastings: 'I have never said anything very bad of Germans'   191

Nietzsche: 'more of a danger than a saviour to post-war Germany'   193

A. M. Ludovici: still 'a convinced Nietzschean'   195

Oscar Levy: the present war is merely a new phase of the French
Revolution'   196

Oscar Levy in Berlin: 'The Old Germany dies hard'   197

Karl Marx: a political critic who 'has seldom been surpassed'   199

Psychoanalysis: the hopeful science of the dawning era'   200

Paul Selver: Germany, 'where poetical translation has been so
widely cultivated as to become traditional   203

Books for wartime: an increasing number of 'English heroines who
married Prussian officers just before the war'   204
War poetry: 'bombs thrown at society'   205
The Music Criticism of William Atheling (Ezra Pound): 'more a
personality than a nom de plume'   205

6. Germany and the *New Age*: November 1919-September 1922   207

The *New Age* in decline: 'The Great War put an end to many things
and many ideas'   209
The A.B.C. and the X.Y.Z of Economics   211
The *New Age*: 'A Socialist Review of Religion, Science and Art'   212
M. M. Cosmoi: Regarding the war 'as an attempt at synthesis'   212
C. H. Norman and the War: 'the killing of men does not settle any
question'   214
Postwar Germany: 'the shadow of 1921 with its attendant bogey is
here'   216
Notes of the Week: France threatens to stir 'the ashes of the dead
militarism of Germany into a possible flame'   217
Allied bankers 'are driving Germany upon the rocks as rapidly as
possible'   219
Ezra Pound: the League of Nations is 'too important an affair to be
based merely on a detestation of the Hun'   221
Janko Lavrin and the Germans: 'a race which has given the world
Goethe, Kant, Bach, Beethoven, Mozart, Wagner'   223
The Nietzscheans: A. M. Ludovici, Paul V. Cohn, Oscar Levy   225
Oscar Levy: appealing for a 're-opening of the Nietzsche controversy
in the interest of philosophical thought'   226
Nietzsche: not guilty of causing 'the most senseless and idiotic
war ever recorded among the monumental follies of humanity'   229
A. R. Orage: Nietzsche 'purged of his colossal errors by the Great
War' has 'a considerable future'   230
Nietzsche 'was only a battle trumpet, and the battlefield lies in the
Mahabharata'   231
Distinguishing 'Nietzscheanism from real Nietzsche'   233
Psychoanalysis and the *New Age*: seeking 'a more profound
analysis and synthesis of human psychology'   235
Treatment for War Shock: Psychoanalysis 'is frequently the last
rope one can fling a man'   238
A. E. Randall: 'Psychologically, we were not prepared for war;
psychologically, we are not prepared for peace'   240
'Readers and Writers': 'Bleeders and Blighters'   241

Paul Selver: 'it is certain that there are now more Englishmen
capable of ordering their lunch in German' 242
Herbert Read and German literature: Goethe's work is 'literary
lumber among which the modern reader must proceed warily' 244
Edwin Muir: 'our values before the war and our values now are so
different' 246
The New Spirit in Germany: 'Those three considerable writers,
Hans Vaihinger, Hermann Graf Keyserling and Oswald Spengler
are in the sun' 249
German Art: 'some very good things indeed are emerging under the
banner of Expressionism' 253
The German Theatre in Wartime: 'Hymns of Hate and spy plays were
not a prominent feature' 254
Post-war German drama in England: evidence of a 'John Bullish'
reaction 255
Bernard Shaw: 'Brawling in the Theatre' 256
Books for Peacetime 257
Music: 'it is sheer pig-headed stupidity to pretend that there are no
other song-writers than Brahms, Schumann and Schubert' 257

Conclusion 259

Germany and the *New Age*: 'our wretched German cousins' 259
German Culture: from 'the period before the Fall' to the post-war era 263
Orage and Nietzsche: 'A little Nietzsche is a dangerous thing' 265

Illustrations 269

Appendix 1 277

Poems by Nietzsche in Translation

Appendix 2 283

Goethe in Translation

Bibliography 287

List of Illustrations

Cover

'Nietzsche! Nietzsche! I must read tha fellow.' (sic)
Cartoon and caption by Ray Lewis (29 October 1914; *NA* XV, 26, p. 623)

Illustrations Section   *Page*

1	Front cover of the *New Age* (3 May 1917; *NA* XXI, 1, p. 1)	269
2	Mr. Bernard Shaw (13 July 1911; *NA* IX, 11, p. 24)	270
3	Mr. Holbrook Jackson (6 March 1913; *NA* XII, 18, p. 440)	270
4	Mr. G. K. Chesterton (13 July 1911; *NA* IX, 11, p. 247)	271
5	Mr. Cecil Chesterton (17 April 1913; *NA* XII, 24, p. 596)	271
6	Mr. Arnold Bennett (24 October 1912; *NA* XI, 26, p. 624)	272
7	Mr. H. G. Wells (13 July 1911; *NA* IX, 11, p. 247)	272
8	Mr. Hilaire Belloc (22 May 1913; *NA* XIII, 5, p. 104)	273
9	Mr. Ezra Pound (9 October 1913; *NA* XIII. 24, p. 712)	273
10	Mr. C. H. Norman (23 October 1913; *NA* XIII, 26, p. 776)	274
11	Mr. J. M. Kennedy (7 March 1912; *NA* X, 19, p. 456)	274
12	Mrs. Beatrice Hastings (1 May 1913; *NA* XIII, 1, p. 12)	275
13	Mr. Ramiro de Maeztu (15 June 1916; *NA* XIX, 7, p. 168)	275

With the exception of the drawing of Ramiro de Maeztu, which is the work of F. Sancha, all the caricatures of contributors shown here are by Tom Titt, the pseudonym of Jan de Junosza Rosciszewski.

List of Abbreviations

NA..The *New Age*
NW...The *New Witness*
Werke..............Nietzsche, *Werke*, edited by Karl Schlechta, 3 vols (Munich, 1956)

Acknowledgements

My research was greatly facilitated by the help I received in both public and university libraries. In particular, I would like to thank the staff of Leeds City Reference Library, Manchester Central Library, Birmingham Central Library and Edinburgh Central Library for finding me copies of the *New Age*. The assistance of the librarians in the Brotherton at Leeds University has proved invaluable. I am grateful to Mr Peter Kelly of Leeds City Reference Library for agreeing to photographs from the *New Age* to be reproduced here, and to Mr David Sheard for his painstaking photography. In addition, I am indebted to the Harry Ransom Research Center at the University of Texas at Austin for allowing me to quote from manuscripts in the Orage Collection and to Mrs Anne Orage for kindly granting me permission to consult her father-in-law's letters.

I would like to extend my thanks to Graham Loud for patiently enduring more than a fair share of discussion about German literature, and to my father Eric Milburn for supporting me throughout my studies.

Finally, I should like to express my profound gratitude to my supervisor Fred Bridgham for his all advice and encouragement, as well as for his efforts to secure funding from the British Academy to enable me to complete this thesis.

Introduction: Alfred Richard Orage:
'a desperado of genius'

When Alfred Richard Orage died on 6 November 1934,[1] tributes to the former editor of the *New Age* flowed from the literary establishment. Invariably known to readers and writers alike simply as A. R. Orage, his greatest achievement had been to give the *New Age* 'a prominence and publicity out of all proportion to its size and circulation'.[2] He had edited the journal 'with remarkable verve and originality' and was best known for his 'strong sympathy for mystical thought', his 'vivid', if not always 'lucid economic exposition', and for having been 'one of the earlier English admirers of Nietzsche', even though 'such admirations as these always kept him a long way from orthodoxy in the Socialism which for the greater part of his adult life he professed'.[3] Bernard Shaw remembered him fondly as 'a desperado of genius' who had kept his weekly periodical 'living on air for fifteen years' between 1907 and 1922, and who had been 'inexhaustible both as a writer and a speaker'.[4] The news struck G. K. Chesterton 'like a thunderclap', so shocked was he to learn that Orage, 'whose very name was The Storm, had passed as suddenly as he appeared in stormy times'. The latter had been 'a man who wrote fine literature in the course of writing fighting journalism, who wrote it in so excellent literary style, yet managed somehow to avoid the awful fate of looking like a literary man'.[5] H. G. Wells reflected that 'We disagreed about everything and I can truly hope that he liked and admired me half as much as I liked and admired him'.[6] The poet Richard Aldington recalled that before the First World War there were three periodicals to which an aspiring writer would hope to contribute: Ford Madox Hueffer's *English Review*, Harold Munro's *Poetry* and Orage's *New Age*. Orage had accepted Aldington's articles on Italy and some

---

1   Orage died in his sleep after having given his first radio broadcast. He had been troubled by a suspected heart condition for some weeks previously. See Philippe Mairet, *A. R. Orage: A Memoir* (London, 1936), pp. 118-20. The transcript of his lively BBC radio talk on 'Social Credit' in the series 'Poverty in Plenty' is to be found in the *New English Weekly. A. R. Orage Memorial Number*, VI, 5 (15 November 1934), pp. 103-4.

2   *The Times*, 7 November 1934, p. 21.

3   'Editor's Collapse after Wireless Talk', *Manchester Guardian*, 7 November 1934, p. 18.

4   *New English Weekly. A. R. Orage Memorial Number*, VI, 5 (15 November 1934), pp. 99-100.

5   Ibid., pp. 98-9.

6   Ibid., p. 110.

translations of 'Latin-Italian poets' between 1912 and 1913 and probably 'paid for these out of his own pocket'.[7] Although he never paid his more famous contributors, such as Chesterton or Wells, Orage did encourage younger writers by paying for their work. Frank Swinnerton appreciated Orage sending him ten shillings for an article in 1909 or 1910 when 'they were like doubloons'.[8] Ezra Pound never forgot that it was Orage, 'whose weekly guinea fed me when no one else was willing to do so'.[9] According to Paul Selver, a regular contributor to the literary columns of the *New Age*, Orage's 'influence was the most precious boon that a young man with literary ambitions could possibly hope to find. The encouragement and guidance which he so lavishly bestowed had the stimulating effect of developing manifest talents and of revealing latent ones'.[10] The novelist Storm Jameson believed that Orage had 'no wish to be an intellectual dictator. You could have the help of his mind if you asked for it, freely, but he did not wilfully impose his mind on other younger or less developed minds'.[11] The conscientious objector C. H. Norman admired Orage for having maintained 'a standard of independence which has almost completely vanished from Fleet Street under the control of the vulgarians. He expected his contributors to be competent, honest and accurate: but beyond that, he did not care what they wrote'.[12]

Despite these glowing eulogies, Orage was soon forgotten after his death. Even the site of the office at 38 Cursitor Street, where he ran the *New Age*, was obliterated by the German bombing of London in the Second World War.[13] Yet those writing at the time of the First World War considered the *New Age* influential. One contemporary commentator claimed that its readership comprised 'men and women who count - people who welcome daring and original thought, who hold important positions in the civic, social, political and artistic worlds, and who eagerly disseminate the seeds of thought they pick up from the *New Age*. Tens of thousands of people have been influenced by this paper who have never even heard its name. It does not educate the masses directly: it reaches them through the medium of its few but exceedingly able readers'.[14] Amongst the contributors, several writers took a keen interest in German politics and literature (including the translators of the first complete edition of Nietzsche in English) and regularly supplied Orage with articles. The *New Age* would

---

7   Ibid., p. 112.
8   Ibid., p. 119.
9   Ibid., p. 109.
10   Ibid., p. 111.
11   Ibid., p. 110.
12   Ibid., p. 120.
13   Cursitor Street was badly bombed on 13 August 1944.
14   Gerald Cumberland, *Set Down in Malice* (London, 1918), p. 130.

therefore appear to have contributed to the perception of Germany of a whole generation of writers and thus played an important role in Anglo-German literary relations.

Early Life and Development of the 'swordsman of the mind'

A. R. Orage was born on 22 January 1873 in Dacre near Harrogate.[15] He was part of a generation that grew up at a time when political events were causing a radical revision of the British perception of Germany. The Franco-Prussian War (1870), with the crushing defeat of the French at the Battle of Sedan and the annexation of Alsace Lorraine, followed by the founding of the German Empire (1871), did not appear as the work of the peaceable German cousins, the musicians and philosophers of early nineteenth century literature, but the work of a new breed of aggressive militarists. Although this deterioration in the *Deutschlandbild* took place gradually, it accelerated after 1900, culminating in the rabid propaganda tracts of the First World War.[16]

Following the death of Orage's father in 1874, his mother, who was probably Irish, moved the family back to her husband's native Fenstanton in Huntingdonshire, where Orage spent his childhood and adolescence in straitened circumstances.[17] He attended the local non-conformist school where he excelled and attracted the attention of his teacher, Howard Coote, the local squire's son. Coote gave him access to his library, where Orage read Ruskin, Carlyle, Arnold and Morris, and arranged for him to take French lessons. He subsequently provided the funds for Orage to attend Culham training college in Oxfordshire to qualify as a teacher and where, incidentally, he learnt how to be an editor. Through Coote's patronage Orage secured his appointment as a schoolmaster in Leeds on 26 October 1893.[18]

---

15 The youngest of four children, Orage was actually christened James Alfred, but even at school was known as Dickie and later abandoned James and chose Richard to make the initials A.R.O. See John Carswell, *Lives and Letters* (London, 1978), p. 15.

16 Günther Blaicher, *Das Deutschlandbild in der englischen Literatur* (Darmstadt, 1992), pp. 157-8.

17 In his last years, Orage's father, who had been a schoolteacher in Dacre, had become an alcoholic and left his wife little money to raise their family. See John Carswell, op. cit., p. 15.

18 Tom Steele, *Alfred Orage and The Leeds Arts Club 1893-1923* (Aldershot, 1990), p. 25. He taught at Ellerby Lane Boys, Leyland Mixed School, Harehills Board School and Roundhay Road Boys.

In Leeds, Orage developed the intellectual interests which would later sustain him as 'a swordsman of the mind'[19] when he edited the *New Age* in London. In 1894 he joined the Leeds branch of the Independent Labour Party, became a regular speaker at ILP meetings and contributed articles to the ILP weekly *Labour Leader* and edited a local radical journal called *Forward*.[20] Through his wife Jean Watson, whom he married in 1896 - to the outrage of his benefactor Squire Coote,[21] he became involved with the Theosophical Society, lecturing at meetings and writing articles on the subject.[22]

Holbrook Jackson: 'My dear Jackson....'

However, it was Orage's encounter with Holbrook Jackson that brought about a crucial development in his thought. Jackson, a Liverpool lace merchant, Fabian and freelance journalist, first met Orage in 1901 at a Leeds bookshop where both were seeking to find in literature 'that community of ideas which we were unable to find locally among men'.[23] According to Jackson, Orage at this time was 'restive under the thrall of elementary school teaching, for although he was a born teacher, his setting under the Leeds educational authority was as incongruous as that of Swinburne at Eton, or Shelley at Oxford'.[24] It was Jackson who cured Orage's restiveness by introducing him to the work of Nietzsche, then only just appearing in English translation. The German philosopher, as we shall see, was to exert a profound influence on Orage in both Leeds and London.

Orage's acquaintance with Holbrook Jackson was probably his first important intellectual friendship. Their correspondence from the Leeds period shows that they were soon on the closest terms. In the early 1900s they regularly exchanged letters between their Leeds addresses and from boarding houses on the North Yorkshire Moors when on holiday.[25] When Orage moved to London in

---

19   George W. Russell, *New English Weekly. A. R. Orage Memorial Number*, VI, 5 (15 November 1934), p. 97.

20   Tom Steele, op. cit., pp. 29-33.

21   Coote disapproved of this early marriage and declined to finance an undergraduate course at Oxford as Orage had hoped. See John Carswell, op. cit., p. 19.

22   Ibid., p. 34.

23   Holbrook Jackson, *Bernard Shaw* (London, 1907), 'Prefatory Letter', p. 9.

24   *New English Weekly. A. R. Orage Memorial Number*, VI, 5 (15 November 1934), p. 114.

25   Invariably beginning 'My dear Jackson', Orage covers a variety of subjects, ranging from philosophy to domestic matters.

1906 his letters to Jackson reveal his initial loneliness in his new surroundings. On 27 May 1906, for example, Orage admits that he is 'glad' to learn that Jackson is finding that Leeds is 'beginning to get on your nerves' and looking forward to the latter's arrival in London, admitting 'I'm damned if I don't feel lost without you'.[26] Just how stifled Orage became in Leeds is clear in a letter of 1907 when he writes: 'Give me, in fact, a roving commission among the intelligent aristocracy and I'll undertake to make a nucleus of Samurai - for London, by God, is not a wilderness of asses like Leeds!'[27] On 22 December 1905 he was granted six months' leave of absence from his teaching post 'in order to write a book', although he never returned.[28]

Plans for the New Age: 'I like the idea of a magazine'

Whilst in Leeds, Orage was giving careful consideration to the idea of running his own journal. In spring 1904, for example, he confides in Jackson 'I like the idea of a magazine'.[29] The following year he informs Jackson that he agrees with the latter's suggestions about the size of a magazine but that the proposed title, *The Hammer*, with its Nietzschean overtones of 'Wie man mit dem Hammer philosophiert', 'is too plebeian, too young - I mean, silly!' With a quarterly bearing this title it would be impossible to 'hammer' to great effect: 'four taps a year wouldn't bend a hair of the Philistine cocoanut!'[30] When Jackson offers further proposals for a possible title, Orage replies that he prefers *The Watchers, Phaedrus, The Centaur* or *The Flame*.[31]

In the 1900s there was no shortage of periodicals on the market, all catering for the steady increase in the reading public. The Education Acts of 1870, 1876 and 1889 had resulted in larger numbers of the population than ever before being able to read.[32] They showed an enormous appetite for popular novels, newspapers and periodicals. Printing costs were cheaper because of the

---

26 Letter from 57 Weltie Road, Hammersmith, No Date, Harry Ransom Humanities Research Center, the University of Texas at Austin (hereafter HRHRC), Manuscripts by and relating to A. R. Orage.
27 Letter dated 27 February 1907, HRHRC.
28 Tom Steele, op. cit., p. 28.
29 Letter dated 3 April 1904, HRHRC.
30 Letter from Broxa, Hackness, Yorks, dated Monday Evening (1905?), HRHRC.
31 Letter from East Acklam, dated Monday, HRHRC. *The Flame* is possibly a reference to Karl Kraus' *Die Fackel*.
32 Wallace Martin, *The New Age under Orage: Chapters in English Cultural History* (Manchester, 1967), p. 6.

introduction of mechanical typesetting and the fall in wood pulp prices, making a large circulation possible.[33] The periodical press in the early twentieth century often offered a more lively presentation of material than that found in the older newspapers and reviews. Political weeklies and 'Little Reviews' flourished, the latter sustaining serious and experimental literature. In addition to the *New Age*, journals such as the *Nation*, the *New Statesman*, the *Commentator* and the *New Witness* were founded.[34] Circulation was relatively small, exact figures were kept secret and the journals usually ran at a loss, but it is likely that the *Spectator*, whose title had origins in the early eighteenth century,[35] enjoyed the largest circulation, selling between 22,000 copies in 1903 and 13,500 copies in 1922.[36] By the end of 1907 the circulation of the *New Age* ran to 5,000 copies, but by autumn 1908 this figure had been increased to 20,000.[37] During Orage's fifteen years as editor of the *New Age* over thirty English periodicals were launched, although few survived for long.[38] When comparing the fortunes of Orage as editor with his contemporaries, Samuel Hynes has observed that Ford Madox Hueffer ran the *English Review* for little over a year, lost £5000 and was dismissed: Hueffer 'was brilliant, but Orage lasted'.[39]

Bernard Shaw: 'The Philosopher'

When Orage and Jackson heard that an ailing journal called the *New Age* was being put up for sale at a reasonable price by its editor Joseph Clayton,[40] they turned first to Bernard Shaw for financial assistance. The *New Age* had been founded in the 1890s and although Shaw had been invited to join the regular staff, he had declined.[41] However, he greeted the appeal from Jackson and Orage with rather more enthusiasm.

Bernard Shaw played a pivotal role in Orage's early career as a writer. Originally, Orage and Jackson planned to collaborate on a book about Shaw.

---

33   Cate Haste, *Keep the Home Fires Burning. Propaganda in the First World War* (London, 1977), p. 29.

34   Wallace Martin, op. cit., pp. 9-10.

35   Richard Steele founded the *Spectator* on 1 March 1711.

36   Wallace Martin, op. cit., p. 10.

37   John Carswell, op. cit., pp. 38-9.

38   Wallace Martin, op. cit., p. 13.

39   Samuel Hynes, *Edwardian Occasions. Essays on English Writing in the Early Twentieth Century* (London, 1972), p. 43.

40   Philippe Mairet, op. cit, pp. 36-7.

41   See Michael Holroyd, *Bernard Shaw, Vol. I, 1856-98. The Search for Love* (London, 1988), p. 328.

Orage was in no doubt that Shaw was 'the first intellectual mind in England', if not 'a forty acre mind', and warned Jackson that if they were to carry out their plans to write a monograph on him 'We shan't walk round him without a good deal more sweat'.[42] The book was mainly the work of Holbrook Jackson, although letters from Orage reveal that it was Orage's cajoling that made Jackson sit down to write.[43] Orage contributed a chapter on Shaw entitled 'The Philosopher'. However, he did not wish to be known as co-author on the following grounds:

> 'Foulis is willing to consider a book by me on Shaw, and I want to do it. (Of course it wouldn't be published till the spring at the earliest). But I couldn't offer him the book if I were already known as the co-author with you of this. I suggest therefore that you should have *your name only* as author, and simply acknowledge my services in the preface. *I* shall be best pleased with that arrangement'.[44]

When he moved to London Orage read and corrected Jackson's manuscript, urging him to send it to the publisher because 'Now's the time. Let the damned cat jump; and may she jump to send glory!'[45] However, Orage's chapter on Shaw met with less glory. Mrs Shaw, who probably did know that Orage was the author, disapproved of it and it was therefore withdrawn. In 1907 the monograph *Bernard Shaw* was published under Holbrook Jackson's name only. Shaw then offered to help Orage with his first book, *Nietzsche: the Dionysian Spirit of the Age* (1906).[46] He would continue to offer assistance throughout the period that Orage was editor of the *New Age*.

---

42   See Letter from East Acklam, no date, and Letter from Broxa, Hackness, Yorks, dated Monday Evening, 1905, HRHRC.
43   Orage sympathises with Jackson: 'Sorry you are not getting G.B.S. done: I shall have to telepathise you strongly.' Letter dated 14 July 1905, HRHRC.
44   Letter from 57 Weltie Road, Hammersmith, no date, HRHRC.
45   Letter dated 26 September 1906, HRHRC.
46   Tom Steele, op. cit., p. 48.

Chapter 1: Germany and the *New Age*:
May 1907 - October 1908

Reducing 'Leeds to Nietzscheism'

In 1903 A. R. Orage and Holbrook Jackson launched an ambitious scheme whose avowed aim was 'to reduce Leeds to Nietzscheism'.[1] This took the form of founding the Leeds Arts Club where the latest developments in literature, philosophy, music and painting were to be discussed. In this respect the interests of the Arts Club anticipate some of the cultural questions debated on the pages of the *New Age* when Orage became editor. The Club was ambitious on two counts. In the first place, it was a platform for the avant-garde, based not in London, where English cultural life was traditionally centred, but in the provinces. In the second place, speakers were often dealing with subjects little discussed outside the metropolis. Nevertheless, the Club was well supported, mainly by teachers, but also by journalists, clergymen, architects and some university lecturers. Guest speakers were invited to attract larger audiences. The Superman'. Such luminaries included Edward Carpenter, W. B. Yeats, Bernard Shaw and G. K. Chesterton, who in the autumn of 1904 spoke on 'Man - The Great Man'. Programmes of talks given at the Club reveal something of a predeliction for Germanic subjects. Lectures were given on Richard Wagner, Hugo Wolf, Heine's poetry, German Romanticism and, of course, Nietzsche. In addition, the Club encouraged members to learn European languages, promoted Esperanto and organised lectures on Ibsen, Strindberg and Turgenev. The concerns of this provincial society were far from parochial. By comparison, syllabuses at Leeds University confined themselves to earlier periods of study. The course on modern thought in the Philosophy Department, for example, ended with Kant, whilst the German Department under Professor Schüddekopf concentrated on Middle High German, Lessing, Herder, Klopstock, Wieland, Goethe and Schiller. Not until 1910 did Gerhart Hauptmann's *Die versunkene Glocke* (1896) creep onto the syllabus as a concession to modernity. Meanwhile at the Arts Club Orage was lecturing almost monthly on Nietzsche,[2] occasionally offering an impromptu talk on the German philosopher as well. Clifford Bax recalled a meeting in 1906 when:

---

1   Holbrook Jackson, quoted by Patrick Bridgwater, 'English Writers and Nietzsche', in *Nietzsche: Imagery and Thought*, edited by Malcolm Pasley (London, 1978), p. 225.

2   See Tom Steele, *Alfred Orage and the Leeds Arts Club 1893-1923* (Aldershot, 1990), pp. 71-2.

'The lecturer had sent a last-minute message to say that he was too ill to come. The Chairman was in a fix. Orage then got up from his seat in the hall and offered to give a lecture on "Three Great Philosophers". They were, I think, Plato, Schopenhauer and Nietzsche: and I shall always remember the brilliant manner in which he gave the discourse which completely saved the awkward situation'.[3]

Schopenhauer's *Die Welt als Wille und Vorstellung* had first appeared in English between 1883 and 1886, when Richard Burdon Haldane (later Viscount Haldane of Cloan) and John Kemp collaborated on a translation. The first English translation of Nietzsche's *Also sprach Zarathustra* had not been published until 1896 and at the time of Orage's lectures no complete edition of Nietzsche's works was available. As Tom Steele observes, Orage's lectures in Leeds mark 'the first sustained attempt at a popular introduction to Nietzsche'.[4]

The Leeds Arts Club: developing 'supermania'

Orage, who was employed as a schoolmaster at Ellerby Lane Boys in one of the worst slum areas of Leeds, lived in the more comfortable suburb of Chapel Allerton.[5] In 1900 he borrowed a copy of Thomas Common's translation of *Also sprach Zarathustra* from Holbrook Jackson. He read it in a single night, then walked from his home in Chapel Allerton to Jackson's house in Headingley, fired with enthusiasm for his new intellectual master.[6] In the course of the next seven years he was to make a detailed study of the philosopher. Moreover, there is evidence to suggest that he was not wholly dependent on the English translations. Orage knew both French and German and, according to Jackson, whilst in Leeds translated Nietzsche's poems into prose for Jackson to render into

---

3   Clifford Bax, *New English Weekly. A. R. Orage Memorial Number*, VI, 5 (15 November 1934), p. 117.

4   Tom Steele, 'From Gentleman to Superman: Orage and Aristocratic Socialism', in *The Imagined Past. History and Nostalgia*, edited by Christopher Shaw and Malcolm Chase (Manchester, 1989), p. 114.

5   See Tom Steele, *Alfred Orage and the Leeds Arts Club 1893-1923* (Aldershot, 1990), pp. 25-6.

6   Holbrook Jackson, *New English Weekly. A. R. Orage Memorial Number*, VI, 5 (15 November 1934), p. 114.

poetry.[7] As an adolescent he had been a voracious reader of Carlyle and Arnold - both important intermediaries for the reception of German literature and thought in England. Arnold, for instance, had written on Heinrich Heine; A. J. Penty, who knew Orage in Leeds, remembered the latter's interest in the German writer at this stage.[8]

However, it would be a misrepresentation to suggest that Orage was solely interested in German culture. Throughout his life his interests spanned a wide range of fields. In Leeds he divided his time between the Independent Labour Party, Plato, Theosophy and the eastern mysticism contained in the *Mahabharata* and the *Bhagavadgita*. It was possibly the concept of eternal recurrence found in *Also sprach Zarathustra*, with its evocations of eastern notions of spiritual transcendence and reincarnation, that initially attracted Orage to Nietzsche. Commenting on the interests of Orage and the Leeds Arts Club Holbrook Jackson acknowledged:

> 'Orage went over the top and so did the group. We all
> developed supermania. He wanted a Nietzsche circle in
> which Plato and Blavatzky (sic), Fabianism and
> Hinduism, Shaw and Wells and Edward Carpenter should
> be blended, with Nietzsche as the catalytic (sic)'.[9]

It was certainly a potent mixture. Perhaps it was too potent, for in 1906 Orage came to the conclusion that 'Dionysos and Leeds would not mix'[10] and, armed with what were reputed to be the only three English translations of Nietzsche in Leeds,[11] borrowed indefinitely from the Arts Club,[12] moved to London with Jackson. Here he helped H. G. Wells, Eric Gill and William Rothenstein form the

---

7   Two notebooks of Orage's translations of Nietzsche's aphorisms survive.
     Dated 1902 they run to twenty four and nineteen pages respectively. See
     Tom Steele, *Alfred Orage and the Leeds Arts Club 1893-1923* (Aldershot,
     1990), p. 49.

8   A. J. Penty, *New English Weekly*, VI, 5 (15 November 1934), p. 113.

9   Holbrook Jackson, ibid., p. 114.

10   Quoted by Tom Steele, 'The Leeds Arts Club: A Provincial Avant-Garde?',
     Literature and History, 14, 1 (1988), p. 98.

11   Mary Gawthorpe, *Up the Hill to Holloway* (Maine, 1962), p. 201. By 1906
     only four volumes were available in English translation: *Thus spake
     Zarathustra* (1896), *The Case of Wagner. Nietzsche contra Wagner, The
     Antichrist* (1896), *A Genealogy of Morals. Poems* (1899) and *The Dawn of
     Day* (1903).

12   Ibid., p. 191.

Fabian Arts Group which was based on the Leeds model. He returned regularly to the Leeds Arts Club, which continued to flourish under Michael Sadler, Frank Rutter and Jacob Kramer, and occasionally published reports on the Club's activities in the *New Age*. He wrote two volumes on Nietzsche - *Friedrich Nietzsche: The Dionysian Spirit of the Age* (1906) and *Nietzsche in Outline and Aphorism* (1907) - both of which were well received in the press. However, it was as editor of the *New Age* that he would be best remembered.

Bernard Shaw and Germany: 'I can neither claim knowledge of the German language nor plead ignorance of it'

During the period that A. R. Orage edited the *New Age* from May 1907 until September 1922 the list of contributors to this weekly periodical reads like a directory of figures from English literary life. More remarkable still was Orage's ability to secure articles from his established contributors without payment, so high was their esteem for him. Writers from whom he coaxed contributions, paid and unpaid, included: Arnold Bennett, H. G. Wells, G. K. Chesterton, Hilaire Belloc, William Archer, Ashley Dukes, Bernard Shaw, Hubert Bland, Edith Nesbit, Holbrook Jackson, Oscar Levy, Anthony M. Ludovici, J. M. Kennedy, T. E. Hulme, Havelock Ellis, Edward Carpenter, A. J. Penty, Herbert Read, Paul Selver, Ezra Pound, John Middleton Murray, Katherine Mansfield and Edwin Muir. Of these, several already had links with Germany: prior to 1900 Havelock Ellis had written a penetrating series of essays on Nietzsche in the *Savoy*. The scholar, Oscar Levy, was editing a complete version of the German philosopher's work, with Ludovici and Kennedy, amongst others, as translators. Kennedy's first contribution to the *New Age*, for instance, was a review of the German edition of *Ecce Homo* in October 1908, although his interests were not confined to literature. From 1911 he reported on foreign affairs for the *New Age*, signing himself S. Verdad (from the Spanish 'es verdad', meaning 'it is true'). Of the younger generation of writers encouraged by Orage, some would later play an important role in Anglo-German literary relations. Edwin Muir as an early translator of Kafka is a prime example. In 1910 Orage showed the foresight to publish Katherine Mansfield's short story *The Child who was Tired* (entitled *Bavarian Babies* in the *New Age*). It was not until the following year that this appeared in book form as part of the collection *In a German Pension* which was based on the writer's experiences in Bavaria.

The £1000 necessary to enable Jackson and Orage to buy the *New Age* was put up by Bernard Shaw, a personal friend of Jackson,[13] and Lewis

---

13   Shaw agreed to be the second backer on condition that they 'raid the City first'. See Philippe Mairet, *A. R. Orage: A Memoir* (London, 1936), p. 37.

28

Wallace, a banker known to Orage through Theosophist circles. Although Shaw might have hoped to be investing in a journal which would propagate his views, it soon became clear that editorial policy was to keep the review independent and to give contributors *carte blanche* to disagree with one another. Nevertheless, the link with Shaw was important because of his own connections with both German music and philosophy. In the 1890s, as the music critic of *The Star*, Corno di Bassetto, Shaw was acknowledged as the perfect Wagnerite, promoting the German composer to English audiences when Wagnerism was at its height. Furthermore, his play *Man and Superman* gave rise to suggestions that the dramatist had been influenced by the most recent developments in German thought, although he was swift to deny to both English and German audiences that he was merely repeating Schopenhauer and Nietzsche parrot-fashion.[14] The question of his knowledge of German is debatable. In the same article for *Die Neue Rundschau* in 1911 he claims that he has 'every intention of learning German one day; it is something everyone should do', but as he is 'not yet fifty five, there is no hurry'.[15] Admittedly he was being somewhat economical with the truth. Although, as his biographer Michael Holroyd points out, he read the first volume of Marx's *Das Kapital* in French (no English version was available in the British Museum in 1883), his German 'not being up to deciphering an original text',[16] by the 1890's he had accompanied May Morris to German classes and gained some knowledge of the language. Shaw probably gave the most accurate description of his acquaintance with German when he asserted

> 'I can neither claim knowledge of the German language
> nor plead ignorance of it. I am like most literary persons:
> I have spent several holidays in Germany (mostly in
> Bayreuth), and have just managed to ask my way, and get
> what I wanted in the shops and railway stations, without
> the aid of an interpreter. The proverbial bits of Goethe
> and Wagner and Nietzsche are familiar to me; and when a

---

14   See Bernard Shaw, 'Was ich der deutschen Kultur verdanke', *Die Neue Rundschau*, 22 (Berlin, 1911), p. 335. However, Shaw did inform his Austrian translator, Siegfried Trebitsch, on 26 December 1902: 'I want the Germans to know me as a philosopher, as an English (or Irish) Nietzsche (only ten times cleverer).' See Patrick Bridgwater, op. cit., p. 225.

15   See *Die Neue Rundschau*, 22 (Berlin, 1911), p. 336.

16   Michael Holroyd, *Bernard Shaw, Vol. I, 1856-98. The Search for Love* (London, 1988), p. 130.

German writes to me I can generally make out what he wants provided he uses the Latin and not the Gothic script. And that is all'.[17]

The implication that 'most literary persons' of Shaw's generation had either knowledge of the German language or contact with German culture is significant for an understanding of the outlook of contributors to the *New Age*. It was this generation of writers that was to play such a large part in the war of words against Germany in 1914.

The New Age: 'An Independent Socialist Review of Politics, Literature and Art'

By the early years of this century journalism had become an integral part of a writer's activity. Matters would be debated in print with fellow authors over a period of weeks, perhaps months if the editor of the periodical was lucky enough to elongate the discussion and keep the contributions flowing. Such long-running debates secured the interest of readers and helped guarantee the precarious sales of weekly journals which invariably ran at a loss.[18] In this respect, one of Orage's triumphs in the early days of the *New Age* was to publish an article by Arnold Bennett entitled 'Why I am a Socialist'. This sparked off a series of replies from the pens of Chesterton, Belloc, Wells and Shaw. There was no shortage of readers for such literary jousting. More people learned to read and looked to Fleet Street as well as to popular fiction for their sustenance.[19] Thus, in the years leading up to the First World War journalism helped shape popular perception of contemporary events more than ever before.

Compared with the *English Review*, which was launched by Ford Madox Hueffer 'with the definite design of giving imaginative literature a chance in England',[20] the 'design' of the *New Age* was much broader. Its concerns were both literary and political. Indeed, it was no accident that its subtitle should be 'An Independent Socialist Review of Politics, Literature and Art'. This was precisely the order in which the publication was arranged, beginning with a commentary on the week's events in politics, originally called 'The Outlook', later 'Notes of the Week'. There followed longer articles of topical interest on both national and international affairs; often these articles formed the inspiration for

17   Bernard Shaw, *Translations and Tomfooleries* (London, 1926), p. 5.
18   Wallace Martin, *The New Age under Orage: Chapters in English Cultural History* (Manchester, 1967), p. 10.
19   Ibid., p. 8.
20   Arthur Mizener, *The Saddest Story. A Biography of Ford Madox Ford* (London, 1971), p. 154.

the shorter commentaries in this section. Then came book reviews, drama, art and music criticism and essays on cultural matters. Several contributors preferred to remain anonymous or disguised themselves behind exotic pen-names. Between 1908 and 1911 Arnold Bennett, calling himself Jacob Tonson, wrote the column 'Books and Persons'; after Bennett's departure Orage took over this 'causerie' under the alias R.H.C., an allusion to R. H. Congreve. In the first year, when Orage and Holbrook Jackson were joint editors, Jackson wrote many of the book reviews, and he continued to contribute to this section after he relinquished his editorship. On the political side Orage wrote little in the early issues, except for a series of articles entitled 'Towards Socialism'. For the political commentaries he relied on more experienced journalists. In this context the part played by Cecil Chesterton cannot be underestimated. In 1907 it was Chesterton who alternated with Clifford Sharp (later editor of the *New Statesman*) and Holbrook Jackson to write the political notes of 'The Outlook'. In addition to longer, signed articles on Socialism, Chesterton was also responsible for 'Notes of the Week'. Cecil Chesterton, Orage's 'first friend amongst London journalists',[21] remained with the *New Age* as assistant editor until 1912 when he left to edit his own journal, the *New Witness*.

Orage's 'Socialist Spectator'

Orage conceived of the periodical as a kind of 'Socialist *Spectator*'.[22] In terms of style he was indebted to the original editors of the *Spectator*. Herbert Read, who as a student at Leeds University had joined the Leeds Arts Club where Orage 'was a name and a legend' long after he had left the city, contributed to the later issues of the *New Age*. Of his impressions of Orage he recalled:

> 'I used to think he had an eighteenth century cast of mind;
> a brilliant occasional writer, like Steele or Addison. He
> rarely ran to a sustained essay, but no better *paragraphs* in
> literary criticism have ever been written'.[23]

Coincidentally, it was the *Spectator* of Addison and Steele that had so impressed German writers to translate it, and, subsequently inspired the *Moralische Wochenschriften* of the eighteenth century. In the twentieth century,

---

21   Philippe Mairet, op. cit., p. 37.
22   Ibid., p. 48.
23   Herbert Read, *New English Weekly. A. R. Orage Memorial Number*, VI, 5 (15 November 1934), p. 112.

Orage's work as editor bears comparison with that of his Austrian contemporary, Karl Kraus. Both *Die Fackel* and the *New Age* appeared at a time when the press was enjoying increased power in public affairs, when news agencies and press bureaux facilitated access to news items, and ownership of the press was still in the hands of individuals whose financial stakes in their newspapers often enabled them to influence editorial policy. Indeed, 'newspaper barons' such as Northcliffe, Hearst and Hugenberg were able to influence governments. Population increases and improved literacy ensured mass circulation so that the owners of the press had 'power without responsibility'.[24] This 'power without responsibility' was a concern of both Kraus and Orage as *independent* owner-editors, watching their countries coming ever closer to the brink of a war, apparently fanned by a press which did not acknowledge or which paid little heed to moral obligations in the years leading up to 1914.

Armament: the need to resist 'the wanton aggression of other nations'

However, on the subject of pacifism, the *New Age* diverges sharply from the views expressed in *Die Fackel*. Whilst Karl Kraus opposed military aggression, political commentaries from the pen of Cecil Chesterton reveal an anti-pacifist stance from the outset. As early as May 1907 he criticises the Labour Party for protesting against the Army Bill of Lord Haldane, the War Minister. He argues 'one need not be a Jingo to recognise that so long as nations exist they must be prepared to resist by force if necessary the wanton aggression of other nations. And it is rather illogical for Socialists to deny the possibility of such aggression on the part of other nations when they are continually accusing their own of habitually practising it. We must have an army, and we may be sure that the British people will refuse to entrust power to any party that will not promise to provide one.' (2 May 1907; *NA* I, 1, p. 2)

In this argument Chesterton was wholly consistent. He did not simply adopt it in order to oblige the propaganda effort in 1914. In *The Prussian hath said in his Heart*, which he wrote at the beginning of the First World War, his position was one which he had repeatedly advocated on the pages of the *New Age* since 1907. In 1914 he still contends that 'all nations have always had armies of some kind to defend themselves against their neighbours, and support such claims as those neighbours might challenge. There is nothing abnormal in that; it is an imperfection, incidental to the organization of men in nations, and can only be destroyed by destroying nations - an idea as unthinkable as it is odious. But there is something abnormal about the frantic piling up of armaments, the wild race to

---

24   See Edward Timms, *Karl Kraus: Apocalyptic Satirist* (London, 1986), p. 30ff for a discussion of the changes in journalism.

secure more men and more guns, which has gone on with ever-increasing speed for the last forty years'.[25]

Disarmament is not a viable alternative. For Chesterton, belief in the need to defend one's country is fundamental. It is only the pre-war arms race which he finds deplorable. On the question of national defence, even as a committed Socialist and former member of the Fabian Executive, he clashed with both Liberals and Socialists.[26] Indeed, his admiration was for the German Social Democrats, who at their Stuttgart conference in 1907 'were almost Jingo in their assertions of loyalty and patriotism' (24 October 1907; *NA* I, 26, p. 311). Although this is part of the unsigned commentary 'The Outlook', the argument is consistent with Chesterton's reasoning and it is therefore likely that he was the author. Advocacy of a system of national defence is an assertion of loyalty and patriotism. This is an example which Chesterton feels the English counterparts of the German Social Democrats would do well to follow.

In an essay for the *New Age* entitled 'Socialism and the Soldier', Chesterton clarified his concept of an ideal army. It would be based on that of the Swiss: nationals of each country would be trained at school in the use of arms and be prepared to mobilize in time of war. If each nation adopted this system of defence, he argues, wars would no longer be fought on the whims of the ruling elite, because an army comprising citizens, the majority of the population, would not take up arms against their opposite numbers abroad without a real cause. Chesterton is careful to distinguish between this kind of national defence and the brand of sabre-rattling jingoism propagated by certain sections of the press. He clearly states that the 'really vile Jingoism is a frivolous and irresponsible Jingoism, the gladiatorial emotion which is evoked by reading accounts of slaughter inflicted by and upon other people. It is not the least of the merits of a citizen army that this vile spirit would once and for all be exorcised.' (25 July 1907; *NA* I, 13, p. 199)

Chesterton's condemnation of jingoism aroused by reading 'accounts of slaughter' is strangely prophetic. In the early stages of the First World War unconfirmed reports of German 'atrocities' against the civilian population of Belgium, as contained in the Bryce Report, stirred both the reading public and the writers of propaganda to more fervent support for the Allied campaign and outrage at enemy action.[27]

---

25   Cecil Chesterton, *The Prussian hath said in his Heart* (London, 1914), pp. 211-12.

26   Brocard Sewell, *Cecil Chesterton* (Whitefriars, Faversham, Kent 1975), pp. 20-9.

27   See Peter Buitenhuis, *The Great War of Words. Literature as Propaganda 1914 and After*, (London, 1989), p. 27 for impact of the Bryce Report.

According to Chesterton, wars were to be fought for ideals. In 'My Utopia' he contends that there can be no complete federation of Europe because differences in the national character of countries must necessarily remain. He believes that 'no good thing is ever secure if men are not ready to fight for it. An ideal is a fragile thing and always menaced by the powers of darkness. I think men will do well to keep the sword sharp.' (28 December 1907; *NA* II, 9, p. 170)

What one defines as an ideal worth fighting for is, of course, a highly subjective matter and Chesterton here declines to elaborate on what he considers worth shedding blood over. In 1914 he would justify the war as a Christian crusade against the evil menace of a Prussia inspired by what he quaintly termed the 'atheism' of Frederick the Great. However, the Germans of 1914 were equally convinced that they were fighting for ideals that were firmly on the side of right.[28]

Cecil Chesterton: 'Artistically it would be an anti-climax to assassinate the German Emperor'

In the context of German affairs, in the column 'Notes of the Week', Cecil Chesterton is at pains to draw attention to financial difficulties experienced by the German Government. On 29 February 1908, for example, he notes the poor state of the German Imperial finances and suggests that this would be an opportune moment for the Foreign Secretary, Sir Edward Grey, to negotiate with Prince Bülow on arms reductions (*NA* II, 18, p. 343). He presses the issue again on 9 May 1908, prompted by the German Government's recent admission in the Reichstag of its need to raise £50,000,000 in the following five years. Since the new Chancellor of the Exchequer, Herr Sydow, has called for a reduction in expenditure, Chesterton observes that this can be done best by cutting arms and once again urges Sir Edward Grey to seek negotiations. Both countries should make reductions in expenditure on weapons (*NA* III, 2, p. 81). Chesterton is well aware that England is equally guilty of stockpiling arms. In less than a month he twice reminds readers that it is time to call a halt to the frantic building up of the Navy. The idea that the German Navy has amassed a larger fleet of Dreadnoughts is a myth because, according to recent naval estimates discussed in Parliament, 'Navy construction for Navy construction, practice for practice, England is at least not behind Germany'.[29]

Cecil Chesterton's contributions to the *New Age* reveal a distrust of all systems of government in Europe. He consistently attacks the policies of the Liberal Government in England, and its attempts at an Anglo-Russian alliance in

---

28   See Fritz Fischer, *Griff nach der Weltmacht*, (Düsseldorf, 1961), p. 184ff.
29   15 August 1908; *NA* III, 16, p. 301. See also 25 July 1908; *NA* III, 13, p. 242.

1907. This, he declares, would be a pact with the Tsar, the oppressor of the Russian people, with which he sides. He even goes so far as to counsel the German Social Democrats, as the true representatives of the German people, to watch carefully the 'coquettings between William and Nicholas' when there are rumours of a *Kaiserbund* in August 1907. He reminds the German Socialists that they 'do not want the German people to incur the indelible disgrace of taking part against a neighbouring people rightly struggling to be free, or the German flag to be stained by the memory of a war waged against the cause of humanity' (15 August 1907; *NA* I, 16, p. 242). Just as Chesterton makes a distinction between the Russian ruler and the Russian people, so too does he view the German Kaiser in a different light from the German people. His attitude towards Wilhelm II is somewhat ambiguous. In his column 'Bombastes in Fleet Street' he dubs the Kaiser 'the bitterest enemy of England that the Continent has produced' (24 October 1907; *NA* I, 26, p. 242). This view is prompted by the Kaiser's anti-British statements which Chesterton thinks are divorced from the true sentiments of the German nation.

On the political front, the *Deutschlandbild* of the *New Age* owes more to concern with the activities of the German Socialists than serious preoccupation with the German Emperor. On occasions Chesterton is capable of depicting this bitter enemy of England almost as a figure of fun. In a commentary on recent social unrest abroad, Chesterton postulates such disturbances might encourage a violent *coup d'état* in Germany. He notes that 'artistically it would be an anti-climax to assassinate the German Emperor; he is too good a comedy character to have a tragic ending. Morally, we hasten to add for the credit of Socialist ethics, it would be an act of which we should feel bound to disapprove' (30 May 1907; *NA* I, 5, p. 66). Indeed, Cecil Chesterton's ironic depiction of the Kaiser here approaches that found in the fiction of his brother. For instance, in the 1911 story *The Blue Cross* in the collection *The Innocence of Father Brown*, G. K. Chesterton suggests a parallel between the arch-villain, Flambeau, and Wilhelm II: 'But in his best days (I mean, of course, his worst) Flambeau was a figure as statuesque and international as the Kaiser. Almost every morning the daily paper announced that he had escaped the consequences of one extraordinary crime by committing another.'[30]

Concern about 'the fear of sudden attack which now animates the pens of English sensational journalism'

The daily papers had a momentous year for announcing the Kaiser's crimes in 1908. An interview with Wilhelm II in the *Daily Telegraph* fuelled

---

30   G. K. Chesterton, *The Innocence of Father Brown* (London, 1911), p. 2.

speculation in the press that war with Germany was imminent. Nevertheless, the commentaries of the *New Age* remained clear-headed. They argued that the enemy of England was not Germany, but rather some of the sensationalist outpourings of Fleet Street journalists, intent on stirring up anti-German feeling. On 14 March 1908 'Notes of the Week' attacked *The Times* over its leader of 7th March. *The Times* had claimed that it was an act of patriotism to bring to public attention the contents of the Kaiser's private letter on naval matters to Lord Tweedmouth, the First Lord of the Admiralty. Chesterton dismisses this claim as 'a deliberately calculated attempt to create a sensation at the expense of the Kaiser and generally damage Anglo-German relations.' (*NA* II, 20, p. 381)

Cecil Chesterton proceeds to argue that *The Times* is on the wane, up for sale to the highest bidder[31] - a fact that is well known on the Continent, he claims.[32] The paper 'no longer represents the feeling of the English nation' and 'its consistent anti-German attitude has been a real source of alarm to friends of peace'. Although not a pacifist, he clearly sees no justification for war at this stage. He concludes with the observation that the views expounded in *The Times* are supported by the *Daily Express* - a publication which Chesterton had already singled out for derision over its condemnation of German Socialists.[33] In the months that followed, the *New Age* attacked other contemporary papers, including the Socialist *Clarion*, for printing articles by Lord Cromer and H. M. Hyndman that claimed war with Germany was unavoidable. Chesterton ventures to suggest that the *Clarion* is just as guilty of war-mongering as *The Observer*[34] and the *National Review*, a paper which continually fell foul of the *New Age* because of its anti-German stance.[35] Following his attack on the *Clarion* Chesterton concedes the volatile nature of the international situation, but calls on Socialists of all nations to unite in opposing war between England and Germany. Any Anglo-German conflict will be the result of ill-considered press reports.

---

31   In 1908 the Walter family, which founded *The Times*, put the newspaper up for sale. See *The Newspaper in Britain: an annotated bibliography*, edited by David Linton and Ray Boston (London and New York, 1987), p. 328.

32   In 1908 there were rumours that a German syndicate, possibly headed by the Kaiser himself, was trying to buy *The Times*. See Oliver Woods and James Bishop, *The Story of the Times* (London, 1983), p. 196.

33   24 October 1907; *NA* I, 26, p. 311.

34   Owned by Lord Northcliffe and edited by J. L. Garvin, *The Observer* was notoriously anti-German. See Richard Cockett, *David Astor and the Observer* (London, 1991), p. 59.

35   For attacks on the *Clarion* see *NA* III, 16, p. 301. Criticism of J. L. Maxse's Germanophobia in the *National Review* was voiced in *NA* III, 3, p. 58 and *NA* III, 7, p. 136.

Chesterton is sufficiently detached to suggest 'Is it not conceivable that the fear of sudden attack which now animates the pens of English sensational journalism may be precisely the same force which is now moving the facile pens and brains of German journalists?' (15 August 1908; *NA* III, 16, p. 301)

Events in 1908 were serious enough for the *New Age* to send one of its correspondents to Nuremberg at the end of August to report on German reaction. The correspondent, William Saunders, an alderman on London County Council, had already contributed four articles to the *New Age* on the Social Democrats in Germany. From Nuremberg he sent three articles on the attitudes of the German Socialists to the war scare, as well as a report on their annual congress.[36] Throughout the articles he argues in favour of cooperation between Socialists in England and Germany to combat jingoism. On 5 September 1908 he notes that the German Social Democrats' paper, *Vorwärts*, has quoted 'at considerable length' from the *New Age's* attacks on war-scaring in the English press during the crisis (*NA* III, 19, p 363). Interest in opinion in Germany ran high, with a further essay on the war scare by C. H. Norman using the pen-name Stanhope of Chester, as well as a report by Ashley Dukes on an address to the German Socialists given by August Bebel. In addition, the *New Age* published an article by Louis Cahen entitled 'Der Drang nach Osten', discussing the future of the Austrian policy of expansion in the Balkan peninsula in the event of the death of the Austrian Emperor.[37] Thus, the concerns of the *New Age* were far from insular at this stage.

Book Reviews: Die sexuelle Frage 'a book for cultured persons'

A similar lack of insularity is to be found on the arts pages of the periodical, where the emphasis is on European culture. The book reviews, for instance, attempt to find a wider readership for works by Italian, French and German authors. They refer to the English translations, when available, but otherwise to the originals - thus assuming a reading knowledge of German, in particular, on the part of subscribers to the *New Age*. In the first three volumes alone reviews appeared of Max Stirner's *The Ego and his Own*, the second volume of Marx's *Capital*, Eugene Richter's *Pictures of the Socialist Future*, Elie Metchnikoff's *The Prolongation of Life*, Paul Eltzbacher's anthology *Anarchism*, Clara Viebig's *Absolution*, Auguste Forel's *Die sexuelle Frage*, Hans Plehn's *Nach dem englisch-japanischen Bündnis*, Nietzsche's *Ecce Homo*, Helen

---

36   See *NA* II, nos. 14, 17 and *NA* III, nos. 4, 8. For Saunders' reports from Germany see *NA* III, nos. 18, 19, 20 and 22.
37   See 15 August 1908; *NA* III, 16, pp. 303-4, 17 October 1908; *NA* III, 25, p. 491 and 1 August 1908; *NA* III, 14, p. 264.

Zimmern's translation of *Jenseits von Gut und Böse* and the second edition of *Thus spake Zarathustra*, reviewed by A. R. Orage himself.[38] Occasionally the reviewers criticised the poor quality of the English translations or pointed out the need to translate a work into English when it deserved a wider audience. In the case of Auguste Forel, it was a campaign by the *New Age* that prompted the issue of an English edition of *The Sexual Question*, although when it was reviewed, criticism was levelled at certain mistranslations of the German, the most glaring example being the work's subtitle: 'Ein Buch für Geliebte', rendered into English as 'A Book for Cultured Persons'.[39] Evidently this mistranslation was the result of confusing 'Geliebte' with 'Liebhaber', which, as well as meaning 'lover', could also mean 'amateur'.

Nietzsche 'will always appeal to the Latin more than the Teutonic temperament'

Perhaps not surprisingly, given the interests of the editor, the early volumes of the *New Age* devoted much space to Friedrich Nietzsche. Without wishing to turn this into a discourse on Nietzsche alone, some discussion of the reception of the philosopher by the *New Age* is crucial to an understanding of the periodical's dissemination of German culture in England. One of the main concerns was to obtain a complete English edition of the works of Nietzsche. In an article on Helen Zimmern's translation of *Beyond Good and Evil* the unsigned reviewer, who is most probably Orage, poignantly remarks that this is only the fifth English translation of Nietzsche to appear in eleven years since the first translation of *Also sprach Zarathustra* by Thomas Common in 1896. By comparison, in France, the full sixteen volumes are available in French translation. To make matters worse, the English volumes are expensive, with *Thus spake Zarathustra* retailing at a daunting eight shillings and sixpence. The reviewer considers it a reflection of the insular English national character that few will bother to read Nietzsche either in the original or in French translation, and questions whether Nietzsche will ever receive a proper understanding in England. A further problem is the nature of Nietzsche's appeal, which fits uneasily into the English cast of mind. According to the reviewer, there is 'a flame in his style and ideas which easily communicates itself to imaginative minds, and just as readily

---

38   See *NA* I, 16, p. 250; *NA* I, 24, p. 412; *NA* II, 3, p. 54; *NA* II, 10, p. 196; *NA* III, 6, p. 114; *NA* III, 12, p. 236; *NA* III, 21, p. 413; *NA* II, 4, p. 74; *NA* III, 26, pp. 513-14; *NA* I, 25, p. 398 and *NA* III, 8, p. 153.

39   Arnold Bennett had complained in his column about the absence of an English translation of Forel's *Die sexuelle Frage*. This sparked off a debate in the journal, with the New Age Press eventually obtaining an English edition and printing it at the end of July 1908.

alarms the pedants who dislike nothing so much as heat, even when luminous. Hence Nietzsche will always appeal to the Latin more than the Teutonic temperament. The latter, indeed, will probably never understand Nietzsche; or understanding him, will become obsessed after the faithful Teutonic way. Unfortunately, however, there is not much danger of an obsession with Nietzsche in the mind of England. When so elementary a nature as Mr. G. K. Chesterton utterly fails to grasp the elementary distinction between the relative Bad and the absolute Evil,[40] there is little wonder if the majority of his contemporaries, temperate in mind and almost frigid in the climate of drama, gape with horror at the bare suggestion that Good and Evil are only relative terms after all, and in the absence of any defined aim in life meaning nothing more than that Mrs Grundy has usurped the throne of Jehovah.' (17 October 1907; *NA* I, 25, p. 398)

Since at least 1904, with his speech at the Leeds Arts Club, G. K. Chesterton had been a consistent opponent of Nietzsche, arguing with both Orage and Bernard Shaw. The argument spilled into print in *Heretics* (1905), *Orthodoxy* (1908) and *George Bernard Shaw* (1909), as well as into his fiction, most notably in *The Man Who Was Thursday* (1908)[41] and later in the short stories involving Father Brown.[42] With such a prolific and influential writer as Chesterton lobbying against the German philosopher, it is little wonder that the *New Age* circle was concerned about the detrimental effect that this quintessentially English author was having on the *Nietzschebild* of his countrymen.

A. R. Orage: 'the difficulties of Nietzsche in England'

Orage's review of the second edition of *Thus spake Zarathustra* takes up the issue of the need for more, cheaper editions of Nietzsche's work. Although he admits that the English reading public is generally unadventurous, he lays the blame firmly on the English publishers, Unwin. He calls into question the wisdom of making *Also sprach Zarathustra* the first, rather than the last, of the Nietzsche canon to be translated into English. Orage argues that in the 1890s, at a time when Ibsen's dramas were being translated and produced on the English stage and when tragedy was much discussed, the obvious work to translate would have been *Die Geburt der Tragödie*, which would have gradually accustomed the English reader to Nietzsche's views. Instead, *Thus spake Zarathustra* was overpriced and sold badly. Orage contends 'If *Zarathustra* had been as dull as say,

---

40 In the first section of *Zur Genealogie der Moral* Nietzsche had distinguished between the terms 'bad' and 'evil'. See Nietzsche, *Werke*, II, p. 785ff.

41 See G. K. Chesterton, *The Man who was Thursday* (London, 1908), pp. 110-11.

42 See, for example, *The Secret of Father Brown* (London, 1927), p. 159.

Kant, the price might have been justified. But *Zarathustra* had a good many of the elements of popularity. At a reasonable price and with judicious advertising, the first edition might have been sold in a year or two at least. By this time, instead of the four or five of Nietzsche's works, we should now have had the complete set, as they have long had in France.' The first work to be translated into French, *Richard Wagner in Bayreuth*, had appeared as long ago as as 1877, only a year after its first German publication. Orage also notes that the translation of *Zarathustra*, unaltered since the first edition, is still not as good as it should be. Alexander Tille's introduction is a further drawback because 'One would suppose from the tone of it that the Professor was introducing a learned dunce to an audience of dons. Except for a few phrases, there is nothing to indicate the meaning or value of the colossal poem that *Zarathustra* really is. It merely adds to the difficulties of Nietzsche in England' (20 June 1908; *NA* III, 8, p. 153). The German, Alexander Tille, a professor at Glasgow University in the 1890s, had edited the first four volumes of the English translation of Nietzsche. However, a conflict with his students over the Boer War had precipitated his return to Germany and caused a lapse in the translations. These were not resumed until the Helen Zimmern translation in 1907, edited by Thomas Common, and again in 1909 when Dr Oscar Levy,[43] a German Jew living in London, took over the general editorship.

Between 1907 and 1908 Oscar Levy contributed three articles to the *New Age*, reviewing Leo G. Sera's *Sulle Tracce Della Vita*, John Morley's *Miscellanies* and a French edition of the letters of Stendhal. Wherever possible Levy makes at least passing reference to Nietzsche, although not always wholly accurately.[44] Nevertheless, he was esteemed by his *New Age* colleagues as an expert on the philosopher. Indeed, his name was so closely associated with Nietzsche that in 1914 this became a source of harassment as Germanophobia swept the country.[45] As we shall see, what had once been a position of honour for Levy became a burden as armchair philosophers looked for a scapegoat for German actions in patterns of German thought, particularly in popularized form.

---

43 See M. E. Humble, 'Early British Interest in Nietzsche', *German Life and Letters*, 24 (1971), pp. 328-9.

44 In discussing Stendhal's alienation from his native country, Levy quotes Nietzsche (in German): 'Ein guter Deutscher sein, heisst sich entdeutschen.' The exact quotation in *Menschliches, Allzumenschliches* is 'Gut deutsch sein heisst sich entdeutschen'. Nietzsche, *Werke*, II, p. 85.

45 See Oscar Levy, 'Nietzsche im Krieg' (1919), in *Nietzsche und die deutsche Literatur. Texte zur Nietzsche-Rezeption 1873-1963*, edited by Bruno Hillebrand, 2 vols (Tübingen, 1978), I, p. 193.

Possibly the most original aspect of the literary pages of the *New Age* in the early volumes was the appearance in translation of five Nietzsche poems, quite independent from those contained either in the existing English edition of his work or in the later Levy edition. The translator chose anonymity, signing himself cryptically E. M. It is easy to speculate that these initials might have belonged to Edwin Muir, although unlikely that they did, as Muir did not contribute to the periodical until 1912 and probably did not know German at this stage.[46] Perhaps a more likely source would be Orage himself, who in Leeds had been translating some of the poems;[47] for the six hundred or so aphorisms contained in his book of this period *Nietzsche in Outline and Aphorism* (1907), he must have been engaged in at least some translation work. There was certainly a need for a good translation of Nietzsche's poetry. A version of sorts by John Gray had appeared in 1899 when it was included in Alexander Tille's edition of *A Genealogy of Morals*, which was translated by William A. Haussmann. However, the English was heavy, in places almost unreadable, as well as severely hampered by basic errors and mistranslations. Nor was the edition complete. Of the *Dionysos-Dithyramben* three poems - *Nur Narr! Nur Dichter, Die Wüste wächst: weh dem, der Wüsten birgt* and *Klage der Ariadne* - were omitted. In 1907 the *New Age* published new translations of *Unter Feinden (nach einem Zigeunersprüchwort), Letzter Wille, Das Feuerzeichen*, extracts from *Ruhm und Ewigkeit* and selected verses from the *Bruchstücke zu den Dionysos-Dithyramben* - this latter selection was receiving its first English translation. Indeed, in order to make this selection more accessible to English audiences, it was entitled *Fragments and Parables 1. The songs of Zarathustra which he sang to himself in order that he might endure his last loneliness*, thus alluding to the third part of *Also sprach Zarathustra*.[48] What is perhaps most striking about *Fragments and Parables* and the other poems in the *New Age*, which are reproduced in Appendix 1, is that they all work as perfectly acceptable English poetry, rather than as translations of German verse.

Max Nordau and 'his gospel of Entartung'

In the early years of the twentieth century attempts were made at biography in which works of art were attributed to pathological sources.

---

46   Edwin Muir, *Autobiography* (London, 1957), p. 126.

47   See pp. 26-7.

48   See Nietzsche, *Werke*, II, p. 404.

Lombroso had elaborated a pseudo-scientific theory of the degenerate nature of the man of genius, inspiring Möbius to write so-called 'pathographies' of Goethe and Nietzsche, in which their ideas were traced to pathological origins. Such an approach was attempted by Max Nordau, author of *Entartung* (1895), which had severely damaged Nietzsche's reputation in Germany and in England by suggesting that his philosophy was that of a madman. The *New Age* vociferously repudiated this diagnosis when it published an open letter from Bernard Shaw to Max Nordau that was in fact a reprint of an article in the *Frankfurter Zeitung*. Nordau had complained to the German paper that Shaw had referred to him as a Jew and was therefore guilty of anti-Semitism. Shaw denied the charge, contending that for Nordau to be known as a Jew in England would do him credit because people would conclude that he was 'an able man, a rich man, a cultivated man, and a man of pedigree'. Shaw continued to argue: 'The fact is you do not know your people very well. Otherwise you would not have been offended by that "einer jener" of which you complain. "Einer jener kosmopolitischen Juden, die gegen die moderne Kultur ausziehen." You are amazed at this. You exclaim "Der gegen die moderne Kultur ausziehende kosmopolitische Jude ist also ein Typus, eine bekannte klassierte Gattung, auf die man nur hinzuweisen braucht, damit jeder wisse, was man meint". Is it possible that you are the only man in Europe who does not know this? Have you never heard of Karl Marx and Ferdinand Lassalle? Do you seriously believe that your gospel of Entartung was received by Europe as a dithyramb of modern culture instead of a fierce attack upon it? Why, you actually drove me, a professed Socialist and malcontent, to defend Civilization against you. You will tell me next that Jeremiah was a Christian courtier and optimist'. Shaw claims he was compelled to 'demolish' Nordau because Nordau's theories were misleading the English and the Americans. He suggests that Nordau branded Wagner, amongst his other targets in *Entartung*, as a lunatic, without really reading the works of those he attacks. His knowledge is derived from Lombroso, who 'having studied nothing at first hand but criminal lunatics, has made the discovery that criminal lunatics are human beings'. Nordau has 'made the discovery that men of genius are human beings also' and come to the conclusion that 'men of genius are criminal lunatics' (18 January 1908; *NA* II, 12, pp. 223-4). A few months later Karl Kraus gave Nordau's approach equally dismissive treatment. When specifically attacking Möbius' 'pathography' of Goethe, Kraus mused that 'Neurologists, who write pathologies on genius, should have their skulls smashed with their collected works'.[49]

---

49   Karl Kraus, *Die Fackel*, 256 (5 June 1908), p. 21.

German Drama in London: 'Anyone who has ever been through a German reading primer should catch on at once'

Drama criticism in the *New Age* was much preoccupied with Ibsen, at a time when the Norwegian dramatist was enjoying a vogue in England. In addition to regular articles by the resident drama critic, Dr. Leslie Haden Guest, the periodical published a three-part transcript of an address delivered at Pen-y-ralt by the translator of Ibsen, William Archer, in September 1908 on the subject of 'Fabianism and the Drama'. Part of Archer's aim in the address was to introduce new European drama to English audiences. In the course of discussing foreign plays 'that spring either from poverty or the actual fear of it', Archer recommends Hauptmann's *Weavers, Hannele* and *The Thieves Comedy* and Sudermann's *Die Ehre* (10 October 1908; *NA* III, 24, p. 469). There was certainly an interest in the German theatre, as reviews of plays being produced in London reveal. In September 1908, for example, Beerbohm Tree produced Goethe's *Faust* at His Majesty's Theatre, taking the role of Mephistopheles. However, Haden Guest has to report that 'only in a very snobbish mood could it claim any relationship with Goethe'. In his opinion, the difficulty lies in the production which in Tree's hands is too conventional, the Brocken scene, in particular, relying too much on scenic effect. Haden Guest advocates a modern, contemporary setting, far removed from the traditional sets associated with the Devil's surroundings. Only then can audiences take the Devil seriously. (19 September 1908; *NA* III, 21, p. 416)

If this attempt at staging mainstream German drama met with a lukewarm reception in the *New Age*, plays by more modern, experimental writers were greeted with interest. In addition to William Archer's concern with German Naturalism, Haden Guest drew attention to productions *in German* at London theatres. In May 1908, for instance, he reviews a German company's production of *Der Weg zu Hölle* by Gustav Kadelburg (1851-1925) at the Royalty Theatre.[50] His review is favourable, although he regrets the sparseness of the audience for the comedy which is 'riotously excellent'. He ponders 'Doubtless the German language had something to do with it, but the Company act so remarkably well, and pronounce their words with such fine distinctness that the play is extremely easy to follow. Anyone who has ever been through a German reading primer should catch on at once.' The only real problem for English theatregoers, according to the critic, is coming to terms with German humour, which allows

---

50   This largely forgotten comedy, which enjoyed great popularity in its day, was first performed in 1905 in Berlin. See J. P. Wearing, *The London Stage 1900-1909: A Calendar of Plays and Players*, 2 vols (London, 1981), II, p. 651.

men and women to be 'rather mercilessly laughed at' (9 May 1908; *NA* III, 3, p. 38). It is a theme which he had already touched on when reviewing the New Stage Club's productions of Arthur Schnitzler's *The Farewell Supper* (now part of *Anatol*) and *Literature* at the Bijou Theatre. Whilst attempting to make Schnitzler's name known to a wider public in England, Haden Guest admits 'One imagines the dramatist like a giant butterfly collector, watching his victims writhe on the stage where he has pinned them, with a grim smile. The Schnitzler mood hardly allows sympathy, it is hard, it is exhilarating, it is gay mockery, and without remorse'. This so-called Schnitzler mood is wholly lacking in modern English comedy, Haden Guest notes, whilst debating whether a three or four act drama by Schnitzler would demand more sympathy than these one act plays. He concludes that there is a need to see more Schnitzler one-acters, as curtain raisers, in the hope that this will arouse sufficient interest for theatre managers to risk mounting longer dramas by Schnitzler. (21 March 1908; *NA* III, 21, pp. 417-18)

Music: 'Oh! for an English Nietzsche'

The relationship of the music critic of the *New Age*, Herbert Hughes[51] to Germany might best be described as one of *Haßliebe*. His first concern is for British music to be taken seriously, and to promote Elgar as a composer of world rank, while praising Henry Wood's Promenade Concerts for stimulating an interest in British composition[52] and Thomas Beecham's New Symphony Orchestra for performing important works by contemporary composers. His targets are orchestras such as the London Symphony Orchestra, which looks 'askance at anything post-Wagnerian',[53] and English composers who are too dependent on German models.[54] Further attempts were made to reject Wagnerism with a series of essays by Edward Carpenter, entitled 'Music-Drama in the Future',[55] although it must be said that Carpenter offered no real concrete alternative for future trends in music, once the yoke of Wagner was overthrown. Herbert Hughes, on the other hand, was in no doubt about what was needed in order to shake up contemporary attitudes to concert repertoire that accepted without question the preference for established, German composers. In one of his earliest columns in the *New Age* Hughes confided in his readers 'Oh! for an

---

51   Hughes (1882-1937) contributed music criticism to the early issues of the *New Age*, but left in 1911 to join the staff of the *Daily Telegraph*.
52   See *NA* I, 8, p. 134 and *NA* I, 16, p. 254.
53   *NA* III, 1, p. 18.
54   See, for example, Hughes' criticism of a book entitled *Sechs Lieder von Edward Agate*. (24 October 1907; *NA* I, 24, p 411)
55   See *NA* III, 16 and 17.

English Nietzsche, who would make music while the kettle was boiling over; who couldn't care whether they liked his "programmes" or not; who could put the Labour Party to music; who could leave his little wooden hut and ask for gin-and-bitters in dotted crotchets and quavers; who could solve the Education problem in a *Scherzo*; who could expose the immorality of *Parsifal* in a *Danse Macabre*' (27 June 1907; *NA* I, 8, pp. 134-5). Nietzsche cherished hopes of becoming a composer. In 1872 he sent a score to the conductor Hans von Bülow. It was returned with the advice that he should abandon a musical career.[56] This episode in Nietzsche's life was clearly ignored by Hughes, who viewed Nietzsche as a byword for iconoclasm and mould-breaking. English music needed a new set of values, to be freed from the pattern of German composers who had so dominated the music scene.

In addition to seeking new values, Hughes also championed the latest developments in German music when he considered they deserved attention. For this reason, he promoted Richard Strauss to English audiences. Whilst decrying the surfeit of established composers in the concert repertoires of 1907, there is equal evidence in his columns of that period to indicate his fascination with Richard Strauss. He was, for example, particularly enthusiastic about Strauss' *Salome Dances* when reviewing a concert given by the New Symphony Orchestra under Fritz Cassirer (7 December 1907; *NA* II, 6, p. 118). Only the dances from *Salome* could be performed, since both the Strauss opera and the Oscar Wilde play were banned in England at this time.

---

56   Bülow's criticism of Nietzsche the composer is evident in a reply drafted by Nietzsche but never sent to Bülow. See draft letter of 29 October (or shortly before), in *Werke*, III, pp. 1075-7.

Chapter 2: Germany and the *New Age*:
November 1908-October 1910

Between 1908 and 1910 the *New Age* underwent a number of changes that had a significant effect on the *Deutschlandbild* of the journal. By 1909 Orage had moved away from party politics, devoting less space to pieces by the established socialists and more to literary matters.[1] In 1909 Orage took over from Cecil Chesterton as sole author of the political commentary, 'Notes of the Week', with which the periodical always opened.[2] This section now concerned itself primarily with home affairs, whilst a separate column dealt with events abroad. Initially this foreign affairs commentary was written by Stanhope of Chester, an alias of the radical writer C. H. Norman,[3] then S. Verdad, the latter a pseudonym of the former *Daily Telegraph* journalist and translator of Nietzsche, J. M. Kennedy. Cecil Chesterton remained as assistant editor until the autumn of 1911 and during this time he contributed a variety of signed articles on subjects ranging from the licensing laws to votes for women. In addition, he found time to conduct a heated argument over Socialism with his brother G. K. Chesterton.[4] Perhaps most indicative of the swing in emphasis from political to literary concerns was the appointment of Cecil Chesterton, this most pugnacious of political journalists, as drama critic of the *New Age* for a brief period from January until April 1909. Indeed, under Orage's editorship the periodical devotes considerable attention to the latest developments in German drama. This is most evident in the articles written by Chesterton's successor as drama critic, Ashley Dukes. After the First World War Dukes became an important intermediary for the reception of German Expressionist drama in England, although his contribution to Anglo-German literary relations begins much earlier with his articles for the *New Age*. Dukes was not the only writer indebted to Orage for the opportunity to publish at an early stage. In 1910, for example, Orage published a series of short stories by Katherine Mansfield, based on her experiences in Bavaria. It was not until the following year that they appeared in the anthology *In a German Pension*. At the same time, as in the earlier volumes, the *New Age* continued to review recent publications in Germany and translations of German authors into English. There was discussion of the problems arising from

---

1   John Carswell, *Lives and Letters* (London, 1978), p. 45.

2   Wallace Martin, *The New Age under Orage: Chapters in English Cultural History* (Manchester, 1967), p. 121.

3   In 1911, following complaints from the Foreign Office, Stanhope of Chester was removed from the *New Age*. Ibid., p. 123.

4   See *NA* IV, 22, pp. 439-40 and *NA* V, 1, pp. 8-10.

translation, particularly verse translation, as well as articles on music, although these were no longer a weekly feature in the later volumes. In addition, the *New Age* continued to discuss Nietzsche with articles by Oscar Levy, J. M. Kennedy and A. R. Orage. However, it would be a misrepresentation to view the periodical solely as a vehicle for the propagation of Nietzschean thought. The German philosopher represented only one aspect of the journal's interest in German culture.

'Scare' Novels: The Coming War with Germany

Political commentary in the *New Age* focused not so much directly on events in Germany as on contemporary British publications and their position vis-à-vis Wilhelm II and his policies. Ever since the early volumes the *New Age* had singled out for attack Leo Maxse, editor of the fiercely Germanophobic *National Review*. In 1909 Robert Blatchford, editor of the Socialist *Clarion*, met with censure over a series of six articles he had written for Northcliffe's *Daily Mail*, in which he argued that there was a very real threat posed by Germany. In the *New Age* Stanhope of Chester responded with the comment: 'The moment England and Germany begin to overcome their mutual jealousies, those crazy politicians Mr. Maxse and Mr. Robert Blatchford stir up blood with their renewed chatter about "The Coming War with Germany".[5] After all, what would the editor of the *National Review* do for a living if there were an Anglo-German alliance?' (18 November 1909; *NA* VI, 3, p. 53). As early as 1909 Robert Blatchford, in his articles about the German peril, stirred up enough blood for them to be republished in 1914 as a propaganda tract entitled *Germany and England: the War that was foretold.* Arguing that Wilhelmine Germany is pursuing 'the Bismarckian policy of deliberate and ruthless conquest, with world-dominion for its goal', whilst Britain is merely maintaining the balance of power in Europe, Blatchford, imbued with old-soldier sentiments, advocates the introduction of conscription, preferably under the leadership of Lord Kitchener. The threat to England of German invasion is so dire that 'on the day when the king of Prussia was declared German Emperor Britain ought to have adopted compulsory military

---

5   Ever since the Franco-Prussian War in 1870 there had been concern in England about the ineviatbility of a war at some stage in the future. After 1900 Germany was invariably depicted by English writers as the most likely enemy in a future conflict. See Bernard Bergonzi, 'Before 1914: Writers and the Threat of War', *Critical Quarterly*, 6 (Summer, 1964), p. 129.

service'.[6] However, in 1909 the potential consequences of this type of scare-mongering are so devastating that Orage explicitly states that 'there neither is, was, nor will be any real German peril to England; but an artificial peril is always there to be created. In truth, as we would explicitly warn our German friends, the real peril is precisely the contrary. There is far more likelihood of England being goaded to make war upon Germany than of Germany making an unprovoked war upon England.' (13 January 1910; *NA* VI, 11, p. 243)

It is the press that wields the power to stir up emotions and bring England to the brink of war. Nevertheless, fear of invasion had been a characteristic of English popular fiction for some time. Practically from the moment Germany achieved unification English writers started to produce 'scare' novels. As early as May 1871 in *The Battle of Dorking: Reminiscences of a Volunteer* Chesney narrated the cautionary tale of England being conquered by Germany. The vogue for this type of fiction continued until the First World War. Erskine Childers' *The Riddle of the Sands* (1903), for example, took as its theme the threat of German naval superiority, whilst in *The War in the Air* (1914) H. G. Wells depicted an attack on England by German forces made invincible through great technological advancement. Although there clearly was a popular belief in the German peril, Orage came close to the view of certain modern historians when he asserted that the government in Berlin did not seek war with England. As Fritz Fischer observes, whilst there was rivalry between Germany and England with the Kaiser vying with the Prince of Wales as a modern monarch who dealt with businessmen and scientists, the policy was not to invade England. Even the controversial building of the German fleet was intended to guarantee Germany the status of a world power on the grounds that: 'This seemed the only possible means of both ranking alongside England as a world power and of being recognised as an equal by the other world powers'.[7] It was certainly true that Germany had raised herself to third place amongst the capitalist nations after England and the United States.[8] As an increasingly important political and economic power Germany felt some justification in regarding herself as a new nation, destined to claim her 'place in the sun' amongst the older powers. It could be argued that the desire to compete on an equal footing with England does not necessarily signify a plan to mount an invasion. Indeed, even as late as the July crisis of 1914 Bethmann Hollweg still counted on the neutrality of England in the event of a war

---

6   Robert Blatchford, *Germany and England: The War that was foretold* (1914), p. 7 and pp. 34-7.

7   Fritz Fischer, *Griff nach der Weltmacht* (Düsseldorf, 1961), p. 17.

8   Klaus Schröter, 'Chauvinism and its Tradition: German Writers at the Outbreak of the First World War', *The Germanic Review*, XLIII (March 1968), p. 121.

in Europe. Between 1912 and 1914 he remained consistent in his argument that if Russia could be seen to provoke a European war and thus made to assume guilt for the war, England would not intervene. Germany would then be able to invade France without engaging in conflict with England.[9] Although the German Ambassador in London, Graf Lichnowsky, warned that this belief was an illusion, it suggests that the government in Berlin did not view England as a target for invasion in the pre-war years. Even so, there existed more sinister voices within the 'broader' government, such as Jagow, the *Staatssekretär*, who was plotting with Berchtold, the foreign minister, in Austria.[10]

The German peril which preoccupied Blatchford provided the stimulus for a series of inspired replies from contributors to the *New Age*. W. R. Titterton, for instance, responded with a humorous piece on the benefits which England would reap from a German invasion.[11] In 'Why not surrender to Germany?' Titterton invites the Germans to invade England. Once they had conquered, the Germans would merely 'dismantle Tilbury, appropriate a fat indemnity and a morsel of South Africa, and march away'. They would leave because England would prove too difficult to govern as a German province, since 'even if there were enough German officials to go round, the task of making the English people speak German would be colossal.' Apart from this language difficulty, the English would profit enormously from German occupation. They would have a freer press and access to a wider variety of books since the German reading public enjoys both serious and frivolous reading matter. Germans satisfy their literary appetite on 'poems, essays, philosophical, ethical, scientific books and squibs, as well as novels, and actually prefer the books that contain ideas they disagree with.' In addition, England would gain first-rate theatres, a love of art and an adoration of music 'with and without beer'.[12] England under the Germans would also gain state support for scientific research and a social life comparable with that found in the cafes and beer halls of Southern Germany - a feature which might even engender tolerance amongst Londoners. Since Germany comprises small states, all very different in character, England, by becoming a German state, would not lose her identity. Titterton contends that 'the Bavarian national character differs more from the Prussian than the Prussian does from the English'

---

9   Fritz Fischer, op. cit., p. 45. See also p. 82.

10   Ibid, p. 46.

11   W. R. Titterton had considerable experience of Germany and had contributed to the *New Age* since the early issues, often writing articles of a light-hearted nature.

12   Possibly this reference was an allusion to Nietzsche, who in *Götzendämmerung* had observed that the Germans had stultified themselves with German music and beer. See *Werke*, II, p. 984.

(14 April 1910; *NA* VI, 24, pp. 562-3). Thus, Titterton argues, using a technique reminiscent of Jonathan Swift in *A Modest Proposal* (1729),[13] it would be in the best interests of England to surrender as soon as possible to a German invasion force.

On a more serious level, in his signed article 'A Study in Jingoism', C. H. Norman illustrates the war-mongering taking place in the press of both England and Germany by citing extracts from English chauvinists alongside translations of their German counterparts. He prefaces his article with the comment: 'Mr Robert Blatchford, Mr Leo Maxse, the Imperial Maritime League, Lord Cawdor, and others deliberately lie when they pretend that the Pan-German school of writers voice the German people. The Pan-German school, the Kaiser, von Bülow, Count von Moltke, Herr Harden, and von der Goltz equally lie when they allege that the utterances of Mr Robert Blatchford, Mr Leo Maxse, the Imperial Maritime League, and Lord Cawdor represent the beliefs and ambitions of the British people.' There follow bellicose comments from Maxse, Blatchford, von Bülow, Hollweg, Bismarck and the Kaiser, although the last two are only quoted for condemning August Bebel and the German Social Democrats as unpatriotic. Despite the introductory comment, no quotation is attributed to Maximilian Harden specifically. Somewhat prophetically in view of what would be written in 1914 Norman includes a citation from the German professor Treitschke (spellt Treitsche in the article). Treitschke's contribution to this study in jingoism is his claim: 'We have settled our accounts with Austria-Hungary, with France, and with Russia. The last settlement, the settlement with England, will probably be the lengthiest and most difficult' (6 January 1910; *NA* VI, 10, p. 223). In 1914, English writers looking to the traditions of German thought to explain German actions pointed accusingly at Treitschke, Hegel and Bernhardi 'with Nietzsche in reserve for those who wished to leave nothing to chance'.[14] Treitschke had lectured in Berlin since 1874, often voicing anti-English sentiments. His argument was based on the belief that natural laws govern historical events, with social and cultural phenomena thus historically determined. Essentially this would follow the Hegelian precept of accepting laws of historical development, which claim the necessity in historical processes and which have the effect of subduing or undermining the belief in human intervention. In these terms, it was argued that the rational processes of history were bringing Germany to the status of world power. The means employed to achieve this position to

---

13   In this savage tract, Swift, making allegedly positive reference to what most people would consider a disaster, suggests that the children of the poor should be fattened to feed the rich.

14   Stuart Wallace, *War and the Image of Germany. British Academics 1914-1918* (Edinburgh, 1988), p. 47.

such neo-Hegelians were immaterial - even war could be justified under these circumstances. The main tenets of Treitschke's doctrine were therefore 'acquiescence in the amorality of political action and unquestioning belief in the rights of a rising nation'.[15] For the English historians who contributed to the series *Oxford Pamphlets*, there was little doubt that Treitschke and the Prussian School of German history represented the decay that had taken place in German intellectual life since 1870. Writing in this series Ernest Barker, Professor of History at Oxford, argues that 'the cult of power and the praise of war are as much articles of faith with Treitschke as they are with Nietzsche; but the power is the power of Prussia and the war is the war of Prussia.'[16] Yet within German intellectual circles Treitschke had been neglected since his death in 1896, and the younger generation of historians such as Erich Marcks and Max Lenz looked to Ranke instead.[17] Even Thomas Mann's work in support of Germany's involvement in the First War, *Betrachtungen eines Unpolitischen*, with its amazing intellectual jugglings and contortions, contains only four quotations from Treitschke, although the Berlin professor was frequently quoted in German newspapers and periodicals of the time.[18]

S. Verdad: Germany seeks 'a war with England'

Until May 1910 the political section of the *New Age* suggests a certain continuity of approach towards Germany. The articles, from a variety of contributors are sympathetic. However, the appointment of S. Verdad as foreign affairs correspondent marks a dramatic change in outlook. His articles are violently anti-German in tone, although he denies accusations from readers that he is part of the 'alarmist tribe' that write for the *National Review*. He is adamant that Germany seeks war with England and warns his readers: 'I can testify from my own personal experience of Germany within the last few years that nothing would be more popular throughout the Empire than a war with England' (12 May 1910; *NA* VII, 2, p. 27). The 'Empire' is clearly the German Empire that competes with its fiercest rival the British Empire for world-power status. What is most surprising is that this Germanophobic article should come from the pen of a journalist familiar with Germany. His *New Age* colleagues who had spent time in Germany denied rumours of German war-mongering. S. Verdad was a pen-

---

15   T. J. Reed, *Thomas Mann. The Uses of Tradition* (Oxford, 1974), p. 216.
16   Ernest Barker, 'Nietzsche and Treitschke. The Worship of Power in Modern Germany', *Oxford Pamphlets* (1914), p. 18.
17   Stuart Wallace, op. cit., p. 68.
18   Hermann Kurzke, 'Die Quellen der *Betrachtungen eines Unpolitischen*', *Thomas Mann Studien*, VII (Bern, 1986), p. 294.

name for J. M. Kennedy who was engaged in translating Nietzsche into English for the Levy edition. He had worked for the *Daily Telegraph*, spoke most European languages fluently, was 'an assiduous reader of foreign periodicals' and rarely missed any 'articles of political significance'.[19] His negative opinion of Wilhelmine Germany is therefore all the more striking.

Nietzsche in English

Between 1908 and 1910 Nietzsche continued to receive much coverage in the *New Age*. In addition to the editor's own interest in the German philosopher, the periodical could boast several of the leading Nietzschean experts and translators as its contributors by 1910. Oscar Levy, editor of the complete English translation of Nietzsche's works, had written for the paper since the early volumes. He was joined by J. M. Kennedy, author of the study *The Quintessence of Nietzsche* (1910), and A. M. Ludovici. who in the autumn of 1908 delivered a course of lectures on Nietzsche at University College London.[20] In 1934 Ludovici recalled his first meeting with the editor of the *New Age* in October 1908:

> 'It must have been twenty six years ago last month that I first met Orage. It was about the time that I was preparing to deliver my lectures on Nietzsche at University College. We sat together in a tea-shop close to Gower Street and discussed Plato, particularly the *Gorgias*, with reference to Nietzsche's *Will to Power*.'[21]

Both Ludovici and Kennedy were engaged in what Levy vaunted as 'the most complete and voluminous translation of any foreign philosopher into the English language'.[22] For the Levy edition Ludovici translated *Unzeitgemäße Betrachtungen*, *Der Fall Wagner*, *Götzendämmerung*, *Der Antichrist* and *Ecce*

---

19 Wallace Martin, op. cit., p. 123.

20 Ludovici lectured on 'Nietzsche - The Immoralist', 25 November 1908, 'Nietzsche's Superman', 2 December 1908 and 'Nietzsche - The Moralist', 9 December 1908.

21 A. M. Ludovici, *New English Weekly. A. R. Orage Memorial Number*, VI, 5 (15 November 1934), p. 115.

22 Oscar Levy, 'The Nietzsche Movement in England. A Retrospect, a Confession, and a Prospect', in *Index to the Complete Works of Friedrich Nietzsche*, edited by Levy, (London, 1913), p. x.

Homo, as well as a volume of Nietzsche's letters. He also translated a further two volumes as *The Will to Power* and *The Eternal Recurrence* for this edition. Kennedy translated *Morgenröte* and *Über die Zukunft unserer Bildungsanstalten*, whilst H. B. Samuel translated *Zur Genealogie der Moral*, W. A. Haussmann *Die Geburt der Tragödie* and M. A. Mügge *Die Philosophie im tragischen Zeitalter der Griechen.* Thomas Common, who had worked on the earlier Tille edition, translated *Die fröhliche Wissenschaft* and *Also sprach Zarathustra* and wrote the introduction to Helen Zimmern's translation of *Jenseits von Gut und Böse*. Together with Paul Victor Cohn, who was responsible for rendering the poems into English, Helen Zimmern also translated *Menschliches, Allzumenschliches*. She held the distinction of having been Nietzsche's own choice for the English translator of his work. In 1888 Nietzsche confided in a letter to Peter Gast that, having found a possible French translator for his *Götzendämmerung*, he thought that a suitable English translator might be Helen Zimmern, who at that time was living in Geneva and was in immediate contact with his friends Fynn and Mansouroff. According to Nietzsche, through her translations she had 'revealed Schopenhauer to the English: why should she not do the same for his absolute opposite?'[23]

Helen Zimmern had translated Schopenhauer into English and known Nietzsche before the onset of his insanity. Indeed, he described her as part of his circle of 'old friends'.[24] Her translation of *Jenseits von Gut und Böse* was complete in the 1890s, but because of the difficulty in finding a publisher, did not appear until 1907 when Levy, at private risk, assumed editorship of the complete edition of Nietzsche's work in English.[25] In the earlier Alexander Tille edition, the only translations published were *Thus spake Zarathustra* (1896), *The Case of Wagner, Nietzsche contra Wagner, The Antichrist* (1896), *A Genealogy of Morals, Poems* (1899) and *The Dawn of Day* (1903). The Levy edition of the complete works, together with an index, was finished in 1913.

Nietzsche was well aware of the difficulties of translating his work. In 1888 he discussed the problem with August Strindberg. He would prefer to see *Ecce Homo* appear simultaneously in German, French and English. However, having sent the manuscript to the printer the previous day, he still does not know which translators should be allowed to tackle his printed work. He praises the 'excellent French' and 'masterly translation' undertaken by Strindberg himself in his play *The Father* (1887) and hopes to enlist the Swedish dramatist in the translation of his own *Ecce Homo*. Such an undertaking, he confides

---

23   9 December 1888, in *Werke*, III, p. 1339.
24   Letter to Frank Overbeck, Summer 1886, in *Werke*, III, p. 1241.
25   Oscar Levy, op. cit., p. x.

'requires a first-class poet; in the expression, in the refinement of feeling, it is a thousand miles beyond all mere "translators" [...] On the question of the English translation. What would you propose? - An anti-German book in England...'[26]

Amidst all this frenetic publishing activity, the *New Age* kept abreast with the latest works on Nietzsche to appear. It ran reviews of M. A. Mügge's *Friedrich Nietzsche: His Life and Work*, Ludovici's *Who is to be Master of the World? An Introduction to the Philosophy of Friedrich Nietzsche*, which was based on his lectures at University College, and J. M. Kennedy's *Quintessence of Nietzsche*.[27] In addition, Orage printed an extract from Elizabeth Förster-Nietzsche's publication of her brother's letters to J. B. Widmann in order to illustrate Nietzsche's impartial attitude to his critics (10 December 1908; *NA* IV, 7, p. 134). The source was an article which had originally appeared in *Bohemia* in September 1907. In 1909 Orage secured an article by Karl Heckel, translated from the German by J. M. Kennedy, entitled 'Genius or Superman?' (20 May 1909; *NA* V, 4, pp. 72-3 and 27 May 1909, *NA* V, 5, pp. 95-6). It was reproduced in the *New Age* 'with the special permission of Mr Maximilian Harden', in whose paper, *Die Zukunft*, it had originally appeared. This would therefore suggest some form of contact between the editor of the *New Age* and Harden in Berlin. At the very least it is highly probable that Orage and his circle were familiar with *Die Zukunft*. Harden's biographer has observed that even before the notoriety surrounding the Eulenberg trials Harden, as the editor of *Die Zukunft*, was known far beyond Germany's borders. Although his importance nor that of his periodical can be judged by circulation alone, in 1900 *Die Zukunft* already had 10,000 subscribers, several times more than similar literary and political periodicals of that time. Harden's *Die Zukunft* was quite simply 'a guide to the ideas and problems of a generation'.[28] The *New Age* had already discussed Harden's role in the Eulenberg trials (31 October 1907; *NA* II, 1, p. 2), so it is likely that English writers had been looking to this 'guide to the ideas and problems of a generation' for some time when seeking comment on German literature and politics.

---

26   Letter to August Strindberg, 7 December 1888, in *Werke*, III, pp. 1337-8.
27   See 26 April 1909; *NA* IV, 26, p. 526, 31 December 1908; *NA* IV, 10, p. 208 and 27 January 1910; *NA* VI, 13, pp. 304-5.
28   Harry F. Young, *Maximilian Harden. Censor Germaniae. Ein Publizist im Widerstreit 1892 bis 1927* (Münster, 1971), pp. 137-8.

The review of Kennedy's *Quintessence of Nietzsche*, although unsigned, was probably by Orage himself. The reviewer takes issue with both Kennedy and Ludovici for mistaking Nietzsche's poetic visions for literal truths with the result that they see Nietzsche as a biological philosopher like Spencer or Bergson, try to make Nietzsche consistent and assume the finality of his judgements. In an earlier signed article, 'Towards Socialism IX. The Infant Democracy', Orage had already discussed Nietzsche's inconsistency (30 November 1907; NA II, 5, p. 89). Not only does Orage take issue with the commentators on Nietzsche in 1910, but he takes issue with Nietzsche as well. The article is called 'Nietzsche: The Lyrical Bismarck', he informs us, in order to 'draw attention to what has hitherto been overlooked in him, though in truth it is the wood of which all his political ideas are the trees. Namely, the essential Prussian, and Imperial-Prussian, character of his political speculations. It was not for nothing that Nietzsche's first book appeared two years after Sedan. In fact he was Bismarck's intellectual executor, Bismarck's justification, Bismarck's 'Apologia pro Vita Sua.' According to this argument, Nietzsche shared not only Bismarck's anti-socialist views but provided the basis for Bismarck's state as well. Thus, the dictum contained in *Also sprach Zarathustra*, 'Man shall be educated for war, and woman for the recreation of the warrior. Everything else is folly',[29] comes to signify 'Bismarck's Prussian system in a sentence'. It will conscript every man into the army and turn every woman into a 'combined child-bearer, housewife and mistress! The Prussian drill-sergeant and the German hausfrau, with a quiverful of young Germans, to ensure the future of the empire. And for what? That Bismarck's Germany, Germany should be over all.' Nietzsche cannot be taken seriously as a political philosopher if this is the practical outcome of his thinking. Only as a poet, psychologist and preacher does he merit admiration (27 January 1910; NA VI, 13, pp. 304-5). In a signed article Orage puts the divergence between Nietzsche the political thinker and Nietzsche the supreme poet even more succinctly when he declares: 'Nietzsche as a poet learned more than Nietzsche as thinker could ever express. His doctrine, besides, is vulgarly Imperialist. Nietzsche was the German Eagle!' ('Unedited Opinions', 11 March 1909; NA V, 20, p. 399). Whilst Orage is here suggesting that the German eagle has negative associations with imperialism, it is worth remembering that in Nietzsche's *Also sprach Zarathustra* the eagle, along with the snake, is one of Zarathustra's companions. Flying high above the ground, the eagle symbolises pride whilst the snake stays close to the earth and represents cleverness. Both are presented as positive attributes and in the course of the

---

29   See Nietzsche, *Werke*, II, p. 328.

narrative Zarathustra learns from his animals. The eagle and the snake intertwine, suggesting 'the overcoming of the old dualisms of light and darkness, heaven and earth, good and evil; their intertwining is beyond good and evil, a harmony of earth and sky'.[30] Zarathustra prizes the qualities of the eagle and reproaches those who consider themselves wise for being 'no eagles' and for never having known 'the happiness that is in the terror of the spirit'. Those who are not birds, 'should not build nests over abysses'.[31]

The equation of Nietzsche with the German Eagle in 1909 suggests a modification in Orage's thought. Previously he had shown no opposition to German nationalism, nor voiced any reservations about Nietzsche, whom he had wholeheartedly embraced as 'the greatest European event since Goethe'.[32] Indeed, when he made this statement only three years earlier in 1906, he was greatly impressed with German nationalism and outlined a proposal dangerously close to National Socialism. On 6 March 1906, after the failure of the German Social Democrats to win the 1906 election, Orage wrote in the *Leeds Mercury* that Socialism had lost its way, was incapable of inspiring society or redeeming man. It had become diluted into Labourism. Salvation was only possible in the form of 'a national movement, even in its Chauvinist form of "Germany over all".' According to Orage such a movement displayed 'splendour', 'imagination', 'wholeness' and 'sanity'.[33] His use of the refrain 'Germany over all' is particularly revealing. In 1906 it epitomizes a praiseworthy nationalist movement. By 1909 it has acquired negative connotations for Orage, emphasizing his disillusionment with German nationalism. His articles in the *New Age* betray an increasing alienation from his earlier political thought and a more cautious admiration for Nietzsche.

Although the editor of the *New Age* was revising his *Nietzschebild* in 1909, he continued to make his periodical a forum for free discussion of the German philosopher. The latest volumes of the Oscar Levy edition - *Thoughts out of Season* and *The Birth of Tragedy* - were reviewed (May 1909; *NA* V, 2, pp. 38-9) and a previously unpublished fragment from *Jenseits von Gut und Böse*

---

30   Laurence Lampert, *Nietzsche's Teaching. An Interpretation of Thus Spoke Zarathustra* (London, 1986), p. 29.

31   Nietzsche, *Werke*, II, p. 362. See also Philip Grundlehner, *The Poetry of Friedrich Nietzsche* (Oxford, 1986), pp. 195-6.

32   A. R. Orage, *Friedrich Nietzsche: The Dionysian Spirit of the Age* (London, 1906), p. 11.

33   Tom Steele, 'From Gentleman to Superman: Alfred Orage and Aristocratic Socialism', in *The Imagined Past. History and Nostalgia*, edited by Christopher Shaw and Martin Chase (Manchester, 1989), p. 120.

appeared in a translation by J. M. Kennedy.[34] The nine fragments in the *New Age* compare the Europeans, who, according to Nietzsche, imagine themselves as representing 'the highest types of men on earth', with the Oriental who, unlike the European, 'is true to himself in daily life'. Europeans are inconsistent because Christianity 'has abandoned the class from which it sprang'. The Renaissance attempted honesty in order to benefit the arts. Michelangelo's conception of God as the 'Tyrant of the World' was honest. Thus, Nietzsche rates Michelangelo higher than Raphael because he saw 'a culture *nobler*' than that conceived by Christianity or Raphael. The latter only 'glorified the values handed down to him, and did not carry within himself any enquiring, yearning instincts'. Leonardo da Vinci had a 'super-Christian outlook', having seen 'too wide a circle of things good and bad'. Nietzsche goes on to discuss the 'German Mephistopheles', who is 'more dangerous' than Goethe's conception: bolder, more wicked and cunning 'and *consequently* more open-hearted'. The real German Mephistopheles 'crosses the Alps, and believes that everything there belongs to him. Then he recovers himself'. He wonders whether the Germans have grown up in the wrong climate, arguing that 'there is something in them that might be Hellenic! - something that is awakened when they are brought into touch with the South - Winckelmann, Goethe, Mozart'. The Germans are 'a dangerous people' because they are 'experts at inventing intoxicants, such as, Gothic, Rococo, Hegel, Wagner and Leibnitz'. The 'smallness and baseness of the German soul' are not the result of the system of small states, since 'it is well known that the inhabitants of much smaller states were proud and independent; and it is not a large state *per se* that makes souls freer and more manly'. (16 December 1909; *NA* VI, 7, p. 156)

Book Reviews: 'to most Englishmen modern German poetry is virgin soil'

The latest publications from Germany were followed assiduously and a miscellany of reading matter discussed. German Socialist publications continued to arouse interest, with reviews of *Was will die Zeit?*, an anthology of articles by early Socialist writers compiled by Kurt Barclay and Erich Max, and August Bebel's *Aus meinem Leben*, the first volume of memoirs by the recently retired leader of the German Social Democrats, covering Bebel's involvement in German Socialism from 1860 until 1870.[35] There were also reviews of German authors in English translation, most notably Clara Viebig's *Our Daily Bread* and a version of *Faust* by Stephen Phillips and J. Comyns Carr. Unfortunately *Faust*

---

34   The fragments appeared in the thirteenth volume of the Levy edition (1913), following a translation of *A Genealogy of Morals* by Horace B. Samuel.
35   See 25 February 1909; *NA* IV, 18, p. 367 and 19 May 1910; *NA* VII, 3, pp. 62-3.

proved to be an expensive 'travesty of Goethe's great work' in the hands of these translators, since the 'vulgar, licentious and blasphemous' sections had been deleted - possibly as a concession to English prudery. As a result, Beerbohm Tree's production gives the English public a spectacle of fireworks, quick changes and storms.[36] Further works to be reviewed included Calvin Thomas' *A History of German Literature*, a survey of German literature from the Nibelungenlied to Sudermann and *Die englische Literatur im Zeitalter der Königin Victoria* by Professor L. Kellner.[37] Of the regular contributors to the *New Age*, only Arnold Bennett, who wrote the weekly column 'Books and Persons' under the pseudonym Jacob Tonson (an allusion to Samuel Johnson's publisher), showed little concern with German literature. His real interest lay in finding a wider public for French authors.

German verse attracted much attention, with reviews of collections by poets from various periods, Goethe and Heine, the poets most usually associated with the 'Land der Dichter und Denker', were discussed alongside less well-known contemporary poets as the *New Age* attempted to find a wider audience in England for modern German writing. On 5th August 1909, for example, J. S. Flint discussed *German Lyricists of To-day*, translated by Daisy Broicher, an anthology of poetry by Stefan Georg, Hugo von Hofmannsthal, Ernst Hardt and Karl Vollmoeller (*NA* V, 15, p. 289). The following year Flint devoted rather more space to *Contemporary German Poetry*, selected and translated by Jethro Bithell, a lecturer at Manchester University. Bithell's volume is singled out for particular praise because 'to most Englishmen modern German poetry is virgin soil' (14 April 1910; *NA* VI, 24, pp. 567-9). Bithell is breaking new ground because not only has he translated Hofmannsthal and Dehmel, who, according to Flint, already have a few admirers in England, but also because he has introduced poets who have never had a hearing outside their native country. Thus, the English at last have access to the work of Else Lasker-Schüler, Peter Hille, Peter Baum, Maximilian Dauthendey and Alfred Mombert. In the same article, involving a rather long and tedious discussion of the theory of translating poetry, Flint also examines a translation of Heinrich Heine's poems and ballads by Robert Levy (apparently no relation of Oscar). In January 1910 Robert Levy became a contributor to the *New Age* with a new translation of Goethe's ballad *Der Gott und die Bajadere*, which is reproduced in Appendix 2.

---

36   7 December 1908; *NA* IV, 8, Literary Supplement, pp. 1-4. Haden Guest
       had already panned Tree's performance of *Faust*; *NA* III, 21, p. 416.
37   See 29 July 1909; *NA* V, 14, p. 273 and 13 May 1909; *NA* V, 3, pp. 57-8.

Orage was not only interested in publishing German writers and translations from the German in his periodical, he was also concerned to introduce his readers to work by English writers with experience of Germany. In 1910 Katherine Mansfield's talent was recognised by Orage. He printed her poem *Loneliness* and eight short stories based on her experiences in Bavaria. The stories appeared between February 1910 and June 1911 and were later collected in the anthology *In a German Pension*, which was published in December 1911.[38] Katherine Mansfield knew German,[39] had read Heine and Nietzsche and was a relative of Countess von Arnim, the renowned author of *Elizabeth and her German Garden*.[40] She was therefore another of Orage's contributors with first hand knowledge of German language and culture. Nevertheless, the tone of the stories that now form *In a German Pension* is not particularly Germanophile - possibly as a result of Katherine Mansfield's personal circumstances at the time of her stay in Bavaria.[41] The mood of *Germans at Meat*, for example, is especially hostile towards one type of German encountered by Katherine Mansfield in the Bavarian boarding-house. Anglo-German antagonism comes to the fore at the dinner table when Kathleen, the English narrator of the story, falls into disagreement with Herr Rat. Arguing that the English have every reason to worry about being invaded because they 'have got no army at all - a few little

---

38　The poem *Loneliness* was published on 26 May 1910; *NA* VII, 4, p. 83. The stories appeared in the following order: *The Child Who Was Tired* (24 February 1910; *NA* VI, 17, pp. 396-8), *Germans at Meat* (3 March 1910; *NA* VI, 18, pp. 419-20), *The Baron* (10 March 1910; *NA* VI, 19, p. 444), *The Luft Bad* (24 March 1910; *NA* VI, 21, p. 493), *At Lehmann's* (7 July 1910, *NA* VII, 10, pp. 225-7), *Frau Brechenmacher attends a Wedding* (21 July 1910; *NA* VII, 12, pp. 273-5), *The Sister of the Baroness* (4 August 1910; *NA* VII, 14, pp. 323-4), *Frau Fischer* (18 August 1910; *NA* VII, 16, pp. 366-8), *A Birthday* (18 May 1911; *NA* IX, 3, pp. 61-3) and *The Modern Soul* (22 June 1911; *NA* IX, 8, pp. 183-6). *In a German Pension* included a further three stories, hitherto unpublished, *The Advanced Lady*, *The Swing of the Pendulum* and *The Blaze*.

39　See Claire Tomalin, *Katherine Mansfield. A Secret Life* (London, 1987), pp. 21-3 and Jeffrey Meyers, *Katherine Mansfield. A Biography* (London, 1978), pp. 13-16.

40　John Carswell, op. cit., pp. 54-6.

41　Her view of Germany may have been coloured by the fact that she was recovering from the premature birth of a stillborn child. See Jeffrey Meyers, op. cit., p. 51.

boys with their veins full of nicotine poisoning', Herr Rat 'fixed his cold blue eyes upon Kathleen with an expression that suggested a thousand premeditated invasions'. Herr Hoffmann from Berlin increases the tension when he adds 'Don't be afraid. We don't want England. If we did we would have had her long ago. We really don't want you' (3 March 1910; *NA* VI, 18, p. 419). In *The Baron*, a story which is not quite so overtly hostile as *Germans at Meat*, Katherine Mansfield takes the opportunity to mock what she considers the excessive respect for titles and social status of the Germans. The Germans at the guest house are filled with awe at the arrival of 'one of the First Barons'. Although a regular visitor, this nobleman has never yet spoken to any of the other guests. However, the Herr Oberlehrer, who cherishes the hope that one day the Baron might indulge in 'some splendid upheaval of that silence', dreams of a 'dazzling exchange of courtesies in a dim future, a splendid sacrifice of a newspaper to this Exalted One, a *danke schön* to be handed down to future generations' (10 March 1910; *NA* VI, 19, p. 444). Such a negative depiction of Germany did not meet with whole-hearted approval from *New Age* readers. The stories sparked off a series of letters to the editor, questioning whether Katherine Mansfield had any real know-ledge of Germany.[42] It is curious that the complete anthology did not appear in German translation until as late as 1983, although certain individual stories that were less hostile towards Germany had been published earlier in German translation.[43] Katherine Mansfield quickly grew dissatisfied with these short stories and in 1914 refused £500 to republish *In a German Pension* on the grounds that she did not wish 'to be increasing the odium against Germany'.[44] She came to consider the youthful bitterness and cynicism of her work to be untrue and unworthy of her talents. Nevertheless, she owed her first opportunity to publish to A. R. Orage and for this privilege, like so many contributors to the *New Age*, she received no payment.[45] Bernard Shaw, for example, contributed over two dozen articles to the *New Age* between 1907 and 1921 entirely free of charge, so high was his regard for Orage's ability as editor.[46] There is no doubt that Orage's periodical was attracting a relatively large readership at this time. In autumn

---

42 See, for instance, *NA* VI, 19, p. 545 and *NA* VI, 20, p. 478.

43 B. J. Kirkpatric, *A Bibliography of Katherine Mansfield* (Oxford, 1989), pp. 198-204. In 1952 *The Sister of the Baroness*, *The Luft Bad* and *Frau Brechenmacher attends a Wedding* appeared in Germany.

44 John Middleton Murray, 'The Literary Review', *New York Evening Post* (17 February 1923), p. 41. Quoted by Ruth Elvish Mantz, *Critical Bibliography of Katherine Mansfield* (New York, 1968), p. 30.

45 Ibid, p. 30.

46 See Shaw's tribute to Orage in the *New English Weekly*. *A. R. Orage Memorial Number*, VI, 5 (15 November 1934), pp. 99-100.

1908, for example, circulation rose from less than 4000 per week to 20,000,[47] although the *New Age* still ran at a loss.[48] This rapid increase in circulation is not only a tribute to Orage's merits as editor, but provides further evidence that the periodical, with its profound interest in German culture, played an influential role in the reception of German literature and thought in England.

Ashley Dukes: 'the German-speaking public takes its theatre seriously'

Orage was probably at his most innovative in his choice of drama critics for the *New Age* between 1908 and 1910. W. R. Titterton, who, as we have seen, had already contributed a number of articles relating to Germany, was also employed as theatre critic in 1908. He compared two recent productions at the New Theatre: W. B. Yeats' *Deirdre* (1907) and Hugo von Hofmannsthal's *Electra* (1904) in an English translation by Arthur Symons. Titterton contrasts the treatment of similar themes, one 'in the delicate allusive manner of the Celt', and the other in 'the heavy definite brutal manner of the German'. The production of *Electra* prompts him to observe that Hofmannsthal, 'like Goethe in *Iphigenie*, has modernised' Greek Tragedy by deciding not to make Destiny a person in the drama (10 December 1908; *NA* IV, 7, p. 42). Prior to 1910 there were dramatic societies in England that occasionally put on plays by contemporary Continental dramatists, such as this performance of *Electra*, but in general audiences had scant awareness of new writers.[49] Under Orage's editorship the *New Age* sought to rectify this situation by promoting contemporary dramatists, who in certain cases had not even been translated into English. Although Titterton was followed for a brief period by Cecil Chesterton, who did not reveal himself to be particularly adventurous in his choice of theatre, it was Chesterton's successor, Ashley Dukes, who proved most able at pursuing this avant-garde policy.

Between the two world wars Ashley Dukes made a considerable contribution to Anglo-German literary relations, translating and adapting modern German drama for the English stage. After the First World War, for example, Dukes tried to bring innovations in the German theatre to English audiences, still bitter towards their wartime enemy. He translated Georg Kaiser's *Von morgens bis mitternachts* (1916) which holds the distinction of being the first play by a German writer to be produced on the English stage after 1918.[50] There followed a

---

47   See John Carswell, op. cit., p. 41 and Wallace Martin, op. cit., p. 10.
48   Antony Alpers, *The Life of Katherine Mansfield* (London, 1980), p. 107.
49   See Wallace Martin, op. cit., p. 74.
50   J. M. Ritchie, 'Ashley Dukes and the German Theatre Between the Wars', in *Affinities. Essays in German and English Literature*, edited by R. W. Last (London, 1971), p. 103.

translation of Ernst Toller's *Maschinenstürmer* (1923) and of his long poem *Das Schwalbenbuch* (1924), Alfred Neumann's *Der Patriot* (1927), an adaptation of Lion Feuchtwanger's *Jud Süß* (1929), an English version of Ferdinand Bruckner's *Elizabeth of England* (1931)[51] and in 1938 an ill-fated plan for an English version of *War and Peace* to be written by Alfred Neumann and Erwin Piscator and directed by Piscator.[52]

However, Dukes' contribution to Anglo-German literary relations began much earlier and can be traced back to his pre-war articles for the *New Age*. In 1907 he resigned as lecturer in science at London University. He moved to Munich, where he became fluent in German and immersed himself in the arts, particularly the theatre. He saw 'almost the entire list of controversial plays of the period', including works by Hauptmann, Maeterlinck, Strindberg, Ibsen, Gorki, Shaw, Schnitzler and Hofmannsthal.[53] Carrying only a postcard from Bernard Shaw as his means of introduction, Dukes managed to get himself invited to rehearsals of all foreign plays and to persuade *Die neuesten Nachrichten* to publish two of his articles on English and Irish drama, written in German.[54] After holidaying in Vienna and Budapest to take in more German plays, he moved from Munich to Zürich, where he read Goethe's *Faust*, Stefan Georg's poetry and Nietzsche's *Also sprach Zarathustra* and *Die Geburt der Tragödie*. He read both volumes of Nietzsche 'in the lyrical German' and regarded them as 'an Old and New Testament'.[55] During this period he met Auguste Forel who held the Chair of Psychiatry at Zürich University. It was from this Swiss base that Dukes sent his first contribution to Orage's periodical in the summer of 1908: a translation of a series of articles by Forel on the sexual question.[56] He also contributed translations of speeches by the German Socialists August Bebel and Georg Ledebour, as well as a report on the celebration of May Day in Zürich and extracts from his own plays.[57] Nevertheless, Dukes' most important work for the *New Age* came in his drama criticism. He recalled that Orage was in no doubt as to the sort of plays he should be reviewing:

---

51   Ibid, p. 102.
52   See John Willett, *The Theatre of Erwin Piscator* (London, 1978), pp. 147-50.
53   Ashley Dukes, *The Scene is Changed* (London, 1941), p. 17.
54   Ibid., p. 23.
55   Ibid., pp. 29-30.
56   See *NA* III, 17, p. 328, *NA* III, 19, p. 363, *NA* III, 21, p. 407 and *NA* V, 18, pp. 328-9.
57   See *NA* III, 25, p. 491, *NA* VI, 20, pp. 461-2, *NA* V, 2, p. 31 and *NA* III, 21, pp. 410-11.

'Orage, who was always a good editor, suggested that instead of gnashing my teeth weekly over plays that his readers would never go to see, I should write about the Continental stage and its dramatists. This suited me perfectly, and the series began with the Scandinavians and went on with Germans, Austrians, Frenchmen, Russians, Dutchmen and Italians, with Shaw, Barker and Galsworthy as the three [Royal] Court Theatre playwrights planted in the midst of them!'[58]

From 7 October 1909 Dukes went on to discuss approximately two hundred plays, and of these less than thirty had already been reviewed in England.[59] He wrote on Sudermann, Wedekind, Schnitzler, Strindberg, Björnson, Chekhov, Gorki and D'Annunzio, complying with Orage's directives.

Bernard Shaw in German: 'every German book seems to have a new vocabulary of its own'

Dukes' first article as theatre critic concerned the success of Bernard Shaw at home and abroad. He notes on 7 October 1909 that *Mrs Warren's Profession* 'is now nearing the end of its second run in Berlin, and has become by far the best known of his plays in Germany and Austria. This very striking success is another proof, if proof were needed, that the German-speaking public takes its theatre seriously. I have seen several Shaw plays very indifferently acted in Germany, but the performances of *Frau Warrens Gewerbe* by the Hebbel-Theater company keeps a high standard. Several actresses have already made big reputations in the part of Mrs Warren. When all the other European capitals have seen and approved it this play may perhaps be tolerated in London' (*NA* V, 24, p. 432). Through his Austrian-born translator, Siegfried Trebitsch, Shaw had become a household name in Germany. Trebitsch had met Shaw for the first time in 1902, armed with a letter of recommendation from William Archer, who had introduced the Austrian writer to Shaw's work in the first place.[60] He had begun by translating into German *The Devil's Disciple*, *Candida* and *Arms and the Man*. By February 1903 he had persuaded the director of the Raimund Theater in Vienna to stage *The Devil's Disciple*, whilst in the same year Cotta in Stuttgart

---

58   Ashley Dukes, op. cit., p. 32.
59   Ibid, p. 74.
60   Michael Holroyd, *Bernard Shaw, Vol. II, 1898-1918. The Pursuit of Power* (London, 1989), p. 48.

published all three plays in Trebitsch's translation. In 1904 the Deutsches Volkstheater produced *Candida* and *Arms and the Man*, and in the course of the next four years German audiences were able to see *You Never Can Tell*, *Mrs Warren's Profession* and *Man and Superman*.[61] Thus, by 1909 *Frau Warrens Gewerbe* was firmly established in the German theatrical repertoire. The translation of Shaw into German brings us back to the question of the dramatist's own knowledge of the language. Although he had read Delville's French translation of Marx's *Capital* and relied on Ashton Ellis's translation of Wagner's *Prose Works* at the time of writing *The Perfect Wagnerite*, when he acquired a German translator for his own work he duly found himself investing in 'a devil of a big dictionary, also a grammar' that caused him to complain that 'every German book seems to have a new vocabulary of its own. None of Trebitsch's words are in the dictionary!'[62] Nevertheless, as time went on, he found enough of the words in the dictionary to be able to castigate Trebitsch for littering the German version of *Caesar and Cleopatra* with so many misunderstandings as 'to make it necessary that I should go through every sentence carefully' and for filling the translation of *Arms and the Man* with 'hideous and devastating errors'.[63] Although Shaw resolutely defended Trebitsch from public criticism, the quality of the German translations in the first edition of Shaw's work left much to be desired. Michael Holroyd cites the example of Trebitsch's misinterpretation of the Waiter's remark in *You Never Can Tell*: 'I really must draw the line at sitting down'. After the Waiter has delivered this line, in Trebitsch's German stage directions, he is made to go to the windows and, before taking his seat, draw the curtains.[64] Ashley Dukes was clearly aware of flaws of this nature when he observed that 'there seems to be a very good case for the formation of a Society for the Protection of Authors from Translators. Bernard Shaw has suffered badly enough in Germany, and nearly all modern European authors of repute have been vicariously slaughtered in England'. In this respect, Hauptmann's *The Sunken Bell* has often fallen victim to the 'many bunglers' who have 'attempted the impossible with that incomparable poem' (31 March 1910; *NA* VI, 22, p. 523). *Die versunkene Glocke* (1896) has largely faded into obscurity. Although popular in its day as a reaction against the bleakness of Naturalism, this five act verse drama was over-dependent on the use of myths and symbolism in its depiction of the tragedy of the artist. Significantly, Dukes' discussion of the need for accurate translations in both English and German comes in the context of a review of the Stage Society's production of a cycle of one-act plays by the Viennese dramatist Felix Salten. In

---

61   Ibid, p. 51.

62   Ibid, p. 49.

63   Quoted by Michael Holroyd, op. cit., p. 49.

64   Ibid, pp 53-4.

1926 Salten became Dukes' German translator, adapting Dukes' comedy *The Man with a Load of Mischief* for the Burgtheater in Vienna.[65]

August Strindberg: 'there is hardly a repertory theatre in the smallest German town where some of his plays at least have not been performed'

On 4th November 1909, Ashley Dukes devoted his column to August Strindberg in honour of the Swedish dramatist's sixtieth birthday. Although familiar to theatre-goers on the Continent, Strindberg was still practically unknown in England. Dukes comments wryly that the English know about the latest developments in European politics almost immediately, 'but a European influence in literature, a centre of radiant intellectual power, is passed by unnoticed for whole decades. This neglect of Strindberg in England, however, is quite exceptional. There is hardly a repertory theatre in the smallest German town where some of his plays at least have not been performed. They may be bought in book form at every bookseller's shop' (*NA* VI, 2, p. 41). When discussing Strindberg's dramas, Dukes refers to their German titles, such as *Glückspeter, Fräulein Julie* and *Gläubiger*, citing extracts from the German edition (*Elf Einakter*) in Dukes' own English translation. It was not until 1912 that the Adelphi Play Society first performed *Miss Julie* in an English translation by Maurice Elvey and Bernard Shaw's sister, Lucy, that Strindberg caught the interest of English audiences.[66] Apart from the number of Strindberg plays being performed and the easy availability of his works in Germany, the Swedish writer could boast several prominent German admirers from an early stage. Nietzsche, for example, wrote to Strindberg as early as December 1888 to express his admiration. He confessed: 'After reading your *The Father* for the second time I wrote to you at once, deeply moved by the penetrating psychology.'[67]

By contrast, Strindberg had made little impact in England. Dukes concludes his piece by quoting from an article by Maximilian Harden that had appeared in his journal *Die Zukunft* in September 1907. Harden had asked: 'Need the gentlemen of Stockholm delay any longer in bestowing the Nobel Prize upon their greatest countryman - an artist of as high achievement as any to whom it has been given; a writer who gives us more life and individuality in the slightest sketch than Björnson does in whole volumes; a poet indeed, who has already won a place among the immortals' (*NA* VI, 2, p. 42). Harden had been instrumental in the reception of Strindberg in Germany. In 1895, for instance, the Berlin editor had called for a fund to be set up in order to enable the impoverished Strindberg

---

65   Ashley Dukes, op. cit., p. 104.
66   Michael Holroyd, op. cit., p. 197.
67   7 December 1888, in *Werke*, III, p. 1336.

to come to Germany and continue his work.[68] This was over ten years before Strindberg was beginning to receive anything like comparable attention in England.

Ludwig Thoma: 'a decatholicised, altogether unmoral, Rabelaisian Chesterton'

Alongside his interest in serious dramatists, Dukes revealed a liking for discussion of more popular, contemporary playwrights. In June 1910, for instance, he brought his readers' attention to the Bavarian writer Ludwig Thoma (1867-1921). Today, rather unfortunately, Thoma is best remembered for his anti-semitism, although he was first known as the author of *Ein Münchner im Himmel*. Prompted by a production of his play *Moral* (1909), translated for the Stage Society's performance as *Champions of Morality*, Dukes discusses as a whole the work of this ironic satirist of Bavarian life. Dukes readily admits that Thoma is 'a jovial spirit', but 'not a great dramatist', who, as a Bavarian writer, is well qualified to adopt an ironic stance towards the Prussian Kaiser. According to Dukes, *Moral* abounds with the same 'jack-in-the-box irreverence as his other work'. In Munich, we are informed, Thoma is compared to Bernard Shaw, although Dukes considers it more accurate to describe him as 'a decatholicised, altogether unmoral, Rabelaisian Chesterton, brimming over with vitality, and ready at any moment for a game of intellectual leapfrog'. Thoma is popular with the Bavarians because he represents 'the quintessence of physical indolence and mental irresponsibility, detestation of control and love of laughter'. Dukes advises his English readers that further examples of these qualities in Thoma's work may also be found in his contributions to the periodicals *März*, *Simplicissimus* and *Jugend*. (2 June 1910; *NA* VII, 5, pp. 113-114)

Recent German Drama: Gerhart Hauptmann, Hermann Sudermann and Frank Wedekind

Dukes' concern with the German stage extended to discussion of more serious contemporary dramatists. In his article 'Recent German Plays' he features Gerhart Hauptmann's *Griselda* (1909), Hermann Sudermann's *Strandkinder* (1909) and Frank Wedekind's *Oaha* (1909). Dukes opens his article with a general comment on the state of the English stage. He perceives a trend amongst theatre managers for importing French plays, whilst neglecting German drama because 'the *Daily Mail* does not like Germany, and that settles the question. It means that the public will not like plays about German people with German names.' He

---

68   Harry F. Young, op. cit., p. 35.

argues that had Sudermann been a Frenchman, at least ten of his plays would be enjoying long runs on the London stage. So far English audiences have only seen Sudermann's *Heimat* (1893), rather misleadingly rendered into English as *Magda*, yet *Die Ehre* (1890) and *Rosen* (1907) would transfer perfectly acceptably to theatres in England. However, this is not to say that Dukes admires every play written by Sudermann. He goes on to condemn *Strandkinder* as 'the later work of a playwright-millionaire - of an author who now writes from habit rather than impulse'. Sudermann was at the height of his literary powers between 1880 and 1900, when his works were compared favourably with those of Ibsen. In the Ibsenite battle then raging in Germany Sudermann was regarded as one of the leaders of the modern movement, especially when his *Sodoms Ende* (1891), with what Dukes rather oversimplistically calls its criticism of the bourgeoisie, was banned in Berlin. By contrast, Hauptmann has had extravagant praise lavished on him by German university professors, who turned from 'the interminable study' of the second part of *Faust* to *Rose Bernd* (1903) and *Jungfern von Bischofsberg* (1905). In Dukes' opinion, only the plays written at the beginning of Hauptmann's career - *Die Weber* (1892), *Die versunkene Glocke* (1896), *Fuhrmann Henschel* (1898) and *Michael Kramer* (1900) - are truly worthy of merit. *Griselda* is simply mediocre. Contrary to the current trend of thought in German criticism that presents Hauptmann as the equal of Goethe, Dukes perceptively refuses to make such connections. He contends that comparison with the sage of Weimar can be detrimental to the future career of a rising author. As for Wedekind, his drama is the result of debasing ideas into a mere vogue for freethinking. Although his *Frühlings Erwachen* (1891) contains 'many scenes of rare beauty', as a work for the stage it is 'a distinguished failure'. It is interesting that Dukes is so unperceptive here, although the play remained forgotten until Kenneth Tynan recommended it for production in the 1960s. Wedekind's latest play *Oaha* is 'as ugly as its title', a glaring example of 'satire without wit' (23 June 1910; *NA* VII, 8, pp. 183-4). From these observations Dukes is forced to conclude that the later work of these three major German dramatists is disappointing. Whilst his aim is to promote the newest developments in German drama, he clearly does not embrace all the latest theatrical fashions without question. Ashley Dukes' judgements on modern German drama therefore remain objective and his criticisms constructive.

Despite his reservations about contemporary German dramatists, Dukes continued to be fascinated by them, devoting two longer articles to Wedekind, a feature on Sudermann and a piece on Schnitzler, all in the autumn of 1910. When discussing Wedekind, Dukes observes that in his home country the German dramatist has a reputation for having 'slain morality' because his plays represent 'the last word in unconventionality and daring' by dragging 'pathology, sex perversion and insanity relentlessly upon the stage.' However, Dukes counters that in fact Wedekind preaches a stern morality in his dramas and that this aspect has earned him the nickname 'Frau Nietzsche'. Although his plays are often tasteless and formless, they are valuable because of their sheer power, offering a rare criticism of modern life by presenting it from a new angle. He therefore cannot be dismissed as a 'hawker of cheap optimistic philosophy like Sudermann', or even be said to share Hauptmann's 'sympathy with the common man', since the common man is a member of the public whom he despises as 'an animated doll built of cowardly prejudices' (6 October 1910; *NA* VII, 23, p. 544). As an iconoclast, Wedekind in the theatre resembles Nietzsche's 'Zarathustra in the market place'. Of Wedekind's plays, Dukes considers *Oaha* and *Hidalla oder die Moral der Schönheit* (1904) to be purely autobiographical, exploiting personal grievances. *Die Büchse der Pandora* (1904) is flawed by its third act, written in an idiosyncratic English which 'is calculated to impress Berlin rather than London.' Wedekind's most successful work, in Dukes opinion, is *Frühlings Erwachen* which is treated with 'rare delicacy and beauty'. The appearance of 'der vermummte Herr' in this work is one of the most beautiful scenes in the Wedekind canon, although Dukes argues that this scene is not really designed for the stage because the change from realism to fantasy is too sudden. Indeed, Dukes regards this as a criticism which can be levelled at all of Wedekind's plays, because 'over and over again, in his modern plays, the characters who begin as real persons become the vaguest shadows, and pass into a dream world of their own' (6 October 1910; *NA* VII, 23, p. 544). Throughout his articles, Dukes refers to Wedekind's dramas only by their German titles. In 1910, with the exception of a performance of Wedekind's *Kammersänger* (1899) by the Stage Society and an American edition of *The Awakening of Spring*, none of his work had been translated into English, much less performed on stage in England.[69] Thus, in his discussion of Wedekind in the *New Age* Ashley Dukes was breaking new ground, even if some of his views on Wedekind were surprisingly unperceptive.

Dukes reserves his most scathing criticism for Sudermann. He condemns him as 'a pedlar of stale wares'. In 1889, the same year as the Freie Bühne pioneered the work of Ibsen and Hauptmann, audiences at the Lessing-theater received Sudermann's *Simoon* 'beyond its merits'. His next play, *Sodoms Ende* (1891), proved 'as trivial a piece of work as *Die Ehre*' and *Heimat* was 'sentimental to the point of nausea'. Dukes concedes that Sudermann displays 'wit, geniality, real gifts of dialogue, sense of the theatre', the only attribute that he lacks is 'the mind that can choose a worthy subject and handle it finely' (20 October 1910; *NA* VII, 25, p. 591-2). Dukes was no stranger to Sudermann's work. At this time, perhaps a touch hypocritically given his views, he was

---

69   Letter from Dukes to the *New Age*; *NA* VII, 24, p. 573.

engaged in translating Sudermann's *Johannisfeuer* (1900) for Miss Horniman's theatre in Manchester.[70]

Arthur Schnitzler: 'nothing to do with moralists or morality'

By contrast, Schnitzler met with great approval from Dukes, who distinguished between the German and the Austrian drama. Hauptmann and Wedekind reflect something of the German national character in their work, whilst Sudermann reveals himself to be 'heavily Prussian.' Schnitzler, on the other hand, is distinctively Austrian. In terms of drama, Berlin belongs to the bourgeoisie, whereas Vienna is a city of aristocrats. It is to the latter category that Schnitzler belongs - at least in spirit, if not by birth. Dukes considers *Liebelei* (1896) to be Schnitzler's most famous play, although the English translation of the title as *Light of Love* does not really convey the true meaning of 'flirtation'. The Austrian dramatist has 'nothing to do with moralists or morality'. His theme is invariably the same, namely 'the lover and a mistress or two', as is exemplified in *Komtesse Mizzi* (1909) and the seven scenes that comprise *Anatol* (1893). Schnitzler treats the theme gracefully, 'with little passion and much gentle melancholy, little humour and much wit'. His power lies in his ability to create atmosphere. His plays operate mainly on the level of comedy, whilst catastrophe is always 'intimately personal' and 'accepted with ironical resignation by the aristocratic hero'. Dukes concludes that tragic problems only occasionally arise in Schnitzler's dramas. He cites *Der einsame Weg* (1903), *Der Ruf des Lebens* (1906), *Freiwild* (1898) and *Das Vermächtnis* (1899) as representing 'the nearest approach that Austrian drama has made to the social problem play and the modernity movement of other countries. In social problems, however, Schnitzler is really out of his element' (27 October 1910; *NA* VII, 26, pp. 611-12). This was not the first time that Schnitzler was discussed in the *New Age*. Leslie Haden Guest had reviewed productions of Schnitzler at the Bijou Theatre in March 1908 (*NA* II, 21, p. 417), but Ashley Dukes was the first drama critic on Orage's periodical to treat the Austrian writer in such detail.

Music: The Hallé Orchestra is so 'intensely German' that 'English composers need not apply'

While there was an increase in discussion of modern German drama, reviews of concerts ceased to be a regular feature in the *New Age*. Although Herbert Hughes continued as music critic, promoting Richard Strauss and urging

---

70   J. M. Ritchie, op. cit., p. 98.

English composers to free themselves from Wagner's influence, he no longer contributed every week after 1908. Attention switched from the German-dominated concert hall to the ballet, particularly when Diaghilev's company performed in London for the first time in the summer of 1910. When concerts were discussed, the predominance of German composers in the English repertoire came to the fore. The composer Havergal Brian devoted an article to the 'Orchestral Crisis in England'. He concedes that there is much activity in English music, but regrets the absence of first rate English composers. Only Elgar can be classed in this league. Although several new orchestras have been formed, the figure is negligible when compared with Germany, a country able to boast two hundred good orchestras and numerous first class opera houses. As Brian notes, Weimar, which is smaller than Stoke-on-Trent, was the centre for Wagner, Liszt and Berlioz. This only proves once again 'how intensely musical is Germany'. England, by comparison, is too centralized, with London and its one decent opera house, Covent Garden, housing most of the best English orchestras. German composers enjoy a natural advantage over their English counterparts in that they live in an atmosphere that has produced a line of great composers from Bach to Wagner and Strauss.

Brian observes that London is the home of four permanent orchestras - the London Symphony, the New Symphony, Beecham's orchestra and the Queen's Hall - but they cannot all pay, so the question arises as to how they can all survive. The picture looks even bleaker in the provinces where the Birmingham Symphony and the Liverpool Symphony orchestras are run on co-operative lines, and Leeds Municipal Orchestra has been forced to become self-supporting. The Hallé Orchestra in Manchester, now firmly established, seems to offer the only ray of hope. However, even the Hallé has the advantage of being 'intensely German' and carrying 'an imaginary notice-board, "English composers need not apply". Dr Hans Richter conducts, and draws a large salary: with the exception of Elgar's works, he does not help modern English music at all' (8 July 1909; NA VI, 11, p. 225). The periodical reveals the dependence on German music by English orchestras in the years leading up to the First World War. In the wave of Germanophobia that accompanied the outbreak of war, calls for a total ban on 'enemy' music and 'enemy' performers would pose a serious threat to the English concert repertoire.[71] The perception of Germany as 'intensely musical' crept into the English wartime tracts. In *The Prussian Hath Said in his Heart*, for example, Cecil Chesterton distinguishes between what he terms the 'Atheist' state of Prussians descended from Frederick the Great and now waging war on

---

71   See Anne Dzamba Sessa, *Richard Wagner and the English* (New Jersey, 1978), p. 140.

England, and the true German people who 'specially love and can create music'.[72] Since Cecil Chesterton worked on the *New Age* for five years, it is probably that he owed much of his *Deutschlandbild* to contact with Orage and his circle.

---

72   Cecil Chesterton, *The Prussian Hath Said in his Heart* (London, 1914), p. 60.

Chapter 3: Germany and the *New Age*: November 1910-August 1914

During the build-up to the First World War there were several changes on the staff of the *New Age*. What might best be described as the older generation of writers who had contributed to the earlier issues turned their attention to other ventures. In June 1911 Hilaire Belloc, who had written for the *New Age*, gave up his seat in Parliament and started his own weekly periodical, the *Eye-Witness*.[1] He was joined by one of Orage's assistant editors, Cecil Chesterton. When, in the following year Belloc ran into financial difficulties, he was bought out by Cecil Chesterton who took over the paper as owner and editor, renaming it the *New Witness*. Chesterton continued to write features on politics for the *New Age* until August 1911, and many of the contributors to the *New Witness* - Hubert Bland, Edith Nesbit, Arthur Ransome, H. G. Wells, W. R. Titterton and G. K. Chesterton - had already written for the *New Age*.[2] In October 1916, when Cecil Chesterton was called up, his elder brother, G. K. Chesterton, assumed editorial responsibility until the *New Witness* folded in 1923, only a year after Orage relinquished editorship of the *New Age*. In view of their almost parallel period of publication and the interchanging of contributors between the two journals, the *New Age* and the *New Witness* may be seen as the closest rivals. It seems likely that the circulation and the financial position of the *New Age* suffered a severe blow when the *Eye-Witness* was founded.[3]

The New Statesman: 'as dull as a privet hedge in Leeds'

Chesterton and Belloc were not the only contributors to diversify their interests. In April 1913, only five months after the launch of the *New Witness*, Beatrice and Sydney Webb, with financial backing from Bernard Shaw,[4] set up the *New Statesman* as a rival Socialist weekly committed to Fabianism. They engaged as their editor Clifford Sharp, who had formerly been an assistant editor on the *New Age*.[5] Alienated by Orage's refusal to give unqualified support to the

---

1   Michael Ffinch, *G. K. Chesterton: A Biography* (London, 1986), p. 193.
2   Brocard Sewell, *Cecil Chesterton* (Faversham, Kent, 1975), pp. 38-41.
3   See Wallace Martin, *The New Age under Orage: Chapters in English Cultural History* (Manchester, 1967), p. 121.
4   Michael Holroyd, *Bernard Shaw, Vol. II, 1898-1918. The Pursuit of Power* (London 1989), p. 319.
5   See John Carswell, *Lives and Letters* (London, 1978), p. 91. Also Antony Alpers, *The Life of Katherine Mansfield* (London, 1980), p. 110.

Fabian movement in his journal, the Webbs and the Fabian backers who transferred their allegiance from Orage to the *New Statesman* hoped to capture the corner of the market held by the *New Age*. Shaw held a financial stake in both publications. In 1907 he had put up the first £500 to enable Orage and Holbrook Jackson to buy the *New Age*, which ran at a loss of more than £1000 a year whilst Orage drew a modest salary of £4 a week[6] and privately renamed his periodical the *No Wage*.[7] However, in order to pose a serious threat to the circulation of the *New Age* the Webbs' publication would have to fend off strong competition from its respected rivals. H. G. Wells had no doubt about its inferiority to both the *New Age* and the *New Witness*. After reading the first issue of the *New Statesman* he described it as

> 'a stagnant marsh of dull print without any current in it at all. It is duller than the *Spectator* at its dullest. It is duller than indigestion. It is as dull as a privet hedge in Leeds [...] Ideas! There is not so much as a tenth of an Orage in the whole enterprise. The *New Statesman* is not a fresh beginning but an epilogue.'[8]

Further resignations from the *New Age* during this period included Arnold Bennett, author of the literary column 'Books and Persons', and the theatre critic Ashley Dukes, who claims to have cast off Socialism, the Fabians and the *New Age* in order to pursue an independent career as playwright, translator and freelance critic.[9] These departures meant that Orage was writing more articles for his paper and relying heavily on the Nietzscheans, J. M. Kennedy and A. M. Ludovici, for contributions on a variety of issues, although at this stage the *New Age* was not transformed into the one-man venture that it eventually became during the First World War when many of the contributors were away at the front.[10] Between 1910 and 1914 Orage managed to recruit a remarkable number of new writers of the younger generation. Amongst them were Katherine Mansfield, John Middleton Murray, T. E. Hulme, Paul Selver and Edwin Muir (writing poetry under the more English-sounding pen-name of Edward Moore). Katherine Mansfield, for example, was born in 1889, whilst Paul Selver was still a student touring Germany when the first volumes of the *New Age* were

---

6   See Antony Alpers, op. cit., p. 108 and p. 237.
7   Claire Tomalin, *Katherine Mansfield. A Secret Life* (London, 1987), p. 81.
8   H. G. Wells, 'On Reading the First Number of the *New Statesman*', *New Witness*, 24 April 1913. Quoted by Brocard Sewell, op. cit., p. 42.
9   Ashley Dukes, *The Scene is Changed* (London, 1942), p. 40.
10   See Antony Alpers, op. cit., p. 237.

published. By comparison, Shaw was born in 1856 and G. K. Chesterton in 1874, a year after Orage. Thus, it was a younger generation of writers who were contributing to the *New Age* in the years leading up to the First World War. Storm Jameson, who wrote for the *New Age* during this period, recalled how important Orage was for this generation of writers:

> 'On the "young generation" of 1912 he had, I suppose, more influence than any other single person and it was unmitigatedly good influence, working for an intellectual integrity and honesty'.[11]

The involvement of this 'young generation' in the periodical helped stimulate receptiveness to new ideas and techniques, particularly in art. Thus, the *New Age* in this period gave a hearing to the emergent Cubist and Futurist movements and introduced readers to the philosophy of Henri Bergson, even if the editor was not always in agreement with the theories put forward by his contributors. In terms of Anglo-German literary relations, several of the younger contributors already had first-hand experience of Germany. Katherine Mansfield, for example, had lived in Bavaria, whilst John Middleton Murray had studied in Heidelberg.[12] Others such as Edwin Muir, the translator of Kafka, would later play an important role in Anglo-German literary relations. Both he and his wife Willa were also friendly with Hermann Broch (1886-1951). In 1932 they overcame the difficulties of Broch's language to translate his trilogy of novels *Die Schlafwandler*,[13] but declined his request to work on an English version of *Der Tod des Vergil* (1945).[14]

As the threat of war grew more tangible, the number of articles on foreign affairs increased. From August 1912 onwards 'Military Notes' by Romney argued that war was a necessary part of human society, whilst December 1913 saw the first in an anti-pacifist series entitled 'Letters on War by a Rifleman'. The *New Age* also published more general articles on modern German life, such as a series in March 1912 by C. E. Bechhofer, using the pseudonym Carl Erich. The author reported on a student *Burschenschaft* drinking session, followed by 'Auf die Mensur' (sic), an account of a duel amongst students. This in turn prompted the author to translate the 'Duelling Code of a German Student

---

11 Storm Jameson, *New English Review. A. R. Orage Memorial Number*, VI, 5 (15 November 1934), p. 110.

12 Claire Tomalin, op. cit., p. 96.

13 See Edwin and Willa Muir, 'Translating from the German', in *On Translation*, edited by Reuben A. Brower (Harvard, 1959), p. 94.

14 See P. H. Butter, *Edwin Muir: Man and Poet* (London, 1966), p. 177.

Corporation', followed by 'O Academia', an article describing the deliberations on whether the honour of the regiment had been discredited by either of the duellists.[15] In addition, there was a two part series dealing with 'The Germanization of Switzerland' by Senex in May 1913.[16] However, by far the most important political column in terms of shaping the *Deutschlandbild* of the periodical was J. M. Kennedy's 'Foreign Affairs', written every week under the pseudonym S. Verdad.

J. M. Kennedy: in the grip of the 'German eagle's talons'

Kennedy's position vis-à-vis Germany was an ambivalent one. On the one hand, he was extremely wary of the aims of modern Germany. Politically, he described himself as a Tory Democrat, so he was unable to accept the reassurances of the German Social Democrats about German intentions that pacified some of his Socialist colleagues on the *New Age*. In this context, in December 1910, he poured scorn on Georg Ledebour of the German Social Democrats for proclaiming in the *Reichstag* that his party wished the German Empire to be a republic. Such an announcement is tantamount to political suicide, Kennedy argues, since 'the monarchical instinct is more strongly developed among the Germans than any other nation in the world; and the mere sound of the word Republic is sufficient to turn indifference for the Kaiser into sympathy for him. To let the cat out of the bag at such a juncture was a bad piece of electioneering tactics; for in the campaign preceding the polling of next spring the anti-Socialists are not likely to omit the use of this useful political ammunition. The *Berliner Tageblatt*, indeed, has already practically admitted defeat, and even *Vorwärts* is discreetly silent'. Although the Kaiser has recently alienated some of the population by laying special emphasis on what he regards as his divine right to govern Prussia, Kennedy contends that Ledebour's approach is not the best way to drum up support for his opposition party. In plain terms, Socialism is making no progress in Germany. Kennedy also observes that the German Emperor is popular throughout his country - even among the intellectuals - because he has attempted to encourage painters, philosophers and writers, including Houston Stewart Chamberlain, whose *Grundlagen des neunzehnten Jahrhunderts* (1899) found particular favour with the Kaiser. By comparison, the English royal family has done nothing to encourage intellectuals since the eighteenth century. (8 December 1910; *NA* VIII, 6, p. 125)

---

15   See 14 March 1912; *NA* X, 20, pp. 469-70; 18 April 1912; *NA* X, 25, pp. 590-2; 25 April 1912; *NA* X, 26, pp. 613-14 and 9 May 1912; *NA* XI, 2, pp. 41-2.

16   See 8 May 1913; *NA* XIII, 2, pp. 31-2 and 15 May 1913; *NA* XIII, 3, p. 53.

Fritz Fischer points out that after the historians Heinrich von Treitschke (1834-96) and Heinrich von Sybel (1817-95), it was Houston Stewart Chamberlain (1855-1927) who, exerted the greatest influence on the ideas current in Wilhelmine Germany.[17] His *Grundlagen des neunzehnten Jahrhunderts* maintained that race was the dominant principle of history. The Germanic race, Chamberlain claimed, had been civilised since the third century. If it was to survive in the future it must first free itself from anti-Germanic elements, especially Jewish elements. Germanic peoples were destined for world power - if they failed to achieve this, they would be condemned to decline, or, as Chamberlain predicted: 'If Germany does not dominate the world, it will disappear from the map; there is no alternative'.[18] In 1911 Kennedy saw the Germans faced with no such choice. In his preface to his translation of Nietzsche's *Morgenröte*, which Orage printed in the *New Age*, he takes issue with the author of the recently translated *Foundations of the Nineteenth Century*. Although an Englishman, Chamberlain appears to have written in German and not translated his work into English himself. This 1911 translation, for instance, was the work of John Lees. Kennedy argues that contrary to what Chamberlain claims, the Teutons are not superior to all the other peoples of the world and they have not kept their race pure. Although Kennedy considers Chamberlain's case 'plausible' when he argues that Jesus Christ was not a Jew but an Aryan, a member of the family of which the Teutons are a branch, he contends that Nietzsche 'has constantly pointed out that the Teutons are so far from being a pure race that they have, on the contrary, done everything in their power to ruin even the idea of a pure race for ever'.[19] However, Nietzsche was not always as exemplary in his views as Kennedy would have us believe. The opening section

---

17 Fritz Fischer, *Krieg der Illusionen* (Düsseldorf, 1969), p. 66. Sybel, like Treitschke, was an academic who wrote in support of Prussia. Fischer's claim is, of course, an arguable point. Nietzsche must have a strong claim to this title, if not Wagner as well, in Pre-War Socialist circles.

18 Houston Stewart Chamberlain, *Politische Ideale*, third edition (Munich, 1926), p. 39. Quoted by Fritz Fischer, op. cit., p. 66.

19 12 October 1911; *NA* IX, 24, pp. 561-2. In *Morgenröte* Nietzsche makes the following observation about purity of race: 'Es gibt wahrscheinlich keine reinen, sondern nur reingewordene Rassen, und diese in großer Seltenheit'. The Greeks exemplify a race and culture that have become pure and Nietzsche hopes that one day a pure European race and culture may be achieved. See *Werke*, I, p. 1182.

of *Zur Genealogie der Moral* reveals him to be rather shaky in his genealogical etymologies.[20]

Nostalgia for the old Germany: 'a land where the inhabitants were lost in the clouds of abstract, idealistic, romantic thought'

On the other hand, Kennedy did admire Germany, but it was the Germany of the early nineteenth century, the *Allemagne* of Madame de Staël. With rather more than a tinge of nostalgia he frequently sets this Germany against the Germany of the early twentieth century in order to demonstrate to his readers how the German nation has deteriorated since 1871. In April 1911 he argues that whilst pacifism has attracted some support in England, it has utterly failed in Germany. Indeed, 'the great impulse given in Germany to the development of philosophy during the nineteenth century has resulted in a class of professional men and students who are uninfluenced by the strict theological scruples that play havoc in England. A German who feels himself to be above mere dogmatic theology, and who can give evidence of his intellectual capacity, is not looked at askance'.[21] Germans of this ilk include the Chancellor, Bethmann Hollweg, and the Foreign Minister, Alfred von Kiderlen-Wächter, who, following his appointment in the summer of 1910, was viewed by the German right as the 'new Bismarck', who would finally breathe life into German foreign policy.[22] We are therefore, in Kennedy's view, faced with a strange anomaly, the discrepancy between a nineteenth century view of Germany and the present reality. 'Up to the present', Kennedy argues, 'we have always considered Germany as a land where the inhabitants were lost in the clouds of abstract, idealistic, romantic thought, a land whence no "practical" proposal ever emanated'. The English, on the other hand, always prided themselves on their 'worldly success', their 'inability to understand abstractions' and their 'practical nature'. The German was simply 'an amiable sort of clumsy animal whom we thoroughly practical people could not take seriously'. The tide turned without us noticing, with Nietzsche, perhaps, as its harbinger, although 'we could not understand how a German philosopher could curse his predecessors and assail all the romanticists with so many hard thwacks.

---

20   See W. D. Williams, 'Notes', in *Zur Genealogie der Moral*, edited by W. D. Williams (Oxford, 1972), pp. 142-4.

21   Kennedy's view that pacifism has failed in Germany is interesting, since in 1911 Franz Pfemfert was just beginning *Die Aktion* in Berlin. Although concerned mainly with *belles lettres* before 1914, throughout the First World War this journal took a strongly pacifist line, with Pfemfert as virtually sole contributor.

22   Fritz Fischer, op. cit., p. 118.

We failed to observe that we ourselves were fast becoming - nay, had already become - the romanticists and idealists; and when a few papers caught the peace fever the contagion was rapidly spread'. Indeed, 'contagion' has defied 'our sturdy British common-sense, and has now taken hold of many of our public men; and, most glaring anomaly of all, its common-sense refutation does not come from any of our Ministers who have escaped the disease, but from hard, matter-of-fact, common-sense Germany, whose philosophic, man-of-the-world Chancellor makes merry at our expense, what time the whole Continent is wondering what these mad Englishmen are coming to.' (13 April 1911; *NA* VIII, 24, p. 555)

Kennedy's pieces of literary criticism also reveal his adherence to the notion of two Germanies. On 6 April 1911, for instance, he reviewed E. A. Brayley's *The House of Hohenzollern* with the observation: 'During its forty years of peace since the humiliation of France the German Empire has made gigantic strides; but its progress has been materialistic and philosophy and art have been elbowed out of the way. The advancement of German culture, the development of the old German spirit ceased with the founding of the German Empire. History repeats itself and Rome may once again be overrun by the barbarians.' (*NA* VIII, 23, Literary Supplement, p. 4). In the wake of the Franco-Prussian War, English observers viewed France as the victim and the newly-formed German state as the aggressor. Subsequent events in the Boer War and the Morocco crisis only served to reinforce the view that Germany had come to embody the spirit of Potsdam rather than Weimar. 'Das Land der Dichter und Denker', the Germany portrayed so enthusiastically by Carlyle, Arnold, Lewes and Madame de Staël, was deemed extinct and the early nineteenth century concept of Napoleonic France menacing European territorial rights was completely overturned. It was a view which extended to popular literature. In 1910, for example, E. M. Forster treated the theme of two Germanies in *Howards End*. Here Ernst Schlegel, who epitomizes the old Germany of culture and philosophy, has fled the materialistic and militaristic Germany that has existed since 1870. Forster explicitly states that Schlegel is not the aggressive German type, but the countryman of Kant and Hegel, 'the idealist, inclined to be dreamy, whose Imperialism was the Imperialism of the air'.[23] At home in the realm of the imagination, Schlegel finds himself at odds with the new naval, commercial and colonial Germany as embodied by his 'haughty and magnificent nephew'. Pan-Germanism, like British

---

23   E. M. Forster, *Howards End* (London, 1986; Penguin edition), p. 42.

Imperialism, stifles the imagination, according to Schlegel, who perceives no German poet or musician able to 'rekindle the light within'.[24]

Kennedy did not confine himself to the single pen-name of S. Verdad to voice the opinion that creative thought in Germany ended with the founding of the German Empire. On 5 June 1913, for example, when using the pseudonym Leighton J. Warnock to reflect on 'The Soul of Germany', Kennedy argues that creativity in Germany is dead - all her great creative writers are the products of a bygone era. Although Prussia has produced fine creative talents such as Kleist, Herder, Humboldt, Schleiermacher, Schopenhauer, Tieck and Heine, they were all born before the most recent period of Prussian expansion - Kennedy conveniently omits to mention that Frederick the Great was also a Prussian expansionist. He reminds his readers that in the first half of the nineteenth century the states were independent, so that it is only fair to speak of Goethe, Börne and the Grimm brothers as natives of Hesse-Nassau; Körner, Gellert, Lessing, Ranke and Nietzsche hailed from Saxony, Jean Paul Richter from Bavaria and the Schlegels from Hannover, whilst Schiller, Wieland, Hauff, Uhland and Hegel all came from Württemberg. Bismarck was 'one of the last creative Prussians'. Modern Prussia has unleashed a 'sense of business' which has 'seized the Germans, a nation not adapted to business at all'. Because Wilhelmine Germany is founded on such materialism, it has no soul. (*NA* XIII, 6, pp. 146-7)

French Civilisation versus German Culture

In dealing with what they considered the negative aspects of Wilhelmine Germany commentators invariably pointed accusingly at Prussia. According to Kennedy the state called Germany is really a euphemism for Prussia. During the Moroccan crisis of 1911 he claims 'Prussia takes the initiative, Prussia supplies the energy, and the remaining states follow her lead. The army wants an opportunity for distinguishing itself; the Prussian junkers and nobles want to maintain their privileges and powers. There is, too, the Prussian bureaucracy, which wants to retain the Government of the German Empire without being troubled by representative government'. Because the French army is now in peak condition the time is ripe for France to go to war with Germany over the Moroccan crisis. Although this would have 'awful consequences for civilisation', Kennedy believes that such a war would enable the allies to 'look

---

24   Ibid., p. 43. See also Meinhard Winkgens, 'Die Funktionalisierung des Deutschlandbildes und seiner Konnotationen einer idealistischen Kultur in E. M. Forster's *Howards End*', in *Images of Germany*, edited by Hans-Jürgen Diller (Heidelberg, 1986), especially pp. 125-30.

forward to a period of virility in European affairs.' (7 September 1911; *NA* IX, 19, p. 435)

European culture, Kennedy maintains, would reap great benefit if France were to win a war against Germany over Morocco. A French victory would break up the German Empire into small states again. Each German state has a separate identity and therefore fits uneasily into this unnatural conglomeration of states that have been welded together by Prussia to form the German Empire. The old German spirit once found in the separate German states has disappeared, Kennedy argues. Although 'homely', this spirit 'was helpful to the type of culture peculiar to Germany' because it produced, in different parts of Germany, 'a Heine, an Uhland, a Lessing, a Schopenhauer'. However, the 'modern spirit' now being cultivated in Germany is 'thoroughly anti-cultural, anti-poetic, anti-philosophic' and 'it is impossible to imagine another Heine or another Goethe being developed in it'. Wilhelmine Germany is 'too materialistic, too Imperialistic; too modern, in short. By becoming an Empire, the German states have cut themselves away from their roots. They have withered, and there is no health in them. But it is not yet too late to return to the old order of things; and a French victory would have helped to bring about a result to which every cultured man and woman must look forward with hopeful eagerness'.[25]

In the wake of the French diplomatic victory over Germany in the Moroccan crisis Kennedy reasons that England was perfectly justified in supporting France. Taking a very selective view of history, he argues that traditionally England always has been an ally of France and that Anglo-French ties have always remained strong. However, he perceives Anglo-German links to be based on much weaker foundations. He contends that the Thirty Years' War, the Seven Years' War and the Napoleonic Wars 'set German civilisation back by at least two centuries'. Normally he considers war to be 'a great civiliser', but in the case of Germany, with all its periods of internecine strife, there has been no war in the sense of conquest. The Thirty Years' War left the country desolate and although the Seven Years' War was 'a campaign of which any country might be proud', Germany did not have time to recover fully before she was subjected to the rule of Napoleon. Even today she is suffering from the after-effects of these conflicts with the result that 'she is one of the most backward of European nations in all forms of culture; and the list of her exceptional and great men is startlingly

---

25   28 September 1911; *NA* IX, 22, p. 510. On 13 June 1912 Kennedy reiterated his view that the German character was deteriorating on the grounds that 'the downfall of the German States meant the downfall of the primitive German character, and that this will at some time in the distant future mean the downfall of the German people. The German Empire is a political expression; it is not an entity.' (*NA* XI, 7, p. 149)

short'. However, England and France were never retarded in the same way, so that 'intellectually and morally we have much more in common with France than with Germany'. All this proves to Kennedy's spurious reasoning that England is 'far beyond' the culture of Germany, although not likely to achieve the level of France. (9 November 1911; *NA* X, 2, p. 30)

The Germans, by comparison, defined Civilization and Culture in quite different terms. Even before the wartime propaganda began, they saw their Culture as comprising inwardness and idealism. This profound *Kultur* contrasted sharply with the rationality and superficiality of French *Zivilisation.* German writers would argue that the Western nations had developed a system of state and culture which, to a greater extent than in Germany, was characterised by the spirit of bourgeois capitalism, although they did not mention that Germany too was a modern capitalist state. Eckart Koester observes that because many Pre-War German writers were basing their ideas on anti-capitalist sentiments, it was inevitable that their wartime polemics would be against capitalist orientated Civilisation, the so-called 'Nützlichkeitskultur' of England and France.[26] Thomas Mann, writing his first wartime tract in November 1914, *Gedanken im Krieg*, was in no doubt about the meaning of the terms *Kultur* and *Zivilisation.* He equated *Zivilisation* with the Enlightenment, reason, moderation, manners, scepticism, mind or *Geist*, and argued that it could actually be repelled by *Kultur*, which had irrational associations of magic, oracles, human sacrifice and witch trials. The antithesis was embodied in the figures of Voltaire and Frederick the Great, who although a friend of the French *philosophe*, was also capable of invading Saxony.[27] The geographical position of Germany in the middle of the continent of Europe meant that it lay between two ideological poles - to the west Civilisation, as represented by France, and to the east Barbarism, as represented by Russia. Since the founding of the German Empire there existed a widespread view that Russia was to be feared. Coupled with a low opinion of the half-Asian barbarism of the Russians was the widespread belief that the economy, culture and military might of Russia were inferior to that of Germany. The alliance between France and Russia and the growth of the Russian economy and population, the evidence of which had been the key-note of Bismarck's foreign policy, fuelled the idea in Germany that war with Russia was inevitable. The recent antagonism between Germany and Russia could be traced back to the late 1880s when emigrants from the Baltic states had published articles in German newspapers, recounting Russian hostility towards Germany.[28] Thus, Russia's

---

26   Eckart Koester, *Literatur und Weltkriegsideologie* (Kronberg, 1977), p. 190.
27   See T. J. Reed, *Thomas Mann: The Uses of Tradition* (Oxford, 1974), p. 181.
28   Fritz Fischer, op. cit., pp. 77-8.

Baltic provinces were portrayed as 'the German guard on the border with Slavdom'[29] and any attempts at Russianisation there were viewed as symptoms of the age-old struggle between 'Slawentum' and 'Germanentum'. A preventative war with Russia was advocated by Baltic journalists and the German Government remained in readiness for hostilities.[30] In 1890, for example, this subject was taken up in *Videant consules, ne quid res publica detrimenti capiat*,[31] published anonymously by General Friedrich von Bernhardi, the subsequent author of the influential *Deutschland und der nächste Krieg* (1912). In his anonymous publication Bernhardi argued that the Germans should wage war in two stages. First, there was to be a reckoning with France that would secure equal power status for Germany. Following that victory all efforts were to be directed towards 'die großen germanischen Kulturaufgaben gegen Rußland'. These great Germanic undertakings in the cause of culture would entail pushing back once and for all 'Slavic barbarism' to the region where it truly belonged, to east and southeast Asia, and protecting Western European *Kultur* from what he terms 'Pan-Slavic violation'.[32] From the 1900s onwards the idea persisted in Germany that there could be no lasting peace with Russia and only armed conflict could decide between an inferior and a superior culture. The idea of attacking France, then turning against Russia before armies could be mobilised properly, was the substance of the Schlieffen Plan. As early as 1892, Count Alfred von Schlieffen (1833-1913), who was chief of army general staff between 1891 and 1906, was planning a strategy for what he then called a 'War of Aggression against France'.[33]. In his plan, which was to occupy him for the rest of his life, Schlieffen proposed that in order to avoid battles in heavily fortified French territory, the Germans should ignore all political implications about violating the rights of neutral countries and march through Belgium, Luxemburg and Holland in order to launch their western offensive. After defeating France, all energies were to be concentrated against the second enemy, Russia. Only then could total victory be achieved in both the west and the east. Schlieffen's successor, Count Helmuth von Moltke (1848-1916) agreed with this strategy, although just before the

---

29   *Ein verlassener Bruderstamm, Vergangenheit und Gegenwart der baltischen Provinzen. Von einem Balten* (Berlin, 1889), p. 212. Quoted by Fischer, op. cit., p. 78.

30   Ibid., p. 78.

31   The title may be translated loosely as *Let the Germans watch out lest the state take harm.*

32   Fritz Fischer, op. cit., pp. 77-8.

33   Ibid., p. 98.

outbreak of the First World War he modified the original plan by abandoning the idea of marching through Holland.[34]

General Friedrich von Bernhardi: Germany and the Next War

The English, Kennedy declares, are not wholly blameless for the present situation in Germany. In the nineteenth century England made the mistake of not checking German expansion sooner. Thus, the balance of power was upset in Europe. He claims: 'It was not until early in the present century that we began to see what we had let ourselves in for by permitting Germany to expand'. He believes that his countrymen failed to see the warning signs in Bismarck's foreign policy and that it is only 'from about 1900 onwards' that 'we find authoritative Germans like General Bernhardi publicly writing and speaking about the inevitable struggle with England' (4 April 1912; *NA* X, 23, p. 533). Probably Kennedy was one of the earliest English readers of Bernhardi's *Deutschland und der nächste Krieg*. In the same month he recommended it to *New Age* readers and appealed for an English translation to bring it to a wider public. It was under the direct influence of the Morocco crisis, in October 1911, that Bernhardi, a member of the German General Staff, had written *Deutschland und der nächste Krieg*, which was published early in 1912.[35] Between spring 1912 and February 1913 Bernhardi's treatise ran through no less than six impressions,[36] followed by an English translation in 1914. He argued that the Morocco crisis had demonstrated to the Germans that they lacked a definite political and national goal to inspire the country to unified action. He attributed Germany's problems primarily to the fact that it had recognised too late the need for an expansionist colonial policy. If Germany were to achieve the world-power status she deserved she must pursue more ambitious colonial policies, even at the risk of war. Geographically Germany and Austria-Hungary already formed 'a united bridge of countries from the Adriatic to the Baltic and the North Sea'[37] which should be made into a central European alliance. Through what he calls the 'sincerity and strength' of German policies the countries bordering the German Reich - Belgium, Holland, Switzerland, Denmark, as well as Austria Hungary, Turkey and the small Balkan states - should be made aware that it would be in their best interests to be allied with Germany. However, Bernhardi admits that such a colonial policy would involve a major European war on three fronts - against England and France as well as Russia, for neither England nor France

---

34   Ibid., pp. 566-8.
35   Ibid., p. 343.
36   T. J. Reed, op. cit., p. 215.
37   Quoted by Fischer, op. cit., p. 344.

would accept an upset in the balance of power in Europe. For this reason France must be defeated so decisively that it would never again stand in the way of Germany, whilst England had to be made to relinquish her current position of supremacy and recognise Germany as a power of equal status.[38]

Although Kennedy disputes the notion that France and England are the dangerous enemies of Germany that Bernhardi makes them out to be, he applauds the German general for emphasizing the 'evil effects of pacifism on the average State' and asserting that it is the 'sacred right' of a nation to 'explain itself by force of arms'. He points out that the general envisages an inevitable war 'not with dread or dismay', but 'with something like relish' on the grounds that war is a salutary experience for the human race, whereas an overlong spell of peace is harmful. Mankind therefore needs a form of 'katharsis' (sic) - whilst Aristotle thought he found this in tragedy, Bernhardi, Kennedy believes, finds it in war. On this point Kennedy draws a parallel with the Italian Futurist, F. T. Marinetti, who 'finds in war also the "hygiene of the world"' (25 April 1912; *NA* X, 26, p. 605). A trifle surprisingly perhaps, Kennedy omits to mention the quotation from Nietzsche, with which Bernhardi's *Germany and the next War* opened:

> 'War and courage have done more great things than compassion. Not your sympathy, but your bravery has hitherto saved the victims.
> What is good? you ask. To be brave is good.'[39]

As we shall see in the following chapter, the English propagandists of 1914, seeking the causes of German action in German thought, seized on Bernhardi, his single quotation from Nietzsche and his extensive references to the work of Heinrich von Treitschke, and alleged that all the brutal and destructive aspects of modern, aggressive Germany took their inspiration from the triumvirate of Bernhardi, Treitschke and Nietzsche.[40]

Kennedy argued not only with German writers on foreign affairs, but with those in England as well. He takes issue, for example, with Bernard Shaw over an article that had appeared in the *Daily News* on 1 January 1914. Here Shaw had voiced the opinion that catastrophe could be averted if England were to 'politely announce' that 'a war between France and Germany would be so inconvenient to England that England is prepared to pledge herself to defend either country if attacked by the other'. The *New Age* columnist counters that the root of foreign policy is self-preservation, which can be secured only by

---

38   See Fischer, op. cit., pp. 344-7.
39   Nietzsche, *Also sprach Zarathustra*, in *Werke*, II, p. 312.
40   See pp. 142-6.

preserving the balance of power in Europe, as England has been doing for more than three hundred years. It is impossible for France, Germany and England to combine as a joint peace-keeping force because France will be satisfied with nothing less than the return of Alsace and Lorraine, whilst the Kaiser is equally determined not to cede these provinces on the principle that 'what the German eagle's talons gripped it never let go.' (8 January 1914; *NA* XIV, 10, pp. 293-4)

Although by spring 1913 Kennedy discounts the possibility of an immediate war - a view he reiterates right up to the outbreak of hostilities - he nevertheless warns that a future war will involve more than the fate of Alsace. In the next war there will be 'a struggle for the hegemony of Europe' that will embroil many nations. Having observed events in the Balkan War of 1912, Kennedy predicts that a war in Europe will include the involvement of the Slav races because Archduke Franz Ferdinand is relying on the Slav element for the preservation of his throne, 'for a German victory in western Europe, immediate or remote, means the absorption of the German part of the Austro-Hungarian Empire by Prussia'.[41]

Orage and Foreign Affairs: 'The brute Bismarck'

What is most striking in foreign affairs commentary in the *New Age* is the intervention of Orage himself as the international situation worsens. Previously, as the author of 'Notes of the Week', he had confined himself to discussion of home affairs. However, after November 1912 he comments much more frequently on foreign affairs. On 14 November 1912 he argues that it is not a German invasion which the English have to fear, but the 'triumphant capitalist'. It has become difficult to prove to the English proletariat that they are in danger of being invaded by Germany, not because they are complacent in thinking that their country is secure, but because 'insecurity has become their normal state' since they have become used to facing dismissal from work every week. As a result they are no longer afraid of 'a German sack' at the end of the month. (*NA* XII, 2, p. 27)

Just as Kennedy does not see war as an immediate prospect in 1914, Orage does not envisage modern warfare as being a long, drawn-out affair. On 2 April 1914 he is sure that 'modern wars are over in a few weeks - certainly by the end of the month the decisive blows are likely to have been struck, as in the case of the Franco-German war and the recent Balkan war'. Should there be a war, he is entirely optimistic about its course and outcome. (*NA* XIV, 22, p. 678)

---

41   20 March 1913; *NA* XII, 20, p. 469, though   Kennedy discounts the
       possiblity of war on 27 February 1913, *NA* XII, 17, p. 397.

Since Kennedy was absent at the beginning of August 1914 and had prepared his 'Foreign Affairs' column in advance, the task of commenting on world events was left to Orage. Two days after the declaration of war, although clearly surprised, Orage is in no doubt about England's right to fight. As a nation wholly devoid of 'aggressive designs' England must look 'primarily to Germany' for the cause of the 'threatened Armageddon'. War, he argues, will dispose of 'the great German lie - the affirmation maintained by Germany, since the days of the brute Bismarck, that force is the final arbiter of the world. Long after the rest of civilised Europe had at least qualified the doctrine of Force by requiring Right to accompany it, Germany revived for herself the ancient and bloody doctrine with no qualification whatever'. In the last forty years Germany has acquired the prestige of a man 'who at a peaceful meeting should go about with a revolver'. This has secured neither the admiration nor the fear of Germany's European neighbours, for 'while Germany, Nietzschean before Nietzsche, was piling armament upon armament and calling upon the God of Battles to be with her, the rest of Europe, in a state of resigned disgust, prepared slowly for the inevitable delirium that should follow the creeping insanity'. There could be no doubt that the 'German military caste, intoxicated with self-importance, blown out with phrases and deluded by their faith in Force, now finds itself at war with nearly the whole of Europe. Of all the nations opposed to her, only Russia can even be suspected of desiring war. France certainly does not. Italy has altogether refused. England has hesitated until the twelfth hour.' (6 August 1914; *NA* XV, 14, pp. 311-15)

Whilst Prussia was regarded as the engineer of Germany's moral decline, attempts were made to see in the Bavarians the true spirit of Germany. W. R. Titterton, who had written articles on German life since the early volumes, contributed an article on 7 September 1911 entitled 'Munich, Catholic and Democrat'. Prompted by what he perceives as the rigid class divisions in England and England's claim to be democratic when 'there never was so little democratic feeling existed in England as existed today', Titterton recommends that more Englishmen take a trip to Munich in order to learn about true democracy from the Bavarians. An English visitor should begin by calling at the Hofbräuhaus where he can enjoy beer, sausage, black bread and radishes. Sitting next to him on one of the long benches in the Biergarten will be a 'Trambahnschienenritzen-reinigungsdame', who, Titterton helpfully informs us, is 'a lady who regulates and clears and cleans the tramlines'. She will greet the intrepid traveller with 'Grüß Gott' and soon they will be 'talking together like brothers and sisters'. Such spontaneous and intimate contact will come as a culture shock to the reserved Englishman, Titterton warns, but he will experience here true equality and democracy. This sense of equality extends to all levels of German life. German intellectuals, for instance, do not suffer from the snobbery of the English intelligentsia and German students come from all classes 'for university education here is a necessity for the cultured man, not a luxury for the rich one'. The Germans are proud of what they are, regardless of their social status.[42]

Book Reviews

Despite the political climate, the review columns of the *New Age* were by no means anti-German. Even as late as the summer of 1913 disdain for scaremongering publications about German invasion schemes continued, with wholehearted condemnation for Colonel H. B. Hanna's *Can Germany Invade England?*, Archibold Hurd's *The Command of the Sea* and a publication of the jingoistic Imperial Maritime League entitled *Britain's Imminent Danger*. (10 July 1913; *NA* XIII, 11, p. 305)

A variety of books on Germanic subjects aroused critical interest between 1910 and 1914, from Mary Hargrave's *Some German Women and their Salons* (20 June 1912; *NA* XI, 8, p. 184) to Richard Wagner's *My Life* and William Ashton Ellis' translation of *Family Letters of Richard Wagner* (23 November 1911; *NA* X, 4, pp. 87-8). Heine remained a popular German writer with the publication of one of his poems and an English translation in 1911, as well as a review of the latest translation of his *Atta Troll* in 1914.[43] In the field of German philosophy, John Middleton Murray, in one of his first articles for the periodical, reviewed MacTaggart's *Studies in Hegelian Dialectic, A Commentary on Hegel's Logic* and *Studies in Hegelian Cosmology* (28 December 1911; *NA* X, 9, p. 204). Psychology also attracted attention, with the *New Age* carrying a review of a work by Sigmund Freud in May 1914.[44] The work in question was *On Dreams*, translated by M. D. Eder (1870?-1936), who was himself a former contributor to the periodical, having written on eugenics in the early issues.

In the build-up to the First World War the contributors to the arts pages of the *New Age* retained the same fascination with German culture that characterised the early issues. Despite the increasing hostility between England and Germany the periodical continued to take notice of publications by German authors or works dealing with Germanic subjects. In November 1910, for example, Arnold Bennett, who invariably promoted French rather than German literature, devotes some attention to the latest Sudermann novel to be published in

---

42 *NA* IX, 19, pp. 440-1. Ashley Dukes, who lived in Munich in 1907, also draws a very warm and affectionate picture of the city in his autobiography, op. cit., p. 12ff.

43 See 9 March 1911; *NA* VIII, 19, p. 443, 20 April 1911; *NA* VIII, p. 586 and 8 January 1914; *NA* XIV, 10, p. 311.

44 *On Dreams* was reviewed by A. E. Randall on 14 May 1914. (*NA* XV, 2, p. 40)

English, *The Song of Songs*. Although 'streaked with sentimentality' Sudermann's novel prompts Bennett to comment: 'We seem to have less curiosity about foreign fiction than we had a dozen years ago' (17 November 1910; *NA* VIII, 3, p. 60). Not only are the English becoming more insular in their reading matter, but more subject to censorship as well, since within a fortnight of its appearance on English bookshelves, Bennett notes, the same novel has been banned by all libraries in England.[45]

With the departure of Arnold Bennett from the *New Age* in September 1911, Orage lost one of his most able literary columnists. 'Books and Persons', written under the pen-name Jacob Tonson, had been a regular feature of the periodical since March 1908. Just how influential Bennett's contributions were can probably be gauged best by the apparent difficulty experienced by Orage in finding a replacement. Following Bennett's departure Orage made space for no less than three new literary columns. Two of these were written by newcomers to the periodical, A. E. Randall and Paul Selver, whilst the third, 'Readers and Writers', was in the main the work of Orage himself, writing under the pseudonym he had used in earlier articles, R.H.C. - an allusion to R. H. Congreve.

Paul Selver: guilty of a 'wholly romantic' attitude towards Germany

As a columnist, Paul Selver was probably one of the most cosmopolitan contributors to the *New Age*. He had a Polish background, knew Czech and was fluent in German. He confessed to a 'wholly romantic' attitude to Germany, inspired no doubt by successful tours he had made of the country. In 1907, as a student, he had visited Berlin, then travelled east as far as the Russian frontier, returning via Leipzig, Thuringia, Frankfurt and Cologne. In 1910 he made a further trip to Germany, concentrating this time on Munich and the south. His impressions were so favourable that in 1914 he felt unable to take seriously the notion that Germany was planning a war.[46] Although he had already contributed some verse translations and lampoons, he did not play a major role in the periodical until Orage approached him to review foreign publications for his 'Readers and Writers' column and write features on specialist aspects of foreign literature. These included 'Hebbel in English', in which he regrets the fact that the

---

45   1 December 1910; *NA* VIII, 5, p. 111. Sudermann as prose writer again came under scrutiny in 1912 when a collection of his stories, entitled *The Indian Lily*, fell foul of the anonymous reviewer as the 'epitome of Teutonic eroticism', at times so sordid that it could only be termed 'Sudermanure'. (6 June 1912; *NA* XI, 6, p. 136)

46   Paul Selver, *Orage and the New Age Circle* (London, 1959), p. 55.

dramatist is rarely translated into English, though acknowledging that an Everyman edition of 1913 has tried to make amends for this oversight (16 July 1914; *NA* XV, 11, p. 257). In addition, there was a selection of aphorisms by Bismarck, translated from the *Vossische Zeitung* by Selver himself. (18 December 1913; *NA* XIV, 7, pp. 204-5)

A favourite theme in Selver's articles for 'Readers and Writers', to which he contributed about once a month, is translation. He observes that in general the Germans can boast of good translations of English writers, especially the renderings of Shelley and Tennyson by Freilgrath and Strodtmann. There are certain exceptions, however, most notably the 1912 edition of Keats's poems translated by Alexander von Berus, an associate of Stefan Georg and his circle of Symbolists - a connection, according to Selver, which gave the translator 'the great advantage of being able to contort German and misunderstand English'. Still, a translator does not have to associate with Georg in order to accomplish this feat. Bernard Shaw's translator, Siegfried Trebitsch, had been responsible for some absurd mistranslations into German. Selver reminds his readers that in the first German edition of Shaw's plays, which comprised *Candida, Arms and the Man* and *The Devil's Disciple*,[47] Trebitsch had offered 'Unternehmer' for 'undertaker', 'ein öffentliches Haus' for 'public house', 'benütze ihn für ein Buch' for 'bring him to book', 'Was haben die für ein Glaubensbekenntnis?' for 'What's the subscription?' and 'Ein Teufelskerl' for 'The Devil's Disciple'. In this respect the state of literary translation had changed little since the mid-eighteenth century, when some of the German translators of Pope, Gray, Thomson and Bolingbroke 'were already anticipating in a mild degree the linguistic feats of Herr Siegfried Trebitsch'. Selver points out that this prompted Lessing to complain in 1759 in *Briefe, die neueste Literatur betreffend*: 'Unsere Übersetzer verstehen selten die Sprache; sie wollen sie erst verstehen lernen; sie übersetzen, sich zu üben, und sie sind klug genug, sich ihre Übungen bezahlen zu lassen'.[48] It is a complaint which might equally well be levelled at Trebitsch.

Selver takes up the subject of translation again in March 1914 when he discusses Paul Wiegler's *Geschichte der Weltliteratur*. He observes that it is easier for Germans to write a book of this nature as there are plenty of German translations of foreign writers at hand. Moreover, they are within the budget of the average reader: both Swinburne and Wilde can be bought cheaply in German translation. By contrast, in England, 'Schnitzler at six shillings and Hauptmann at

---

47   In 1903 Cotta published the three plays in one volume entitled *Drei Dramen*. See Michael Holroyd, *Bernard Shaw, Vol. II, 1898-1918. The Pursuit of Power* (London, 1989), p. 51.

48   See 2 October 1913; *NA* XIII, 23, p. 666.

several more' are beyond the means of most readers. (5 March 1914; *NA* XIV, 18, p. 563)

Selver's predominant interest lay in modern rather than classical German literature. In September 1913 one of his earliest pieces for 'Readers and Writers' discusses contemporary Austrian writers. He considers P. K. Rosegger (1843-1918), the author of dialect poems such as *Zither und Hackbrett* and sketches of Alpine life that 'set a dubious fashion in *Heimatkunst*'. In the same article Selver praises the Austrian critic and novelist, Hermann Bahr (1863-1943), for having discovered Hugo von Hofmannsthal in his essay *Loris*, recently reproduced in the *Hermann-Bahr-Buch* in honour of the author's fiftieth birthday. (4 September 1913; *NA* XIII, 19, p. 548)

During the months leading up to the outbreak of war Selver continued to follow the latest publications in Germany. In addition to praising Hermann Bahr, Selver also turned his attention to the poetry of Arno Holz, singling out *Phantasus* and *Das Buch der Zeit* for particular commendation (19 March 1914; *NA* XIV, 20, p. 626). This piece was soon followed by a feature on Karl Bleibtreu's two-volume *Geschichte der deutschen National-Literatur von Goethes Tod bis zur Gegenwart* (2 April 1914; *NA* XIV, 22, p. 691). He also noticed the appearance in *Das literarische Echo* of an article on 'Nietzsche in England' by Professor Leon Kellner, who gives credit to the efforts of Oscar Levy (2 July 1914; *NA* XV, 9, p. 205), whilst as late as 6 August 1914 he admits to reading German fiction for pleasure. In order to emphasise this point he goes on to recommend Hermann Bahr's novel *Theatre*, a volume of stories by Schnitzler entitled *The Greek Dancer* and Georg Hermann's *Kubinke* as 'A German Mr. Polly'. The article concludes with a discussion of Thomas Mann, who, according to Selver, is virtually unknown in London. The few English readers who have heard of Mann know him only as the author of *Buddenbrooks* (1901), which Selver does not consider his best work. He argues that it is as a writer of short stories that Mann excels, giving particular commendation to *Luischen*, *The Railway Accident* and *Those who Hunger*. (*NA* XV, 14, p. 325)

R.H.C.: 'Readers and Writers'

However, it would be misleading to suggest that Selver alone was interested in German literature. He was, after all, an *occasional* contributor to 'Readers and Writers'. It was very much Orage's column and he too reveals a certain interest in the German publishing world. On 5 June 1913, for example, within a month of the column's inception, Orage criticises the approach of Professor Schüddekopf, Head of German at Leeds University, who writes on contemporary English literature for *Das literarische Echo* in Berlin. In the German periodical the German professor generally 'conducts himself with truly German caution. That is, he catalogues the books which appear, with as little adventure at selection as possible, and for his judgements depends upon the the safe sagacities of the *Saturday Review*, the *Spectator* and the *Nation*'. In addition to familiarity with current German periodicals, Orage goes on to discuss a recent reprint of the work of Georg Christoph Lichtenberg (1742-99), a writer who had found favour with Nietzsche. Indeed, in Orage's opinion, Lichtenberg's aphorisms were of such a high standard that they 'might well be, and probably have been, credited to Nietzsche himself'; he notes that Nietzsche copied Lichtenberg's aphorism: 'God created man in his image; that probably means, man created God in his' (5 June 1913; *NA* XIII, 6, p. 145). In *Menschliches, Allzumenschliches*, for instance, Nietzsche ranks Lichtenberg's *Aphorismen* as one of the few works of German literature that deserve to be read again and again.[49] Although Orage no longer adheres so absolutely to Nietzschean thought, he still clearly admires the aphorisms of Nietzsche. In this context, it is worth remembering that one of Orage's first publications on the German philosopher was *Nietzsche in Outline and Aphorism* (1907), which was for the most part a collection of hitherto untranslated aphorisms, taken mainly from what Orage entitles *Inopportune Contemplations, Human, all too Human, Joyful Science*, and *Dawn of Day*; with the exception of the latter work, none of Orage's sources had appeared in English at this date, suggesting that he had relied on his own translation of the majority of the aphorisms contained in his collection.

The German philosopher was still being discussed in the *New Age* between 1910 and 1914. Amongst the pieces on Nietzsche that Orage published were three translations of articles from the *Frankfurter Zeitung*, the first by Professor A. Messer of Gießen University on Kant and Nietzsche, the second by Karl Strecker on Nietzsche and Strindberg and the third by Nietzsche's cousin, Dr. Richard Oehler, the librarian of Bonn University, on 'The Zarathustra Jubilee' to commemorate the thirtieth anniversary of the first publication in 1883 of *Also sprach Zarathustra*.[50] Oehler notes that by 1913 one hundred thousand copies of the work had been printed: 'luckily, the number of those to whom Nietzsche has become an inseparable companion is far larger than the number of those who only write about his teachings. For their intellectual as well as for their emotional life we may say what Maximilian Harden once confessed in conversation "Everyone steals from him"'.[51] Harden, too, was no stranger to the pages of the *New Age*. On 5 June 1913, for example, an anonymous reviewer of *Men around the Kaiser: Makers of Modern Germany* by the Berlin correspondent of the *Daily Mail*,

---

49   Nietzsche, *Werke*, II, p. 921.
50   29 February 1911; *NA* X, 18, p. 419; 10 April 1913; *NA* XII, 23, pp. 559-60 and 22 January 1914; *NA* XIV, 12, pp. 367-8 (the article by Oehler originally appeared in Germany in December 1913).
51   Ibid., p. 367.

Frederick W. Wile, comments that some of the Germans treated are 'almost human', including the editor of *Die Zukunft*, 'a paper which is almost the *New Age* of Germany'. (*NA* XIII, 6, p. 151)

The Nietzscheans: J. M. Kennedy and A. M. Ludovici

The translators of Nietzsche - Ludovici and Kennedy especially - occupied much space in the periodical. A. M. Ludovici followed the latest works on Nietzsche assiduously - often looking abroad for his material. In February 1911 he reviewed *The Life of Friedrich Nietzsche*, translated from the original French of Daniel Halévy. Ludovici is pleased to report that the impact of the original is not lost in translation. He recommends this interpretation of Nietzsche by a Frenchman rather than those of English critics, maintaining that Max Nordau's attack on Nietzsche in *Degeneration*, apart from being a good ten years out of date, is 'still the source to which most English critics have to go in order to refresh their critical faculty before the stupendous task of valuing an unknown quantity' (23 February 1911; *NA* VIII, 17, p. 403). The following month he turned his attention to Claire Richter's *Nietzsche et les Théories Biologiques Contemporaines*. He notes that English, and also many German scholars 'scoff at Nietzsche's incursions into the realm of science, simply because he spoke with the divination and authority of a prophet and a poet, just as Heraclitus, Leonardo da Vinci and Goethe had done before him', whereas Claire Richter clearly demonstrates that Nietzsche's biological views are taken seriously in France, where he is considered to have been more influenced by Lamarck's school than Darwin's (14 September 1911; *NA* IX, 20, pp. 473-4). The translators of Nietzsche also reviewed each other's books, with Kennedy discussing Ludovici's *Nietzsche and Art* in August 1911, and Paul V. Cohn, a fellow translator for the Levy edition, reviewing Kennedy's *English Literature 1880-1905* in June 1912. In addition, there was a favourable review for *The Nietzsche Calendar*, a collection of aphorisms compiled by J. M. Kennedy from the Levy edition, apparently issued to coincide with the translation of the Nietzsche canon being completed in 1913.[52]

J. M. Kennedy was engaged in reviewing a number of books for the literary pages of the *New Age*. In January 1911, for instance, he commends a 'longish pamphlet' by the professor of Political Science at Gießen University, Magnus Biermer, entitled *Die politische Krise in England*. Despite being written in 'what is at times rather trying German', Kennedy approves of the work on the grounds that the author has put his experience of living in England to good effect

---

52   10 August 1911; *NA* IX, 15, p. 350; 13 June 1912; *NA* XI, 7, pp. 154-5 and
      28 November 1912; *NA* XII, 4, p. 88.

in order to produce some penetrating observations and an admirable denunciation of the Liberal press (26 January 1911; *NA* VIII, 13). Kennedy was not the only Nietzschean to be undertaking different activities on the *New Age*. Ludovici began to write a weekly column on art in the summer of 1912, whilst Levy contributed occasional reviews, including a critique of Oscar Schmitz' *Lord Beaconsfield oder die Kunst der Politik* and a discussion of a recent lecture on German literature given by Lord Haldane at Oxford University. This diversification in the interests of the Nietzscheans would suggest that Orage as editor was trying to shift the emphasis of his periodical away from Nietzsche as he developed a more critical approach to the German philosopher.

A. E. Randall: August Bebel is 'the enemy of democracy'

Works on German political life continued to attract critical interest. In 1911, for instance, an anonymous review of G. A. C. Sandeman's *Metternich* rates this politician as the third greatest nineteenth century statesman after Disraeli and Bismarck, likening Disraeli's Tory Democracy to Bismarck's policy in Germany. At the other end of the political spectrum there were notices on Werner Sombart's *Socialism and the Socialist Movement*, Adelheid Popp's *Autobiography of a Working Woman*, as well as August Bebel's *My Life*. The latter was in 'Views and Reviews' by A. E. Randall,[53] a new recruit to the *New Age*, marking one of several attempts by Orage to find a replacement for Arnold Bennett's 'Books and Persons'. Whereas previous commentators on August Bebel (1840-1913) had been highly sympathetic towards the leader of the German Social Democrats, Randall proves sharply critical of his achievements. He begins by questioning why Bebel can lead his party to landslide victories at elections, yet is repeatedly excluded from exercising power by the German government.[54] His flaw, according to Randall, was to strive for social democracy through the Social Democratic Party because it meant that though he gained control of the party, he fell far short of achieving the ideal of social democracy. It is on this point that Randall is most caustic: 'When you see a design, infer a designer, was Paley's maxim;[55] and it has survived all the onslaughts of the Rationalists. So when we

---

53 5 October 1911; *NA* IX, 23, p. 545 and 23 May 1912; *NA* XI, 4, pp. 88-9.

54 Although Bismarck's *Sozialistengesetze* had banned Socialist meetings and publications, Socialist electoral activity was still allowed and Socialists spoke freely in the Reichstag. See William Carr, *A History of Germany 1815-1985*, third edition (London, 1987), pp. 131-3.

55 The Anglican priest and Utilitarian philosopher William Paley (1743-1805) argued that the existence of God could be proved by observing the design apparent in natural phenomena.

see Herr Bebel reaching what he set out to reach, and then telling his followers that there is really no room for more than one of himself, we see him, not as the friend, but as the enemy of democracy. His appeal is not to the free instincts of men, but to the instincts of the herd. The display of his own virtues in this book will not deceive anyone who has read Nietzsche.' Bebel's Social Democrats have therefore achieved nothing (21 November 1912; *NA* XII, 3, p. 65). The following year Randall once more sets out to explode what he sees as the myth of Germany being a Socialist utopia. He uses his review of William Harbutt Dawson's *Industrial Germany* to argue that Germany is a 'servile state with a vengeance' where workers are just as badly exploited as in England. (29 May 1913; *NA* XIII, 5, p. 122)

Randall's view of the German Socialist movement was very much in accordance with Orage's own at this time. In an obituary note on August Bebel on 21 August 1913 Orage expressed a similar sentiment when he remarked that Bebel's death 'lucidly enforces the conclusion that German political Socialism is as barren and futile as its British counterpart'. Bebel died leader of a party with four million supporters but never managed to improve conditions for ordinary workers. He failed as leader of the Socialists 'just as Keir Hardie failed in England' (*NA* XIII, 17, pp. 474-5). In the late 1890s Orage spoke at meetings of the Independent Labour Party, met the party's leader, Tom Mann, and supplemented his income as a school teacher in Leeds by writing 'A Bookish Causerie' for Keir Hardie's paper, the *Labour Leader*.[56] His disillusionment with Socialism springs from what he views as the failure of the movement in England and Germany. He is roused to scathing criticism of Socialists in both countries. In May 1911, in an essay entitled 'On Sentimentality', he accuses Socialists of hypocrisy, branding them 'frauds trading on emotional credit'. The worst offenders in this category are the German Social Democrats. He contends that of all the ill things he hears about Germany the worst is this that it contains a very large number of voting Socialists but no Socialism (4 May 1911; *NA* IX, 1, p. 13). The historian William Carr has also made the point that although there were some extreme left-wingers in the Reichstag, most German Socialist deputies, including Bebel, were centrists. Committed to democratic socialism, they tried to repress the fervour of extremists and thus alienated left-wingers, such as Rosa Luxemburg. At the same time, they reiterated revolutionary slogans and refused to give absolute support to the established political parties, with the result that they set themselves at odds with the middle classes, whose support they needed if they were ever to secure a majority in Germany.[57]

---

56   Philippe Mairet, *A. R. Orage: A Memoir*, (London, 1936), p. 15.   See also John Carswell, op. cit., p. 19.

57   See William Carr, op. cit., p. 184.

At the same time as Orage was reconsidering his political views he was also subjecting his philosophical outlook to rigorous re-examination. This involved much discussion of his former intellectual master, Nietzsche, in the pages of the *New Age*. Between 1910 and 1914 Orage's perception of Nietzsche becomes increasingly complex. As his articles show, he took issue not only with the theories of the German philosopher, but also with the interpretations given to those theories by the English Nietzscheans. He did not break with Nietzsche altogether, however, and attempted to shatter some of the myths about Nietzsche's thought through plain argument in his columns 'Unedited Opinions' and 'Readers and Writers' and, on one occasion, in his fictional series of 'Tales for Men Only'.

On 14 September 1911 the *New Age* printed a letter signed 'R. M.', denouncing the Nietzscheans for stubborn persistency in the face of repeated defeats in their struggle to find wide acceptance for Nietzsche in England. This letter was probably the work of Orage himself because in it Nietzsche is branded 'a lyrical Bismarck' - the exact expression used by Orage in an unsigned article early in 1910.[58] In the letter Orage contends that Nietzscheism 'is only a German name for romantic eugenics'. By good art Nietzsche meant: 'art that conduced to an increase of a healthy population; and by bad art that which discouraged procreation. In this respect I contend that not only was he a good German in the Kaiser's sense of the word (the Kaiser should sculpt a statue to him in common gratitude), but he embodied as well as intensified the tendency of the Germany of our day. Everybody knows that Germany alone among the civilised nations is adding to its population at an indecent rate (nearly a million a year). A procreative effort of this kind needs some justification when all the rest of Europe, and in particular the most intelligent parts, are learning to dispense with numbers in favour of quality. Nietzsche supplies Germany with that justification. He marshals the most elaborate sophistries and the most resounding theories to excuse and to glorify the philoprogenitiveness of the German, thus lulling to sleep their suspicions and giving them a good conscience for their reaction. To this same end he interprets art and everything else. Never was such a missionary, and one of whom civilised people should stand more in fear' (14 September 1911; *NA* IX, 20, p. 479). Certainly there had been a population explosion in Wilhelmine Germany. Between 1871 and 1914 the population rose from 41 million to 66 million, whilst in France the rise over the same period was only from 38 million to 40 million and in Great Britain between 1870 and 1910 from 26 million to 40 million. This dramatic rise in the German population since 1871 seemed to

---

58   'Nietzsche: The Lyrical Bismarck', 27 January 1910; *NA* VI, 13, pp. 304-5.
      See Chapter 2, pp. 56-7.

justify the view that Germany was a new, rising nation, destined to supersede the old powers and claim world power status.[59] Nevertheless, Orage's suggestion that Nietzsche supplied the Germans with the justification for the expansion of the population is dubious.

Nietzsche's concept of the *Übermensch* was a source of great contention to Orage. On 1 December 1910, for example, he devotes a whole article in his series 'Unedited Opinions' to the Superman. First he attacks the Nietzscheans as 'parasites on the weaknesses of Nietzsche, parasites on his defects and mistakes'. These weaknesses are the theories of a new aristocracy and of the Superman. According to Orage 'Nietzsche is only at his best when he is demonstrating that man is a caged animal, and is seen beating his head against the bars; when one can hear him saying: "Thus and thus, we people of earth are confined and hemmed in; thus and thus are we subjected by our human nature to servitude, imprisonment and degradation; yet let our redemption be that we remain for ever dissatisfied with it." As a preacher of human discontent in our very depths Nietzsche is comparable with Job. As a reformer he is ridiculous'. Nietzsche is ridiculous because 'he had no notion of bursting the bars and of liberating the mind by the creation of new faculties, but simply returned to the old exploded human way of physical procreation'. Having demonstrated that the human race was doomed and damned Nietzsche had no right to expect us to believe in his new physical race. Because the Superman is the product of man and woman, he must be human. Although he may be endowed with better health, greater strength, sharper intellect, because he is basically human he will not be vastly different from men and women of today. The concept of the Superman signifies 'no more than providing the lions at the zoo with bigger cages and a more nourishing diet, and then pretending that they are more than lions.' (*NA* VIII, 5, p. 107)

In his fictional series of 'Tales for Men Only', Orage also attacked the concept of the Superman and the interpretation of a new aristocracy which certain followers of Nietzsche put on his theories. In 'A Fifth Tale for Men Only', which ran in August 1912, the narrator, Congreve, introduces us to a group whose common purpose is 'to form a communal mind which, by its nature and powers, shall constitute a new order of being in the hierarchy of intelligent creation'. In the course of their quest, the members make the acquaintance of Mr. Lessing, 'a youngish to middle-aged man whose fresh complexion announced him to be an incorrigible idealist'. Matters take a downward turn when the narrator realizes that Mr. Lessing's hobby is 'the philosophy of that colossal pastichist (sic) Nietzsche'. Congreve perceives that the unfortunate Lessing wishes to be an aristocrat since he displays 'contempt for the plebeian, hatred of manual labour,

---

59   Fritz Fischer, op. cit., p. 18.

fastidiousness in manner and dress, the profession of the connoisseur of women. Each of these qualities which Nietzsche somewhere or other noted as aristocratic virtues Lessing had quite ludicrously, to my mind, cultivated in the hope, it would seem, he might become visible to the naked eye.' Presently Mr. Lessing becomes involved in an argument with Congreve when he expresses the view that the first condition for becoming a Superman is to be a man. The Superman will develop out of the perfection of man. Congreve, the narrator, counters that the Superman means the death of man. He argues that Lessing has forgotten that the 'philosopher-scholar-artists' were Nietzsche's preparatory school for the Superman. (22 August 1912; *NA* XI, 17, pp. 398-9)

This view of the Superman was in keeping with the concept put forward by Orage in his 1907 book *Nietzsche in Outline and Aphorism*, where he had highlighted Nietzsche's three phases of existence: the camel, the lion and the child. The present stage was that of the camel - slow, reponsible, reliable, but ripe for change. The camel phase was to be destroyed by the generation of the lion. 'If the watchword of the camel is Others', Orage explained, 'the watchword of the lions is Ourselves'. However, in 1907 few men in Europe had reached the lion stage, therefore 'few are available as the nucleus of Nietzsche's race of philosophers, who should prepare the way for the Superman. Yet few as they are, their influence is already being felt'. Orage foresaw that in the coming decades there would emerge more adventurous iconoclasts, 'laughing lions' of Nietzsche's ilk, who would destroy the old ideals of duty and service and deliver Europe from the camel phase. However, not until the lions were replaced by the child would the Superman be born. In the child, according to Orage, there exists 'no human consciousness of within and without, no conscious responsibility or rejection of responsibility, no will to serve or will to command. All in him is instinctive. He rules because he is; his service is his presence; his duty is to be'.[60] Whether Orage was familiar with the work of Freud when he wrote this in 1907 must remain open to conjecture. No reference is made to the Austrian publicly in his circle until 1912, when A. E. Randall discusses 'Freud and his school' in an article for the *New Age*.[61]

By May 1914 there was no doubt in Orage's mind about Nietzsche's shortcomings. In 'Unedited Opinions' he defines Nietzsche as a nihilist in the practical, rather than the philosophic sense. He calls a practical nihilist one 'who destroys with no notion of what is to take its place'. Nietzsche succeeded in

---

60   A. R. Orage, *Nietzsche in Outline and Aphorism* (London, 1907), pp. 156-
       7. See also Tom Steele, 'From Gentleman to Superman: Alfred Orage and
       Aristocratic Socialism', in *The Imagined Past: History and Nostalgia*, edited
       by Christopher Shaw and Malcolm Chase, (Manchester, 1989), p. 119.
61   See Wallace Martin, op. cit., p. 140.

destroying morality as commonly conceived, but never defined the standards of conduct that were to succeed it. 'In so far as he attempted to do so', Orage argues, Nietzsche 'fell into the very errors he had just demonstrated; in other words, he never really transcended his negative doctrine at all, but remained a moralist even when he was beyond morality'. Nietzsche succeeded in destroying the morality of good and evil, although 'he never succeeded in destroying the morality of right and wrong.' Orage contends: 'Good and Evil are terms relative; but Right and Wrong are terms absolute. Good and Evil are related either to some end desired or not desired by us; or to some feelings peculiar to ourselves. Right and Wrong, on the other hand, are independent of our predelictions or aversions and are the nature of things. What Nietzsche did was to prove that Good and Evil are not absolute terms. What he failed to affirm was that Right and Wrong *are*. Indeed, the one was comparatively easy to prove: the other is much more difficult.' (28 May 1914; *NA* XV, 4, p. 84)

Orage's argument - if it can be called an argument - seems wilfully wrong-headed for one who allegedly has read Nietzsche systematically. Nietzsche defines the terms 'gut und böse', 'gut und schlecht' most succinctly in the first part of *Zur Genealogie der Moral*. He accuses 'English Psychologists' of having attributed an incorrect history to the origin of our moral values, so subverting the meaning of 'good' and 'bad'. These historians of morals maintain that man originally termed altruistic acts conferred on others 'good'. Now altruistic acts are called 'good' out of sheer habit. However, the origin of the word 'good' was not among those to whom goodness was shown, but among those who applied the term. It is not the lowly, but the high-ranking, powerful and aristocratic members of society who created the values. These people were able to set the criteria for moral values. It is only because of the decay of aristocratic values that the antithesis between 'egotistic' and 'altruistic' weighs more heavily on the human conscience. Originally the root idea of 'good' was what the 'noble' or 'Vornehmen' thought themselves to be, namely 'aristocratic' or 'privileged'. A similar form of evolution took place with the word 'bad'. Initially the German 'schlecht' was synonymous with 'schlicht', meaning 'simple or common' - the opposite of 'aristocratic' or 'priviledged'. Only after the Thirty Years' War did the term acquire a moral meaning.[62] The antithesis 'Good' and 'Bad' is the invention of the weak and therefore relative, not absolute. According to Nietzsche the 'gut' in the 'gut/schlecht' antithesis of the 'Vornehmen' could be construed as absolute in the sense that the 'Vornehmen' took it for granted and did not need the weak to give themselves meaning.

---

62   Nietzsche, *Werke*, II, p. 771ff.

Orage and the Nietzscheans: 'parasites on the weakness of Nietzsche, parasites on his defects and mistakes'

However, Orage did not adopt a wholly negative view of Nietzsche in this period of transition in his ideas. Already disenchanted with political alternatives, he hoped to find in Nietzsche's thought in 1914 the basis for a satisfactory system of government. This was odd given Orage's very negative and misunderstood view of Nietzsche's ethics outlined above. In January 1914 his column 'Readers and Writers' opens with Nietzsche's aphorism from the second volume of the *Will to Power*:

> '*Concerning the future of the workman*: Workmen should learn to regard their duties as *soldiers do*. These receive emoluments, incomes, but they do not get wages! There is no relationship between work done and money received; the individual should, *according to his kind*, be so placed as *to perform the highest* that is compatible with his powers'.[63]

Orage questions why neither Levy, nor Ludovici, who translated this work, have mentioned this quotation before as the germ of the National Guilds System, which would later so preoccupy Orage. He comments: 'like many of his disciples, [Nietzsche] was satisfied with glimpses into economic reality and never, to the end, appreciated the importance of half the observations he made. My own view, nevertheless, is that Nietzsche and his specific problems must wait upon the economic problems he affected to despise. Until, in fact, workmen have become "soldiers", the military order of society with its grand campaigns of culture and science will never be possible.' (22 January 1914; *NA* XIV, 12, p. 370)

On several occasions Orage openly criticises the English Nietzscheans in the *New Age*. It is significant that Oscar Levy, in his introduction to the complete works of Nietzsche - which, incidentally, was printed in the *New Age* during December 1912 and January 1913 - makes no mention of Orage when acknowledging the efforts of writers and translators to make Nietzsche a household name in England. Levy's plans to erect a monument to Nietzsche in Weimar, as part of a joint venture with Elisabeth Förster-Nietzsche, for example, met with particular scorn from Orage. On 14 May 1914 Orage reflects: 'An age that only likes great men as the Americans like their Indians -

---

63   See Nietzsche, *Aus dem Nachlass der Achtziger Jahre*, in *Werke*, III, p. 558.

dead - needs first to have its wits sharpened on its living contemporaries before it can really honour even the dead'.[64]

Henri Bergson: 'the intellectual has no energy, no élan vital, no "go" in him'

In addition to Nietzsche, the *New Age* devoted considerable attention to the French philosopher Henri Bergson (1859-1941), whose theories of the *élan vital* owed something to Nietzsche's ideas. For Nietzsche, life, given purpose and direction by 'the will to power', represents the highest product of Nature. Bergson also regarded life as the highest phenomenon of Nature and, like Nietzsche, evolved a philosophy that was anti-rationalist and placed emphasis on intuition. The main distinction between Bergson and Nietzsche is that Bergson's vital principal or *élan vital* is conceived as a senseless, directionless, totally unpredictable force - closer to Schopenhauer's 'will' than Nietzsche's.[65] Bergson's influence was widespread, inspiring a younger generation of writers. John Middleton Murray, for example, as a student making his first visit to Paris in the winter of 1910, read Bergson there, although he did not attend the French professor's highly popular lectures.[66] It is significant that Bergson's appeal was to a younger generation of writers. In the *New Age* serious commentary on Bergson did not come from the established contributors, but from a new recruit, T. E. Hulme.

T. E Hulme had established himself as a writer on philosophy and translator of Bergson, and between 1912 and 1913 shared a flat off Oxford Circus with the *New Age* drama critic, Ashley Dukes. Together with Dukes he frequented the circle of the sculptors Epstein and Gaudier-Brzeska, where the conversation invariably turned on 'the inevitability of war, Marinetti's Futurism or Ezra Pound's verse, or the paper that Wyndham Lewis was bringing out called *Blast*'. Dukes describes the atmosphere of the group as 'authoritarian', with the ominous prediction that had Hulme survived the First World War he 'would

---

64   *NA* XV, 2, p. 37. Levy was not the only Nietzschean to come under fire. On 5 February 1914, as R.H.C., Orage wrote a letter to the *New Age* attacking A. M. Ludovici specifically, but by implication, the Nietzscheans as as a group. He contends that 'it is said that no Christian can read the Bible; but it is equally clear that the Nietzscheans cannot read Nietzsche', since they 'twist and distort and misread his various opinions as if, somehow or other, Nietzsche would be disgraced if they did not make them all fit.' (*NA* XIV, 14, p. 440)
65   See R. G. Collingwood, *The Idea of Nature*, (Oxford, 1945), pp. 135-8.
66   Claire Tomalin, op. cit., p. 96.

probably have embraced some form of fascism'.[67] Fascism, at the time, of course meant Italy. In no way were Hulme's views the product of his understanding of German literature or experience of German culture. His colleague, Paul Selver, recalls that Hulme 'had spent some time in Berlin where, from what he said, he disliked the Germans and they had disliked him. Also, under circumstances which remained obscure, he had fallen foul of Prussian authority. And he came back with anti-German feelings which could scarcely have been stronger if he had foreseen that he was to be killed by a German shell in 1918'.[68]

Interest in Bergson began on the pages of the *New Age* in July 1911 with a review of A. D. Lindsay's *The Philosophy of Bergson*. Although in the previous weeks there had been letters in the paper debating the importance of the French philosopher, this review by Belford Bax marks the first detailed study of Bergson in the *New Age*. This was soon followed by T. E. Hulme's first article, 'Bax on Bergson', and then a further six on the French philosopher that established Hulme as the periodical's chief spokesman on Bergson between 1911 and 1912.[69] On 2 November 1911, for example, Hulme confesses that before he read Bergson he believed the world 'was nothing but a vast mechanism'. However, Bergson's criticism could enable man to escape from 'this mechanistic nightmare'. What he terms Bergson's 'theory of intensive manifolds' leads man to a world-view which replaces the mechanistic one. (*NA* XI, 1, p. 39)

However, Orage was not particularly impressed with Bergson. In May 1914, after having made his periodical a platform for the followers of the French philosopher, Orage spoke out on 'The Popularity of Bergson', or more precisely, on what he terms, 'Bergsonism' as 'the chief reactionary movement in the present spiritual politics of the world'. Orage classes philosophers, especially popular philosophers, as 'the spiritual politicians of the day; and it behoves us to consider them quite as carefully as we find we have to consider our temporal politicians. They do not, it is true, legislate in the technical sense; but none the less they do legislate by changing our beliefs'. For Orage, the categories of

---

67   Ashley Dukes, op. cit., pp. 40-1.

68   Paul Selver, op cit., p. 26.

69   For Belford Bax's review see 20 July 1911; *NA* IX, 12, pp. 280-1. Hulme's piece on Bax appeared on 3 August 1911; *NA* IX, 14, pp. 328-31, followed by a series explaining Bergson's ideas - 19 October 1911, *NA* IX, 25, pp. 587-8; 26 October 1911; *NA* IX, 26, pp. 610-11; 2 November 1911; *NA* X, 1, pp. 38-40; 23 November 1911; *NA* X, 4, pp. 79-82; 30 November 1911; *NA* X, 5, pp. 110-12 and 22 February 1912; *NA* X, 17, pp. 401-3. There were other contributions, albeit more sporadic, from a variety of hands, including A. M. Ludovici discussing *Le Rire* (3 October 1912; *NA* XI, 23, pp. 547-8).

'popular philosopher' and 'spiritual politician' must certainly include Nietzsche in view of his recent criticism of the German philosopher for supplying the political ethos on which Bismarck's Germany is based. Contending that the chief duty of mankind is the perfection of reason, since it is only when we have perfected reason that we can dispense with it, Orage charges Bergsonism with having undervalued reason. For intellect Bergson has substituted intuition, but according to Orage, 'impulse in its vulgarest sense is the meaning Bergsonism carries with it'. Reason has been cheapened by being renamed intellectualism, whilst the estimation of impulse has been raised by being renamed intuition. Originally the purpose of reason or intellect was to inhibit or control certain impulses. Orage believes that the 'anti-intellectualists' have countered that 'the intellectual has no energy, no élan vital, no "go" in him; and they not only do not like this state, but they fear it means the end of the world. Decadence, I think, poor old Nietzsche used to call it'. Orage contends that intellect will not suppress intuition because intuition is more powerful than intellect, which in turn is more powerful than impulse. Bergsonism makes the mistake of 'denouncing intellect *before* impulse has been completely subdued'.[70]

F. T. Marinetti: 'We wish to glorify war'

Henri Bergson was not the only modern European thinker to come under the scrutiny of Orage's periodical. In 1914 the theorist of the Futurist movement, F. T. Marinetti, was the subject of much discussion in the *New Age*. Marinetti had first come to prominence in Europe with the publication of his *Declaration of Futurism* in *Le Figaro* on 20 February 1909. This had contained not only a glorification of the machine and speed, revelling in vigour and vitality, but also the following exhortation: 'We wish to glorify war - the only true hygiene of the world - militarism, patriotism, the destructive gesture of the anarchist, the beautiful Ideas which kill, and the scorn of woman'. Marinetti took dynamism as the basis for his ideological system and believed that his theories were confirmed by the discoveries of modern science.[71] In Bergson's writings Marinetti saw the value of intuition, whilst in the the figure of Nietzsche's Zarathustra, who seeks to create a world based on new, different and superior values, he saw a parallel with himself. He was also impressed with the subtitle of *Götzendämmerung*, 'Wie man mit dem Hammer philosophiert', although he tried to play down suggestions of his

---

70   7 May 1914; *NA* XV, 1, p. 12. A few weeks later Orage confesses that 'M. Bergson has the knack of intriguing me against my inclination', before taking up this argument again. (28 May 1914; *NA* XV, 4, p. 85)

71   Jean-Pierre de Villers, *Le premier manifeste du futurisme* (Ottowa, 1986), p. 28.

having been greatly influenced by the German philosopher.[72] Certainly his own exhilarating prose style and startling imagery suggested philosophizing with a hammer. Only six months after the *Declaration* appeared in French it had been published in English translation in the *Daily Telegraph* and in German translation in the *Kölnische Zeitung, Frankfurter Zeitung* and *Vossische Zeitung*. Whilst intended as a rousing call for *Italian* poets and painters to look to the present rather than the past of Ancient Rome, this *Declaration of Futurism* with its emotive language and powerful imagery lends itself easily to misinterpretation.[73]

From late 1913 onwards the *New Age* carried articles on the Futurists by T. E. Hulme, A. M. Ludovici and Oscar Levy - the experts on Bergson and Nietzsche. This would suggest that Marinetti was being seen in the context of a wider discussion of vitalism. Admittedly Ludovici was not particularly favourably disposed towards the aesthetic theories of Futurism and became embroiled in a battle in print with T. E. Hulme on the subject in the course of 1914, whilst Levy set about denying any great similarity between Marinetti and Nietzsche.[74] Perhaps more importantly, as late as May 1914, the *New Age* printed a translation of Marinetti's 'Geometric and Mechanical Splendour in Words at Liberty' from the *Futurist Manifesto* (1910), which expanded some of the ideas set out in the original *Declaration of Futurism*. In the manifesto we learn that earlier notions of beauty associated with the Romantic, Symbolist and Decadent movements, have been superseded by what Marinetti calls 'Geometric and Mechanical Splendour'. The essential elements of this new beauty are 'power under control, speed, intense light, happy precision of well-oiled cogs, the conciseness of effort, the molecular cohesion of metals in the infinity of speeds, the simultaneous concurrence of diverse rhythms, the sum of independent and convergent initiatives in one victorious direction'. He first observed this beauty from that most potent symbol of the early twentieth century - the bridge of a Dreadnought. Marinetti recalls the minutest details of the sensations that the German warship aroused, the 'geometric splendour' of 'the speeds of the ship, the distance of the shots calculated at a great distance from the bridge in the fresh breeze of warlike probabilities, the strange rebellion of the orders transmitted by the admiral.' (7 May 1914; *NA* XV, 1, p. 16)

---

72   Ibid., p. 185.
73   For details of Marinetti's expansive declarations that would prove unfortunate in the light of events in 1914, see Jean Pierre de Villers, ibid., pp. 126-7.
74   See January-July 1914; *NA* XV.

Although not necessarily in agreement with either Bergson or Marinetti, Orage was sagacious enough an editor to publish articles on them that would attract readers. As he was turning away from Socialism, losing faith in the German Social Democrats and criticising Nietzsche, the question arises as to where he was looking for intellectual sustenance. It was certainly not to France. On 21 September 1911 he cries 'Down with the tricolour' and denounces liberty, equality and fraternity as wrong-headed on the grounds that 'in every sense, individual, social, national, these three ideas have done more harm and less good than any trinity ever invented. The world will never be sane until it forgets them' ('Unedited Opinions', *NA* IX, 21, pp. 489-90). However, on 11 December 1913 Orage was convinced he had found an alternative thinker in Benedetto Croce, hailing the Italian as 'the philosopher of the *New Age*'. Orage admits to having once 'delighted' in Plato for seven years, followed by Nietzsche for a further seven until the German's 'whimsicality became a burden'. However, since Nietzsche he claims to have 'read nothing to compare with Croce'.[75]

Katherine Mansfield: the English as a nation 'are dying for war'

In the course of 1911 Orage continued to publish Katherine Mansfield's short stories, based on her experiences in Bavaria. These included *A Birthday* and *The Modern Soul*, which, together with the earlier stories,[76] appeared in 1911 as part of the collection *In a German Pension*. In addition, Orage printed work not included in the *Pension* anthology, namely *The Festival of the Coronation*, *The Breidenbach Family in England*, *The Journey to Bruges*, *Being a Truthful Adventure* and the poem *Love Cycle*.[77] Although the later stories did not deal exclusively with Germany, two are particularly significant in terms of Katherine Mansfield's perception of Wilhelmine Germany. In *The Modern Soul* she reveals herself to be fascinated with German titles and sentence

---

75 *NA* XIV, 6, p. 177. In a later article he qualifies this statement by confessing that Croce's novelty lies in his form rather than his content. (8 January 1914; *NA* XIV, 10, p. 308)

76 *A Birthday* appeared on 18 May 1911 (*NA* IX, 3, pp. 61-3) and *The Modern Soul* on 22 June 1911 (*NA* IX, 8, pp. 183-6). For a discussion of the stories which had already appeared see Chapter 2, pp. 60-2.

77 29 June 1911; *NA* IX, 9, p. 196; 17 August 1911; *NA* IX, 16, p. 371; 24 August 1911; *NA* IX, 17, pp. 401-2; 7 September 1911; *NA* IX, 19, pp. 450-2 and 19 October 1911; *NA* IX, 25, p. 586.

structure. Thus, in the Bavarian guest house, the 'Herr Professor' addresses Kathleen, the narrator, as 'gnädige Frau' and when another guest, Frau Godowska, bursts into tears, the Professor exclaims 'Ach Gott! Gracious lady, what have I said?' At mealtimes the 'Herr Professor' wishes his companions at the table 'good appetite', whilst at a musical soirée put on by the guests 'Frau Ober Lehrer Weidel' (sic) sings so beautifully that the audience claps and cries 'Ach, how sweet, how delicate' (22 June 1911; *NA* IX, 8, pp. 183-5). Katherine Mansfield's tone is gently ironic towards the Germans, rather than openly hostile. Her concern is not only with the English living in Germany, but also with Germans living in England and the attitude of the local community to them. Thus, *The Breidenbach Family in England* deals with 'Herr Doctor Breidenbach' (sic), his wife and his daughter, Maria, adapting to English life after leaving Munich. They take a walk in the countryside near their lodgings, 'the stout Herr Doctor with stick and scarf, his wife in navy print and a smart hat and a stick, and Maria in white muslin and a stick' and all the while 'rural England giggled audibly from behind its window-curtains'. Even against this pastoral background Anglo-German antagonism threatens. The conversation between the Breidenbachs inevitably turns on the likelihood of war when they notice a farm labourer staring at them. Although Breidenbach discounts such a possibility, his wife is convinced by the 'enmity' of the labourer's gaze that the English as a nation 'are dying for war' (17 August 1911; *NA* IX, 16, p. 371). This is almost a complete reversal of one of the earliest stories to be published in the *New Age*, *Germans at Meat*, in which the 'Herr Rat', a guest in the German pension, fixes 'his cold blue eyes' on the English narrator 'with an expression that suggested a thousand premeditated invasions' (3 March 1910; *NA* VI, 18, p. 419). Because *The Breidenbach Family in England* is sympathetic towards Germans, its omission from the collection *In a German Pension* is all the more noticeable.

Katherine Mansfield was no stranger to the German language. Even before she spent five months in 1909 undergoing a *Wasserkur* at Bad Wörishofen in Bavaria, she knew German. As a pupil of Queen's College in London between 1903 and 1906 she was taught German by Walter Rippmann,[78] who introduced her to the work of Richard Dehmel. She was also taught history by J. A. Cramb, whose postumously published lectures, *Germany and England* (1914), would help link General Bernhardi's name with Prussian military strategy.[79] During her stay in London Katherine Mansfield met her cousin, Countess von Arnim, whose

---

78   Antony Alpers, op. cit., p. 25.
79   M.E. Humble, 'The Breakdown of a Consensus: British Writers and Anglo-German Relations 1900-1920', *Journal of European Studies* (March 1977), p. 45.

Elizabeth and her German Garden (1898) had greatly impressed her.[80] On her return to New Zealand she read Heine's *Ideas*[81] and Nietzsche's *Dawn of Day* and during her visit to Bavaria she was particularly keen on the Munich based magazine, *Jugend*.[82]

Ashley Dukes: the 'Art of Theatre'

Ashley Dukes continued his series on European dramatists until early in 1911, extending his scope to include Tolstoi, Gorki, D'Annunzio, Maeterlinck, Brieux, Capus, and Heijermans. Just as Katherine Mansfield's pieces for the *New Age* were later published in book form, so too were Dukes' articles on drama printed as *Modern Dramatists* in March 1911. His book was praised by Charles Carrington in the periodical for bringing to the attention of English playgoers dramatists of whom 'less than fifteen per cent' are known to English readers and even fewer of which have been produced on the English stage. Dukes ranks as the first serious critic of drama since William Archer. Thanks to Archer and Dukes, drama criticism is no longer a dilettante's occupation or the stepping-stone to a more fruitful career in journalism. It has become a genre in its own right.[83]

In November 1910 Dukes devoted his column to the Austrian dramatist Hugo von Hofmannsthal (1874-1929). He observes that a recently opened German provincial theatre bears an inscription to Goethe, Hauptmann, Schiller and Hofmannsthal above its proscenium. To many Germans, Dukes maintains, Hauptmann and Hofmannsthal 'are already canonised among the classic poets'. Hofmannsthal's first work was published in 1891 when he was only seventeen. Although this was the time of the Berlin Freie Bühne and independent Ibsenite theatres throughout the rest of Europe, the main influence on Hofmannsthal was Italian art. Writing under the pseudonym Loris he gave the critic Herman Bahr the impression that he was a Frenchman writing in German. By the time he was nineteen Hofmannsthal had already published poems, essays and two verse dramas - *Gestern* (1891) and *Der Tod des Tizian* (1892). He reacted against modern realism and turned deliberately to a more heroic age in search of beauty. Dukes considers Hofmannsthal's verse untranslateable, remarking that not even Arthur Symons was wholly successful in rendering Hofmannthal's *Elektra* (1904) into English. Because of the difficulties in literary

---

80   See Antony Alpers, op. cit., p. 33 and Claire Tomalin, op. cit., p. 11.

81   In *Ideen, Das Buch Le Grand* (1826) Heine talks about the dream of democracy and a united Europe. This prose work forms part of Heine's *Reisebilder*.

82   Antony Alpers, op. cit., p. 101.

83   6 April 1911; *NA* VIII, 23, pp. 544-5.

translation 'only once in a millenium can a Schlegel be found to translate a Shakespeare, and for the most part poets are best left to their own language. With Hofmannsthal, who is as Viennese as Schnitzler in the delicacy of his moods and atmosphere, translation must always be something of a travesty.' (3 November 1910; *NA* VIII, 1, p. 16)

In addition to his interest in contemporary German dramatists, Dukes was also concerned with problems of stagecraft and revealed himself very much aware of the shortcomings of English producers in staging modern drama. On 19 January 1911 his column deals specifically with the 'Art of the Theatre'. Except for Max Reinhardt's staging of *A Midsummer Night's Dream* in Berlin 'all recent attempts at Shakespearian production are crude and amateurish'. Chekhov and Hofmannsthal have not only exerted great influence on European theatre, but they have also given the enormous impetus to new forms in stage decoration. They came into a world 'avowedly realistic in its creed, and encountered a bourgeois drama full of ideas, brimming over with moral indignation and political rhetoric, but utterly out of touch with the accessory arts. Beauty of speech counted for little; beauty of setting was barely considered. Ugliness, indeed, was often a matter of deliberate choice'. In an astonishing judgement, Dukes attacks Wedekind for objecting to 'new-fangled devices of decoration', and argues that this 'spirit of restriction' has always been implicit in the modern 'drama of ideas'. He warns that unless this spirit is crushed theatrical innovation can make no headway. Thus, the plays of Shaw, Hauptmann, Ibsen, Sudermann, Brieux, Gorky and Schnitzler are all performable with any type of stage sets as long as they provide 'the necessary two doors and a French window'. Revolutionary modern productions in Berlin and Vienna owe much to Hofmannsthal and reveal that 'there is more opportunity for the stage artist in a single scene of *Venice Preserved* or *Oedipus and the Sphinx* than in all the plays that Sudermann has ever devised' (*NA* VIII, 13, p. 281). In his autobiography Dukes castigates the Royal Court Theatre for its lifelike style of presentation at this time under Harley Granville-Barker's direction. Surrounded by staging that was 'rather common-place in its naturalism' English producers were 'scarcely aware, even by report, of the richer development of theatre art which was then proceeding under Reinhardt's direction at the Deutsches Theater in Berlin'.[84]

Huntley Carter: theatre-goers are tired of 'hyper-modern perversities and mortuary atrocities'

1911 was an important year for theatrical innovation. There was the first production of Chekhov in London when the Stage Society put on *The Cherry*

---

84   Ashley Dukes, op. cit., p. 7.

Orchard at the Aldwych Theatre. In addition, the arrival of two companies from Europe widened the horizons of the English theatre. On 21 June the Imperial Russian Ballet performed at Covent Garden. Earlier in the year, on 30 January, Max Reinhardt (1873-1943) and his company had opened at the London Coliseum. The production of Friedrich Freska's *Sumurûn*, by the Berlin director was a momentous occasion for Dukes. He saw the first performance in the afternoon, the second in the evening, the third the following afternoon and continued in this way 'while funds and opportunity lasted'.[85] Later in the year Reinhardt triumphed again in London with his production of Karl Gustav Vollmöller's *The Miracle*.

Certainly the latest developments in continental stage production were followed assiduously by the *New Age*, no doubt spurred on by the impetus originally given by Ashley Dukes in his series on modern European dramatists. However, Dukes did not undertake the task of reporting on the developments he encouraged. He left the periodical in the spring of 1911 and was replaced as drama critic by John Francis Hope, a pseudonym for the literary critic, A. E. Randall. However, after 1911, the periodical devoted less attention to reviewing plays by German dramatists or discussing the work of contemporary German playwrights. Instead, it looked to Germany as the centre for innovation in the techniques of staging plays, with Huntley Carter writing features from various European capitals, reporting directly on theatrical developments there.

Both performances by the Russian Ballet and productions by Max Reinhardt were high on Carter's agenda. On 2 March 1911, for instance, he notes that the production of *Sumurûn* by the Deutsches Theater under Reinhardt is finding great favour with London audiences, whilst on 29 June 1911 he discusses the Russian Ballet in Paris and London.[86] In Berlin he saw Max Reinhardt's production of the second part of *Faust* which 'has been the despair of German producers ever since Goethe completed it'. He attacks both parts of Goethe's drama as 'undramatic from beginning to end' on the grounds that Goethe was not a natural dramatist but 'a poet with metaphysical leanings'. Goethe 'swallowed Rousseau', whom he re-expressed as far as it is possible for 'the Teutonic temperament to express the philosophy of the Latin one'. Every other line of *Faust*, according to Carter, requires 'a satisfactory commentary by a learned person to whom the statement of scientific facts has become a matter of special knowledge'. The true home of Goethe's drama is the lecture theatre. Nevertheless, Carter notes that Reinhardt's ambitious eight-hour production, which has now been cut down to a mere six hours, has enjoyed great success and is visually stunning (19 October 1911; *NA* IX, 25, pp. 292-3). In 1912, reporting

---

85   Ibid., p. 34.
86   *NA* VIII, 18, Literary Supplement, p. 3 and *NA* IX, 10, pp. 222-4.

on a production by Reinhardt in Berlin of *Much Ado About Nothing*, Carter suggests that London's actor-managers should be compelled to study the German director's Shakespearian productions (14 March 1912; *NA* X, 20, p. 467). However, Huntley Carter was not always in favour of productions in the manner of Max Reinhardt. On 11 April 1912 he criticises the Covent Garden Theatre and the Kingsway Theatre for producing Greek drama after Reinhardt because Greek drama will not work in a modern setting. (*NA* X, 24, p. 565)

In the *New Age* Carter had already campaigned for a new national theatre in England and encouraged new theatrical forms. July 1911 marked the first in a series of reports on the theatre sent direct by him from Berlin, Leipzig, Bayreuth, Nuremberg, Munich, Vienna, Budapest, Crakow, Warsaw, Moscow and Paris. From Berlin, the first stop on his tour, he notes that the German capital possesses some excellent theatres, most notably the Hebbeltheater, built about four years previously by the architect Oskar Kaufmann who also designed the new opera house for Berlin and a theatre for Bremerhaven. Carter praises the Hebbeltheater on the grounds that its 'pose of dignity and gravity is just suited to serious plays. Its absence of tinsel and freedom from offence from box-office to dressing-room is a new sensation' for English performers and theatregoers alike. Berlin has become the centre of a 'strong romantic and classic dramatic movement which promises to restore a much needed emotional expressivenness to the drama'. Realism has ceased to be fashionable because the public has tired of 'hyper-modern perversities and mortuary atrocities' and lost interest in Wedekind's *Frühlings Erwachen* and Shaw's *Mrs Warren's Profession*. Berlin shows no 'feverish demand for studies of the psychology of the beer-drinking German proletariat, for glorious records of filth and outrage in low places, or for plays of unholy social deposits'. In the same article Carter notes that Berlin's Lessingtheater has been devoted to performing the work of Ibsen for several years. By comparison, productions of Ibsen in London rank as mediocre. The same theatre is also presenting Hauptmann's *Die versunkene Glocke* (1896) and *Hanneles Himmelfahrt* (1893), Karl Schönherr's historical drama *Glaube und Heimat* (1910), as well as works by Sophocles, Lessing, Schiller, Goethe and Shakespeare. In this context Carter observes that the English dramatist 'has become a naturalised German' with 1141 performances of his works in Germany during the course of 1910. He therefore ranks as the third most performed dramatist in Germany after Wagner and Schiller. (27 July 1911; *NA* IX, 13, pp. 293-4)

The following week Huntley Carter was in Leipzig, reporting that music, like drama, is in a state of transition, and that the birthplace of Wagner is now revelling in Bach. Younger critics in Leipzig now consider Wagner out of date. The composer's autobiography, which has recently been published, reveals him to be 'a very small and unpleasant character', not the colossal figure his followers would like him to be. Such revelations can only erode his reputation.

Wagner is also declining as a thinker since his philosophical speculations are viewed as less valuable than his music. Ironically, as Leipzig turns away from Wagner, the composer's ideas are beginning to influence the development of the drama and the theatre (3 August 1911; *NA* IX, 14, pp. 323-4). Carter also visited the Bayreuth festival in the course of his travels for the *New Age*, although he was more concerned with the commmercialization of the Wagner Festival. However, he sees one ray of hope in the fact that 'a theatre devoted to the representations of music-drama of the highest order' has been established through the generosity of the King of Bavaria. The Wagner theatre is therefore 'further evidence of the great interest taken in the theatre and drama by the German aristocracy. The theatre in England could also advance, Carter argues, if 'the cultured aristocracy recognised its duty' and gave both financial and moral support to the aesthetic movement in England. (17 August 1911; *NA* IX, 16, pp. 368-9)

From Bayreuth Huntley Carter travelled to Nuremberg (24 August 1911; *NA* IX, 17, pp. 392-3) and Munich, a city he extolled for being 'saturated with art and culture'. He singles out the 'Künstler-theater' as typical of what he terms 'the contracting tendency' in the theatre. He recommends that every town in England follows the example of Munich for this is the ideal sort of theatre for experiment and suggestion and can be built for minimum cost. Although only transitional, it would be perfectly adequate until the coming of the new theatre. The amphitheatre of the 'Künstler-theater' is modern, rejecting the 'old system of circles and galleries and was originated by Wagner in his search for sensations of unity'. Thus, the amphitheatre is designed to remove all friction and 'induce to a state of mental concentration in the spectator'. To this end, the seats rise gently to a single row of boxes, the orchestra pit is sunken, scenery is minimal, whilst side lights and footlights have been practically abolished in favour of overhead lighting to create the illusion of an unseen sky or ceiling. The new system aims 'to reduce stage setting to the simplest proportions, and to call in the aid of suggestion in the attempt to abolish modern extravagances and over-elaboration'. (31 August 1911; *NA* IX, 18, pp. 425-7)

Music: Strauss and Schönberg

Music criticism was no longer a regular, weekly feature of the *New Age* between 1910 and 1914. Critics ceased to view German composers as innovators in music. On 19 October 1911, for example, the journal's music critic, John Playford, observes that apart from Richard Strauss German music has nothing new to offer. He welcomes the return of the Russian Ballet to Covent Garden and suggests that only this company can be called innovative in terms of contemporary music (*NA* IX, 25, p. 593). On 31 October 1912 he argues that Schönberg is a composer worthy of serious attention like Richard Strauss and suggests there are analogies to be drawn between Schönberg and the Futurist painters. (*NA* XI, 27, p. 644)

Chapter 4: Germany and the *New Age*: August 1914-December 1916

With the surge of patriotic fervour that accompanied the outbreak of the First World War, the governments in both Berlin and London found enormous public support for their respective causes. In Germany there already existed a belief, developed by a whole school of historians after Ranke, that twenty years of German 'Weltpolitik' proved that Germany had a legitimate claim to the status of world power.[1] Starting from this premise, German publicists in 1914 hailed the 'German war'[2] as their country's opportunity to realise this claim which had been denied her for so long by the older nations of Europe. This idea took root in the German consciousness, and in the face of military setbacks in the winter of 1914/15, hardened into a determination to continue fighting until this aim was achieved.[3] There arose an intellectual movement that was inspired by professors in both the humanities and economics and charged with the mission of providing the war with a positive philosophy. The so-called 'Ideas of 1914',[4] ignored the practical causes of the war and, instead, sought reasons in national intellectual traditions. Divorced from any realistic political thought, such an interpretation depended on an entirely emotional appeal to mobilise German public opinion.[5] The war was conceived not only as a defensive struggle by Germany against the enemies surrounding her, but as a higher, predestined necessity rooted in the antithesis between German spirit, German culture, German political forms, and the life and forms of her alien enemies.[6] England was a mere nation of 'shopkeepers' opposing German 'heroism'.[7] Thus, the conflict was depicted as

---

1   Fritz Fischer, *Griff nach der Weltmacht* (Düsseldorf, 1961), p. 184.

2   Ibid., p. 184. The term comes from a collection of political pamphlets edited in 1914 by Ernst Jäckh entitled *Der Deutsche Krieg*.

3   Ibid., p. 184.

4   Ibid., p. 185. Rudolf Kjellén coined the expression 'Die Ideen von 1914' in *Zwischen Krieg und Frieden* in 1915.

5   Ibid., p. 186.

6   In *Friedrich und die große Koalition*, which was written in 1914 and published early in 1915, Thomas Mann argued this was the situation confronting Frederick the Great and intended that the reader make comparisons with Germany in 1914/15. See Thomas Mann, *Das essayistische Werk. Taschenbuchausgabe*, edited by Hans Bürgin, 8 vols (Frankfurt am Main, 1960), V, p. 48ff.

7   In 1915 Werner Sombart described the war in these terms in his tract *Händler und Helden*.

being between the culturally superior German mind and its shallow enemies. France was a superficial and rational 'civilisation', whilst Russia was the land of 'barbarism'.

This 'great war of words', as it has recently been called,[8] was fought by both creative writers and academics. At the beginning of October 1914 Ulrich von Wilamowitz-Moellendorff, an expert on German classical philology, who had previously been in close contact with colleagues in British universities,[9] collected the signatures of ninety three eminent Germans for a manifesto he had drawn up, denying that Germany had caused the war or been unwarranted in violating Belgian neutrality. The document, the so-called 'Declaration of the 93', read like a directory of German men of letters and science, with names such as Gerhart Hauptmann, Emil von Behring, Karl Lamprecht, Max Liebermann, Max Reinhardt, Max Planck and Wilhelm Röntgen, whilst further support came from teachers and university rectors.[10] The signatories later swelled to about four thousand - practically every university professor in Germany.[11] It proved to the Allies that German intellectuals were staunch supporters of their country's militarism and, as a result, severely damaged the high esteem in which German universities had been held by British intellectuals before 1914.[12]

English writers on the Germans: 'a people who had suddenly become incredible'

In England, as in Germany, Romain Rolland's appeal to the European intelligentsia to view events with detachment by remaining 'au-dessus de la mêlée'[13] generally went unheeded. In 1914, most intellectuals leaped to the defence of their nation, spurred on by hitherto untapped resources of patriotism. While some writers, such as Herbert Read, chose active military service, others preferred to channel their new-found political awareness into fighting a war of words against their German counterparts. Perhaps the mood sweeping English

---

8   Peter Buitenhuis, *The Great War of Words. Literature as Propaganda 1914 and After* (London, 1989).

9   Stuart Wallace, *War and the Image of Germany: British Academics 1914-1918* (Edinburgh, 1988), p. 33.

10   M. E. Humble, 'The Breakdown of a Consensus: British Writers and Anglo-German Relations 1900-1920', *Journal of European Studies* (March 1977), p. 44.

11   Fritz Fischer, op. cit., p. 186.

12   Stuart Wallace, op. cit., p. 4.

13   In an anthology of war essays that appeared in October 1915 under the collective title *Au-dessus de la mêlée*, Rolland appealed to intellectuals not to let passions sway their rational judgement.

intellectual circles in August 1914 is best evoked by H. G. Wells in his fictional account of the First World War, *Mr. Britling sees it through* (1916). In this novel he recalls that 'the effort to understand a people who had suddenly become incredible' was 'one of the most remarkable facts in English intellectual life during the opening phases of the war'. It provoked 'an enormous sale of any books that seemed likely to illuminate the mystery of this amazing concentration of hostility' and 'the works of Bernhardi, Treitschke, Nietzsche, Houston Stewart Chamberlain, became the material of countless articles and interminable discussions' with 'little clerks on the way to the office and workmen going home after their work earnestly reading these remarkable writers'.[14]

Initially, there was a sense of disbelief that war could actually break out. England in 1914 was preoccupied with trouble at home rather than abroad.[15] Admittedly, armaments had been piling up since 1870 as rivalry between England and Germany intensified, while invasion and war scares had abounded in the press and popular fiction ever since Chesney's *Battle of Dorking* in May 1871 had identified Germany as the country most likely to invade England. Although the enemy was occasionally depicted as France or Russia, after 1900 it was invariably Germany,[16] the most notable examples being Erskine Childers' *Riddle of the Sands* (1903) and H. G. Wells' *War in the Air* (1908). However, the public appetite for such literature had apparently led to a certain indifference and a feeling of confidence that war between European nations was a thing of the past. The generation of 1914 had no direct experience of a European war; the last conflict between European powers had been in the Franco-Prussian War in 1871, while Britain, perhaps with the exception of the Crimean War and the Boer War, had not fought in a major war for over a century. People associated war with soldiers in uniform, military parades, decisive battles and, most importantly, rapid victory.[17] A long, drawn-out trench war of attrition with eight million dead was not envisaged in the early stages on either side.

It soon became apparent that written material had a vital role to play in shaping public opinion. Before the war, neither Germany[18] nor Britain had

---

14 H. G. Wells, *Mr. Britling sees it through* (London, 1916), p. 273.

15 See Bernard Bergonzi, 'Before 1914: Writers and the Threat of War', *Critical Quarterly*, 6 (1964), p. 126.

16 Ibid., p. 129. See also Chapter 2, p. 49 ff.

17 Paul Fussell, *The Great War and Modern Memory* (New York and London, 1975), p. 21.

18 Klaus Schröter, 'Chauvinism and its Tradition: German Writers at the Outbreak of the First World War', *The Germanic Review*, XLIII (1968), p. 120.

mounted an organised propaganda campaign,[19] in spite of the existence of a far larger reading public than ever before, helped in Britain by the 1867 Reform Act, the 1870 Elementary Education Act and the further acts of 1888, 1891 and 1902.[20] Improved standards of literacy led to public opinion being better informed, as well as a boost in sales for popular daily newspapers and novels. It was not until late August 1914 that Charles Masterman, then Chairman of the National Insurance Commission, was invited by Asquith to establish a system of organised propaganda. Charged with the task of justifying wartime policy decisions, Masterman organised two conferences at Wellington House. On 7 September 1914 journalists met to agree on a code of practice for the press in wartime,[21] although it was the conference on 2 September that attracted most publicity. This was a meeting of prominent literary figures, including William Archer, Thomas Hardy, Rudyard Kipling, J. M. Barrie, Harley Granville-Barker, Rider Haggard, Arnold Bennett, John Galsworthy, John Masefield, Anthony Hope Hawkins, Arthur Conan Doyle, Ford Madox Hueffer, H. G. Wells and G. K. Chesterton. A patriotic declaration signed by fifty three writers was subsequently published in *The Times* on 17 September 1914 - just preceding the 'Declaration of the 93' which appeared at the beginning of October in Germany.[22] Both creative writers and academics subsequently wrote propaganda tracts for Wellington House. British scholars, shocked by the support shown for official German policy by hitherto revered German academics,[23] responded in kind by writing their own pamphlets, such as the series by Oxford historians.[24] They were certainly prolific. Between September 1914 and June 1915 Wellington House published two and a half million copies of books and pamphlets by British writers and academics in seventeen different languages, and by February 1916 seven million copies had been circulated.[25]

Spurred on by such emotive issues as Germany's violation of Belgian neutrality, alleged German atrocities against Belgian women and children, the torpedo attack by a German submarine on the passenger vessel the *Lusitania* in April 1915, and the execution of the British nurse, Edith Cavell in October 1915,[26] British participants in the war of words against Germany filled their tracts

---

19   M. L. Sanders and P. M. Taylor, *British Propaganda during the First World War, 1914-18* (London, 1982), p. 15.
20   Ibid., p. 2.
21   Ibid., pp. 38-9.
22   See p. 114.
23   Stuart Wallace, op. cit., p. 5.
24   Ibid., p. 60.
25   M. L. Sanders and P. M. Taylor, op. cit., p. 108.
26   Peter Buitenhuis, op. cit., pp. 27-9.

with denunciations of the German 'Ideas of 1914' as incongruous with German deeds, accounts of the discrepancies between German militarism and German culture and explorations of German traditions of thought as the source for Germany's actions.

Bernard Shaw: 'both armies should shoot their officers and go home'

There were, of course, certain notable exceptions to the general desire to take part in a war of words against the enemy. They too proved far from idle in the literary debate. In September 1914 Hermann Hesse, for example, pleaded 'O Freunde, nicht diese Töne!', and with allusions to Schiller's *Ode to Joy* and Beethoven's Ninth Symphony, called for human brotherhood.[27] In Britain Bernard Shaw was a vociferous opponent of the hostilities. From the outset he faced a dilemma which, to a considerable extent, sprang from his own close ties with Austria and Germany. When Britain declared war on the Central Powers he immediately telegraphed his Austrian translator, Siegfried Trebitsch:

'WHAT A HIDEOUS SITUATION CIVILIZATION TEARING ITSELF TO PIECES... YOU AND I AT WAR CAN ABSURDITY GO FURTHER MY FRIENDLIEST WISHES GO WITH YOU UNDER ALL CIRCUMSTANCES'.[28]

His essay *Common Sense about the War*, which was first published on 14 November 1914 as a supplement to the *New Statesman*, caused outrage in Britain because he suggested that 'both armies should shoot their officers and go home'[29] and equated the British ruling class with the Prussian Junker. Suspicions that he was a pro-German sympathiser were confirmed when he forwarded a copy of his controversial tract to Trebitsch, who promptly translated it into German.[30] In addition, because Shaw had given Trebitsch the rights to the world première of *Pygmalion*, with the result that the play was first performed in Germany before it was seen in Britain, it was alleged that the dramatist had snubbed the British and

---

27 T. J. Reed, *Thomas Mann. The Uses of Tradition* (Oxford, 1974), p. 214.

28 Quoted by Michael Holroyd, *Bernard Shaw, Vol. II, 1898-1918. The Pursuit of Power* (London, 1989), p. 346.

29 The essay is contained in Shaw's collection *What I really wrote about the war* (London, 1931), p. 23.

30 Siegfried Trebitsch, *Chronicle of a Life*, translated by Eithne Wilkins and Ernst Kaiser (London, 1953), p. 258.

amused the Germans.[31] To make matters worse, because Shaw never wrote anything hostile about the Central Powers, for some time his most successful plays, *Candida* and *Pygmalion*, were allowed to stay in the theatrical repertoire in Germany and Austria.[32] Not only did he remain popular in enemy countries, but he was also guilty of having interpreted such representative German philosophers as Nietzsche and Schopenhauer, championed Wagner, defended Richard Strauss in a recent newspaper controversy with Ernest Newman, and given a favourable review to Houston Stewart Chamberlain's *Foundations of the Nineteenth Century*.[33] His box office appeal plummeted in the war[34] and in 1916 the *New Statesman*, which he had helped set up, refused to publish his articles.[35] It was his other press venture, the *New Age*, which published his next essay, 'The Case Against Germany' - a rather less outspoken attack on Britain - on 25 May 1916.[36]

By that time Orage was desperately in need of material to fill his periodical. He had already lost some of the most promising members of the younger generation of writers, such as T. E. Hulme and Herbert Read, who had joined up for active service soon after war was declared, although both did send occasional articles back. He could not always turn to writers who were too old for military duties since Chesterton, Wells and Bennett, who had contributed to the early issues, were engaged in writing tracts for Wellington House. Contributors of German extraction became equally elusive, with Oscar Levy, the editor of the first complete English edition of the works of Nietzsche, eventually being forced into exile in Switzerland, depriving the *New Age* of another valuable columnist. The problem became more acute as the war progressed and Orage was forced to write, and occasionally translate,[37] more and more articles himself, rely on such stalwart regulars as J. M. Kennedy, A. E. Randall and Paul Selver, and, where possible, coax material from former contributors, such as Bernard Shaw[38] and Katherine Mansfield.[39] Although the contributors were less varied, in terms

---

31   Ibid., p. 173.
32   Ibid., p. 230.
33   Michael Holroyd, op. cit., p. 356.
34   Ibid., p. 376.
35   Ibid., p. 359.
36   *NA* XIX, 5, pp. 77-80.
37   In November 1916, for example, Orage translated from the French an article by Professor Yves Delage on 'Germany and Science' - a rather unfavourable discussion of Haeckel's work in Zoology, Weismann's in Biology and Freud's in Psychology. (9 November 1916; *NA* XX, 2, pp. 39-41)
38   Michael Holroyd, op. cit., p. 192.
39   On 4 November 1915 Katherine Mansfield contributed a short story entitled *Stay-laces*; *NA* XVIII, 1, pp. 14-15.

of Anglo-German literary relations the periodical could not have been more productive, with an increasing number of articles on Germany appearing.

J. M. Kennedy: the war as 'racial conflict between Slav and Teuton'

At the beginning of the war commentators in the *New Age* attempted to define its causes and predict its length, although their calculations often proved woefully inaccurate.[40] J. M. Kennedy, writing his 'Foreign Affairs' column under the pseudonym S. Verdad, was no exception, filling his articles in the autumn of 1914 with predictions of Germany's imminent defeat. On 17 September 1914, for example, he anticipates decisive allied victories over the German army in November and December, and even draws up the terms of a possible peace treaty (*NA* XV, 20, p. 468). He reassures his readers that Great Britain stands to lose 'much less than any other Power actually concerned in the fighting' and explains that 'the conflict has spread from a little dispute between Austria and Servia (sic) to the long-expected racial conflict between Slav and Teuton'.[41] Kennedy is convinced that in this racial conflict Britain should take the side of 'the Slavs plus the Latins', since this is a more natural combination for the British than 'an alliance with the Teuton'. (6 August 1914; *NA* XV, 14, p. 316)

Marmaduke Pickthall (1875-1936), a recent recruit to the *New Age*, also viewed the war in terms of a conflict between Slav and Teuton. On 20 August 1914 he agrees with Kennedy that Britain has no part in the racial quarrel allegedly at the root of the First World War. He argues that Britain is not fighting for Slav against Teuton, but simply supporting a French ally and maintaining her naval supremacy. He is not wholly unsympathetic towards Germany, and attacks the vilification of the Germans in the British press as 'brutal' on the grounds that the Germans 'are as conscientious, upright, patriotic and the rest of it as ourselves, only more sentimental in devotion to the Fatherland'. Pickthall recalls visiting Germany in 1912 in the wake of Slav atrocities against Germany and Austria in the Balkan War, in which Russia had supported the Balkan States and France and

---

40 As early as 13 August 1914 a columnist using the pen-name A.B.C. confidently estimates that the war will end 'about six weeks from Sunday last' (*NA* XV, 15, p. 354). Orage could well have used this pseudonym which was possibly an allusion to the ABC tea-rooms in Chancery Lane, where the editor and his staff met every Monday to discuss the layout and content of the *New Age* that would appear on the Thursday of that week.

41 6 August 1914; *NA* XV, 14, p. 316. The spelling was still Servia at this time, but because it suggested servility, the name was elevated to Serbia by the press 'sometime between August 1914 and April 1915'. Paul Fussell, op. cit., p. 175.

England had supported Russia. He reminds us that Archduke Ferdinand was assassinated by what he calls 'barbaric' Slavs, with the inevitable consequence that Germany lent its support to Austria as a fellow 'civilised' nation in a war against 'barbarism'. Germany, he declares, is 'one of the three great civilised Powers the world possesses', and 'to wish for her annihilation is to wish for untold evil', and he continues that while 'we wish to see the French re-take Alsace Lorraine', this should only involve checking the Germans, not crushing them lest Russia should achieve greater power in Europe. (*NA* XV, 16, pp. 366-7)

The idea of a conflict between Slav and Teuton was no figment of the imagination of English publicists. Since at least 1912 there existed in Germany a general belief that if a war broke out it would be essentially a 'racial conflict', a battle of Teuton against Slav for both 'the future of the Hapsburg monarchy' and for the very 'existence' of Germany.[42] Early in 1913 Count Helmuth von Moltke, the chief of the German general staff, was sure that a European war would come, although he cautioned that the Slavs must appear to have provoked it. To prepare for this conflict between Slav and Teuton was the duty of all states in the vanguard of Germanic culture.[43] Even after the war broke out the German Chancellor, Bethmann-Hollweg, held so firmly to this conviction that he was prepared to combine forces with France and England in the belief that such an alliance would provide 'the best guarantee against the dangers threatening European civilisation by the Russian colossus'.[44] The need to defeat the Russian colossus, the traditional protector of the Slavs, was integral to Austrian as well as German wartime policy - a fact that tended to be overlooked in British propaganda tracts and by some of the commentators in the *New Age*. In the autumn of 1914, the Austro-Hungarian foreign minister, Count von Berchtold (1863-1942), twice asserted that one of his country's war aims was the 'lasting weakening of Russia'.[45]

With Germany vilified, commentators frequently looked to Russia as Britain's true ally. On 15 January 1915 Humphrey Morgan Browne rejects

---

42   This was the prediction of the Kaiser in a conversation with his friend Albert Ballin on 15 December 1912. See Bernhard Huldermann, *Albert Ballin*, fourth edition (Oldenburg, 1922), p. 272. Quoted by Fritz Fischer, *Krieg der Illusionen* (Düsseldorf, 1969), pp. 270-1.

43   These sentiments were expressed in a letter of 10 February 1913 from Moltke to Conrad von Hötzendorf, his Austrian counterpart between 1906 and 1911. See Conrad von Hötzendorf, *Aus meiner Dienstzeit*, Vol. III, p. 146. Quoted by Fritz Fischer, ibid., p. 271.

44   See Berhard von Bülow, Hollweg's forerunner, *Denkwürdigkeiten*, Vol. III, p. 148. Quoted by Fritz Fischer, ibid., p. 758.

45   See Fischer, ibid., p. 756.

Germany's claim to excellence in science on the grounds that in chemistry the Russians strike him as more original. He reminds readers that 'Madame Curie is of Slav descent' (*NA* XVI, 11, p. 276). When Geoffrey Dennis investigates 'The "Darkest Russia" Bogey', he attacks those who extol Germany as the 'Land of Luther'. Luther, he informs us, was 'a coarse, uninteresting fellow, great perhaps in a rough elephantine sort of way, a strong-minded German of the more offensive type, from whom nobody with a knowledge of even the barest outline of religious history could pretend that English Protestantism derives its greatness, its love of clean and godly living, and its nobler Puritan fervour'. Germany's culture as exemplified by Goethe, Beethoven and Heine belongs to what he regards as 'the un-Prussianised past'. By contrast, modern Russians are 'spiritual, with faith and compassion' and hate their autocratic government, whilst the ideal of modern Germany is 'Machtpolitik, materialism, physical cruelty, brute force'. With such watchwords it is only to be expected, Dennis concludes somewhat simplistically, that in this Prussianised Germany men 'despise women as in no other European country' and coachdrivers flog their horses 'with unequalled cruelty.' (17 September 1914; *NA* XV, 20, p. 473)

J. M. Kennedy is no more generous in his views on the Germans, finding them guilty of placing 'emphasis on Teutonism as the supreme standard'. They have neglected European traditions to 'rummage among Teutonic and Scandinavian mythologies for peculiar and highly unedifying gods of their own'. The Terms of a peace treaty must therefore bring Germany 'spiritually in line' with the rest of Europe, by placing Schiller below Virgil and 'German Christianity' below the traditional Christianity of Europe. Kennedy argues that the only way to defeat Germany is to defeat German principles, because 'so long as German professors are let loose to preach a non-European morality of supremacy and so long as the people of Germany, from Social Democrats upwards believe in them, just so long will Europe sleep on an uneasy couch'. This Germany has 'deliberately cut herself off from the classical tradition on which the rest of Europe has been built up', although Kennedy admits that this is only a 'relatively modern' development, calling it 'a Germany dating from Kant and Hegel' (1 June 1916; *NA* XIX, 5, pp. 100-101), an unusual grouping since commentators tended to praise the Germany of Kant at the expense of that of Hegel.[46]

What Kennedy really means by 'this modern Germany' is the German Empire with 'Prussia at its head'. The Empire cannot just be dismantled into

---

46   See Ernest Barker's tract, 'Nietzsche and Treitschke. The Worship of Power in Modern Germany' (1914), p. 3ff. This *Oxford Pamphlet* concludes with a plea for a return from Treitschke's 'praise of war', which took its inspiration from Hegel, to Kant's 'vision of permanent peace', p. 28.

separate states again because Prussia will rise again sphinx-like. He even goes so far as to advocate the inclusion of the German provinces of Austria in the post-war German Empire with Vienna, not Berlin, as the new German capital! He justifies his opinion by lumping together Austrians, Bavarians and Southern Germans as 'nearly the same race' and a 'peaceful people', the very antithesis of the Prussians. In this sweeping generalisation he claims that southern Germans only tolerate the Prussian army in the belief that the Prussian army is there to protect them. With Prussia crushed, he is sure, the other German states and Austria would return to a love of the arts and humanities. Indeed, Kennedy's faith in the Austrian national character is so resolute that he confidently claims that had Austria been successful in contesting the leadership of the German states in 1864, there would have been no Franco-Prussian War in 1870 and no European War in 1914. (1 October 1914; *NA* XV, 22, pp. 515-16)

Fanciful as this view may appear, Kennedy is not alone in gazing nostalgically at non-Prussian states as the epitome of all that was laudable in the German character. While not always singling out Austria for praise, commentators often distinguish between northern and southern Germany. In his column 'Military Notes' on 1 October 1914, Romney asserts that tension between the Prussians and the Bavarians has reached breaking point (*NA* XV, 22, p. 517), and six months later he rashly claims that the 'God punish England tomfoolery' appears to be confined to 'the gentry to the North of the Main'. He suggests that the Bavarians and the Württembergers are less savage than other Germans since they were the only ones to 'fraternise' with the enemy in the trenches at Christmas.[47] He even ventures to suggest that when a Saxon regiment is to be relieved by a Prussian one, the Saxon puts up a sign to that effect to warn the English enemy to prepare for Prussian treachery. (11 March 1915; *NA* XVI, 19, p. 501)

Romney claims that the German people are 'militarist' but not 'military', since 'the larger and better part of Germany - the centre and the south' has always shown itself to be 'profoundly averse to war'. Only with Prussia in control are the Germans militarist and Prussia is 'about as typical of Germany as Ulster is of England'. The inhabitants of Bavaria, Württemberg and Baden, he reassures us, are 'most agreeable persons, but even in 1870 their fighting qualities were a joke', whilst only the Prussians, the Hanoverians, the Saxons and the Hessians ever displayed an aptitude for war. (24 December 1914; *NA* XVI, 8, p. 189)

The belief that the southern German states were less interested in military, territorial or material issues proved just as dubious as the view that

---

47   On Christmas Day 1914 German and Allied soldiers laid down their arms, crossed the front lines and shook hands.

Austria was any more pacific than Prussia. On 15 August 1914 King Ludwig III of Bavaria laid claim to the whole of Alsace as a Bavarian war aim to revitalise the economy of southern Germany, in addition to demanding that Belgium disappear and that the mouth of the Rhine become German. Not to be outdone, Wilhelm III of Württemberg and the Grand Duke Friedrich of Baden demanded compensation for the lives and material which the war was costing them.[48]

Kennedy rejects the notion that this is the 'war to end all wars', but hopes that it might put an end to 'the coarse German doctrine that brute force is everything'. He claims that he has always tried to show that speeches by monarchs and statesmen need not always be taken at face value, and that, in particular, he aimed to demonstrate from everything he knew of Germany that 'any reference to peace in the mouths of German statesman or the German Emperor were simply hypocritical and deceitful lies'. He notes that the Germans talk at great length about 'Deutsche Kultur' and that 'since 1870 they really do believe, these people, that they have something to give the world in the shape of culture - something that the world lacks, something that must, if necessary, be forced upon other nations and races at the point of the bayonet, at the toe of the jack-boot'. Kennedy feels at a loss to comprehend exactly what the Germans mean by 'Kultur' but believes that Germany and the Germans 'merely wish to make the ideals of the military caste predominant everywhere - the principle that not even the written word is to bind one, nationally or internationally; that the world was made for the benefit of the Prussian officer and the German Emperor - and "Deutsche Kultur" - that the Germans alone are "virile" and other nations degenerate; and that these elemental facts, beliefs, call them what you will, must be brought home to every inhabitant of the five continents. In short, Germany has stood this forty years for the principle that might is right, and for all that such a principle implies'. Europe has risen in arms against this 'pernicious culture'. Apart from Austria, Germany has no allies. Bismarck would never have allowed his country to become so isolated, Kennedy feels sure. Instead, the 'Iron Chancellor' - who is not generally admired by *New Age* commentators - would have 'succeeded in making his opponents appear wrong as he did in 1864, 1866 and 1870, although in 1914 'Bismarckianism (sic) without Bismarck is dangerous.' (20 August 1914; *NA* XV, 16, p. 364)

By contrast, German publicists defined *Kultur* in rather different terms. The poet and essayist Rudolf Borchardt (1877-1945), for example, argued that *Kultur* was 'a purely German concept' that could not be translated adequately in any European or American language. A victory for Germany would put an end

---

48   Fritz Fischer, *Griff nach der Weltmacht* (Düsseldorf, 1961), p. 217.

to what he calls 'civilisation' or 'European civilization'. Because no other country had a word for *Kultur*, it could only be propagated by Germany.[49]

Ramiro de Maeztu: war as 'the organisation of adventure'

During the early period of the war information about events at the front was limited and coverage in the press tended to be sketchy. The *New Age* was not particularly critical of military strategy. Kennedy, for example, calls Verdun 'another tremendous tactical success' (13 July 1916; *NA* XIX, 11, p. 245), when, in fact, the French defence of Verdun cost so many lives that the main offensive had to be made by the British on the Western Front instead.[50] Similarly, no mention is made of the 60,000 British troops killed or wounded on the first day of the Somme offensive on 1 July 1916,[51] though the first writers and journalists were allowed to go to the front and publish their observations in May 1915.[52] Arnold Bennett, John Galsworthy, Rudyard Kipling, Hilaire Belloc, Conan Doyle and Bernard Shaw were among those sent on such tours.[53] On 3 February 1916 the *New Age* published its first report on 'Men at War' from a correspondent signing himself B. and describing a visit to a military hospital in Flanders (*NA* XVIII, 14, pp. 324-5), whilst seven months later Herbert Read offered Orage a rather less circumspect account, as we might expect from someone actually involved in the fighting. On 12 October 1916 Read sent 'Extracts from a Soldier's Diary', relating his arrival in France in the previous November and his first encounter with 'the real thing', a trench in winter, 'wet and cold, the stench of decay, and even ghastly death', to his being wounded and sent back to England the following April. He retains vivid impressions of Ypres, 'the ruins cut like silver silhouettes against the sky', whilst 'over all broods Desolation, gathering to her lap her leprous children', and a sunset gives out flames that 'rise and fall against the dusking sky.' (*NA* XIX, 24, p. 576)

However, the regular reports from the front were sent back to the *New Age* every week between September and November 1916 by Ramiro de Maeztu, who since January 1915 had covered a variety of subjects for the periodical. He begins at an unnamed military hospital dealing with head wounds for those so

---

49   Rudolf Borchardt, *Der Krieg und der deutsche Selbsteinkehr*, p. 14. Quoted by Eckart Koester, *Literatur und Weltkriegsideologie* (Kronberg, 1977), p. 221.

50   Paul Fussell, op. cit., p. 12.

51   Ibid., p. 13.

52   Cate Haste, *Keep the Home Fires Burning. Propaganda in the First World War* (London, 1977), p. 32.

53   See Peter Buitenhuis, op. cit., p. 80ff.

seriously injured that they are unable to return to Britain (28 September 1916; *NA* XIX, 22, pp. 510-11), then moves to Loos in Flanders and the Somme where the British are currently advancing. The experience prompts him to comment 'suddenly I have the intuition that war cannot be so unendurable as it has been depicted by humanitarian novelists', such as Tolstoi or Zola. If war were unendurable, he claims, 'men would not endure it'. He recognizes the 'horror' of passing months of alternating between the trenches and rearguard villages, 'to go to the trenches every five or six days with the conviction that the company will not return'. Despite the horror of shells and torpedoes, the commentator alleges that 'one must feel all the time that one's will is asserting itself.' (5 October 1916; *NA* XIX, 23, p. 533)

On 26 October 1916 Ramiro de Maeztu describes the military operations 'On the North of the Somme'. He is most impressed with the number of British balloons making observations, whilst the Germans appear to have no such advanced technology, and concludes that 'the British are now absolute masters of the air'. The British quickly shoot down any German aircraft, yet miraculously they are able to 'fly over the enemy lines every day'. He attributes this deficiency in German aviation not to lack of machines, but to lack of personnel because 'the aviator is born of the spirit of adventure, and adventure is not the spirit of organisation. And yet could not war be defined as the organisation of adventure?' (*NA* XIX, 26, pp. 604-5)

This rather blinkered definition of war seems to be coloured by a view of the Germans he had already advanced from the safety of his office early in 1915. In that article he defines English culture as 'a culture of men' whose ideal is the gentleman, whereas German culture is 'the culture of things'. A gentleman must embody such qualities as strength, courage and self-discipline, 'hence arises the cultivation of sport, of physical exercise, and of danger', although a gentleman exercises such self-control that he only exerts strength 'when justice demands it' and, perhaps most importantly of all, is always aware 'of the fact that his neighbour exists and is worthy of all respect'. Given such a fundamental demand for correct behaviour, 'the master of an English public school takes so much care to see that his charges become gentleman that only in the second place does he see that they study'; furthermore, he will teach them to be 'clean, healthy energetic, truthful, incapable of betraying their comrades or of lying, respectful towards others and self-respecting'. Other social classes always imitate the upper classes, therefore de Maeztu is convinced that 'English culture culminates in the gentleman'. In Germany, on the contrary, work comes first and man second. Thus, 'it is, above all, important that the student shall master his subject, of war, or philosophy, or classics, or mathematics. It is a secondary matter if he is a blabber, talks at the top of his voice, ill-treats his servants, or drinks himself dead drunk'. The Germans 'do things well because they subordinate themselves to them'. Even the writing of a *Festschrift* in honour of a German scholar deals only with 'things' such as music or painting or science or politics, depending on the branch of learning to which he has devoted his life, although no mention will be made of the life of the man. By contrast, in England, we are informed, no-one would dream of honouring a great man with a collection of essays. Instead, a biography will be written, discussing not his work, but concentrating on details from his private life. Only a German judges a man by his works and considers 'things a measure of man'. Indeed, the ideal German 'would be one who should entirely enter into and disappear among his things. For that reason the Germans give themselves up so thoroughly to their vices, their wealth, and their wars'. De Maeztu concludes optimistically that the war will convey to the English the true meaning of German culture as 'inhuman but efficient', whilst the Germans will learn that English culture is 'dilettante but loveable.' (21 January 1915; *NA* XVI, 12, pp. 303-4)

Only the sight of Fricourt, a scene of fierce trench warfare, causes Ramiro de Maeztu to look more critically at what is actually happening on the battlefield and admit to feeling overwhelmed by 'the desolation of the whole thing' when he sees once green forests 'half-covered with ashes' and finds that he cannot 'take four steps' without sinking into the mud of a shell hollow. Of the village of Fricourt 'nothing remains but heaps of dust. The very bricks were pulverised by the shells. Not a single tree is left standing in the wood. Nothing but stumps and fallen branches, covered with dust'. The shock of this awesome sight forces him to comment: 'to turn a whole countryside of woods, villages, and wheat-fields into a rash of dust it has been necessary to pour hell itself over the face of the earth' (26 October 1916; *NA* XIX, 26, pp. 604-5). However, when the author returns to England in order to tour a Birmingham munitions factory, he forgets his horror at the front and concentrates on the heroic enterprise of the Allies. (16 November 1916; *NA* XX, 3, pp. 53-4)

As a counterbalance to Ramiro de Maeztu's highly coloured reports, Orage also published a series of translations by his literary columnist, Paul Selver, of 'German Letters Home'. These letters, written by German soldiers at the front and very much biased in favour of German successes, had originally appeared in the *Berliner Tageblatt, Berliner Lokal-Anzeiger, Frankfurter Zeitung, Vossische Zeitung, Kölnische Zeitung* and *Der Tag*.[54] In one letter, for instance, a German soldier describes his reaction to shelling as 'a gruesome, horrible spectacle, if you think as a human being while it lasts; but you don't. You have rather an ardent feeling of joy and delight having all that whistling, crashing, bellowing, and blazing around you', although, rather improbably, with enemy shells dropping

---

54   See *NA* XIX, 21, pp. 499-500; *NA* XIX, 22, pp. 525-6; *NA* XIX, 23, pp. 549-50; *NA* XIX, 24, pp. 573-4; *NA* XIX, 25, p. 597 and *NA* XIX, 26, pp. 616-17.

'between 50 to 200 yards' behind the German line, the soldier claims that only three infantrymen were killed and 'a few wounded'. The Germans then begin shelling in retaliation, at which point the enemy stops 'at once, for our artillery shoots magnificently' (21 September 1916; *NA* XIX, 21, p. 500). The following week an Uhlan recalls the 'splendid, memorable days of victory' on entering Antwerp, when 'a kind fairy' guarded his unit for twelve days of constant patrol and attack with loss of 'neither man nor horse' and achievements which he describes as 'brilliant'. On the same page, a German officer describes this event as proving that 'no other army in the world could have been a match for Germany by taking the strongest fortress with a garrison of over 100,000 men in nine days.' (28 September 1916; *NA* XIX, 22, p. 525)

T. E. Hulme: 'the German army offers a career...'

T. E. Hulme, who had enlisted immediately after war was declared, contributed 'A Notebook' from the front, together with a series of 'War Notes', written between November 1915 and March 1916 whilst he was in England convalescing from a war wound, and using the pseudonym North Staffs, an allusion to his birthplace in North Staffordshire.[55] Wounded in April 1915, he did not return to the front until the following March and was killed in 1917. When the 'War Notes' series was subsequently published in the *Cambridge Magazine*, he became embroiled in a heated debate with Bertrand Russell over pacifism. His strident attacks on pacifism, liberalism and what he called 'sentimentalism' found little favour with Russell. On 7 February 1916 Russell complained to C. K. Ogden, the editor of the *Cambridge Magazine*, that Hulme was 'rude, bumptious, and grossly inaccurate',[56] although there is no record of him lodging such a complaint with Orage in whose paper the articles originally appeared. In January 1917 Russell was approached by the *New Age* to write a series of articles on the problems of the post-war period; he apparently agreed, although no article was ever published in Orage's periodical.[57] Thus, one of Britain's leading pacifists never actually wrote for the *New Age*, although he was sometimes discussed, by Hulme amongst others, in the pacifism debate on its pages.

North Staffs makes his first appearance on 11 November 1915, when he criticises the failure of the British civilian population to grasp the seriousness of war. This he ascribes to the difficulty of British Liberal opinion 'to eradicate

---

55 *The Collected Papers of Bertrand Russell*, Volume XIII, *Prophecy and Dissent 1914-16*, edited by Richard A. Rempel (London, 1988), p. 321.

56 Ibid., p. 322.

57 Ibid., p. 580.

from its mind the assumption that Germany is Liberal at heart', when, in fact, the reverse is true. He continues: 'knowing Germany as I do from residence there as well as from history, past and present, I affirm that the mind of Germany is neither Liberal nor even Liberalising, that is not disposed to become Liberal'. The German Social Democrats are 'without power' and their only hope of victory is if there is a victory of the Allies (*NA* XVIII, 2, pp. 29-30). There is a certain justification for Hulme's argument; Liberalism in Germany appeared to have died with the outbreak of war since the German government found support from all parties in the Reichstag, including the Social Democrats who voted in favour of war credits[58] - much to the dismay of allied observers who had looked to the Socialists as a party of opposition.

On 16 December 1915 Hulme complains that two of the greatest handicaps in the war are 'the atrociously bad staff work and the age of our commanding officers', the average age of a brigadier being fifty to sixty. He argues that 'all the new ideas and all the initiative and inventiveness has been on the side of the Germans'. According to Hulme, it is because the Germans had prepared for war that they were able to spring surprises on the enemy. He observes that the typical English soldier goes out to the front 'with his head full of ideas of Germany presented to him by his daily newspapers'. He invariably arrives at night because the troops are shelled in the day if they are seen. Thus, long before he is actually close enough to hear the shells, he sees them in the night sky. English equipment is often defective and no match for German rockets, Hulme alleges. The rookie is quickly disillusioned because the Germans are not at all like those portrayed in the English papers, and soon comes to respect his enemy's greater military expertise. According to Hulme, German commanding officers are more intelligent than their British counterparts because 'the German army offers a career in times of peace for men of ability', whereas the British army does not. 'You cannot expect an army suddenly to improvise brains', Hulme reflects wistfully, suggesting that he is one of the few contributors to the *New Age* to favour conscription. (*NA* XVIII, 7, pp. 149-50)

Conscription: 'the essential feature of the Prussian system'

In the autumn of 1915, following heavy losses in the first year of the war, the British Government, faced with a dwindling supply of volunteers, started to consider conscription as the only means of swelling the ranks of the army sufficiently to win the war. Appeals for volunteers, such as the one made by Lord

---

58   William Carr, *A History of Germany 1815-1985*, third edition (London, 1987), p. 213.

Kitchener in October 1914[59] that brought in 300,000 eager recruits, could no longer be relied upon when the nation had understandably grown weary of war.[60] When the Military Service Act was passed early in 1916 it brought an end to the tradition of the British army comprising volunteers who joined of their own free will, and helped convince 16,500 men that they should not be forced to fight. Although the pacifist movement in Britain had really begun in 1914, it was the introduction of conscription that made pacifism a political issue for the first time.[61] Whilst the *New Age* was not a pacifist journal, Orage nevertheless allowed pacifists to air their views and published more general articles opposing conscription, or 'compulsion' as it was commonly known amongst contributors. As early as 19 August 1915, Belford Bax had argued against 'compulsion' because the introduction of a conscripted army would mean purchasing 'material victory over the Prussian armies at the price of becoming morally like Prussia' (*NA* XVII, 16, p. 376). Since the Allies were supposed to be fighting 'militarism', there was a certain anomaly in adopting one of the most obvious features of the militarist state, namely an army of conscripts.

Argument against conscription on the grounds that it would turn the British army into a mere imitation of the enemy German, or more precisely the 'Prussian' army, was common in the *New Age*. When Lloyd George shows himself in favour of conscription, for example, J. M. Kennedy responds on 30 September 1915 with a startling denunciation of the then Chancellor of the Exchequer as 'the Welsh champion of Prussianism in the Cabinet' who has dared to lend support to that 'essential feature of the Prussian system'. In Kennedy's view, 'compulsion, enslavement, subjection, the unquestioned acceptance of the motives of a bureaucracy: these have always been German characteristics; and on this foundation a German superstructure of brutality, inconsiderateness, and bad manners has been built up. All the evil characteristics of the German mind can be traced to this spirit and its resultant concentration of power in the hands of the "State" ie., in the hands of the relatively few individuals who control the German Administration'. This war, he is convinced, is a 'war of ideas' between the British 'principle of freedom' and the German 'principle of subjection'. Because Lloyd George seeks to introduce Britain's first conscripted army, he must be regarded as 'Prussian to the backbone' (*NA* XVII, 22, pp. 519-20). Kennedy is not alone in

---

59   Voluntary recruiting for Kitchener's Army relied on a poster campaign. The now famous poster picured Kitchener, with forefinger outstretched, saying: 'Your country needs YOU'.

60   Most of Kitchener's volunteers were killed on the Somme in 1916; Paul Fussell, op. cit., p. 10.

61   Martin Ceadel, *Pacifism in Britain 1914-1945: The Defining of a Faith* (Oxford, 1980), p. 31.

this extraordinary opinion. In his column 'Notes of the Week', Orage also attacks conscription by charging Lloyd George with being 'a kind of Prussian Tory - a Welsh Bismarck' (23 September 1915; *NA* XVII, 21, p. 490). There is evidence to suggest that this attack on Lloyd George took its inspiration from G. K. Chesterton, who in 1911 had taken up arms against the Insurance Bill. He argued that because the system of national insurance had first been invented in Prussia, Lloyd George, who introduced the Bill, was guilty of importing the principles of German state welfare into British life.[62] Although it is difficult to prove that Chesterton was directly responsible for Orage's equation of conscription with Prussia, it seems that from about 1910 onwards Orage was increasingly influenced by Chesterton, most especially in his criticism of socialism, literary realism, Shavian drama[63] and even of Nietzsche.[64]

However, in more reflective mood when discussing 'The Compulsion of Men' on 4 May 1916, Orage concedes that whilst a man should do his duty, it is better that a man does his duty voluntarily than be compelled to do it. Thus, 'Voluntaryism (sic) is the principle of which Compulsion becomes only the support in case of need. Compulsion is the policeman of Voluntaryism; not a principle in itself, not a thing to be admired or adopted for its own sake, but the only alternative left when men refuse to do their duty voluntarily'. He favours the 'Conscription of Personal Service' and the 'Conscription of Wealth', as both of these are duties owing to the state. (*NA* XIX, 1, p. 5)

Pacifism: an outrage to 'the proprieties of language'

Despite his qualified opposition to conscription, the editor of the *New Age* was far from espousing the pacifist cause. Only if he had been a German would Orage have been 'a pioneer of pacifism in the world', because he would have realised that war was already obsolete among the 'Elder Powers of Europe' and therefore unlikely to bring any 'solid advantage'. Even if he cannot quite envisage a 'Prussian as Pacifist', Orage still holds to the nineteenth century view that the German 'is essentially a man of peace' because war is 'not the trade at which or in which Germany excels'. Since 1870 Germany has been at peace and has flourished. 'Say Germany anywhere', he argues, 'and at once the image rises of skilled industrialists, practical scientists, indefatigable workers -

62   Jay P. Corrin, *G. K. Chesterton and Hilaire Belloc: The Battle Against Modernity* (London, 1981), p. 41.
63   John D. Coates, *Chesterton and the Edwardian Cultural Crisis* (Hull, 1984), pp. 235-44.
64   Tom Steele, *Alfred Orage and the Leeds Arts Club 1893-1923* (Aldershot, 1990), p. 162ff.

characters, that is, of peace above everything'. It is only the 'hegemony of militarist Prussia in Pacifist Germany' that has disrupted this peace (16 March 1916; *NA* XVIII, 20, pp. 461-2). Indeed, so impressed is he with this practical side of modern Germany that when looking ahead to replan and restructure England after the war, Orage argues that the laissez-faire Liberal policy on industry must be replaced by German 'methods of industry' that are well organised and based on a productive principle. (7 October 1915; *NA* XVII, 23, p. 539)

Nevertheless, Orage sees no reason to become a pacifist in Britain. On 20 April 1916 he contends 'these pacifists outrage the proprieties of language when they refer to war as murder', because 'if war is murder, think what a devilish race we must be; and a very inconsistent race, too: for, on the one hand, we erect statues and write poems to the "happy warrior," while, on the other hand, we hang the unhappy murderer'. The difference between war and murder lies in the concept of duty; men believe that 'war is sometimes a duty, but they never believe that murder is a duty' ('The Ethic of War', *NA* XVIII, 25, p. 581). In the early days of the war Orage claims to have welcomed pacifists 'as evidence of our national peaceableness. A nation could not have had a war in its heart that harboured so many pacifists as England possessed, and withal treated them so tolerantly'. Love of peace is an admirable quality. However, pacifists 'misunderstand the real nature of man. They assume that man is not only (as I agree) a perfectible creature, but a creature that naturally seeks perfection'. There exist 'men who hate peace, hate truth, hate brotherhood, hate, in fact, all the things the others love. Mankind is not, therefore, the homogeneity that pacifists conceive'. Although he likes to think that reason is the best means to resolve differences, he perceives that it has failed and other less peaceable means must be employed. ('Pacifists and Pacifism', 27 April 1916; *NA* XVIII, 26, p. 605)

However, Orage was quite prepared to allow those who outraged the proprieties of language to explain themselves in his paper. One pacifist to be given almost free reign to say what he liked was C. H. Norman, who had once written the foreign affairs column as Stanhope of Chester prior to J. M. Kennedy. On 29 July 1915, for example, Norman explains 'Why I think the War should be stopped', a strident argument interspersed with a series of counter-arguments from an anonymous commentator on behalf of the *New Age*. This was probably the longest and fiercest denunciation of the war to be published by Orage between 1914 and 1916. Eleven months into the hostilities, Norman blames the Liberal Government for plunging the nation into war. Indeed, the 'military position is no more advanced today than it was many months ago' and both governments will go on with the fighting to 'save their own faces', even at the cost of turning Europe into 'one vast cemetery, Britain a mourning house, and the whole world a bankruptcy court'. Norman argues that is time to bring to account a government that has caused the loss or maiming of 'the hundred thousand lives' in a war 'which could have been prevented by the British statesmen just as the Crimean

War could have been and which is far more insane and purposeless than that disastrous war was'. Negotiation with Germany over Belgium would therefore be a much saner policy than force. (*NA* XVII, 13, pp. 302-3)

On 3 December 1914 Norman, together with Clifford Allen and Fenner Brockway, had founded the No Conscription Fellowship whose aim was to gather like thinkers and oppose conscription, subsequently giving assistance to conscientious objectors.[65] As a conscientious objector Norman duly found himself in military custody. On 18 May 1916 the *New Age* carried an open letter from Orage, Shaw and Belloc, amongst others, supporting Norman against his harsh treatment at the hands of the military authorities at Caterham. Although all signatories disagree with Norman's pacifist views, they respect his right to express his opinions (*NA* XIX, 3, p. 69). However, it was not until stories emerged of Norman's rough treatment whilst in custody at Wandsworth Detention Barracks that Bertrand Russell intervened and secured more tolerable conditions for him.[66]

Beatrice Hastings: 'no possibility of suddenly hating my German friends'

Ever since the inception of the *New Age*, Beatrice Hastings (1879-1943) had contributed a variety of articles under a multiplicity of pseudonyms.[67] Often she dealt with the question of women and appears to have exerted considerable influence on Orage, with whom she lived between 1907 and 1914.[68] However, her autobiography, with its vitriolic attack on Orage and factual inaccuracies, suggests she is not a wholly reliable source. She claims, for instance, that reviews of foreign books signed R.H.C. were not the work of Orage who, she alleges, was 'incapable of the "grind" necessary to master a foreign language'[69] and therefore preferred to leave such difficult reviewing to J. M. Kennedy, whom, incidentally, she claims to have discovered.[70] Early in 1914 she moved to Paris, initially to send a series of reports on life in the French capital

---

65   Cate Haste, op. cit., p. 147. See also Martin Ceadel, op. cit., p. 33.

66   Richard A. Rempel, op. cit., pp. 408-10.

67   Apart from her own name, she wrote as Beatrice Tina, Robert à Field, T. K. L., D. Triformis, Edward Stafford, S. Robert West, V. M., G. Whiz, J. Wilson, T. W., A. M. A., Cynicus and Alice Morning.

68   See Claire Tomalin, *Katherine Mansfield: A Secret Life* (London, 1987), p. 84 and Tom Steele, op. cit., p. 39.

69   Beatrice Hastings, *The Old 'New Age'. Orage and others* (London, 1936), p. 17. She spoke French fluently and had taken German lessons. See *NA* XV, 24, pp. 574-5.

70   Beatrice Hastings, op. cit., p. 5.

back to the periodical. Caught up in the city at the outbreak of war and seeking permission to travel back to England, she produced probably her most effective pieces of journalism, describing French attitudes towards the Germans and her own ambivalent feelings.

On 13 August 1914 Orage published the first of Beatrice Hastings' 'Impressions of Paris', written under the pseudonym Alice Morning. The French capital, she reports, is rife with rumours and the French are reliving the horrors and food shortages of the Franco-Prussian War. Anti-German sentiment runs high, with the French pillaging shops suspected of being owned by Germans. She recalls having seen gendarmes applauding the pro-war movement and breaking up a peace meeting with 'frenzied faces laughing for war', as well as two separate incidents in which Germans have been battered by the French for shouting, courageously in her opinion, 'Vive L'Allemagne!' Of the Germans who have been interned, she notices that for the most part they show 'bewildered horror and dignity'. In such surroundings she feels alienated, admitting 'I feel so out of things, with no possibility of suddenly hating my German friends.' (*NA* XV, 15, p. 350)

Beatrice Hastings was not slow to give voice to her weariness with the war. On 20 August 1914, when observing the French rejoicing at the defeat of the Germans at Liège, she comments 'it is hard to hate a beaten foe' (*NA* XV, 16, p. 370), whilst the following week, after learning about the treatment meted out by the French to German prisoners of war, she admits 'I wept at reading of the weeping and starved German prisoners - and was glad they were not ours' (27 August 1914; *NA* XV, 17, p. 394). On 15 October 1915 she attacks the 'loathsome commerce' of certain French shops selling German uniforms taken in the field with the apt remark that 'if we heard of this being done in Berlin, what comments we should make!' (*NA* XV, 24, pp. 574-5)

The execution of nurse Edith Cavell by the Germans caused an outcry in Britain, although the *New Age* remained aloof. Beatrice Hastings views Cavell's action, in helping allied prisoners to escape, as 'plainly wrong', an exploitation of the position of trust in which the Germans placed her. She finds no justification for the hypocrisy and hysteria that accompany the case since 'several women have been shot by the Allies in France alone', even when they held less worthy positions than a nurse and were 'miserable, ignorant peasants whose only glory was to be of German birth' and to worship the Kaiser. She levels the charge of hypocrisy at the politicians and journalists 'who know and have not forgotten that we have killed women spies, and who have traded on the death of Miss Cavell. Miss Cavell was the last person in the world whom we ought to heroise for her action' (18 November 1915; *NA* XVIII, 3, p. 59). In this she concurs with Bernard Shaw, who also argued that the Germans were justified in executing Cavell, although he questioned whether 'any commandant with the brains of a rabbit' would have 'outraged popular sentiment by having her shot, instead of locking her up until the end of the war, after passing a formal sentence of imprisonment for life.' ('The Case Against Germany', 25 May 1916; *NA* XIX, 4, p. 79)

By June 1916 Beatrice Hastings was writing on more general subjects; Huntley Carter, who had already reported on drama in various European capitals before the war, took over her column on Paris at the end of August 1916. Even so, her forthright opinions on the Germans could not be silenced. In 'The Enemy in the House', for instance, she speaks out against those who 'think of the Germans as wild animals, rats rather - every one killed so much to the good, every reverse for them an unmitigated good for us, victory one day nearer home. I cannot think like this. Men are being slaughtered and for me the attitude of satisfaction over dead men, German or any other, is impossible'. Thus, she is filled with 'impotent horror' when 'the soul repudiates the natural savage joy over the fallen enemy, and sees no instant way out of his death'. Invariably war is depicted naively as a quick battle between good and evil. She feels no hatred for England's opponents because the German youth 'now being thrown away at Verdun' did not begin the war and cannot be viewed simplistically as the evil enemy. 'Whatever may have been the character of the original combatants', she argues, 'the present ones are fighting because they must; they are all caught in the battle and can dare nothing but fight their way out'. Thus, conscription is 'forced assassination'. In this vigorous denunciation of war she argues that women should speak out against war and praises pacifists for being in advance of nations. (15 June 1916; *NA* XIX, 7, pp. 160-1)

On 20 July 1916, doubtless wishing to develop her comments on pacifism, Beatrice Hastings began a short series of 'Peace Notes', in which she discusses the difficulty we experience in understanding war as 'simply killing' because 'millions of men decorate each other for performing it as though it were an act of almost divine reason. Education instils the glories of war into us as children. The books are half filled with the deeds of conquering heroes' (*NA* XIX, 12, p. 281). The following week, in an attempt to understand war, she launches an attack on her fellow contributor T. E. Hulme for volunteering and demands an explanation for his decision (27 July 1916; *NA* XIX, 13, pp. 304-5), although it appears that even the combative Hulme declined to take on such a formidable opponent.

A. R. Orage: confronting 'the nakedness of the Teuton'

In addition to Orage's weekly political commentary, 'Notes of the Week', with which the journal always opened, his series of 'Unedited Opinions' became a regular rather than an occasional feature during the war. On 13 August 1914 he asks 'What is Civilisation?' and confesses that he regards Germany as 'the least civilised of the four chief Western Powers'. By civilisation he understands 'supremacy in control of the civil population', although this is not the case in Prussia, which, like J. M. Kennedy, he distinguishes from the rest of Germany. Prussia, he warns, is the 'predominant partner in the German Empire', whose ideal is not civilisation but 'militisation' (sic), the subordination of social organisation, morals, manners, 'even what they call culture', to the military ideal. Thus, the civilian is subordinate to the soldier just as the subordination of society to religion means the 'supremacy of the priest'. Orage denies that 'the virtues developed under militarism are either the same or the equal of the virtues we hope to develop under civilisation'. Militarism is inferior to civilisation because it only engenders 'discipline, character, courage, the virtues of the soldier in other words'. However, the distinguishing character of civilisation is intelligence. In the practical world, discipline and character do not imply intelligence, any more than intelligence implies discipline and character. To a militarist state like Prussia, discipline and character are 'external' since they are 'superimposed upon it'. However, discipline and character developed by the intelligence are 'native to the soul, and self-imposed'. The aim of a 'civilised state' is to '*induce* in the citizen the virtues of the soldier'. Orage fairly admits that 'in the mass of citizens' all the inducement possible 'will still fail to make soldierly souls of them', although he considers that 'one volunteer of virtue is worth ten men pressed into its service' and one volunteer in ten justifies civilisation. If society were wise, Orage contends, it would place more and more responsibility on the individual and 'militarism would everywhere give place to civilisation and civilisation to more civilisation. That movement, initiated by the Renaissance, had happily begun to spread over Western Europe when Prussia (the same North Germany that opposed the Renaissance with the Protestant anti-Renaissance of Luther) revived the military system and once again put the citizen under lock and key not of theological but of military dogmas'. Indeed, he is in no doubt that Prussia is 'a threatening anachronism to Western Europe', and must therefore 'be brought in to step with Italy, France and England' or else 'be brought to heel'. To achieve either of these goals, Prussia 'must be de-militarised and re-civilised.' (*NA* XV, 15, p. 348)

Besides attacking Prussian militarism, Orage criticises the German navy for dividing Europe and forcing the British and French into an unnatural alliance with the Russians, whom he clearly does not trust. Unlike some of his contributors, he sees no reason to transfer his allegiance to Russia as a matter of wartime expediency. On 13 August 1914 he suggests that in the previous decade England has been subjected to 'terrorism' by Germany thanks to 'the totally superfluous and provocative creation of the German Navy'. The very existence of the German Navy gives justification to England's support for war against Germany. Orage argues that 'from the moment when Germany decided upon a naval challenge to us, not merely was the Balance of Power in Europe threatened, but our Imperial supremacy as well'. We simply could not afford 'to watch calmly the growth of Germany's navy'. In addition, Germany's naval programme weakened the defences of the Allies against Russia because they were forced to channel all their energies into shipbuilding instead of watching the Russian front. Rather than squander money on a navy, Germany should have invested in defences against 'our common Russian enemy'. According to Orage's rather dubious calculations, the Allies have had to compete with the German navy and have been forced to spend 'a thousand unnecessary pounds'. He brands the German Navy 'a blunder and a crime' because it has 'ranged England and France against a Germany of which we are the natural and predestined allies', and it has 'thrown Western Europe against its will and against its interests into the support of Russia' (*NA* XV, 15, pp. 337-8). We see here something like an anti-Russian barbarism line emerging in Orage, rather approaching the attitude of Thomas Mann.

Only two days after England's declaration of war on Germany, Orage, ignoring the *Entente cordiale* agreed by Russia, France and England, warns against giving unqualified support to France as this might involve replacing the power of Prussia with the power of Tsarist Russia and thus upsetting the balance of power in Europe. England must therefore go into battle with both eyes open, try to behave honourably towards France, yet take care that 'in disestablishing Germany we do not establish Russia', even if this means reaching an agreement with Germany before the war is over. Orage foresees that such an alliance could exist once the war has disposed of the 'German lie' that has circulated since the time of the 'brute Bismarck', namely that force is 'the final arbiter of the world.' ('Notes of the Week', 6 August 1914; *NA* XV, 14, pp. 313-15)

Orage's attitude towards Germany reveals a certain ambivalence. At the beginning of the war, some of his outbursts on the Germans represent little more than the propaganda clichés of the day. In a blanket condemnation of Germany on 20 August 1914 he announces that the Allies are confronted with an 'untamed, snapping, barking brute' which has contributed little to 'humanity at large during the last forty years'. Evidence for this claim can be found in a rather unlikely source, namely the 'social sense' of the Germans, which he condemns for being 'as undeveloped as it was in the seventeenth and eighteenth centuries, when the uncouth antics of the coarse fellows from beyond the Rhine alternately shocked and amused the salons of Versailles, Rome and Madrid'. Only by 'associating through a long period of years with Frenchmen, Englishmen and Italians' were the Germans able to acquire 'some manners and a trifle of elegance'. Thus, aristocratic German women have ordered dresses from Paris and in more recent years the men have come to London for 'clothes that did not look like misfits'. However, we must not be fooled by the apparent ability of the Germans to appreciate the finer points in life, Orage warns, reminding us that Bismarck 'scoffed at the art treasures of Paris and insinuated that they would look better on a bonfire'. Yet, 'this epidemic was mild' compared with its successor, 'an arrogance which has grown more difficult to tolerate from decade to decade'.

Orage is in no doubt that 'with the declarations of war all sense of sociality, even of decency, has been cast off, and we are confronted with the nakedness of the Teuton.' (*NA* XV, 16, p. 362)

However, after two years of being confronted with the 'nakedness of the Teuton', Orage becomes rather more guarded in his remarks. On 9 March 1916, whilst convinced of Germany's 'guilt' in starting the war, he attempts to present to his readers 'The Case for Germany'. In this article he contends that as the English failed to understand their German cousins before the war, it is time to understand them during the hostilities. He finds Germany's objective 'legitimate and necessary to her', even if her methods were 'tragically mistaken'. Germany's 'undertaking of war' was not 'the act of madmen but of reasonable fallible creatures - much as we are.' (9 March 1916; *NA* XVIII, 19, pp. 438-9)

Nevertheless, the following week Orage is careful to make clear what 'The Case Against Germany' is. He argues that although Germany had some excuse for her actions in the sense of 'a ground upon which ordinarily stupid men might act', excuse does not constitute justification, and 'it behoved a professedly philosophical and cultured nation to discover a justification for the use of force, and not to be satisfied with a mere excuse for it'. Although herself a Great Power 'with all the moral responsibility of a Great Power', Germany 'declined to keep step with her peers, and to accept the obsolescence of war as an obligation self-imposed upon the Concert. It was precisely as if a gold-digger in a mining camp that had begun to settle down into civilisation had insisted upon continuing to be armed with a six-shooter'. Germany was thus wrong to carry arms when the rest of Europe agreed that it should not wage war amongst itself, hence the 'incredulity of the world' at the outbreak of war. People no longer believed that a European war was possible, with the result that England was not prepared (16 March 1916; *NA* XVIII, 20, pp. 461-2). Orage's case against Germany is rather different from that put by Bernard Shaw. In his article of the same name, Shaw's main charges against Germany are that it cannot reduce its high rate of infant mortality, it has failed to produce military competence and has sacrificed its education system to 'the idolatrous romance of Hohenzollernisn.' (25 May 1916; *NA* XIX, 4, pp. 78-9)

Although Orage views the hostilities in terms of a war of ideas, he elaborates that 'in ideas this is pre-eminently the war of France'. France's main motive, he explains, is derived from before 1870, namely from 'the refusal of Germany, her neighbour, to be moved by the French Revolutionary ideas of 1848'. In an absurd attack on France, he claims that it was an affront to 'the soul of France' when Germany 'declined to take seriously or to be practically moved by' the 'ideas of 1830-48' which, according to Orage, represent 'the greatest political effort of thought ever made by a nation'. Germany's refusal was a 'slap in the face to the culture of France from which the pride of France has ever since suffered. And, moreover, it was followed by two events that added humiliation to injury: the Occupation of Paris and the attempt to establish in Germany a competing culture'. German occupation was 'a practical demonstration of the fallacy of 1848, and hence a justification of Germany's repudiation of modern Liberalism'. Until 1870 European cultures, including that of Germany, shared 'an identical foundation of standards and tastes'. Before 1870 European culture was 'single-minded, and France was its particular custodian'. However, Orage contends, after 'the German reaction of 1848, confirmed in its wisdom as it appeared to be by 1870, Germany not only ceased to accept France as the judge of European standards of culture, but proceeded to set up standards of her own in competition with all the standards that had hitherto prevailed. Her action was therefore more than a repudiation of the cultural leadership of France, it was a challenge to the culture of Europe'. He perceives that this repudiation of French cultural leadership is supported by German intellectuals who 'see the war as the continuation and triumphant conclusion of 1848 and 1870', with Thomas Mann calling '*Kultur* and Militarism brothers-in-arms against a civilisation hitherto based upon persuasion and peace. For German intellectuals, in fact, the enemy is France, and Europe only through France.' ('The Case for France', 30 March 1916; *NA* XVIII, 22, p. 509)

There is a certain justification for Orage's opinion that Thomas Mann's enemy is France above all other European nations. To the *Entente* propagandists' charge that Germany was divided between barbarous militarism and civilised values, Thomas Mann replied in his essay *Gedanken im Krieg* (November 1914) that civilisation held little appeal for the Germans because it signified politics and superficiality and was therefore too shallow for the profound German soul. His antithesis of *Kultur* and *Zivilisation* was probably influenced by meanings that the terms had acquired since they first entered the German language in the eighteenth century.[71] From the outset, *Zivilisation* was equated with characteristics of the French aristocracy, with politics and elegance. Thus, there already existed an antithesis between *Zivilisation* and *Kultur*, between 'superficiality' and 'depth', 'falseness' and 'sincerity', 'external politeness' and 'true virtue'.[72] After the events of 1789, *Zivilisation* acquired further connotations - it no longer stood for the code of behaviour of the French aristocracy, but also for the main ideas on politics and society of the French revolutionaries. Thus, *Zivilisation* became inextricably linked with the 'Ideas of 1789', with the declaration of human rights and the demand for liberty, equality and fraternity. The French felt themselves to be at the forefront of 'civilisation', fighting for human rights, but to many Germans it had come to mean revolution and for this

---

71   Eckart Koester, op. cit., pp. 269-70. *Kultur* first entered the German language in about 1760 and *Zivilisation* in about 1775.
72   Ibid., p. 271.

reason it was henceforth regarded by conservatives in a negative sense.[73] The ideas contained in Mann's wartime essays were elaborated further in his *Betrachtungen eines Unpolitischen*, which was written between November 1915 and March 1918. This piece of intellectual juggling in support of Germany's involvement in the war was prompted by Romain Rolland's criticism and the attack on German intellectuals made by his own brother Heinrich, whose allegiance lay with France.[74] This would suggest, as Orage perceives, that for Thomas Mann at least the real argument is with France. Indeed, in the *Betrachtungen*, Mann confesses that apart from England's treatment of Ireland, which he finds scandalous,[75] he has no quarrel with England.

Oscar Levy: 'I am an "Alien" of yours'

One of the saddest aspects of the war was the persecution by certain fanatics of people living in Britain whose only crime was to have German surnames or German ancestry. Employers came under pressure to dismiss employees with such enemy connections, and in May 1915 the London Stock Exchange excluded brokers of German birth.[76] The situation became ridiculous when, in a burst of misguided patriotic zeal, German shepherd dogs were renamed Alsatians and on at least one occasion a dachshund was stoned in the street.[77] Amongst Britons who were descended from Germans, opinion was divided on how to tackle the problem. The British royal family surname, Battenberg, was hastily changed to Mountbatten. W. T. Sonnenschein, the Vice Principal of Brasenose College, Oxford, thought it wiser to revert to his paternal grandmother's name of Stallybrass, although his uncle, E. A. Sonnenschein, Professor of Latin at Birmingham, kept the name, whilst his son preferred Somerset as a surname.[78] The Professor of German at Leeds University, Albert William Schüddekopf, a graduate of Göttingen University and a naturalised British citizen, was hounded until the University, bowing to outside pressure, granted him indefinite leave in November 1915 and in June 1916 Michael Sadler, the Vice Chancellor, advised him to resign. He died in a Harrogate nursing home three months later, apparently killed by the 'mental anguish of seeing the two

---

73   Ibid., p. 273.
74   T. J. Reed, op. cit., p. 190.
75   Ibid., p. 211.
76   Stuart Wallace, op. cit., p. 162.
77   Paul Fussell, op. cit., p. 176.
78   Stuart Wallace, op. cit., p. 161.

countries he loved best at war with each other, and by the shoddy treatment he received from the community in which he lived'.[79]

The *New Age* was swift to come to the defence of Germans persecuted in England. On 20 August 1914, for example, A.B.C., who is most probably Orage,[80] condemns pen-knife attacks on Germans in the East End of London and calls on his fellow countrymen to remember that it is the duty of civilians to be 'polite to foreigners' even in time of war (*NA* XV, 16, p. 379). However, it soon transpired that racial abuse was much closer to home than this when one of Orage's regular contributors, Oscar Levy, became a victim. As a German living in England, and having edited the first complete English edition of the works of Nietzsche - who, as we shall see, was a prime target for vilification - Levy was especially susceptible to attack, eventually finding it necessary to flee his adoptive country to the sanctuary of Switzerland for the duration of the war. The irony of the situation was not lost on Levy who recalled in a letter to the *New Age* that twenty years earlier he had left his native Germany, where he practised medicine, because he was boycotted for being a Jew, only to find himself persecuted again for being a German in England (5 November 1914; *NA* XVI, 1, p. 23). Once exiled, Levy continued to send articles to the *New Age* dealing with a variety of literary subjects, as well as a longer series entitled 'The German and the European: A Dialogue'[81] in which he attempts to give insight into the German national character, although perhaps surprisingly, given his wartime experiences, his sympathies ultimately lie not with Germany but with the rest of Europe.

The first indication to *New Age* readers that anything was amiss came on 1 October 1914 when Levy sent a letter to the periodical entitled 'Germans in England: An Appeal'. He admits 'I am an "alien enemy" of yours', even though he has never thought of himself as an enemy and feels more at home in England than anywhere else. He finds himself in the position of many of his countrymen in England, assailed by anti-German feeling that has caused German waiters, clerks and governesses to be 'dismissed wholesale', prompted the Guildhall School of Music to revoke the contracts of all its professors of German, Austrian and Hungarian origin, and provoked Edinburgh University to attempt to dispense with non-naturalised German teachers and cancel the pension of one who has occupied the chair for forty years. (*NA* XV, 22, p. 532)

Even after he left England, Levy was still persecuted by certain Fleet Street journalists, most notably Austin Harrison, the editor of the *English Review.*

---

79   Ibid., p. 163.
80   See p. 119, note 40.
81   See 24 June 1915; *NA* XVIII, 8, pp. 176-9; 22 July 1915; *NA* XVII, 12, pp. 270-1; 26 August 1915; *NA* XVII, 17, pp. 399-402; 30 September 1915; *NA* XVII, 22, pp. 541-3 and 28 October 1915; *NA* XVII, 26, pp. 614-17.

On separate occasions both J. M. Kennedy[82] and Orage came to Levy's defence. Orage, for example, praises Levy in glowing terms for continually 'plotting some good to the intelligence of this country'. According to Orage, 'for years, single-handed and without the smallest expectation of reward, he had devoted himself to counteracting Prussianism in philosophy, literature and politics by means of the publication of the works of Nietzsche'. He even ventures to suggest that had the works of Nietzsche 'been as well known amongst us some years ago', then Prussia 'would not have taken us by surprise as she did.' (18 February 1915; *NA* XVII, 16, p. 430)

Certainly Levy's highly idiosyncratic defence of Nietzsche against his wartime detractors would have given the chauvinists much cause for complaint.[83] In an article entitled 'Nietzsche and this War' that appeared in the *New Age* at the end of August 1914, Levy contends that the controversial German philosopher would not 'have condemned the war itself' because 'for nations that are growing weak and contemptible war may be prescribed as a remedy, if they want to go on living'. In these terms, war is 'a brutal cure' for the 'national consumption' that has swept Europe since the nineteenth century with the spread of 'wrong values', the values of the 'weak, the tame, the lame, the sick, the humble, the crooked, the cunning, the dishonest, the botched and the bungled. These values have poisoned not only the people, but its leaders as well, all over Europe alike, and to such an extent no-one could any longer preserve an upright and honourable peace, and all have drifted into a general conflagration'. At the same time he emphatically denies that Nietzsche has any connection with German militarism. Germany, he observes, was a military country long before Nietzsche wrote, and needed no help from the German philosopher to develop further its militarist aims. He explains that the Kaiser is 'a very romantic personage and devout Christian', who urged his people to go to church at the outbreak of war and 'would certainly take amiss any accusations of "Nietzscheism"'. According to Levy, German academics would also take amiss such an accusation because they still remain 'very hostile to Nietzsche's creed, and would almost to a man repudiate any connection with the teacher of the Superman'. Levy remarks tellingly that although certain German officers speak highly of Nietzsche, so too do many non-German officers: it is therefore ridiculous to accuse Nietzsche of influencing German militarism. The Franco-Prussian war proved nothing to Nietzsche and its outcome, the German Empire, was Nietzsche's 'lifelong bugbear'. Given these views, Nietzsche could never be popular in his own country. Instead, the Germans have chosen a 'very different guide for their exploits, aspirations and enterprises', namely Houston

---

82   4 February 1915; *NA* XVI, 14, p. 369.

83   See Oscar Levy, 'Nietzsche im Krieg' (1919), in *Nietzsche und die deutsche Literatur*, edited by Bruno Hillebrand, 2 vols (Tübingen, 1978), I, p. 193.

Stewart Chamberlain, who is 'more German than a German'. His *Grundlagen des neunzehnten Jahrhunderts* argued the superiority of the Teutonic family to all the other races of the world. For Chamberlain the Teuton already embodies the Superman. It is this work, rather than the writings of Nietzsche, that in Levy's opinion 'has become the Bible of modern Germany' and 'has completely turned the heads of modern Germans, who are only too ready to accept a gospel of conceit and flattery' (27 August 1914; *NA* XV, 17, p. 393). Although it might be an overstatement to call Chamberlain's *Foundations of the Nineteenth Century* 'the Bible of modern Germany', it is true that the work had tremendous impact; a cheap, popular edition of 1906 had sold over 100,000 copies by 1915.[84]

Nietzsche and Treitschke: 'Nitch and Tritch'

In addition to attacking Prussian militarist ideals and condemning German *Kultur* as a threat to French Civilisation, English writers looked to traditions of German thought to explain away modern German strategy. However, they did not necessarily base their assumptions on the work of academic specialists, but instead drew their conclusions from the popular form into which the original philosophy had been filtered. In 1912 General Friedrich von Bernhardi's *Deutschland und der nächste Krieg* had stirred up anti-German sentiment by arguing that Germany must prepare to defeat England in a war that could no longer be avoided. In addition, the title page of Bernhardi's treatise bore a quotation from *Also sprach Zarathustra*.[85] Although this was the only reference made to Nietzsche by Bernhardi, there were extensive quotations from the Prussian historian Heinrich von Treitschke, whose works were first translated into English at the beginning of the war and confirmed English suspicions that he was typical of German greed for power.[86] The potent combination of a sabre-rattling German professor, a mad German philosopher of dubious 'morality' and a member of the German General Staff who endorsed them both, was seized upon by writers of anti-German tracts. All the brutal and destructive aspects of this new, aggressive Germany were alleged to take their inspiration from the triumvirate of Bernhardi, Treitschke and Nietzsche. Thomas Mann, who was far from innocent when it came to distorting Nietzsche for his own propagandist ends,[87] joined

---

84   Geoffrey G. Field, *Evangelist of Race: The Germanic Vision of Houston Stewart Chamberlain* (New York, 1981), p. 225.

85   See Chapter 3, p. 85.

86   Gertrud von Petzhold, 'Nietzsche in englisch-amerikanischer Beurteilung bis zum Ausgang des Weltkrieges', *Anglia*, 53 (1929), p. 148.

87   See T. J. Reed, op. cit., pp. 218-22.

fellow German writers in a vigorous denunciation of this grouping[88] on the grounds that it was a ridiculous association since Treitschke and Nietzsche hated one another, Treitschke had long since ceased to be an influential thinker, and Bernhardi was never influential in the first place. Nevertheless, the trio remained uppermost in popular English perception of Germany.

In the opening stages of the war of words against Germany, Nietzsche and Treitschke found themselves transformed into 'two sinister and influential demons, called Nitch and Tritch'.[89] The campaign against the philosopher and the history professor was so fierce that even when the military hostilities ended 'it was a disappointment to the British public to learn that Nitch and Tritch could not after all be hanged, as they had been dead a good many years'.[90] There were, of course, slight variations on the spelling and pronunciation. One pamphlet advised pronouncing 'Neets-shay' and 'Tritsh-kay',[91] whilst others spoke of 'the execrable "Neech"' and 'the German monster Nietzsky',[92] and one enterprising London bookseller advertised 'the Euro - Nietzschean War. Read the Devil in order to fight him the better'.[93] Evidently this sales tactic met with some success for the *New Age* relates a tale of 'two regular Tommies' who went to a Charing Cross Road bookshop in order to purchase a work by '"this Nich or Nych"'. When shown a book of extracts from Nietzsche they 'examined it together in blank astonishment for a while and then handed it back, saying they couldn't see anything by the Kayzer (sic) in it.' (10 September 1914; *NA* XV, 19, p. 455)

The controversy was wide-ranging, embracing intellectual periodicals, pamphlets, magazine articles and letters to the national press. Of the numerous men of letters enlisted into the propaganda campaign, William Archer, the drama critic and translator of Ibsen, was one of the most outspoken. In 'Fighting a Philosophy' Archer argues that the vast majority of people interpret Nietzsche's ideas as being 'precisely those which might be water-marked on the

---

88   Letter from Thomas Mann to Ernst Bertram, quoted by R. Hinton Thomas, *Nietzsche in German Politics and Society 1890-1918* (Manchester, 1983), p. 128.
89   Recalled by E. R. Dodds, *The Ancient Concept of Progress and other Essays on Greek Literature and Belief*, (Oxford, 1973), p. 104.
90   Ibid., p. 105.
91   Canon E. McLure, *Germany's War-Inspirers: Nietzsche and Treitschke* (London, 1914). Quoted by James Joll, 'The English, Friedrich Nietzsche and the First World War', in *Deutschland in der Weltpolitik des 19. und 20. Jahrhunderts*, edited by Imanuel Geiss and Bernd Jürgen Wendt (Düsseldorf, 1973), p. 287.
92   Patrick Bridgwater, *Nietzsche in Anglosaxony* (Leicester, 1972), p. 203.
93   R. Hinton Thomas, op. cit., p. 128.

protocol paper of German militarism',[94] because together with Treitschke, Nietzsche 'gave articulate voice to the colossal swagger in stone and bronze with which the record of 1870 is written all over Germany'.[95]

Archer's views, which did not appear to damage his friendship with Bernard Shaw, were by no means extreme when compared with some of the outbursts made by his contemporaries. Their more outrageous remarks quickly found their way into the *New Age* where they were held up for derision. During the war, possibly prompted by the need to fill the paper as contributors dwindled, Orage printed a page of selected quotations considered to be so unworthy of their authors as to merit the title 'Current Cant'. Cant was defined by Orage as meaning not only hypocrisy, but 'the will to self-deception as well as to deception' ('Readers and Writers', 23 December 1915; *NA* XVIII, 8, p. 182). Although remarks on Nietzsche were not the only source for 'Current Cant',[96] in the first year of the war they provided the column with a steady supply of material. On 13 August 1914 Arnold White is cited for asserting that 'Nietzsche is chief thinker for the Fatherland... The German war lords have drunk deeply of Nietzsche's gospel of lies and robbery' (*NA* XV, 15, p. 363). Two weeks later J. L. Garvin's *Pall Mall Gazette* comes under fire for accusing Wagner of representing 'the Nietzsche philosophy, which has undermined the German Empire' (27 August 1914; *NA* XV, 17, p. 402). The *Morning Post* is cited for calling 'Nietzsche, that raving and half-insane prophet of Pan-Germanism' (1 October 1914; *NA* XV, 22, p. 531), whilst Sydney Dark merits entry for his allegation that 'Nietzsche is ultimately responsible for the Belgium barbarities' (22 October 1914; *NA* XV, 25, p. 587). Lord Cromer comes in for ridicule for writing in the *Spectator* that 'one of the reasons we are now at war is to prevent the philosophy of Nietzsche from becoming one of the main principles which will serve to guide the future course of progress and civilisation' (30 December 1915; *NA* XVIII, 9, p. 213). Given these comments it is hardly surprising that on 12 November 1914 Orage wonders whether after the war English journalists will actually read Nietzsche. (*NA* XVI, 2, p. 42)

---

94   William Archer, 'Fighting a Philosophy', *Oxford Pamphlets* (November, 1915), p. 4.

95   Ibid., p. 5.

96   Other gems included Amy B. Barland's suggestion that 'the thick neck and lower back head of the average German' provide 'the explanation of the predisposition to sexual licence and sexual depravity' (17 June 1915; *NA* XVII, 7, p. 165) and G. K. Chesterton's assertion that 'there will never again be a true pantomime till the Prussian can be made into sausages exactly as he was made out of them.' (10 December 1914; *NA* XVI, 6, p. 155)

Ironically, during his lifetime Nietzsche had repeatedly criticised modern Germany and Treitschke - a point seized upon by the *New Age*. Nietzsche was so misrepresented that Orage was prompted to publish a selection of quotations to show that Nietzsche despised German 'intellect', derided the Prussian Court for considering Treitschke profound, and looked to France as the only nation with a true culture. Amongst the citations published by Orage were examples from *Ecce Homo*, where Nietzsche comments that '"German intellect" is my foul air: I breathe with difficulty in the neighbourhood of this psychological uncleanliness that has now become instinctive - an uncleanliness which in every word and expression betrays a German', and asks 'Have the Germans produced a single book that had depth? They are lacking in the mere idea of what constitutes profundity in a book. I have known scholars who thought that Kant was deep. I am afraid that at the Prussian Court Herr von Treitschke is regarded as a profound historian'.[97] In the same selection of quotations, Nietzsche also admits 'I believe only in French culture, and regard everything else in Europe which calls itself "culture" as a misunderstanding. I do not even take the German kind into consideration... The few instances of higher culture which I have encountered in Germany were all French in origin... Wherever Germany extends her sway, she *ruins* culture'.[98] (29 October 1914; *NA* XV, 26, p. 625)

With the outbreak of hostilities the *New Age* was swift to defend Nietzsche against the charge of being 'the mind that caused the Great War'.[99] Apart from holding up for ridicule quotations from rival publications about Nietzsche's responsibility, Orage also printed longer articles in defence of the German philosopher. Perhaps this is not surprising given that the paper had always been a platform for the English Nietzscheans - Levy, Kennedy and Ludovici. What is striking is the intervention of Orage himself, when since January 1910 he had been denouncing Nietzsche as 'The Lyrical Bismarck' (*NA* VI, 13, pp. 304-5). On 20 August 1914, in his column 'Readers and Writers', Orage speaks out against the poor quality of anti-German poetry and prose published in contemporary papers, quipping with his own pastiche:

'Drink deep or taste not the Nietzschean spring,
A little Nietzsche is a dangerous thing.'

---

97 Nietzsche, *Ecce Homo*, in *Werke*, II, pp. 1149-50.
98 Ibid., pp. 1087-8.
99 This was the improbable slogan on the front cover of J. M. Kennedy's study *The Quintessence of Nietzsche* when it was reissued in 1914. See 26 November 1914; *NA* XVI, 4, p. 109.

Orage notes that much of the blame for Germany's 'war lust' has been put on Nietzsche, admitting that 'there is no denying that texts can be found in him to justify any war on a large scale. The cause is justified, he said, by the fight that is made for it: a good fight justifies any cause'. However, Orage qualifies this by recalling that Nietzsche warned the Germans in particular against 'taking his doctrines grossly', the Germans needed first to digest more Erasmus, Petrarch and Voltaire. Orage reflects poignantly that it would be 'a tribute to the power of ideas if we could assume that the Kaiser has been Nietzsche-intoxicated'. However, he is convinced that it was not Nietzsche, but 1870 that 'went to the head of Prussia', with the occupation of Paris acting as 'a fatal drug'. Ever since, Germany 'has not produced a single great European'; the single exception Orage allows is Nietzsche, but even Nietzsche Orage now thinks 'dated'. (*NA* XV, 16, p. 373)

On 27 August 1914 Orage criticises the vogue for depicting Nietzsche as 'the author of the present horrible war'. He argues that it cannot be denied that Nietzsche 'anticipated such a war though for a remote future' and only if 'the nation waging war had a true European idea. I think he would not only have absolved Prussia from the crime of war, but he would have glorified Prussia, had the "idea" been to Europeanise Europe instead of merely to Prussianize it'. Nietzsche was 'a European who sought to abolish national distinctions within Europe', whereas Prussia seeks to impose unity and uniformity by spreading Prussian ideas throughout Europe. Nietzsche 'was not so foolish as to imagine that one type of society could ever become general in Europe', therefore he would not have approved of Prussia's present campaign, although he would have favoured a war to 'harmonize Europe and to establish a unity in the midst of its diversity'. Orage argues that Prussia is 'one of the least European of all the countries of Europe', since by virtue of her militarism, her doctrine of force and her materialism 'she is really more Asiatic than European'. Thus, her 'right' is not only 'disputed quite properly by the rest of Europe', but victory for Prussia would mean 'the degradation of the whole continent', for just as 'the victory of Athens saved Europe from barbarism, the victory of the Allies over Prussia (mind, I do not say Germany) will save Europe from rebarbarism' (sic). ('Unedited Opinions: Nationalism and Internationalism', *NA* XV, 17, p. 396)

Bernhardi: war as 'a condition of civilisation'

With the deluge of material on Nietzsche and Treitschke there also came heated debate on General Friedrich von Bernhardi (1849-1930). As we have already seen, J. M. Kennedy had discussed Bernhardi's treatise[100] when it

---

100   See Chapter 3, pp. 84-5.

first appeared in German in 1912. On 27 August 1914 he refers again to *Deutschland und der nächste Krieg*, but refuses to place any blame on Bernhardi for writing the tract. Instead, he attacks the German Government 'for gravely inspiring its people with fears of France, England, and Russia, and then taking advantage of their nobler sentiments to hurl them upon us.' (*NA* XV, 17, p. 388)

It was A. E. Randall in his column 'Views and Reviews' who first discussed the English edition. On 3 September 1914 Randall notes that Bernhardi's *Germany and the next War* is 'now made accessible to the English public in a cheap edition', suggesting that the translation first appeared in August 1914. Randall concedes that the work deserves more serious treatment than it has received in the jingoistic British press. Bernhardi, 'by his insistence on the right and duty of making war, has reminded us of what pacifists would have made us forget, the nature of man'. Because our civilisation 'tends to negate war, it tends to unreality', Randall believes. According to his argument, civilisation is 'a condition of culture', whereas war, 'or willingness and preparedness for war, is a condition of civilisation; and if culture develops in the individual savoir faire and forgets the need of prowess, it has made the fatal error that Disraeli attributed to the English and mistaken comfort for civilisation'. Randall defines civilisation as 'a conspiracy of men to avoid calamity', yet this is a hollow aim because 'calamity cannot be avoided. It has its place in the scheme of things; the process of evolution includes integration, disintegration, re-integration; and the destructive power of calamity is inherent in the process of growth'. He concludes that 'destruction is only an incentive to and an opportunity for creation; militarism and culture do not really stand in antithesis but in sequence to each other; and war remains intrinsic to reality and necessary to civilisation' (*NA* XV, 18, p. 424). In summarising Bernhardi, Randall approaches the argument formulated by Oswald Spengler in *Der Untergang des Abendlandes*; the first volume was written between 1913 and 1914, although not published until 1918.[101]

On 15 October 1914 Randall devotes his column 'Views and Reviews' to 'The Real Issue of the War', in which he defends Nietzsche, Treitschke and Bernhardi against the accusations of wartime propagandists. He reasons that Treitschke began teaching in Leipzig in 1859 when Nietzsche was only fifteen, and when Treitschke delivered his Freiburg lectures in 1863 that now form two volumes of *Die Politik*, Nietzsche was only nineteen. Randall continues: 'If Nietzsche has any relation to this war (and it is interesting to recall the fact that Treitschke regarded him as "a rum fellow," and Nietzsche replied in kind) it is only as the lyricist of valour; "a lyrical Bismarck" he has been called by the *New Age*, with, perhaps, an over-emphasis of certain characteristics that are manifested in Prussia. But if Nietzsche did not make this war, this war will make

---

101   See Chapter 6, pp. 249-53.

Nietzsche; for it is effecting a transvaluation of all values, or, at least, is forcing people to define their ideals of the purpose of civilisation and the nature of man'. In Randall's opinion, Germany resembles all other states in that it is man-made. He is in no doubt that the German state was the creation of one man - the statesman Bismarck, rather than the philosopher Nietzsche. (*NA* XV, 24, p. 576)

Although Orage comes to the defence of Nietzsche in the first two years of the war, he is rather less willing to absolve Treitschke and Bernhardi from all guilt. On 17 September 1914 he warns that 'the culture of the Goethe-Beethoven schools has disappeared from modern Germany. The utterances of General von Bernhardi and Dr. von Treitschke are very far from being the exaggerated opinions of specialists; the whimsical beliefs of eccentric people whose views may be disregarded. Bernhardi, following the example of Treitschke and taking his inspiration from Houston Stewart Chamberlain, holds that it is the heaven-sent task of the German race to rule the world and enforce German culture upon it'. This objective is to be accomplished by military means, yet the majority of Germans are not outraged. Indeed, Orage is convinced that these are not the ideas of 'mere cranks', but are to be found 'at least once in every issue of every German newspaper, magazine and review published during the last thirty years. The Treitschke-Bernhardi school includes every German professor, every German journalist, every pamphleteer, every poet, every dramatist, every scholar'. Only Nietzsche is deemed innocent by Orage because he criticised such people and 'was ostracised and classed with Heine as the enemy of the Fatherland'. At the same time, Orage attacks editors who fill their newspapers with references to General von Bernhardi and 'the influence of such people on modern Germany', along with journalists 'who have never read a line' of Treitschke yet quote him 'as if they knew his every chapter. They ask us solemnly to beware of this bad Germany of our own generation, and to remember the "culture" latent under it all, of Goethe and Beethoven'. However, this is folly, Orage contends, and suggests - a little surprisingly - that 'the world would be greatly the poorer for the loss of German music, but for little else that Germany has ever produced', since the English have always drawn their main inspiration from Rome and Greece and 'in a lesser degree France.' (17 September 1914; *NA* XV, 20, p. 467)

J. A. Cramb: 'an embracing of Bernhardi's big boots'

What had made Bernhardi known to the English public, according to Cecil Chesterton, was J. A. Cramb's *Germany and England*. This book, based on lectures delivered eighteen months earlier and subtitled 'A reply to Bernhardi', constituted 'a whole-hearted welcome to Bernhardi, an enthusiastic endorsement of Bernhardi, an embracing of Bernhardi's big boots'.[102] Cramb (1861-1913) had studied in Bonn in the 1880s, heard Treitschke lecture in Berlin, and subsequently taught Modern History at Queens College, London,[103] although he remained on the periphery of academic life.[104] Cramb's *Germany and England* certainly commanded much attention in this period; it ran through eight reprints between June and September 1914.[105] He discusses Treitschke and Bernhardi with the aim of opening the eyes of the British public to the prevailing trends in German thought and shows that Germany is pursuing more vigorously than England an imperialist mission. He asks readers to apprehend these trends for the purposes of self-defence. Although he makes little reference to Nietzsche, the thoughts expressed, as M. E. Humble argues, would be likely to fuel the belief that these were the German intellectuals who were influencing German policy.[106]

In the *New Age* A. E. Randall reviewed rather more cautiously than Chesterton the work in which Professor Cramb 'did more than prophesy the coming of this war' and 'did more than "reply to Bernhardi" as the publisher vainly declares. He gave to contemporary politics the historical spirit, that sense of fatality that has been almost forgotten since Napoleon died'. Politics is synonymous with destiny, 'the national spirit becoming embodied in one man or a number of men, who communicate the inspiration, intensified and made intelligent by their personality, to the nation'. Cramb saw Anglo-German antagonism as 'a challenge to our dominion of the world', a confrontation of two states, 'each endowed with the genius for empire'. According to Cramb, of all England's enemies, Germany is 'by far the greatest'. Randall thinks this may possibly be true, but argues that Germany's 'political mistakes during this campaign alone show that she is not yet ready to govern an Empire; her reliance on spies, and lying bulletins, betrays the same weakness that will not allow a genius to act according to the heroic dictates of his inspiration; but with the world ranged against her, she is making one of the most gallant fights that history has known. We are back in the sagas, battling with heroes for the dominion of this world. We shall win only because we also regard Christ as the eternally crucified. But although Germany will lose this time, our Empire will be challenged, if not by her, then by some other heroic nation; for it is intolerable to the soul of man that the bourgeois should sit in the seats of the mighty.' (8 October 1914; *NA* XV, 23, pp. 551-2)

---

102 Cecil Chesterton, *The Prussian Hath Said in his Heart* (London, 1914), p. 85.
103 M. E. Humble, op. cit., p. 45.
104 Stuart Wallace, op. cit., p. 68.
105 M. E. Humble, op. cit., p. 45.
106 Ibid., p. 45.

On 15 October 1914 Orage takes issue with Nietzsche's critics. As R.H.C. in 'Readers and Writers', he muses that 'it is strange how many people are discovering their contempt and at the same time displaying their ignorance of German culture'. According to Orage, except for Nietzsche, 'all Germany' has not 'produced a world-thinker since Heine'. Surprisingly, Orage makes no mention at all of Karl Marx, and proceeds to argue that 'German thought has been too exclusively German thought to matter much outside its own borders'. He concedes that 'to pronounce such a judgement' requires 'at least a passing acquaintance with the best that has been said and thought in modern Germany'. Orage had ably demonstrated since the days of the Leeds Arts Club that he was fully conversant with the latest developments in German thought. He contends that a much profounder study of the subject is necessary to 'justify the severe and brutal sentences passed on Germany by our chauvinists' who commit the 'elementary blunder' of assuming that 'Nietzsche is at the bottom of the modern Prussianism of German thought and was actually the master and inspiration of Treitschke'. The popular assumption that Nietzsche has influenced policy in Berlin accords 'too much honour' to Germany, in Orage's opinion, because this assumption necessarily attributes to Germany 'an accessibility to ideas positively admirable'. Germany, he imagines, 'is much like England, and her public opinion under much the same kind of influence', namely that of 'the cheap newspapers, the music-halls, the cinemas and the pulpits'. Indeed, Orage goes so far as to say that it is neither Nietzsche nor Treitschke who has moulded German public opinion, but 'journalists like Bernhardi, Lamprecht and Chamberlain, and the ninety or so German correspondents of the Press who have been domiciled in England. These, it is the more natural to assume, have been at the bottom of the Prussian form of mind; just as in our own country it is not the *New Age* that creates or defines public opinion, but journalists like Garvin, Maxse, and journals like the *Daily Mail* and the *Daily Telegraph*'. Nietzsche, he reasons, 'did not live to see a single one of his sixteen or seventeen works cover the costs of publication in Germany. Did this in Nietzsche seem very popular? And there was good reason too, Nietzsche hated the Germans and German culture from the moment that the defeat of France by Prussia had got on Germany's brain. That this hatred was no affectation may be taken as proven by the fact that the German press almost without exception, during his lifetime, boycotted him as vigorously (far more so, indeed) as the *New Age* is boycotted to-day by our British press'. Although Orage has called Bismarck 'the end of old Germany' and Nietzsche 'its swan-song', he perceives that the German press sought 'the beginning of a new Germany, a Kaiser's Germany that had dropped Bismarck's Germany overboard'. Nietzsche has, if anything, refined the present war by his gentlemanly behaviour. Indeed, 'for any gentlemanly conduct the Prussians have shown, Nietzsche may safely be given the credit.' (15 October 1915; *NA* XV, 24, p. 573)

Ramiro de Maeztu had no qualms about exonerating Treitschke and Bernhardi as well as Nietzsche. On 4 March 1915 he investigates 'The Bellicose Pacifists', making particular reference to Norman Angell Lane's *Prussianism and its Destruction*, which argues that the war is the result of a philosophy propagated in Germany by a handful of professors and literary men. De Maeztu contends that if it were true that 'a few professors and writers like ourselves could, with a single idea, bring about such a great event as a European war, our professional dignity would at once be raised so high that no other social occupation would dare to challenge our primacy'. He does not believe that 'Germany's aggressiveness is due to the influence of a philosophy' and argues that the effect of Treitschke's historical writings 'has not been so great as Professor Cramb, in England, believed it to be, but much less', whilst Nietzsche 'has not had any influence upon Germans beyond that of teaching them how to write beautifully', and Bernhardi 'is only one of hundreds of officers who have used their pen to extol the importance of their trade'. He is convinced that 'what has made the German people the passive tool of a military caste is not a militarist philosophy, but simply the radical pacifism of the German people, its incredible docility, and above all, the mania for abstractions of its intellectual classes, which has withdrawn them from any kind of direct political action.' (*NA* XVI, 18, p. 481)

Nietzsche or Carlyle?

The *New Age* looked rather closer to home when considering thinkers behind the policies of the Wilhelmstraße. A letter from a correspondent signing himself Pteleon,[107] for example, contends that if the English are going to condemn Nietzsche and Treitschke for the war, they might as well condemn their own Carlyle as well. Carlyle was influenced by pre-1840 Germany and 'he in his turn profoundly influenced the modern Germany of discipline and science. His doctrine of heroes, his teaching that will is above law, his praise of despots like Cromwell, became interwoven with German thought. His eulogistic biography of that royal ruffian, that crowned brigand, Frederick the Great, on which he spent fourteen years, had an immense and evil influence on Germany'. Despite Nietzsche's condemnation of Carlyle and his countrymen for lacking all capacity for philosophy,[108] Pteleon contends that in much of his thought Nietzsche is 'merely an exaggerated Carlyle, just as Bernhardi is a concentrated and practical Nietzsche.' (22 October 1914; *NA* XV, 26, p. 603)

---

107 Pteleon or Pteleum is the Latin name for the Greek town of Pteleón in Thessaly, near the Aegean island of Euboea.

108 See Nietzsche, *Jenseits von Gut und Böse* (252), in *Werke*, II, pp. 718-19.

On 18 March 1915 the question of Carlyle's responsibility arises again when a contributor signing himself G. D. asks: 'Nietzsche or Carlyle?'. Although seeking to 'rescue poor old Nietzsche from the brick-pile under which he has been buried', the author 'does not necessarily wish to be identified with the Nietzschean mode of thought', suggesting perhaps that the letter is the work of Orage himself. Nietzsche, he contends, made 'two glaring errors' which 'effectually put him outside the ranks of philosophers worth considering at all'. First, he confused Socialism with Christianity and attacked both as identical creeds. Secondly, he assumed that Christianity was a 'slave religion imposed by the slaves upon society from below'. G. D. further disapproves of a teacher so reliant on 'the means of parables and contradictory aphorisms'. However, he praises Nietzsche for setting on record his dislike of Prussians and German culture. The current attacks on Nietzsche G. D. blames on 'church-going circles' and sections of the Press led by William Archer. He asks if these people 'did not feel at the back of their heads that blameworthy as the Kaiser was, something must be done to switch the public mind off the ominous fact that the Kaiser at least was a God-fearing man, who read his Bible every night, and recommended his nation to read it too? This circumstance must be very discomforting to the religious intellect, and here is Nietzsche, an anti-Christian, ready to hand. To the lions with him!' Soon Carlyle must inevitably appear in this conflict thanks to the similarities between his and Nietzsche's thought. G. D. argues that it is time to state clearly that 'what Nietzsche meant by blonde beast, Thomas Carlyle called hero'. Moreover, Carlyle was not only 'a lover of Germany', but he also 'soaked himself in German culture from youth to old age. He tried to graft it on to England. All his idols - literary, religious and military - were German: Goethe, Luther, Frederick the Great. To a biography and glorification of the latter source and fountain head of all Prussian jack-bootery he devoted the most arduous labour of his life, producing a monument which even now is treasured in every German University'.[109] Although Carlyle refused English honours he had no hesitation in accepting the Prussian Order of Merit. G. D. reflects wryly that Carlyle's words sound so 'terrible' and 'insane' that 'it may be necessary to remove his monument from the Thames Embankment for the present, as the Kaiser, should he ever arrive, will undoubtedly pay it a ceremonial visit and probably decorate it with an Iron Cross'. G. D. assures us that in terms of literary influence, Carlyle 'had undoubtedly more to do with the cause of the present war than Nietzsche', citing as an example 'a recent volume on the bombastic and malevolent Treitschke' which claims that the only Englishman to merit Treitschke's admiration was Thomas Carlyle. (*NA* XVI, 20, pp. 534-6)

---

109   Eckart Koester confirms Carlyle's popularity in Germany. Op. cit., p. 160.

With the outbreak of war fewer books were reviewed in the *New Age*. Even those that did receive notices tended to be wartime tracts, rather than the works by European writers that had so preoccupied reviewers in the earlier issues of the periodical. One of the few exceptions was a review of the English translation of Jung's *Psychology and the Unconscious* (20 July 1915; *NA* XIX, 12, pp. 284-5). However, on 10 September 1914 Orage reflects that the autumn publishing season is likely to be scarce and 'except for some half a dozen works, no book can compare with the daily press' because publishers do not concentrate enough on literature. English literature, he believes, has declined appreciably 'during our idle peace' (*NA* XV, 19, p. 448). Indeed, the section of book reviews was entirely absent from the *New Age* during the first three months of the war. Even when it did return on 29 October 1914, it appeared in much shorter form than its pre-war model which sometimes ran to three or four pages of short notices.

The military conflict brought a spate of war books, outlining the Allies' aims, assessing the German national character and analysing trends in modern German thought, many of which were discussed briefly in the *New Age*. On 18 March 1915, for example, the journal praises the *Oxford Pamphlets* series, with the exception of William Archer on Nietzsche (*NA* XVI, 20, pp. 540-1). Archer is castigated the following month over his gross misrepresentation of the German philosopher's ideas in his *Oxford Pamphlet* 'Fighting a Philosophy'. In it he 'considerably lowers the Oxford average' and reveals himself to be a 'pseudo-philosopher trying to write', only one of many writers currently distorting quotations from Nietzsche's works (22 April 1915; *NA* XVI, 25, p. 673). By contrast, Ernest Barker's pamphlet 'Nietzsche and Treitschke: The Worship of Power in Modern Germany' is singled out for praise as typical of the general high quality of the Oxford series. The author is commended for being one of the first commentators to perceive the origin of Treitschke's thought in Hegel, while his survey of Nietzsche and Treitschke is 'impartial' and 'without bias.' (13 May 1915; *NA* XVII, 2, p. 40)

Not all books undermining Wilhelmine Germany find favour with reviewers. There is, for example, a wholehearted condemnation of William Le Queux' *German Spies in England* as a 'disgrace' and a 'waste of time', since the British Government already knows about German spies (29 April 1915; *NA* XVI, 26, p. 701). Charles Sarolea's *The Murder of Miss Cavell* is censured for failing to recognise that under German military law, the British nurse was guilty of committing crimes and was dealt with accordingly. The reviewer suggests that perhaps 'execution' would be more appropriate, even if less stirring as a title (1 June 1916; *NA* XIX, 5, pp. 114-15). A. S. Elwell Sutton's rabidly anti-German tract *Humanity versus Unhumanity. A Criticism of the German Idea in its*

Political and Philosophical Development is rightly panned for its cursory treatment of the Germans (7 September 1916; *NA* XIX, 19, p. 452), and William Roscoe Thayer's *Germany versus Civilisation* is savaged as typical German atrocity material, comprising 'Huns and Hohenzollerns, Treitschke - Nietzsche - Bernhardi - Wagner, Odin and despotism, Christianity and Democracy.' (21 September 1916; *NA* XIX, 21, p. 499)

Critical attention is also accorded to the work of more established writers. A. E. Randall praises H. G. Wells' novel of wartime disillusion, *Mr. Britling sees it through*, because it is both 'a vivid personal study' and 'an intellectual and emotional history of England during the period of the war'. It is one of Wells' 'most vital' and 'most poignantly sincere' works which leaves the reader in no doubt that the war is, as Wells concludes, 'without point' and 'has lost its soul' because it has degenerated into mere 'incoherent fighting and destruction, a demonstration in vast and tragic forms of the stupidity and ineffectiveness of our species.' (12 October 1916; *NA* XIX, 24, pp. 570-1)

By comparison, G. K. Chesterton came nowhere near concluding that the war was 'without point' in either of his wartime tracts, *The Barbarism of Berlin* (November 1914) or *The Crimes of England* (November 1915), both written to help the Wellington House propaganda effort to secure support for the Allied cause in the United States. The reaction of the *New Age* was mixed. Lionel de Fonseka, the reviewer of *The Barbarism of Berlin*, complains that wartime propaganda tracts of this nature have rendered the English language 'unspeakable'. Literary men of the calibre of Chesterton were 'fools' to issue the manifesto as 'representative men of letters' at the beginning of the war. Instead, they should have 'retired to a monastery' or at least 'sought the monastic gift of silence'. The English language is now 'unfitted not only for the speech but even for the thought of a man of sensibility'. Indeed, the reviewer feels 'afraid to utter the English word *culture*'; if he wishes to 'definitely imply a sneer' he must use the word *kultur*, otherwise he must speak of *the humanities* to avoid all implication of a sneer. In other words, the term *culture*, 'a beautiful English word with beautiful associations has been dragged into the mire'. The author argues that the German militarists 'may have violated the neutrality of Belgium', but English journalists 'have done worse - they have violated the neutrality of words'. Indeed, this is 'a war on English words', and Chesterton with his 'flaming topical pamphlet' is the chief culprit. (31 December 1914; *NA* XVI, 9, pp. 216-17)

Chesterton's next wartime tract was the rather more substantial *The Crimes of England*. It is reviewed by Orage who considers it 'a deplorable misfit'. Although he identifies it as one of Chesterton's two best works, as an exposé of the crimes of England - or even Germany, for that matter - it is 'unconvincing' because 'the *truth* of what Mr. Chesterton says is the last thing that the reader thinks about. So dazzled are we by the verbal sparklings of Mr. Chesterton's wit that it is as if we were trying to read by the light of fireworks; we can read nothing for the explosions and the coloured spectacles'. In wartime, the appearance of G. K. Chesterton 'in all his idiosyncrasies' is 'very nearly an impertinence'. We are never allowed to forget that it is G. K. Chesterton and no-one else who is writing, in much the same way that 'the egoistic interludes of Mr. Bernard Shaw' betray his presence in his writing. Both these literary figures, he concludes, are more suited to writing letters than tracts. (*NA* XVIII, 8, pp. 157-8)

From wartime exile in Geneva Oscar Levy sent 'An Open Letter to British Intellectuals' in which he criticises G. K. Chesterton and Bernard Shaw as writers who 'enjoy a great reputation' both at home and abroad because they are supposedly 'well instructed and well able to lead the "intelligentsia" of their country', yet through certain misunderstandings have inadvertently mis-represented Germany. Chesterton comes under fire for his insistence on 'the modern atheism of Frederick the Great' being the 'military religion of Berlin'. As a young man, Levy had been a member of the Prussian army and argues that religion plays a large role in the army and that it is pretty nigh impossible to be an atheist. Nor will he allow Frederick the Great to be dismissed as an atheist, remembering him as a fine sceptic, freethinker and Voltairian. Shaw is criticised for his article 'The Case Against Germany', in which he illogically respects the pretensions of German culture and civilisation but calls the pretensions of the Hohenzollerns and the Junkers 'humbug'; yet if they were only humbugs, Levy reasons, they could not have produced the civilisation so respected and admired by Shaw. (20 July 1916; *NA* XIX, 12, pp. 273-4)

Werner Sombart: 'Faust and Zarathustra and Beethoven in a rifle-pit'

The *New Age* did not confine its attention to English wartime tracts. On 30 December 1915, for example, T. E. Hulme considers Werner Sombart's *Händler und Helden*. He observes that although German professors enjoy great power and influence in their own country, few people in England would recognise this fact before the war and as a result their books went unread. Professors are accorded great respect and high status in Germany and in English 'scholastic circles' there is often 'blind admiration' for works by German academics. Professor Sombart believes that the war is between two conflicting ideals. He views the English character as essentially pure commercialism that fails to produce art, literature or philosophy of any importance. According to Hulme, Sombart sees militarism as the union of the spirit of Weimar and Potsdam, or 'Faust and Zarathustra and Beethoven in a rifle-pit', and attacks English 'sportsmanship' as suffering from a surfeit of tennis, football and 'Krikett' (sic). In Sombart's opinion, the only profound British writers are Irishmen, such as Wilde, Ruskin and Bernhard (sic) Shaw, whilst English art has only 'the sugariness of Gainsborough and Reynolds'. However, Hulme counters, in equally selective terms, that the Germans have little to offer as an alternative, arguing that 'since

155

Dürer there has been absolutely nothing of any importance whatever.' (*NA* XVIII, 9, p. 198)

By contrast, Orage finds a certain degree of truth in Sombart's indictment. In an article published in the summer of 1915, he argues 'we are for the moment and have been for twenty years incapable, as a nation, of maintaining, still less of transcending, our intellectual traditions'. Germany has some justification in reproaching England, for 'if Germany has never equalled our English culture at its best, Germany can yet maintain that, while she has been striving to do so, we have been falling away'. He notes that 'the majority of cultured Germans certainly know our Newton and our Shakespeare better than do the majority of our own educated classes', and suggests that after the war 'familiarity with our classics should be made obligatory on British citizens.' (19 August 1915; *NA* XVII, 16, p. 382)

R.H.C.: German Literature 'in the period before the Fall'

During the early stages of the war Orage betrays a certain caution in discussing German authors. When he is not defending Nietzsche, he refers only to 'safe' German writers from the eighteenth and early nineteenth centuries, when Germany was still the pacific 'Land der Dichter und Denker'. Thus, on 12 November 1914, using the pseudonym R.H.C. in his literary column 'Readers and Writers', he commends Bohn's classics for reprinting volumes of Lessing and Schopenhauer (*NA* XVI, 2, p. 41). He claims to have 'mentally judged' Schopenhauer to be 'more English than German', citing Schopenhauer's admiration for England and suggesting that he was given an English Christian name, Arthur, because his father had wanted him to be born in England. Orage points out that Schopenhauer was partly educated in England and later chose to live in Frankfurt because it had a large English community. It is therefore hardly surprising, Orage contends, that Schopenhauer is now classed as an anti-Prussian thinker (29 April 1915; *NA* XVI, 26, p. 695). Tinged with the zeal of a propagandist, Orage praises Coleridge for 'discovering' Shakespeare a good two years before Schlegel gave his lectures on the English writer that popularised him in Germany, but ignores charges that Coleridge plagiarised German writers (10 December 1914; *NA* XVI, 6, p. 149). Lessing's *Laokoon* he considers to be 'a fine example of German criticism in the period before the Fall'. He notes that, as a critic Lessing, paved the way for creative artists like Goethe; in the same way as Matthew Arnold 'drudged at much the same task in England' rather than become a great poet. Thus, in 1915 Lessing is still tarred with the brush of his own making, that he was merely showing the way to other writers, a sort of John the Baptist figure. Orage also recommends Chamisso's *Peter Schlemihl: The Shadowless Man*, which he first read 'years ago'. He reminds readers that the author distinguishes himself by being 'one of the few Frenchmen' who 'became a

German' (16 September 1915; *NA* XVII, 20, p. 477). On 27 May 1915, following the republication of Kant's *Perpetual Peace* (1795) which was not translated into English until 1903, Orage recommends that both the English and the Germans 'skip Hegel' for a while and return to Kant for a discussion of international politics (*NA* XVII, 4, p. 85), whilst on 27 January 1916 he commends Goethe's sayings, extracts of which, mainly from *Conversations with Eckermann*, have been republished recently under the unlikely title, *Gleams of Goethe*. (*NA* XVIII, 13, p. 300)

Orage was highly critical of writers who attacked German literature without good reason. Shortly after the outbreak of the First World War he is prompted to remark 'What devils of critics our literary reviewers have now become of German writers! There is not now, it appears a single living German of any account whatever in European culture'. Thus, propagandists brand Hauptmann 'a Galsworthy without talent' and Wedekind 'a Wilde without wit'. Orage questions why, if these opinions are true, critics have waited until the outbreak of war to make them known. At the same time he observes that German critics are making equally vitriolic attacks on other European writers and nations. Hauptmann describes Bergson as a 'superficial feuilletonist' and Maeterlinck as a 'blinded Gallomaniac', and can only think of England 'with pain and bitterness'. Orage asks pertinently 'why only now rather than a few months ago? Bergson has 'not changed, Maeterlinck is still the same. England is what it was.' (10 September 1914; *NA* XV, 19, p. 449)

Orage also discusses recent publications dealing with the German character, choosing wherever possible those which look a little deeper than the hackneyed stereotypes found in so many propaganda tracts, although often these articles are more revealing about Orage's own views than those of the author under discussion. On 14 October 1915, for example, he takes as his starting point the current issue of *Quest* in which Jessie L. Weston investigates 'Germany's literary debt to France'. He comments that until the end of the twelfth century, Germany possessed only 'the usual mythical fragments of almost primitive folk-lore' and, for the most part, was dependent on copying the French troubadours. He argues that there was no German literature until Frederick the Great 'sent to France for Voltaire', suggesting that in literature Germany is 'annexationist' rather than 'a discoverer or an inventor' (*NA* XVII, 24, p. 573). The question of imitation amongst German authors proved controversial. When Paul Selver takes up this theme, he concludes rather differently that it proves that German writers are widely read and have assimilated their reading, indicating that 'general European literature is far more accessible in Germany' than in England. In this respect he commends the Reclam publishing house especially for its initiative in making works by foreign authors readily available. (7 January 1915; *NA* XVI, 11, p. 248)

While Orage is circumspect in his literary column, the pieces contributed to 'Readers and Writers' about once a month by Paul Selver are far from cautious. On 3 September 1914 he is responsible for a remarkably Germanophile piece in which he speculates on the possible effect of the war on the reception of German language and literature in Britain. He argues, somewhat surprisingly, that German will probably rise in status, whilst the following month he asserts that 'German prose has almost come to rival French in polish of expression, in richness and flexibility of phrase' (*NA* XV, 18, p. 421). Despite the political climate Selver was not afraid to air his views. In a letter to the *New Age*, for example, he boasts that he possesses 'more than a smattering of the German language' and 'more than a tourist's knowledge of Germany'. He concedes that Germany has broken treaties, but feels 'heartily sick of the yelp, yelp, yelp about Huns' and 'equally nauseated by the sneer of the half-educated about "culture" (with a damning allusion to Nietzsche not far off).' (8 October 1914; *NA* XV, 23, p. 555)

In a more light-hearted vein Selver commends the appearance in 1915 of a satire on the Pan-Germanists by a 'Professeur Knatschké' suitably entitled *Oeuvres choisis du Grand Savant Allemand et de sa fille Elsa. Recueillies et illustrées pour les Alsaciens par Hansi. Fidelement traduites en français par Dr. H. P. Colli.* The volume is particularly effective when making suggestions for the Germanisation of Paris by renaming well-known landmarks in a way more pleasing to the German ear. Thus, Notre Dame becomes 'Unsere liebe Frau', Place de la Concorde 'Eintrachtsplatz', Tuileries 'Ziegeleien', Bois de Boulogne 'Bolonesisches Holz' and Les Folies Bergères 'Die Schäferischen Verrücktheiten'. Such absurd literal translation is no idle fantasy, Selver informs us, citing a recent 'symposium of throbbing intellects' which met in Germany to find alternative names for 'garments with offensive names' such as knickerbockers, raglans and breeches. The Germans cannot decide whether 'Reithosen, Reiterhose, Knie-hosen or Sporthosen' would best translate breeches, whilst a dinner jacket, hitherto termed a 'Smoking' in German, is 'variously metamorphosed into Rauchjackett, Abendsakko, Frackjacke, Halbfrack, kleiner Frack'! Selver also notes the Anglophobia of various respected German writers, with Hugo von Hofmannsthal penning 'twenty lines of doggerel in a newspaper', Herman Bahr turning out 'a war farce', and Richard Dehmel celebrating the war 'in the worst poem ever written' for which the Kaiser has rewarded him with the 'Order of the Red Eagle (Fourth Class).' (1 April 1915; *NA* XVI, 22, p. 589)

At this time Selver was also engaged in translation from both German[110] and Russian.[111] Increasingly, the *New Age* turned its attention to Russian or French literature,[112] reflecting perhaps wartime political alliances. However, not all contributions on Russia achieved total objectivity; one in particular rapidly descends to the level of propaganda tract so reviled by the *New Age*. On 14 January 1915 John Butler Burke discusses 'Russian versus German Culture'. He argues that the Germans abuse the word 'Culture'. Our false perception of the Germans may be blamed on Carlyle, who extolled their virtues to us. However, Burke claims, Carlyle would turn in his grave if he could see Germany now, whilst 'the lofty-spirited Goethe', Schiller and Heine would 'writhe with shame that the sublime in German culture should perish with Louvain and Rheims in the flames of indignation which German barbarism has kindled in the human breast'. The 'insanity' of modern Germany, he asserts, is supported by the Kaiser who has been driven to 'this exalted state of dementia by a number of crack-brained professors' led by Treitschke, and 'despots of a military caste following Bernhardi under the influence of a pretentious would-be philosopher, who, in fact, despised philosophy and particularly German philosophy, which he did not take the trouble to understand; one who despised the German thought of his time but whose ideas have, nevertheless, somehow prevailed', namely Nietzsche. This 'would-be philosopher', we are told, 'hated Germany but the Germany of to-day follows him in principle by preaching the gospel of hatred'. Nietzsche was 'a fine spinner of epigrams and a manufacturer of paradoxes which half-educated persons, particularly women and effeminate men of little courage and less intellect, are the more likely to appreciate, for the mere reason that his sayings sound well, seem plausible enough, convey some semblance to the truth, and inflict a damaging blow to Christianity and the moral sense in man whilst advocating selfishness and moral cowardice as the "will to power"'. Such ideas were bound to find followers amongst 'the smart set', especially in Vienna and

---

110 In May 1915, for example, Selver adapted epigrams by seventeenth and eighteenth century German writers, including Gryphius, Lessing and Lichtenberg (*NA* XVII, 1, pp. 19-20 and *NA* XVII, 2, p. 42), whilst on 16 December 1915 he translated three short poems by Nietzsche - *At Midnight*, *Star Mortal* and *Third change of skin* (*NA* XVIII, 7, p. 156).

111 On 31 December 1914 Selver translated Chekhov's *The Chameleon* (*NA* XVI, 9, p. 220).

112 In the autumn of 1914, for example, Paul V. Cohn, who had collaborated on the Levy edition of Nietzsche, translated extracts from Stendhal's *De l'Amour*.

Berlin, where 'to be cultured means to be affectedly immoral, and where, in fact, morality is regarded on the whole as mere conventionality of somewhat doubtful good taste and decidedly unartistic'. Russia is truly cultured, not at all barbarous, he alleges, because it produces great literature and music, citing as examples Tolstoy, Dostoievsky, Turgenev, Chekhov, Tchaikovsky and Rubenstein. What is more, Russia does not follow Nietzsche but Christ. (*NA* XVI, 11, pp. 269-70)

Nevertheless, these views are in no way a reflection of those held by the editor of the *New Age*. Just as Orage is wary of Russia in his political commentaries, in his literary column he also displays a certain coolness towards works by Russian writers. On 15 April 1915 he remarks wryly that 'anything *said* against Russia today is resented as savouring of pro-Germanism' (*NA* XVI, 24, p. 642), whilst on 28 October 1915 he comments: 'of culture in the Western European sense - Italy, France, and England are its home - there is less in Russian literature than even in German literature. I scarcely remember a wit or a scholar in all the Russian books I have read'. He is prompted to suggest that the classics of English literature be translated into Russian, for 'Russia has more to learn from us than we from her'. France and England 'will have much to do to bring Russia into the western mood. It will take a century at least!' Only Chekhov ranks as 'the nearest approach to a cultivated writer', but even he was 'little more than a very talented provincial.' (*NA* XVII, 26, p. 623)

Chapter 5: Germany and the *New Age*:
January 1917 - October 1919

When hostilities between England and Germany ceased, Bernard Shaw was delighted. In the autumn of 1919 he announced that 'it is with great pleasure that I find myself able to correspond with my German friends again. I need hardly say that the war did the most painful violence to my personal feelings, and that I was unable to make any distinction between the German casualties and those of the Allies in respect of the loss they inflicted on European civilisation'.[1] Even during the Armistice he had to secure official authorisation to write to his translator Trebitsch.[2] Shaw was therefore delighted when Trebitsch moved to Switzerland: he exclaimed 'At last I have got you in a country which I can write to without being shot at dawn'.[3] Not only was he able to correspond with Trebitsch, but he found himself translating one of his Austrian translator's plays as well. Before the war Shaw had offered to translate one of Trebitsch's plays, when, according to Michael Holroyd, he understood 'hardly a word of German'.[4] Just after the war Trebitsch sent him *Frau Jittas Sühne*. Whilst working on an English version Shaw reflected that Trebitsch 'did not seem to know any German, but to have invented a new language of his own'; not even 'Sühne' could he find.[5] By May 1920 Shaw was writing to Trebitsch that he had now read *Jitta's Atonement* 'though most of your words are not in the dictionary', causing him to 'guess what it was all about by mere instinct'. He took a year to translate, 'using some telepathic method of absorption' in order to 'divine, infer, guess, and co-invent the story of story of Gitta'.[6] Beneath the joking to Trebitsch, according to Shaw's secretary Blanche Patch, he took his translating very seriously, having procured a literal translation from his former secretary and relative Judy Gillmore, who spoke German.[7]

---

1   Quoted by Michael Holroyd, *Bernard Shaw, Vol. III, 1918-1950. The Lure of Fantasy* (London, 1991), p. 64.
2   Ibid., p. 64.
3   Quoted by Holroyd, ibid., p. 65.
4   Ibid., p. 65.
5   Quoted by Holroyd, ibid., p. 66.
6   Quoted by Holroyd, ibid., p. 66.
7   Ibid., p. 66.

However, once the immediate post-war euphoria died down, Shaw, like many of his contemporaries, including A. R. Orage, was overcome by a profound sense of disillusion. As a result Shaw, and, as we shall see, Orage, felt impelled to search for new values. For Shaw, the Treaty of Versailles was 'perhaps the greatest disaster of the war for all the belligerents, and indeed for civilisation in general'.[8] In his despair he spoke of 'the uncertainty of my own position and my impotence in the face of a collapse of civilisation'.[9] He became increasingly opposed to democracy, arguing that government by the people was unworkable. Only 'government of the people and for the people' was workable - and even this could only be achieved by applied communism. In November 1914, he had spoken out against tsardom, arguing that 'when we fight for the Tsar we are not fighting for Tolstoy or Gorki but for the forces that Tolstoy thundered against all his life'.[10] He had conceded that the Allies needed Russian military support, but such an alliance with 'the most barbarous and bigoted autocracy in Europe' undermined the Allies' moral position.[11] In the spring of 1917 he wrote in the *New York Times* of 'the enormous relief, triumph and delight' with which the news of Kerensky's revolution in Russia was received in England'.[12]

However, hopes soon died with Lenin's Bolshevik Revolution. Kerensky had been a lawyer and appointed princes and historians to his provisional government, effecting a bloodless revolution: all this was overthrown by Lenin.[13] Shaw was forced to re-assess his own situation. Having believed that 'artists and intellectuals formed the mind of a country which then gave politicians their mandate', he came to place trust in 'men and women with a genius for action' and in 1920 complained that he was tired of seeing Socialists 'rolling the stone up the hill with frightful labor (sic) only to have it rolled down again'.[14] Shaw concluded that he could 'no longer believe in the Fabians' waiting game'.[15] Change therefore had to be imposed, so he looked to Lenin, 'the only interesting statesman left in Europe',[16] a 'man of action', as opposed to Kerensky, a 'man of

---

8   Quoted by Holroyd, ibid., p. 7.
9   Quoted by Holroyd, ibid., p. 33.
10   Quoted by Holroyd, ibid., p. 221.
11   Quoted by Holroyd, ibid., p. 221.
12   Quoted by Holroyd, ibid., p. 222.
13   Ibid., p. 223.
14   Quoted by Holroyd, ibid., p. 224.
15   Quoted by Holroyd, ibid., p. 223.
16   Quoted by Holroyd, ibid., p. 8.

speeches'. Only Lenin could get things done. He informed Fabians that Democratic Socialism now meant communism and was prepared to indulge in endless intellectual juggling to support Lenin.[17]

Shaw's enthusiasm for the Bolsheviks was not shared by many of his contemporaries, including Orage, who felt unable to espouse the excesses of Lenin's revolution. For many people, war was familiar in that the English had recently survived one and could survive another, whereas revolution was to be feared as an 'unknown, a bloody sequence of events that happened over there on the continent, among foreigners'.[18] Some would see their worst fears about Bolshevism and Revolution confirmed in the 1926 General Strike. During the war, when aristocrats and workmen fought side by side, it was hoped that this would help make for a classless society when the war ended. The General Strike dispelled this illusion, making clear that nothing positive had come from the war.[19]

The New Age: in need of money 'to be frittered away in salaries to the clerical and editorial staff

The problems facing Europe had an effect on the *New Age*. By the last two years of the First World War Orage's journal was showing signs of strain. With fewer contributors and constant financial difficulties, Orage was forced to pad out the *New Age* with a weekly collection of 'Press Cuttings' from rival publications, as well as 'Memoranda', an assortment of the best quotations from the previous week's *New Age*. By January 1917, this type of padding occupied almost two of the journal's twenty four pages. During the wartime paper shortage, the periodical was cut back further to a mere sixteen pages in 1918,[20] and following a campaign to attract more subscriptions the price rose from 6d. to 7d. in 1918. By early 1919, 'Letters to the Editor' could occupy up to four pages in a sparse week.[21] In October 1917, Orage calculates that after printing a total of

---

17 Ibid., pp. 224-30.
18 Samuel Hynes, *A War Imagined: The First World War and English Culture* (London, 1990), p. 408.
19 Ibid., pp. 228-30.
20 On 21 March 1918 Orage warns readers that he may even have to reduce it further to twelve pages. (*NA* XXII, 21, p. 417)
21 Orage delighted in printing his readers' diverse views on the *New Age*. Some complain that it has become 'too much of a Jingo journal' and 'too insular and chauvinist', whilst others think that it is 'pacifist in disguise, is probably run on pro-German money', and condemn it as 'written by foreigners for foreigners'. (31 October 1918; *NA* XXIII, 27, p. 430)

2,250 copies of the *New Age* per week (500 of these are subscriptions, returning the full 6d. to him - those sold in retailers return only 4d.), the *New Age* brings in a total of £37 10s. per week from sales. Out of that there are weekly costs for printing (£20), paper (£7), office and rent charges (£2), office expenses such as stationery and postage (£2), leaving £6 10s. 'to be frittered away in salaries to the clerical and editorial staff'. The margin has only recently shrunk to this level, thanks mainly to a fifteen per cent rise in the cost of printing (10 October 1918; *NA* XXIII, 24, p. 381). His own contributions increased: he continued to take charge of the political commentary 'Notes of the Week',[22] with which the paper always opened, as well as produce the literary column 'Readers and Writers', using the pseudonym R.H.C. In addition, he took over S. Verdad's 'Foreign Affairs' commentary when its author, J. M. Kennedy, died suddenly in the autumn of 1918. The *New Age* between 1917 and 1919 is therefore very much the work of one man - A. R. Orage.

A. R. Orage: 'the jackboot we have taken off the German people is now on the other leg'

For Orage and his fellow commentators, one of the most disturbing consequences of the war was the way in which England appeared to have taken on many of the characteristics of the enemy country she was supposed to be fighting. If they had begun to hesitate about calling that enemy Germany, they were in no doubt that the real villain of the piece was Prussia. They were all convinced that England was emulating the Prussian model.

England's adoption of 'Prussianism' had concerned Orage for some time.[23] On 18 January 1917 he draws a parallel between the 'Prussian mind' and its English counterpart. He contends that the Germans are 'a people capable of reasoning and yet at the same time incapable of reasoning universally, that is, in a manner to appeal to a mind that is not German'. The notion that the Germans are 'incapable of reasoning universally' is unusual, since it is at odds with the early nineteenth century view of the Germans as a people 'inclined to be dreamy, whose Imperialism was the Imperialism of the air'.[24] Orage detects a similar obstinacy in the English 'wealthy classes' who object to the proposal to 'conscript wealth for

---

22   From 6 February 1919 for six weeks Orage's coveted 'Notes of the Week' were written by the theorist of the Social Credit movement C. H. Douglas.
23   See Chapter 4, pp. 129-30.
24   E. M. Forster, *Howards End* (London, 1986; Penguin edition), p. 42. This view of the Germans was also echoed by Orage's colleague J. M. Kennedy. See pp. 170-1 and Chapter 3, pp. 78-80.

the purpose of defraying the financial cost of the war'.[25] He argues that 'exactly as the Prussian mind, obsessed with its own self-importance, is incapable of applying to itself the criticisms it gives to others, the mind of our own wealthy classes is similarly blind to the inconsistency in exhorting men to give their lives while at the same time refusing even to consider the question of giving their own no less necessary money. The duty of giving your life for the nation without hope of reward has nowhere been preached with more fervour than in circles where the duty of giving your capital and income is not so much as dreamed of. And not only is this the case, but the mere mention of the proposal to apply to money the compulsion they themselves have applied to lives is enough - once more after the Prussian pattern - to provoke our wealthy classes to unreasoning abuse.' (*NA* XX, 12, p. 265)

Four months later Orage again reflects on the transformation of England into a state run along Prussian lines. On 17 May 1917 he perceives in the workforce 'a disposition not far removed from despair' caused by 'the prolongation of the war beyond any period imagined by the Government, the strain of overwork during all that time, the experience of the kind of legislation thought necessary to keep Labour working and in order, the defection of its leaders, the rise in prices, the maintenance of profiteering'. He argues that 'there is neither unpatriotism in the mind of Labour, nor the smallest disposition to withdraw from the war, nor the slightest willingness to fail their brothers and sons who are fighting on land and sea. On the contrary, there is unanimity among them, both in public and private, that Prussianism must be destroyed'. The real criminals are 'our capitalist and governing classes', who, 'as the price of destroying Prussianism abroad, are insisting upon establishing Prussianism at home'. He defines Prussianism as 'as state of mind as well as a system', consisting in 'the subordination of a nation to the dominion of a class, whether it be, as in Prussia, in military or, as it is in this country, in economic matters'. In Prussia 'the individual is subordinated to the glory of the Prussian military caste body and soul', whereas in England 'the body and soul of Labour are subordinated to the English capitalist classes for profit'. Both systems use similar means: 'every German is required to sacrifice himself to an end in which as an individual he will never share: and to bear all the burden of a policy destined to glorify the ruling caste at his expense. British Labour, likewise, is called upon to make every sacrifice, while British capital is being not merely spared any sacrifice whatever, but carefully encouraged to add to itself even by means of the most disastrous war

---

25   Orage returned to the subject of the 'conscription of wealth' later that year when he argued that 'the resistance of the wealthy to the conscription of wealth is the pacifism of capitalism'. (1 November 1917; *NA* XXII, 1, p. 19)

ever known to history'. Once Labour perceives this, there could be 'a catastrophe as great as the war itself'. Orage contends that the only way to avert a catastrophe of this nature is to abolish the wage system and profiteering. The elimination of profits would signify 'a revolution in our industrial system'. Unless this happens there is 'no prospect of industrial peace after the war'. He believes that there is 'a divinity in the war that will not permit England to win while the evil of profiteering remains with us. The accursed thing must be removed; our wealthy classes must strip themselves of all their economic privileges; we must become an economic as well as a political democracy before we can dare to pray to be proved superior to our present enemies.' (*NA* XXI, 3, p. 51)

Even with 'Prussianism' abroad apparently defeated, Orage sees his worst fears about his own country confirmed. When discussing the peace negotiations at Versailles, he reveals that he is convinced that the war has changed England into a state modelled on Prussia. In his disillusion he observes succinctly that 'the jackboot we have taken off the German people is now on the other leg'. England has 'adopted conscription both for the Army and for the Navy; we have increased the burden of our colonial responsibilities; we have been confirmed in our Imperialism. The war to end war, which has resulted for Germany in an ability to make war, has resulted for us in an obligation to be prepared for war in every quarter of the world. A tribe can hardly engage in a scuffle in any part of the world but we must be on the strain lest it should jeopardise our precarious balance of power. For every penny our rulers extracted from our labour to spend on "Empire" before the war, we must consent in future to spend a pound. The whole burden hitherto borne by the German people will have fallen upon us, to add its weight to a load already crushing'. He concludes despairingly that 'we, the victors, have assumed the yoke which bound the German people, and from which we have delivered them'. (15 May 1919; *NA* XXV, 3, pp. 33-4)

Indeed, what Orage terms 'Prussianism at home' forms a regular theme of his articles in 1919. He is convinced that the German people 'have gained rather than lost by the war' - not in terms of material possessions or worldly power, but 'in all that makes social life worth living; and one of these days they will be counting their blessings the war has brought them'. By contrast, the English, 'the declared and triumphing victors, have so far no more than the empty dreams and trappings of victory as the spoils of war'. Germany has been relieved of autocracy, Prussianism and militarism, yet the English 'have added these burdens to our former load and are now, in fact, in imminent danger of becoming all that Prussia was'. Whilst Germany has 'every inducement and reason to become the first orderly Socialist commonwealth in the world, to the infinite happiness and welfare of all her people, the lot of the English people appears to be more than ever that of bond-slaves to the capitalist and militarist oligarchy which now feels itself secure beyond its dreams'. He is in no doubt that the war 'that was to have created among us a brotherhood of liberty, justice and equality has dug deeper the old gulfs between the possessing and the working classes.' (10 July 1919; *NA* XXV, 11, p. 173)

Germans 'are men even if they are possessed by a collective madness'

Although Orage sees the destruction of Prussianism as a valid war aim, he is more cautious when discussing Germany as a whole, reminding his readers that Germans deserve to be treated as human beings. On 3 May 1917 he praises the *Times Literary Supplement* for acknowledging that 'Germans are men even if they are possessed by a collective madness; and we are to assure them that when their fit is over we shall treat them again as men rather than as madmen. This view, besides being obviously wise - for the alternative, as we have pointed out before, is a war of extermination - has ample immediate evidence, and evidence, too, which accumulates from day to day'. He suggests that 'the people of Germany are much the same as ourselves with only, perhaps, these differences in their favour: that they are somewhat less of a mere population and more of a people; and that we *can* be driven to a rebellion. How soon, however, we may be deprived of these distinctions nobody can say; but when they are gone our superiority will have gone with them'. It is only 'under the provocation of popular fear and Prussian ambition' that 'our wretched German cousins' have become 'temporarily bestial and insane'. Under normal circumstances the difference in character between the English and the Germans is 'trivial'. Because of this affinity, reprisals and acts of revenge against the Germans 'ought at once to be foresworn.' (*NA* XXI, 1, pp. 1-2)

Prince Lichnowsky: 'the man who first broke the evil spell that has been cast on Germany'

Early in 1918, Orage's confidence in the German people is boosted by the publication in a Swedish journal of Prince Lichnowsky's *Memorandum* (21 March 1918; *NA* XXII, 21, p. 405). When it was published, this document by the former German Ambassador to London caused a stir in both England and Germany. Lichnowsky's account of the diplomatic exchanges between Berlin and London up to August 1914, including details of Germany's encouragement of a harsh Austrian policy against Serbia in order to provoke Russia, as well as the charge that the German government ignored diplomatic advice, firmly placed the guilt for the war on Germany.[26] After reading the *Memorandum*, Thomas Mann

---

26   T. J. Reed, *Thomas Mann. The Uses of Tradition* (Oxford, 1974), p. 212.

was prompted to attempt further intellectual juggling in his *Betrachtungen eines Unpolitischen* by claiming that Germany had restrained Austria, yet England had not tried to restrain Russia, and dismissing Lichnowsky as a product of the Enlightenment, an *Aufklärer*, who would succeed only in disheartening the German people.[27] By contrast, Orage feels sure that Lichnowsky will receive 'an honourable mention in history as the man who first broke the evil spell that has been cast on Germany'. He argues that 'never again during the rest of the war, however long it may last, will it be possible to aggravate in Germany the hatred felt for this country in particular. With every reading of his *Memorandum* by the honest men still left in Germany, their present hatred of us, founded, as it has been, on lies, will tend to give place to a sense of having wronged us, and to a wish to repair their faults. This change of heart in the German people is now as inevitable as it appeared to some of us only a few weeks ago to be improbable. Their eyes are about to be opened. They are to see what most of the world has already seen, that the conduct of foreign affairs cannot be left in the hands of an irresponsible set of militarist criminals without entailing the most appalling consequences. They are, moreover, to see that in all Europe as it existed before the war there was but one clique and one monarch that sought war - the Kaiser and his Junkers.' (11 April 1918; *NA* XX, 24, p. 461)

Allied war aims: to defeat 'the attempt of Militarism to strangle Democracy in the cradle'

Because it was the Kaiser and his Junkers who sought war, Orage believes that if the fighting is to achieve anything, its main aim must be to rid Germany of its militarist Prussian system. As early as 5 July 1917 he observes that any proposal to 'impose peace upon Germany' following 'a military victory over Prussia' will defeat 'the Prussian military caste' temporarily, but could also pave the way for its revival. This sort of peace is precisely the type that President Wilson 'entered the war to avert'. He warns that in the ashes of such a peace 'will remain the live embers of future wars'. A peace that 'leaves the Prussian system intact, though momentarily defeated, can only be regarded as a truce' which will soon be broken. If the war is being fought to protect small democracies, he doubts whether small democracies will be safe after the armistice, if the peace terms allow Prussia to rise again. He warns that 'the hair of Samson will certainly grow again even in prison; and sooner or later militarist Prussia will pull down civilisation once more about our ears'. He rejects the pacifist line of peace at any price as 'short-sighted': although an unpopular approach in 1917, he favours instead a prolonged war, if it will eliminate the threat of Prussia in the future. He

---

27   Ibid., pp. 212-13.

argues that the Allies must regard Germany as 'a dual power, one of whose members is militarist and hostile, against whom we are, therefore, in arms; but the second of these members is the German people, now hostile but potentially friendly, with whom our relations should be diplomatic'. To this end of converting Germany 'from militarist to democratic sentiment we ought to address ourselves with as much care as we are bestowing militarily upon Prussia - for it is ridiculous to imagine that diplomacy is less in need of organisation than war'. He reflects that history 'will view this war as the attempt of Militarism to strangle Democracy in the cradle'. According to Orage, a 'highly developed, powerful and efficient Militarism' is at war with an 'underdeveloped, weak and apathetic Democracy'. He warns that Democracy must decide quickly between two courses: either 'to become militarist and therein die', or 'to become a socialised commonwealth, and therewith to become adult, powerful, intelligent'. (*NA* XXI, 10, pp. 217-19)

One of the anomalies of Germany, according to Orage, is the way in which leading members of its intelligentsia adhere to right-wing politics, yet in their youth espoused more liberal ideals. He contends that 'it is practically true to say that every young and intelligent German has always been a democrat and even a republican. Bismarck and Treitschke both started life as republicans, and the latter, we believe, was publicly fêted in Paris for his republican principles'. He ascribes the change in their views to the fact that 'Prussia was a "success", and by virtue of her success she was always able to present to every talented German the alternative between democracy and exile, and autocracy and honour. Under these circumstances, men being what we know them to be, what else was to be expected of a people thus shepherded but the appearance of connivance with their Prussian rulers?' In other words, it was inevitable that, 'so long as Prussia promised success the German people would appear to be enthusiastic in following Prussia's lead.' (6 September 1917; *NA* XXI, 19, pp. 397-8)

Prussia at war: 'with kultur in one hand and a bomb in the other'

On 28 February 1918 Orage devotes 'Notes of the Week' to the whole question of Germany and the war. He indicates that the war aims of both the Allies and the Central Powers have changed in the wake of Lenin's Bolshevik revolution. The object of Prussia, rather than Germany, is 'unmistakably clear': it is 'to obtain an unfettered freedom to exploit the Slav peoples for the purpose, first, of dominating Europe and, afterwards, of dominating the world'. In an argument not wholly consistent with his comments on England becoming 'Prussianised',[28] he reasons that this, 'having now proved to be the aboriginal

---

28   See pp. 164-7.

purpose of the war', shows not only 'that Prussia is alone responsible for the war', but also that 'the Allies have no other commensurate object but defence'. They must defend 'the liberty of Europe and the world against the domination of Prussia'. The fear of Prussian domination, he cautions us, is no 'mere bogey' for 'the Wolf is at our doors; and between us and it stand only our armies and our wits'. He explains that 'hitherto we have experienced war for glory, war for adventure, war for trade, war for security; but never before have we encountered the spirit of war as a duty and for power'. Both elements enter into what he calls 'the Prussian cult of war'. It is war for power because 'only by perpetually striving after increased power can the spirit of militarism be kept alive'. It is also war as a duty because 'Prussia has come to regard herself as the predestined pioneer of a new world-civilisation - the civilisation of German *kultur*'. From this point of vantage Prussia looks upon the rest of the world, as an object of 'pity and contempt' that 'a superior race must simultaneously exploit and educate. With *kultur* in one hand and a bomb in the other, Prussia thereupon proceeds to attempt, first, to subject us, and afterwards she would attempt to improve us, the one thing being the means to the other'. These notions of superiority and duty give rise to the 'easy conscience with which Prussia has committed any and every crime in the pursuit of civilising the world'. He contends that 'the *kultur* which Prussia means to impose upon the world is assumed to be of such benefice that it will amply compensate and justify all the crimes committed in compelling the world to accept it'. He rejects the notion that the rest of Europe provocatively encircled Germany and goaded the Central Powers into fighting what the Viennese zealot in *Die letzten Tage der Menschheit* (1915-19) calls a 'holy war of defence'.[29] Orage dismisses this as a myth 'invented by Prussia as a means of inducing the German people to submit to militarism'. The German people are now defending 'nothing more than the attempt of their Prussian masters to dominate Europe and the world'. He goes so far as to distinguish 'Prussian Imperialism', which is 'a world-menace', from British and other Imperialisms, which are 'merely troublesome'. (*NA* XXII, 18, pp. 341-4)

J. M. Kennedy, writing under the pseudonym S. Verdad in his 'Foreign Affairs' column, also prefers to single out Prussia for abuse. On 18 January 1917, in an article which draws a clear distinction between Prussia and the southern German states and Austria, he claims that in 1914 there existed a 'genuine feeling of regret on both sides that it should have been necessary for England and Austria to meet in the field as enemies'. England always had 'a considerable amount of sympathy for Austria', yet without Austria-Hungary as an ally, he alleges in a dubious argument, 'it would have been impossible for

---

29   See Karl Kraus, *Die letzten Tage der Menschheit* (Zürich, 1945), I, 1, pp. 55-6.

Germany to carry on the war for a week'. Austria has augmented the German forces by 'at least five million men' and only by forming an alliance with Germany has she convinced Turkey and Bulgaria to side with Germany. Nevertheless, he still hopes to see Austria 'at the head of a South German combination - say with Bavaria and Saxony, and even with Baden, subject to the guarantees of non-interference demanded by the Allies'. He argues that it was only fear of attack that 'impelled Austria to seek Prussian protection after the Berlin Conference nearly forty years ago'. He alleges that 'the ill-feeling between the northern and southern Germanic countries was pronounced even before the war; and nothing but the faith in combination as a means of mutual protection could have led to its maintenance for so long. This belief was based first and foremost on the military power of Prussia; and when that is shattered, the moral as well as the political value of the alliance necessarily disappears.' (*NA* XX, 12, p. 268)

Kennedy returns to the theme of the different characteristics of the German nation when discussing Hermann Fernau's *The Coming Democracy*, which argues that the root of Germany's problem lies with 'a century of intellectual drilling'. Kennedy is prompted to comment that it is not only German professors who have been 'intellectually drilled', but the whole nation as well. He is convinced that 'the ideas initiated by Hegel', and developed by modern-day exponents, such as General Bernhardi and the historian Treitschke, 'have been instilled into the mass of the people with such skill and assiduity that every crackpot theory of Germany's immeasurable superiority to the rest of mankind is implicity believed in as an article of national and even religious faith. And the dynasty is now, as it has ever been, the foundation, the rallying point, the "granite rock", on which these principles of German superiority, of German culture, rest'. Nevertheless, the defects of modern Germany are 'utterly opposed' to the 'spirit of the German people'. Kennedy argues that 'we have known the Germans, by tradition, as solid if somewhat heavy thinkers; as scholars, plodding and accumulative rather than displaying brilliancy and initiative; as musicians; as historians; as poets; as the possessors of simple national songs remarkable for their emphasis on the domestic virtues - and on the virtues of good wine and unlimited food - rather than as the blond beasts of a later period who devote themselves systematically to brutality and crime, whether in peace or in war'. According to Kennedy, the modern German is what his Prussian ruler, acting through his mainly Prussian professors, has made him. (13 September 1917; *NA* XXI, 20, pp. 420-2)

Any man expecting a revolution in Germany 'should have had his mind inquired into'

Britain's wartime alliance with Russia was never an easy one. A pre-war distrust of the Russian autocratic system lingered on and was complicated by fears that figures influential in the Tsarist regime were biased in favour of Germany. On 11 January 1917, for example, Kennedy maintains that the death of Rasputin is a signal that 'the real disappearance of German influence in Russia' has begun, and argues that 'Liberal Russia' always opposed Rasputin's German influences (*NA* XX, 11, p. 244). Kerensky's revolution was therefore welcomed as further evidence of the rise of liberalism and the defeat of German influence in Russia. There were hopes that German radicals would look to revolution as a means of removing the Hohenzollerns from power and bringing the war to an end. Thus, on 22 March 1917, with revolution presenting itself as a viable means of ending the war, Orage confidently predicts that the Russian Revolution will have repercussions in Germany, even though 'the German people are less out of love with Prussianism than the Russian intelligentsia has been with Tsardom'. Germany is unique in that there 'the intellectuals have actually been the agents and the tools of the autocracy.' (*NA* XX, 21, p. 483)

However, Lenin's Bolshevik revolution, which ousted the more moderate Kerensky and his supporters and ultimately stopped Russia from fighting alongside France and England, aroused more ambivalent feelings amongst those who had hoped for revolution in Germany, but had come to fear the extremes of Bolshevism. On 11 July 1918 J. M. Kennedy attacks the Bolsheviks for having 'displayed such astounding ignorance that their opinions are not worth the paper on which the Brest-Litovsk Treaty was written'. He criticises the judgement of Lenin and Trotsky, who entered peace negotiations with Germany, although it was known that the Germans were determined to exact peace terms unfavourable to Russia. Both Lenin and Trotsky had lived in Germany and 'were perfectly familiar (or should have been) with the conditions there'. The Treaty of Brest-Litovsk effectively quashed all hopes a victory for liberalism in Germany. Kennedy concludes pessimistically that 'any man who thought, after the Russian collapse, that there would be a revolution in Germany, should have had his mind inquired into.' (*NA* XXIII, 11, p. 165)

Germany facing 'the choice between revolution and perpetual war'

Despite Kennedy's pessimism, Orage clung on to hopes of the German Social Democrats leading an uprising against Prussia. On 4 April 1918 he plainly states that the only path open to the German Social Democrats is revolution. He contends that while 'the world will never submit to a Prussian hegemony, though it may cost a century of world-war to escape it, there is also before the German people only the choice between revolution and perpetual war'. Although the 'political reputation of the German people' is disgraced, if the revolution comes soon 'much will be forgiven a people who should spare by their exertions the efforts of the coming generation'. He argues that 'the world is not engaged in the present war with any hope of advantage either to civilisation, culture, or, still less, to capitalism. The simple truth is that the world is engaged in the war for the purely negative advantage of saving its liberty and of avoiding the return of itself into the dark ages from which it has so recently emerged after a previous catastrophe. Under these circumstances it cannot be the case, therefore, that we should fail to welcome a new Ally if that Ally were to be the German people. On the contrary, we can truthfully say that no new Ally, not even the military defeat of Prussia, could be more welcome; for, in the end, it is not so much the defeat of Prussia that the world desires as the regeneration of Germany.' (*NA* XXII, 23, p. 446)

German Social Democrats: the only 'section that has not yet been hopelessly ingrained with Prussian theories'

Orage consistently looks to the German Social Democrats as the hope for the future of Germany. As early as 16 August 1917 he discusses the need for the Allies to open talks with 'the *only* section of opinion in Germany with whom a permanent peace is thinkable', namely the Socialist section. He argues that the 'Prussian ruling caste, the professional classes, are all of them autocrats and militarists dyed in the wool. A peace with them to-day would be imperilled to-morrow and break out into war the day after. Two generations of intense and isolated meditation upon power have robbed them even of the capacity of entertaining the notion of democratic liberty. The sword may be struck from their hand at this moment, but they will resume it at the dictation of their thoughts to-morrow, or upon the first opportunity'. Peace with the present rulers of Germany is therefore impossible. He concludes that 'our only hope is in establishing relations with the section that has not yet been hopelessly ingrained with Prussian theories; with, in short, the German Socialist and democratic parties.' (*NA* XXI, 16, p. 338)

Looking forward to 'the democratisation of Germany'

In supporting the German Socialists, Orage hoped that they might bring about 'the democratisation of Germany, with or without a military victory' as 'the *only* condition of permanent peace' and 'the *only* security for democracies everywhere'. It is 'the *only* condition under which any one of the various plans for keeping Prussianism under can possibly succeed - whether they be military plans, economic plans, plans of arbitration, league of nations, disarmament, or what not'. Without the democratisation of Germany 'no plan for pressing peace is worth more than the value of the paper it is written on. Peace will depend upon a scrap of paper'. He concedes that 'it does not take a prophet to foresee that from a "patched-up" peace there must result the permanent militarisation of Europe; by which we mean, to be exact, the retention permanently, in more or less their present form, of measures of conscription, protection, the censorship, espionage, registration, compulsory arbitration, together with the addition of new measures - State-controlled education, for example'. A 'peace with the Prussian caste' is 'a patched-up peace'. He defines the aim of autocracy as power, the aim of democracy as liberty, arguing that Russia's 'direction of endeavour has been changed by the revolution from power to liberty', therefore 'a good half of the popular excuse for Germany's "defensive" war has been got rid of. Not even the most nervous of Germans can pretend any longer that he cannot sleep o' nights for the Russian peril. The Allies have now only to prove that there is no peril to Germany from the western world to rob German popular opinion of its last excuse for a "defensive" war.' (15 November 1917; *NA* XXII, 3, pp. 42-3)

Despite his hopes of seeing the democratisation of Germany, Orage was far from convinced by the cosmetic changes in October 1918 that apparently transformed Germany into a democracy. On 10 October 1918 he reflects that 'the appointment of Prince Max of Baden as Chancellor, the inclusion of Socialists in his government, the terms of his inaugural speech and the fact that he declared himself the spokesman for the majority in the Reichstag, will all be taken as they are designed as evidence in Germany of the democratisation and reasonably pacific intentions of the German Government'. However, not only is Prince Max a Hohenzollern, but 'both his government and his policy are the express creation of the will of the Kaiser acting in concert with the German General Staff'. The new government, far from being the 'creation of the German people', is 'the deliberately created instrument of the powers that governed Germany before the war and that govern Germany still'. Furthermore, the policy outlined by the new Chancellor, is 'little more than the continuation in its main features of the policy laid down by the preceding and militarist Chancellors'. By entering what Orage calls 'the militarist-capitalist Government of Prussia', the German Socialists 'have committed a crime even greater than when they voted supplies for the invasion of Belgium'. The German Socialists are 'now about to be responsible for the collapse of German Socialism; but with German Socialism finally gone, there will be no nucleus left in Germany with which the world can make peace' (*NA* XXIII, 24, pp. 373-5). According to Orage, only the minority Socialists, such as the Socialist theorist Karl Kautsky (1854-1938) and the Spartacist leader Karl Liebknecht (1871-1919), are worthy of praise. 'No German Government', he cautions rather unrealistically, 'can be said to be "safe for democracy" that contains a single Pan-German or that excludes a single minority Socialist.' (17 October 1918; *NA* XXIII, 25, p. 390)

Orage's admiration for Karl Kautsky remained undiminished, although by 1919 he sought to distance himself from the extremes of Liebknecht's Spartacus League. On 30 January 1919, having assumed the pen-name S. Verdad to continue Kennedy's 'Foreign Affairs' column, he denounces the Spartacists as 'the German Bolshevists'. Instead, he accords great respect to Kautsky, under whose guidance 'the Revolution in Germany has been carried out - and will continue, I think, to be carried out - with comparative sanity and humanity'. He commends Kautsky as one of the Germans to have most successfully 'managed to keep their heads cool during the revolution' by providing the thinking behind the revolt and staying 'behind the scenes directing the actors'. Orage admires him 'unreservedly' for thinking that 'only a bloodless revolution is a permanent and real revolution'. According to Orage, had Kautsky's advice been taken by the Spartacus League, 'not only would the Spartacists have escaped useless slaughter, but they would have lived to fight another day - in another way'. Orage praises Kautsky, who, along with the theorists in the *New Age*, considers economic revolution more important than political revolution, and who criticises the Spartacists for seeking only to destroy the existing order. It is 'a revolution against and not for something that they are attempting to engineer. Their plan appears to stoke the fires of destruction to such a heat that the pot will boil, and then to watch for the new society to issue from the fumes. What, however, that new society is, the Spartacists have kept secret, even from themselves'. The probable consequences of a Spartacist success in Germany, Orage cautions, would be 'the destruction of German industry, and the inevitable destruction of the German proletariat', followed by 'a re-declaration of war upon the Allies.' (*NA* XXIV, 13, p. 204)

Armistice: exchanging 'the black flag of militarism' for 'the white flag of surrender'

On 14 November 1918 Orage, in jubilant mood, welcomes 'the democratisation of Germany' as 'an accomplished fact' since 'the black flag of militarism' has been exchanged for 'the white flag of surrender'. He reminds his readers that the Allies should show 'no reluctance in receiving the returning prodigal son of Europe' because 'militarist Germany has ceased to be a menace to the world, while, at the same time, a completely democratised Germany in which the German has prevailed over the Hun, has become for Europe, at any rate, an indispensable factor in the reconstruction of the continent. The relief derived from the disappearance of Prussianism is of little greater value than the assistance Europe needs in the work of reconstruction from the new German democracy. As certainly as it was impossible for Europe to live with Prussianism in her midst, so certainly will it be impossible for Europe to prosper without the willing co-operation of the German people'. He argues that the German Socialist party is different from its English counterpart, which 'has always been jealous of admitting educated men into its governing ranks'. By contrast, the German Socialist leaders 'number among them half a score and more of the ablest men in Germany; and the party has almost a monopoly of the democratic brains of the Empire'. Thus, 'we need not anticipate for Germany the welter of chaos which the Bolshevist revolution in Russia has caused'. The Bolshevists, he observes, implemented 'the subordination of skilled Labour (including brain-power) to unskilled Labour'. However, in Germany 'with the example of Russia before their eyes, the German people, unless driven madly into it, may be counted upon to adopt every precaution against the bloody orgies of the Bolshevist dictatorship of the unskilled proletariat. Under favouring circumstances, indeed, we do not see why the German Revolution should not be almost a model of order, and therewith provide Europe not only with relief from Prussianism but with a new hope for democracy.' (*NA* XXIV, 2, pp. 17-18)

Orage is in no doubt that Bolshevism and Prussianism 'arise from similar fallacies, and with the end of the one the fear of the other may be said to be eliminated. Prussianism, it is obvious, has as its intellectual principle the false absolute implied in the proposition that Might is the *only* creator of Right. Because Might is one of the invariable factors of Right - perhaps the only invariable factor - our Prussian philosophers concluded that it was the sole factor; it became their one and only, their unique, their dogma. But similarly it is no less obvious that the Bolshevist fallacy is its consanguinity with Prussianism. Because Labour (manual Labour we should say) is an invariable factor in production - and, perhaps, the only invariable factor - the Bolshevist mind concludes that it is the one and only factor, the unique, the sole. And from this proposition it would follow that manual Labour is entitled to everything as from the Prussian proposition is followed that Might was entitled to everything'. However, Orage rejects the suggestion that Bolshevism might take root in Germany on the grounds that Prussianism has just been exposed. He views the new Germany in highly optimistic terms: 'she will emerge different from the war, unrecognisably different in many respects, but wiser. To begin with, the excorcism of the Prussian militarist incubus will alone prove to have given release to the latent and hitherto suppressed or distorted powers of the German mind. Having undergone a terrible course of psychoanalysis, she will in all probability find herself proportionally both cured and renewed'. He anticipates that this process will involve 'the removal of the Russian "menace", the probable re-union of German Austria with Germany proper, the re-establishment this time on a popular basis, of German national unity, the creation of a new order and a new personnel of government, and the fresh democratic and perhaps Socialist impetus. It is true that for some years to come the new Germany will be burdened with debt and with obligations involved in the legacy of the past; but relatively we are of the opinion that these will be no greater than a renewed nation can easily bear, above all, when she is inspired with a fresh hope'. He predicts that Germany, as a 'democratic, pacific and disciplined' country, 'planted in the middle of the Continent and surrounded for the most part by Russia and a series of young and ill-disciplined states', will be able to exercise a moderating influence on her neighbours. (21 November 1918; *NA* XXIV, 3, p. 34)

Europe in 1919: 'the cessation of war has not brought peace'

However, Orage's high hopes for the regeneration of Germany were soon dashed. On 27 March 1919 he reflects bitterly that 'the cessation of war has not brought peace'. He contends that the Allies' treatment of Germany is wrong: their policy is only adding to the problems of their defeated foe. The policy being pursued at Versailles causes 'fresh problems to arise every day' and makes 'the problems of yesterday appear to be as nothing in comparison with the prospective problems of tomorrow'. Although France has every right to demand security against 'the repetition of a crime that has decimated her population', the security measures now under discussion strike Orage as being 'rather provocation than safety'. Germany, he observes, is to cede 'considerable slices of her former territories. All her colonies are either withdrawn completely or in tutelage to the League of Nations, and, in addition to this, an indemnity spread, we are told, over half a century'. He reasons that 'only the most pusillanimous or magnanimous of nations could endure to be treated in this fashion after even the greatest of crimes; and only commanding Powers of implacable militarism could avail to force and maintain such treatment upon her. But is Germany either one or the other? And are the Western Powers disposed to turn permanently militarist in order to accomplish this design?' This policy is 'swiftly and surely' convincing Germany that 'there is no salvation in the West for her, and that her only hope lies in a communion of desperate misery with Russia.' (*NA* XXIV, 21, pp. 333-4)

The actual terms of the Treaty of Versailles arouse Orage's deepest suspicion. He observes quite rightly that 'hatred and distrust and fear of Germany are to be found in almost every line of the terms. And since upon a peace of hate it is impossible to build a peace of justice, the pillars of the present peace are certain to moulder and crumble away and to bring down war upon the individual once more'. In this perceptive article he reflects that 'the parties in the war-controversy have exchanged roles. Before and during the war, the patriots were right in demanding the defeat of Germany, as the pacifists were wrong in objecting to it. To-day the patriots were wrong in demanding the destruction of Germany, while the pacifists are right in protesting against it. Unfortunately, however, the prestige acquired by the two parties by their attitude to the war allows the former to be supported and followed now that they are wrong, and the

177

latter to be repudiated as generally now that they are right as when they are wrong. The pacifists indeed, have done nothing for Germany': they have only made the war more bitter and the peace more difficult. He likens the Germans' position over the Treaty of Versailles to that of the Russians over the Treaty of Brest-Litovsk: they have no option but to sign. He accuses the statesmen of having bowed to popular pressure and 'imposed terms of perpetual slavery upon a people that had just cast off militarism and twenty-two kings along with it', although he concedes that without the moderating influence of the politicians the peace terms might have been even harsher. (22 May 1919; *NA* XXV, 4, pp. 53-4)

J. M. Kennedy: 'a bit of a mystery-monger, if not a downright mystery-man'

When J. M. Kennedy died in the autumn of 1918, apparently from overwork at the age of thirty two, Orage assumed the role of S. Verdad to continue the column 'Foreign Affairs'. Curiously, Orage only acknowledges that Kennedy frequently acted as his 'deputy' in this column, when it would appear that Orage only contributed to the column from 1917 onwards, after it ceased to be a weekly feature. Instead, in an obituary note Orage emphasises the contribution Kennedy made under his own name and, latterly under the pseudonym Leighton J. Warnock, although Warnock was responsible for only a handful of articles. (7 November 1918; *NA* XXIV, 1, p. 4)

Kennedy remains something of a mystery figure. Some alleged that he was a government spy, whilst others argued that Orage deliberately circulated rumours that his foreign affairs correspondent had a direct link with the Foreign Office.[30] He left mixed impressions on his fellow contributors at the *New Age*: C. E. Bechhofer remembers him only as 'a fat squeaky man who lived with his mother',[31] whilst Paul Selver is more charitable, recalling that he 'immoderately envied' Kennedy, 'an affable bachelor', who had published books and lived comfortably in a pleasant flat in Bloomsbury. Selver concedes that some people swore that Kennedy 'went round ransacking the contents of waste-paper baskets in foreign embassies and legations', although he personally regards 'this statement, at least, as blatant slander'.[32] Nevertheless, Selver calls Kennedy 'a bit of a mystery-monger, if not a downright mystery-man'. Some said he was an *agent-provocateur*, although Selver argues that if he had been, 'some of the unorthodox remarks on the conduct of the war which were bandied about as a regular thing in the office of the *New Age* would assuredly have produced

---

30   Philippe Mairet, *A. R. Orage: A Memoir* (London, 1936), p. 61.
31   16 November 1949; quoted by Antony Alpers, *The Life of Katherine Mansfield* (London, 1980), p. 114.
32   Paul Selver, *Orage and the New Age Circle* (London, 1959), p. 20.

untoward results'.[33]   When he died his mother gave his private papers to Orage who, with typical concern for individual privacy, destroyed them.[34]   Perhaps the most tantalising comment comes from Beatrice Hastings, who claims that the mystery lies with Kennedy's diaries. Orage wrote to her, presumably after 1918, to say that 'he had gone through Kennedy's papers and discovered that he 'had been betraying the *New Age* for years'.[35]

G. K. Chesterton: 'Prussia like prussic acid; its poisonous essence is a fact'

By assuming the role of S. Verdad after Kennedy's death, Orage was able to write under another pseudonym for his contributions to the *New Age*. This proved particularly useful when he became embroiled with G. K. Chesterton in a heated debate on the rabid Germanophobic views expressed in the latter's periodical, the *New Witness*. The argument, which began at the end of 1917, occupied much space in both the *New Age* and the *New Witness*, and ran into 1919. Although attacks on Chesterton's anti-German outbursts always appeared in S. Verdad's column, when replying in the *New Witness* Chesterton always acknowledges Orage, not Kennedy, as his critic.

Criticism of Germany, particularly Prussia, made by the *New Age* seems tame when compared with some of the vitriolic insults hurled by Chesterton in the *New Witness*. During the course of six months in 1917 alone, Chesterton derides the *Cambridge Magazine* for associating with Bertrand Russell and G. Lowes Dickinson and 'for its defence of the views held by these and other notable pro-Germans' that excites only abhorrence 'among all decent men' (3 May 1917; *NW* X, 235, p. 7). He dismisses the pacifist E. D. Morel as 'the supporter of the Prussian Government' (28 June 1917; *NW* X, 243, p. 198). Prussia, Chesterton roars, is 'like prussic acid; its poisonous essence is a fact, not a theory; and all other theories are labels printed on a bottle' (23 August 1917; *NW* X, 251, p. 387). In an unsigned article, probably by Chesterton, anti-Semitism is combined with Germanophobia to explain 'Why the Jews are Pro-German' (11 October 1917; *NW* X, 258, pp. 561-2). Chesterton, as editor, was equally keen that his contributors produce scathing attacks on the Germans. Edith Nesbit, for example, easily matches some of his own wild assumptions when she argues that 'to cast out the Hohenzollerns and make friends with the German people is as though we should hang Frankenstein and embrace the monster which he has made. The German Emperor set out to make, out of simple, homely, kindly

---

33   Ibid., p. 20.
34   Antony Alpers, op. cit., p. 142.
35   Beatrice Hastings, *The Old 'New Age'. Orage - and others* (London, 1936), p. 22.

peoples, a monster that should devour all good and gentle things, and sprawl diseased and infectious across a blighted world. With almost incredible valour and sacrifice we have fought this monster, and barred its way. We are fighting it, we are driving it back. William of Hohenzollern set out to make that black beast, and for that he deserves a thousand deaths: but he not only set out to create a monster; he did create it'. President Wilson may say that his quarrel is with the Hohenzollerns, not the German people, but, according to Edith Nesbit, the Allies' 'quarrel is with the German people, as well as with the Kaiser; with the Monster, as well as with its maker.' (17 May 1917; *NW* X, 237, p. 60)

Chesterton and the New Witness: seeking 'to merely vilify the Prussians'

Given some of the startling opinions expressed in the *New Witness*, it is little wonder that Orage, as S. Verdad, cautions Chesterton that it is 'useless to merely vilify the Prussians' or 'to declare that they must be exterminated like rats before peace can reign'. He points out that, quite aside from the fact that 'extermination is impossible', there are 'even some Prussian traditions and institutions - a judiciary even less corrupt than our own, a love of scientific knowledge for its own sake, a general disregard for wealth among officials who labour for the benefit of the State - which are too good and rare in the world to be destroyed. If the ruling classes have misapplied these virtues and traditions, that is neither here nor there for the moment. The point is, when the Prussian military system, with all that it connotes in morality, religion, and politics is at length shattered on the battlefield, what do you propose to put in its place? For upon that depends the future liberty of Europe, and not merely of England'. He argues that 'no reasonable man could ask or command another merely to destroy, unless the substitute for the thing destroyed were instinctively, if not rationally, understood. On one point the Allies were agreed when they started to resist Germany, and that was that henceforth all nations, large and small, should be free to dispose of their own destiny, under the recognised public law of the world. This formula, vague though it may appear, was better than nothing; it was an idea against an idea; but in time it became crystallised into something much more definite. It was easy even for people who did not take a very great interest in foreign affairs to notice that German aggression sprang from the German military caste and its civic connections, and that the German military caste had enormous power, because it was autocratic and not representative. Therefore, the demand of the Allies, expressed in varying ways and in varying degrees of emphasis, gradually became this: the democratisation of Germany as the most trustworthy means of ensuring representation in Germany, and, consequently, the very high probability (I say no more) of preventing Germans from undertaking another war.' (1 November 1917; *NA* XXII, 1, p. 4)

To his credit, Chesterton replied in full to the criticism levelled at him by the *New Age*, and the debate went on between the two journals for the rest of 1917. The argument resurfaced the following year, when, on 8 November 1918, in the first of four articles entitled 'At the World's End', Chesterton argues that 'if the Germans relapsed into literal barbarism, into a vague world of tribes with totems and tribal chiefs, I should think that better than Prussianism. If Germany broke up again into small kingdoms, with petty but omnipotent kings, I should think that much better than Prussianism. Even if, like some tragically unfortunate peoples, the Germans came to be ruled by sham representatives who were really the lackeys of the oldest type of Capitalist, if there were no cause but a caucus and no caucus without a millionaire, even if, above all, it had the brazen hypocrisy to call such system Democracy; I should still think this better than Prussianism. For I think it better to worship birds and beasts than to worship demons; better to be governed by childish caprices than by wrinkled perversions; better to be ruled even by men so uneducated as our last crop of barons and viscounts than by men exclusively educated in evil'. Unlike Orage, Chesterton does not want to see a new Germany but one based on past values because 'the rudiment of good Germanism is in the past; in those southern elements softened by French and Italian culture, and retaining only the natural and innocent proportion of native German fancy. What is the matter with modern Germany is that *Kultur* set up a *counter-attraction* to civilisation. A new magnetic pole was found in the North; and the mind was turned from Paris and Rome'. With the aim of turning Germany backwards to its past, he is in no doubt that 'the most benevolent service to the German Empire is to dash it to pieces'. (*NW* XI, 262, pp. 34-5)

On the subject of France, Orage concurs with Chesterton that 'the maintenance and future of France are essential to civilisation; and if I were empowered to choose between the obliteration of France or Germany, I cannot conceive myself hesitating for a moment to obliterate Germany' (13 March 1919; *NA* XXIV, 19, p. 304). However, he takes Chesterton to task for 'reckoning France as the index of the European and the world situation' and forgetting the 'existence of the rest of Europe'. Orage expresses the wish that Chesterton 'were a better European, and less of a Francophile'. He contends, contrary to Chesterton's opinion, that 'it was *not* the defencelessness of France, but the prospect of the rich spoils of Slav exploitation that tempted the German military capitalist to go to war; and equally it will not be by making France impregnable to German aggression that the war can be won or lost.' (27 February 1919; *NA* XXIV, 17, p. 272)

The association of the editor of the *New Age* with Ramiro de Maeztu has been described as 'one of Orage's most important intellectual friendships, during the war period and for some time after'.[36] Beatrice Hastings complained bitterly that after she left for Paris in 1914, Orage filled the *New Age* with articles by the bilingual Spanish journalist.[37] As well as Spanish and English, the latter being his preferred language,[38] he could read French and German, tackling Nietzsche's *Also sprach Zarathustra* in the 1890s, when no Spanish translations were available.[39] In 1905 he was among the first Spanish journalists to be sent to England, reporting for the independent daily *La Correspondencia de España* - previously British news came to Spain via French newspapers.[40] During his stay in London he became acquainted with members of the Fabian Society, including Hubert Bland, Beatrice and Sydney Webb and Bernard Shaw, and in 1907 was prompted to try to explain the Fabians to his Spanish readers.[41] In addition, he expressed considerable admiration for Cecil Chesterton, whom he considered one of the few writers to perceive the need for reform.[42] By June 1914 he had become an avid reader of the *New Age*, which he had first discovered whilst browsing on a railway bookstall some years before, and described to Spanish audiences as 'a progressive journal for use by young and restless people'.[43] He was a close friend of T. E. Hulme, who exerted a profound influence on his philosophy, and probably introduced him to Orage,[44] who published his first article for the *New Age* in January 1915. From that date he contributed regularly on literary and philosophical matters. Between September and November 1916, he went to the front to observe the British at war, sending back a series of reports to both the *New Age* and the Spanish press. Orage, who was considered by de Maeztu to be

---

36   Philippe Mairet, op. cit., p. 71.
37   Beatrice Hastings, op. cit., p. 24.
38   Margaret M. Kilty, 'Ramiro de Maeztu, Journalist and Idealist' (unpublished MA Dissertation, University of Leeds, 1962), p. 9.
39   Ibid., pp. 20-1.
40   Ibid., p. 41.
41   Ibid., pp. 53-7.
42   Ibid., p. 84.
43   Quoted by Kilty, ibid., p. 61.
44   Martin Nozick, 'An Examination of Ramiro de Maeztu', *PMLA*, 69.2 (1954), pp. 723-6.

'one of the most influential minds in England',[45] valued the views of this 'outsider, who culturally at least was a Germanophile'.[46]

De Maeztu was well-versed in German philosophy. Between 1911 and 1914 he spent almost twenty months studying Kant at the University of Marburg, then the best centre for the study of the philosopher, although by 1917 he was becoming dissatisfied with Kant.[47] In his pre-war articles he had expressed admiration for Germany. Writing from Marburg in 1912, for example, he criticises English values in comparison with German, claiming 'I do not believe that English intellectual life is equal to German intellectual life'.[48] Even after the war began, he still preferred the German code of values and was duly accused of being pro-German, although he later came to criticise the German code of values.[49] As Margaret M. Kilty observes, Ramiro de Maeztu's 'attitude, his obvious allegiance to British ideals', made him an unusual war correspondent 'in view of his marked preference for German culture and philosophy'.[50]

In September 1916, Ramiro de Maeztu returned to England to marry the daughter of a professor of languages in London. He did not go back to the front after his marriage, although he continued to write on the war for Spanish publications and the *New Age*.[51] On 31 January 1918, for instance, he turns his attention to 'The Formula of the War'. He rejects the notion that the Allies are fighting to restore to France her lost provinces. Not even France, he argues, 'is fighting to redress the balance of the wrong of fifty years ago, but to defend herself against the invader. We may also go further and say that even if the question of Alsace-Lorraine were a world question, the majority of men outside France would not feel it to be so, and would consider it only a private question between two European nations'. England did not enter the war in 1914 in order to defend Belgian neutrality, or even '*merely* in defence of right', but because 'the conquest of Belgium would have proved a permanent menace to herself'. He contends that in 1918 the war is 'not being fought for the independence of the Slav nations', but because 'the balance of power in the world having been lost, Germany cannot be permitted to control the Slav races, for if she succeeds, there will be no means in a few years of preventing her becoming the master of the world.' (*NA* XXII, 14, pp. 266-7)

---

45   Quoted by Margaret M. Kilty, op. cit., p. 65.
46   Ibid., p. 111.
47   Ibid., pp. 70-3.
48   Quoted by Kilty, ibid., p. 107.
49   Ibid., pp. 107-8.
50   Ibid., p. 106.
51   Ibid., p. 114.

The following month Ramiro de Maeztu warns that 'if Germany, as a result of the war, expands and consolidates the influence she previously exercised over the Slav nations and territories, the world will be confronted by an Empire unvanquished and invincible, placed in the heart of the oldest, greatest and most populous of its continents'. Such an empire, he calculates, would comprise 'seventy million Germans, fifty million Austro-Hungarians, twenty million Balkan Slavs, twenty million Turks and fifty, sixty or seventy million Russians of different denominations'. He predicts that in twenty years time this Empire would be so strong that no other power could oppose it, if it decided to annexe Switzerland, Denmark or Holland. (21 February 1918; *NA* XXII, 17, pp. 323-4)

De Maeztu once more takes up the theme of Germany's expansionist plans on 7 March 1918. He explains that because he has lived in Germany, he knows 'how small is the influence of the wealthy over the military'. The only way for Germany to expand is by taking over other nations. However, he feels that 'to submit to the will of a single nation is to forego consciousness and civilisation'. Nostalgically he recalls that this used to be thought by all educated Germans 'in the times before they dreamed of becoming the rulers of a universal empire themselves. And this is what all awakened minds in the rest of the world still think - and, thank God, many Germans also'. He considers the German virtues to be love of work and pleasure in thinking and in dreaming. However, modern Germans prefer 'to be ruled by a despotic dynasty and a tyrannical caste' and to live in 'a State endowed with the fabulous power of that very work and thought but turned to the fulfilment of dreams of its own'. He calls this 'the German failing', adding that if the German people had been 'poor and insignificant, this accumulation of power in the hands of the state would have mattered little in the world. Had it occurred in a nation differently situated or in a period of the world's history other than the present, or before the railways had superseded sea-power, or the railways themselves had been superseded; or the Slav peoples had been less divided and less weak, the world would still have been more or less complacent.' (*NA* XXII, 19, pp. 371-2)

Ramiro de Maeztu probably contributed his most penetrating study of Germany after the cessation of military hostilities. His article 'Germany Now', which was inspired by a recent visit to occupied Germany, appeared on 9 January 1919. He paints a depressing picture of life in post-war Germany. He has heard of soldiers in uniform selling matches and newspapers or grinding barrel organs in the streets of Berlin, where morale is very low. The German people, he explains, cannot forgive their rulers for waging war against 'a superior strength. And this resentment has inspired and given its characteristics to the German Revolution. I have heard many Germans complain that in the critical hour "the strong man" has not arisen'. As an observer, de Maeztu finds it distressing 'to witness the lack of joy and hope in the Revolution. The Revolution has arrived late and badly. If it had come years ago, and through other causes - for instance, in protest against the invasion of Belgium, or against the use of poison-gases, or against the sinking of the *Lusitania*, or against the first bombardment of London by Zeppelins - Germany could offer to-day the cheering spectacle of a country extending its arms to the world across the body of a dead tyrant. But the Revolution came out of defeat'. What is worse, the German revolution has not inspired new ideas. He contends that the Socialists in Germany are ruling 'at a moment when the experience of Russia has proved to the world that Socialism, unassailable as it is in its criticism of economic parasitism, does not contain a positive method of administrating the economy of an industrial nation. In other words, Socialism has assumed the government of Germany when all the thinking spirits of the world (Germany included) had clearly seen that Socialist principles had not yet produced an efficient system of government'. As they lack methods of their own, the Socialists in Berlin have been forced 'to maintain the capitalist organisation' of industry in order 'to avoid the catastrophe in Germany which occurred in Russia - where, in the absence of competent direction, industry went out of the door when control by the workers came in at the window'. He accuses the German people of not having 'awakened to the problem of the *guilt* of the war'. The German people, he alleges, 'do not accuse the old regime of having been *guilty* of the war, but of having made them wage a war in which they would inevitably be crushed. German intellectuals sincerely believe that all the belligerents share more or less in the guilt of the war'. He ascribes the present 'disorientation of Germany' to the German intellectuals having 'preferred the abstract problems of science and the technical problems of industry to the practical problems of political life'. At the same time, he has a certain respect for the German love of books. After browsing in a Bonn bookshop, already crammed with the latest publications in German, he is filled with awe, 'for in both quantity and quality no country has an intellectual production to rival that of Germany. The German bookshop makes one feel that Germany will somehow find her way'. He speculates that in Germany 'the cause of the catastrophe is the political absentee-ism of the intellectual classes, for it does not seem probable that the German people would have been satisfied with such a poor ideal as Imperialism if the subtle minds of the thinkers had devoted themselves to pointing out its obvious dangers'. He concludes that it is now time for German intellectuals 'to come down from their ivory tower', reasoning that 'the consequent encounter of thinking minds with political realities cannot be unfruitful in Germany, for it has not been unfruitful in any other country.' (*NA* XXIV, 10, pp. 155-7)

George D. Herron: 'the world cannot continue in flames, and so big a house as the United States escape conflagration'

Whilst Orage was keen to publish the opinions of Ramiro de Maeztu as an outsider, he also showed interest in presenting the American perspective on

Germany. In 1917, he printed a series dealing with America's position in the war by a new contributor, George D. Herron. Herron's first article, 'Germany and Woodrow Wilson', appeared on 11 January 1917. In it he observes that Europeans have misinterpreted the American president's Peace Note. Herron believes that it was really intended as an ultimatum to Germany: if the war continues, the United States cannot remain apart because 'the world cannot continue in flames, and so big a house as the United States escape conflagration'. The United States must choose to ally itself with the side of 'hope and progress of democracy'. The terms of the Allies are well known: they wish to restore Belgian neutrality and independence, as well as to restore France and return Alsace and Lorraine to the French. In addition, they seek the 'restoration and reunion of the Serbian peoples in a greater Serbian Kingdom'. Italy wants part of the Italian nation 'still under Austrian dominion', and Russia wants Constantinople. By contrast, Germany has never stated her terms for 'she has only the intention of keeping her hold upon Middle Europe and the road to Baghdad, knowing that, if she succeeds in this, the rest of Europe will ultimately come into her possession'. Herron warns that if a peace conference takes place, Germany will act as conqueror and will use its duration to replenish her supplies and resources. He concludes that 'the end of discussions would be the gain by trickery and treachery of much of that for which Germany began the war. That President Wilson foresaw the German evasion or rejection of this invitation I do not for a moment doubt. And, if Germany persists in her present position, the entrance of America upon the war in fellowship with the Allies is certain'. He argues somewhat vaguely that Germany must set conditions 'as shall win the sympathy and applause of mankind' by completely restoring France, Belgium and the Balkan states and providing adequate compensation, as well as 'full and true re-habilitation of Poland, including the part attached to Prussia'. Germany should also return Schleswig-Holstein to Denmark, 'set Bohemia free' and 'invite all German peoples to unite in fraternal confederation, in one fellowship of freedom and progress'. Herron believes that by this 'sudden realisation of a new kind of national integrity', Germany may 'step into the spiritual leadership of the world'. Providing he has 'the vision and daring', the Kaiser could then become the 'most tremendous and anointed ruler of history', and Germany could be 'the messianic nation of the world, the first-born of the true and universal super-humanity'. (*NA* XX, 11, p. 250)

America's entry into the war, according to Herron, 'is not at all the triumph of militarism: it is exactly the contrary. The entire American nation has mobilised itself, with its immeasurable resources, to bring militarism to its full and final end. And there is no contradiction between America's opposition to militarism and her nearly rapturous determination to assist in exterminating Prussianism and the autocratic principle. The American resolution to help clean up the world, and to make it the dwelling-place of democratic peoples and societies, is the perfect sequence of American anti-militarism'. America did not enter the war during the first two years because the population of America was initially 'largely pro-German in its sympathies', with much American finance under German control, while 'a powerful public Press was advocating an alliance with Germany against England'. Herron believes that President Wilson's achievement has been to guide his nation 'into an understanding of the meaning of war' and thus gain 'the common and hearty support of the people'. America's war aim is to 'make the world safe for democracy' and to create 'a world-State embracing all nations in a League of Peace'. She is therefore waging 'a pacifist crusade'. (12 July 1917; *NA* XXI, 11, p. 242)

In addition to his commentary on American war aims, Herron also displayed tremendous zeal for defining the national characteristics of the enemy. On 22 March 1917, for example, he turns his attention to Austria. Unlike J. M. Kennedy or A. R. Orage, who find positive qualities in Austria, Herron dislikes Austria as much as the rest of Germany. He admits that he was once 'almost captivated by the Austrian illusion' and grew 'remonstrant' when England and France 'threw the Hapsburgs back into the arms of Germany' because he had hoped that Austria would form an alliance with the Entente powers. However, he came to realise that such a union would be impossible on the grounds that there is no 'reformed Hapsburg Empire', and its only claim to continue is that it has existed for a long time. He reminds readers that the Swiss Cantons revolted against Austria, that Austrians marched against the French of the Revolution, that Sobieski's Poland saved Europe from Turkish rule but was betrayed by Austria - after the Poles had saved the gates of Vienna. Again and again the Hapsburgs appealed to the Serbs for help and 'rewarded them with betrayal and butchery'. Thus, 'for a thousand years the Hapsburg blight has lain across Europe, crushing every effort towards liberty, and crowning every political infamy'. Part of his distrust of Austria stems from religious prejudice: he contends that Austria wants a restored Catholic Empire and will trick France and England to get it because Austria constantly seeks 'a renewal of the political power of the Pope in Europe'. He argues that in this venture Germany would be a willing ally of Austria because 'the whole present tendency in Germany is back towards Rome. The Prussian ruling-class is 'steadily moving over into the Catholic fold'. German intellectuals, far from turning to agnosticism, are also moving from Protestant to Catholic. He is convinced that 'Prussianism and Roman Catholicism are but two forms of the same conception of life and authority. They must inevitably, if the power of each prevails, amalgamate again in a Catholic Empire, with the Pope as its spiritual head and the Emperor as its secular chief. Ultimately, the Hapsburgs and the Hohenzollerns would merge their dynasties, and the German and the Catholic Empires would become one and the same'. (*NA* XX, 21, p. 485)

According to Herron, Europe is in turmoil because the 'Latin soul' has been submerged by the German soul. Italy, although poor, has made a great contribution to the war; she has defended her frontiers from Austria and stopped it from 'co-operating with Germany upon the French and Russian frontiers. He finds that the Italians, more than any other nation, are fighting for civilisation against barbarians and want to save the world from the 'Tedeschi'. In this context he praises 'the sublimity of Dante' at the expense of 'the dilettantism of Goethe', by contrasting St. Francis of Assisi with 'the grossness of Luther' and setting 'the dreams of Mazzini' against 'the meanness of Bismarck'. Herron's view is reminiscent of the Italian Settembrini's great tirade against Vienna as the ultimante reactionary power - and against the militant Catholicism of Naphta - in Thomas Mann's *Der Zauberberg* (1924).[52] Herron cautions against intrigues between the Vatican and Vienna, suggesting that the ghost of the Holy Roman Empire must be laid to rest in order to free Italy. A victory for the Pope, he alleges, would also be the victory of Prussia since 'a Prussian capitalist domination of Europe is the basis of the Pope's plan for political power. These two perils, Prussian and Papal, are twin aspects of the one materialist enemy of mankind'. He is sure that the 'occupation of Italy, with a Germanised Pope at the Vatican' is never far from German plans. (*NA* XX, 21, p. 486)

Ezra Pound: 'the Hun must get the word "Macht" out of his occiput'

In addition to Herron's pronouncements, which are at times naive and bellicose, Orage published articles on Germany and America by Ezra Pound (1885-1972). While Pound's pieces occasionally echo the hysteria of Herron, they also contain some astute judgements on the subject. The American writer probably offered more copy than any other contributor to the *New Age*, even if his views were not always in keeping with those of the editor. He was probably first introduced to Orage in the autumn of 1911 by his fellow contributor T. E. Hulme at the latter's London home at 67 Frith Street. Orage was so impressed with Pound's potential that in November of that year he agreed to publish a series of translations from Anglo-Saxon, Provencal and Tuscan poetry, together with prose comments.[53] From this beginning Pound was soon supplying Orage with weekly contributions. Indeed, between 1911 and 1921 Orage published nearly three hundred of Pound's articles - and, contrary to his usual practice, paid for them.[54] Pound was well aware of his debt to Orage, whom he described as 'the best friend I ever had in the editorial office', despite their 'twelve years of almost

---

52   See Thomas Mann, *Der Zauberberg*, (Frankfurt am Main, 1982; Fischer paperback edition), p. 167.
53   Noel Stock, *The Life of Ezra Pound* (London, 1970), p. 104.
54   Humphrey Carpenter, *A Serious Character: The Life of Ezra Pound* (London, 1988), p. 169.

continual disagreement'.[55] Although attracted by the 'unfastidiousness' of the *New Age*, it seems unlikely that Pound was ever influenced by the ideas discussed in the journal. He once retorted 'I hope you don't think I *read* the periodicals I appear in', and in 1935 he admitted 'To this day I haven't the faintest idea who *read* the paper. The only man I ever met who had seen my stuff in the *New Age* was an admiral'.[56]

For a writer discussing the Germans, Pound's experience of their country was extremely limited. In 1911 he had made a short visit to Germany, spending August as a guest of Ford Madox Ford in Gießen.[57] Pound travelled to Gießen from Lake Garda and appears to have regretted the move north from the moment he arrived. In a letter to his mother he complained: 'I was dragged about to a number of castles, etc, which were interesting and about which I persistently refused to enthuse'. Of Germany he said 'I don't approve of it', although he conceded that Gießen was 'a model town'. After Ford took him to Nauheim, the setting of Ford's *The Good Soldier* (1915), Pound dismissed it as 'a spring and baths hell'.[58] On one occasion he ventured a little further afield, taking the train for a day in Freiburg-in-Breisgau, only to spend the time talking to a French scholar, Dr. Emil Lévy.[59] By the end of August he had returned to London.

The United States' declaration of war on Germany met with the full support of Ezra Pound. In one of his most damning articles, entitled 'Provincialism the Enemy', Pound examines German influences on the American university system. He first equates England and France with civilisation because 'they have not given way to the yelp of "nationality"', despite their talk of 'Little England', 'La France' and 'Imperialism'. Nor have these countries 'given way to the yelp of "race"' because France 'is so many races that she has had to settle things by appeal to reason. England is so many races, even "Little England", that she has kept some real respect for personality, for the outline of the individual'. In short, France and England represent 'modern civilisation' since 'neither nation has been coercible into a *Kultur*; into a damnable holy Roman Empire, holy Roman Church orthodoxy, obedience, Deutschland über Alles, infallibility'. Neither France nor England could be duped in the way that 'it has been possible to cook up "the German" so tempting a stew of anaesthetics that the whole nation was "fetched". A certain lurability could be counted on.' According to Pound, Germany is not the only country susceptible to such temptation. America was also tempted, but 'has been hauled out by the scruff of her neck', after having

55   Quoted by Noel Stock, op. cit., p. 261.
56   Quoted by Humphrey Carpenter, op. cit., p. 169.
57   Ibid., p. 160.
58   Quoted by Carpenter, ibid., p. 161.
59   Ibid., p. 161.

189

'imbibed a good deal of the poison'. American universities in particular were 'tainted', but America's 'original ideas', namely those taken from France, 'and her customs, imported from England, won out in the end'. Until this happened, Pound claims, 'it was very difficult to get any American periodical to print an attack on *Kultur*, *Kultur* which will still be found lurking by the grave of Munsterburg in the cemetery of the American universities'. He feels 'distress over a system of education and of "higher education"'. He condemns the German-influenced university system in the United States, which fifteen years earlier succeeded in alienating him totally. According to him, it is 'the only system whereby every local nobody is able to imagine himself a somebody. It is in essence a provincialism. It is the single bait which caught all the German intellectuals, and which had hooked many of their American confrères'. In Germany, 'every man of intelligence nicely switched on to some particular problem, some minute particular problem *unconnected* with life, *unconnected* with main principles (to use a detestable, much abused phrase). By confining his attention to *ablauts*, hair-length, foraminifera, he could become at a small price an "authority", a celebrity. I myself am an "authority", I was limited to that extent. It takes some time to get clean'. Thus, 'the whole method of this German and American higher education was, is, a perversion'. He calls this system evil because 'it holds up an ideal of "scholarship", not an ideal of humanity. It says in effect: you are to acquire knowledge in order that knowledge may be acquired. Metaphorically, you are to build up a damn'd and useless pyramid which will be no use to you or to anyone else, but which will serve as a "monument". To this end you are to sacrifice your mind and your vitality'. This system has 'fought tooth and nail against the humanist belief that a man acquires knowledge in order that he may be a more complete man, a finer individual, a fuller, more able, more interesting companion for other men'. Indeed, 'knowledge as the adornment of the mind, the enrichment of the personality, has been cried down in every educational establishment where the Germano-American "university" ideal has reached' and made the student 'the bondslave of his subject, the gelded ant, the compiler'. In these conditions the student 'has become accustomed first to *receiving* his main ideas without question: then to being indifferent to them. In this state he has accepted the Deutschland über Alles idea, in this state he has accepted the idea that he is an ant, not a human being. He has become impotent, and quite pliable' (12 July 1917; *NA* XXI, 11, p. 245). Pound's analysis is very much in key with the *Erkenntnisekel* of Thomas Mann and Gottfried Benn, whose play *Ithaka* (1916) poured scorn on the indulgence of German academics who sought to acquire knowledge for its own sake.[60]

---

60   See Gottfried Benn, *Ithaka*, in *Gesammelte Werke*, edited by Dieter Wellershoff, 8 vols (Wiesbaden, 1968), VI, pp. 1472-4.

On 19 September 1918 Pound attacks Germany in terms reminiscent of the most cliché-ridden propaganda tracts. In 'What America has to live down', Pound depicts the German as so 'docile' that, 'having been indoctrinated with the idea that he must behave like a machine-containing ourang outang', he has 'imperilled the rest of the world'. What he calls 'a decent doctrine imposed from above' could have been equally successful given the docile nature of the German. The 'civilised world' could possibly accommodate a Germany 'governed by Americans, or even by Germans imbued with American ideals of decency'. He argues that the Germany of the seventeenth and eighteenth centuries would be acceptable, but 'there will be no such place under Prussia'. Indeed, 'what it has taken forty years to drive into the German head will not be driven out in a fortnight. I can conceive no such Germany before a crushing defeat. I can conceive no such Germany as a result of *nothing more than* such a defeat'. He can only conceive such a Germany after a course of 'counter-Kultur', after the Germans have learned that 'some thoughts are made to be thought, but are NOT to be translated into action'. In this context, Pound contends, Nietzsche 'has done no harm to France because France is accustomed to treating all thought as thought, and has not the mania of putting *all* into action'. He is convinced that 'the Nietzschean chaos is all very well in conversation. It is all very well in the works of Nietzsche, from which Prussianism is, conceivably, as far removed as was the Holy Inquisition from conversation in Galilee'. Pound's solution to Germany's problems is simple, not to say simplistic: he argues that 'the Hun must get the word "Macht" out of his occiput. He needs a course in Confucius, the one "founder" who cannot be made the basis of devastating crusades.' (*NA* XXIII, 21, p. 329)

Beatrice Hastings: 'I have never said anything very bad of Germans'

In January 1918 Beatrice Hastings, under the guise of Alice Morning, made a brief appearance for two months with a series entitled 'Notes from France'. It was perhaps no coincidence that Beatrice Hastings should appear again just after a series by Katherine Mansfield had finished, given the rivalry between the two women. In 1910 Katherine Mansfield had taken a sample of her short stories, including *The Child who was Tired*, which was subsequently published in the *New Age*,[61] to the editor's London office, where she met Orage and Hastings and a friendship quickly developed. However, Beatrice Hastings soon became jealous of her younger rival's greater literary success and instigated a series of bitter satirical attacks on her former friend, which appeared in the *New Age* in the

---

61   For a discussion of the short stories which later appeared in the anthology *In a German Pension* see Chapter 2, pp. 60-2 and Chapter 3, pp. 105-7.

course of 1912. Nor were the hostilities confined to a war of words. The young poet Ruth Pitter, whose work appeared in the *New Age*, recalls visiting Orage and Hastings only to find the floor strewn with beads and be told that Katherine and Beatrice had come to blows with their necklaces.[62]

By the end of the First World War, in addition to her long-running feud with Katherine Mansfield, Beatrice Hastings was at daggers drawn with Orage as well. According to her version of events, she was 'a woman who offended Orage's masculine amour-propre, and for this, was made the victim of a social cabale (sic) - that did not matter even to herself - and of a literary boycott that does, or should, matter to every reading person'.[63] She denies that she ever left the *New Age*; whilst she was in Paris a plot was hatched to have her 'jockeyed out'.[64] She argues that at the end of 1915 Orage wrote to her, asking her to discontinue her 'Impressions of Paris' because they 'infuriated people' and she was 'seriously damaging the paper'. Her 'Peace Notes', anticipating the 'first German offer of peace by a month or two', were 'premature and had fallen flat', Orage told her. He then stopped sending her copies of the *New Age* and she was removed from the payroll.[65] She never saw the journal between December 1916 and January 1918: Orage rejected her manuscripts after the third 'Impressions of Paris'. In March 1920 she sent an article signed Alice Morning to the *New Age* and it was accepted. She also sent two poems as Beatrice Hastings: these came back by return of post with a letter saying 'the readers would revolt at seeing the name of Beatrice Hastings in the paper'. She claims that when Orage, or 'this maniac' as she prefers to call him, 'fled' to Fontainebleau in 1922, he spent his time machinating against her amongst her Paris acquaintants, although she never saw Orage again in the flesh after July 1914.[66]

In the last series of her reports from France to appear in the *New Age*, Beatrice Hastings observes that the French middle classes are placing their hopes in a revolution in Germany to bring the war to an end, despite the fact that the Germans 'still seem to think imperially'. She perceives the 'misfortune' of the German to be that he is 'over-educated while politically enslaved'. She concedes that the English are also politically enslaved, but they are not over-educated and 'that saves us'. She argues that the English motto is 'ours not to reason why', whereas 'every unhappy Teuton ever since he first sat on a kindergarten bench has had to reason why from a false Berlin basis. So now in the trenches and else-

---

62   John Carswell, *Lives and Letters* (London, 1978), p. 74.

63   Beatrice Hastings, op. cit., p. 3.

64   Ibid., p. 24.

65   Ibid., pp. 24-6. Possibly this was also in part a consequence of their separation as lovers.

66   Beatrice Hastings, op. cit., pp. 28-9.

where he reasons and constructs Berlin syllogisms: where it goes well with me, there is my Fatherland: it goes well with me in Belgium, in Romania, in Italy, in Servia (sic): therefore, there is my Fatherland. And he sticks, seeing, as yet, no reason for locking his Kaiser in a lunatic asylum and sending back all the deported Belgians and others with fraternal apologies. It remains to be seen whether the Russians will not teach him more in three months of peace than three years of war has achieved. We others, even with all our lack of culture and logic, are yet not capable of teaching him'. Nevertheless, she is ready to admit that 'I have never said anything very bad of Germans, even when their airmen came bombarding Paris; honestly, I couldn't, knowing only nice ones in England, whose worst fault was a confidence in our ideals of liberty which verged on the scandalous'. Because of her liking for Germans she feels alienated by the French, who indulge in what she calls 'armchair-swearing and civilian bosh about the Boches'. (17 January 1918; *NA* XXII, 12, p. 227)

On 14 February 1918, Beatrice Hastings devotes her column to the recent shooting of Mata Hari as a spy - an act of which she strongly disapproves. She argues, as she had done over the execution of Edith Cavell,[67] that it is 'mean to shoot spies, considering that all armies employ them'. She goes on to express her weariness with the war. Although she now lives in a village on the outskirts of Paris, she has experienced air raids on the capital. In such situations, following the sensation of fear, she recalls feeling 'immense weariness, even boredom, the same as nations feel when the stupidity of war comes home stronger than even its wickedness; when the glamour of glory fades from around the spectre of murder and the elderly patriots find that even five per cent is too much for a ruined country to pay'. Reprisals achieve little, since 'a bombardment is a bad exchange for a sense of moral superiority' and does 'nothing to advance the military operations'. (*NA* XXII, 16, p. 308)

Nietzsche: 'more of a danger than a saviour to post-war Germany'

Orage continued to devote considerable attention to Nietzsche, even after the German philosopher had ceased to be the favourite subject of writers of propaganda tracts. One of the translators of Oscar Levy's first complete edition of Nietzsche's work in English, A. M. Ludovici, who in 1917 was a Captain in the Royal Fusileer Artillery, responded to a request from Orage[68] to write again for the periodical, to which he had been a regular contributor before the war. Oscar Levy, who, as a German closely associated with the work of Nietzsche, had spent

---

67   See Chapter 4, pp. 133-4.

68   Wallace Martin, *The New Age under Orage: Chapters in English Cultural History* (Manchester, 1967), p. 194.

the war in exile in Switzerland because of harassment in England, also sent articles on a variety of topics to the *New Age*. Orage himself still devoted much of his own literary column, 'Readers and Writers', to Nietzsche. On 14 June 1917, for instance, Orage notes the appearance in the United States of a reprint of W. M. Salter's 'Nietzsche and the War' in the *International Journal of Ethics*, and reminds his readers of the large number of pamphlets pontificating on whether the philosopher is guilty or innocent of the charge that his ideas influenced German wartime strategy. Orage argues that the question must be 'left open; for there is as much evidence for the one view as for the other'. He suggests, in line with Ezra Pound, that Nietzsche's work is full of ambiguities because Nietzsche himself was not 'a man of action, and, therefore, never being compelled to make up his mind upon any point, he could afford (or he allowed himself) to express contradictory judgements upon almost every problem that occurred to him'. He reflects that 'you can find in Nietzsche anything you choose to look for: the most extreme form of Christianity, the most extreme form of paganism, gentleness and brutality, praise and denunciation of force, the same of the virtues, and the same of various kinds of social life. He was, as he said, an interrogation-mark; and every attempt to define him in more accurate terms must end in an interrogation'. In a nicely balanced judgement, Orage contends that 'there is too much praise of force in Nietzsche to permit us to doubt that *if* the unity of Europe had been achieved by force he would have repudiated it'. Some critics, including Salter, attempt to 'exonerate Nietzsche from any influence upon German militant radicalism; and no doubt it is true that Nietzsche believed himself to hate the German Empire as much as the German Empire neglected Nietzsche. Germany's profession of a War for Kulture (sic) preceded Nietzsche, who, in fact, did no more than spell Kulture (sic) with a C, while approving of war as its method'. Orage concludes that a 'A Lyrical Bismarck' - a term he had coined as early as January 1910[69] - still 'best defines Nietzsche in relation to Germany'. (*NA* XX, 7, p. 158)

Orage takes up the theme again after the war when Oscar Levy reports in the *New Age* that Nietzsche 'is being read as never before in Germany'.[70] Orage is prompted to remark that Nietzsche 'was taken, if at all, in the wrong sense in Germany before the war. The Germans did with him precisely what the mob everywhere does with the satanist: they swallowed his praise and ignored his warnings'. The controversial philosopher, Orage reflects, is still 'more of a danger than a saviour to post-war Germany, since his vocabulary is for the most part militarist. Culture for him is usually presented in terms of combat; and the still small voice of perfection is only heard in the silences of his martial sentences'. He doubts whether 'the new Germany, now that it has begun to re-

---

69   See Chapter 2, pp. 56-7.
70   See 14 August 1919; *NA* XXV, 16, p. 258.

read Nietzsche, will read him any more intelligently than before' for he perceives that there are writers, 'who are most dangerous to the nation in which they appear'. According to Orage, Rousseau has been particularly dangerous in France, Whitman a menace in America, whilst Dr. Johnson 'has been a blight upon English thought'. Nietzsche, he speculates, may be 'only a blessing outside of Germany'. A nation, he warns, 'runs risks in accepting as its own doctrines of the great men who chance to appear among it. On the other hand, a nation runs the risk of missing its real chosen unless it examines all the great men of the world. Chauvinism, in other words, either by choice or by exclusion, is always dangerous'. (4 September 1919; *NA* XXV, 19, p. 310)

A. M. Ludovici: still 'a convinced Nietzschean'

A. M. Ludovici responded to Orage's request with occasional book reviews under his own name, as well as articles on Nietzsche, for which he preferred the pseudonym A Zarathustrian. In 1918 he used this pen-name for two long review articles. In the first, a discussion of John Neville Figgis' *The Will to Freedom*, Ludovici claims that, having experienced three years of war and spent three years in the army, he still remains 'a convinced Nietzschean'. Of the Nietzscheans in England, only Ludovici joined the army in the war; it is therefore hard to conceive that this article is written by anyone but him. As a 'convinced Nietzschean', Ludovici commends Figgis for absolving Nietzsche 'of the charge so ignorantly and fiercely made against him by almost all the poorly cultivated newspapers of this country, of having, by his pro-Germanism and his bellicosity, acted the part of the philosophic Bernhardi behind the ideas of pan-Germanism'. The author has also succeeded in denying the 'contention reiterated with mulish obstinacy by so many more shallow critics of Nietzsche, that the latter panders to mere unbridled egoism of the individual. He elevates Nietzsche above the smart epigrammists who are out to *épater le bourgeois*'. (10 January 1918; *NA* XXII, 11, pp. 215-16)

Nine months later, A Zarathustrian once more sets out to exonerate Nietzsche. He condemns the 'blank cartridges of ignorant abuse which each group of belligerents fired at each other in the early days of the war', proving 'the state of absolute inertia to which mutual interest and sympathy had declined'. The journalists of Europe abetted this ignorance, producing in 1914 'the outburst of indignation against Friedrich Nietzsche, which composed the leitmotif of articles in most of the fashionable newspapers during the early months of the war, and in the face of which Nietzscheans went about almost in danger of their lives'. Some booksellers advertised 'The Euro-Nietzschean War' or 'The Mundo-Nietzschean War' in order to 'attract attention to certain war books they were selling, and there was nobody to object, because nobody "who mattered" really knew how ridiculous was the phrase'. Had England understood Nietzsche, who was really a brutally honest critic of his country, 'there would have been little of that speechless astonishment at German methods in the early days of the war'. In this respect Ludovici praises 'a certain enthusiastic and indefatigable writer on Nietzsche', who before the war was criticised by his 'fellow-Nietzscheans' for having toned down the German philosopher for public consumption. This unnamed writer, who is most probably Orage, always countered that 'there is much in Nietzsche which though never intended to exonerate and give clean consciences to hogs, can nevertheless be twisted by hogs to that purpose'. Ludovici now thinks that Orage was right to give 'as little prominence as possible to this aspect of Nietzschean doctrine' and thus save 'the master from gross misinterpretation'. (14 November 1918; *NA* XXIV, 2, pp. 23-4)

Oscar Levy: 'the present war is merely a new phase of the French Revolution'

In 1919, Oscar Levy rose to the challenge of providing Orage with material for the *New Age*. Between January and February 1919 Orage published Levy's 'The idolatry of words', four essays which had originally appeared in *La Revue Politique Internationale*, but was translated for the *New Age* by Paul Victor Cohn, who had helped translate Nietzsche for the Levy edition. In the first of these pieces Levy argues that Europe can thank democracy for both the war and its long duration. The democrat has a conscience, which tells him 'that the aggressor is a criminal and the sufferer a noble victim'. It is the democrat who 'provides us with "the question of responsibility", that salt which is ever being rubbed into the wound of war as soon as it seems likely to heal'. However, according to Levy, the strong have always attacked 'those whom they thought weaker than themselves: if it is a crime, the criminal can plead a long series of precedents. And before the French Revolution there was no "question of responsibility"'. The question of responsibility did not arise until democracy, or what Levy terms 'the morality of the humble', was proclaimed. (9 January 1919; *NA* XXIV, 10, p. 161)

On 23 January 1919 Levy finds a direct link between 'the present world-war and the Revolution of 1789', seeing 'the close parallel between the exuberant rhetoric of to-day and the hollow verbiage of the past'. In the French Revolution, he argues, Robespierre and St. Just 'looked to the ideal of "justice on earth" which seemed to them well within their grasp; they fancied that only a few heads barred their way'. Unfortunately, despite all the blood-letting, they moved no nearer their goal. In Levy's opinion, 'if we add to the ideals, still current, of "Justice", "Liberty" and "Equality", such phrases of later growth as "Kultur", "the happiness of the many", "securities of peace", "League of Nations", "last war in the annals of humanity"; if we substitute for the few pints of blood that flowed of old on the Place de la Concorde the rivers of blood that the world-war has cost us; if we compare the idealism of a few individuals who valiantly sacrificed themselves with the self-denial of whole nations who to-day are giving up their property and their lives - we cannot but be forcibly struck by the similarity between the present world-war and the Revolution of 1789'. He firmly believes that the 'present war is merely a new phase of the French Revolution' and the 'St. Justs and the Robespierres, find their replicas in the Lenins and Trotskys'. (*NA* XXIV, 12, pp. 196-7)

Oscar Levy in Berlin: 'The old Germany dies hard'

Perhaps Levy's most effective pieces of journalism are to be found in the series of reports he sent in the summer of 1919, based on a visit to Berlin he made at the end of June which enabled him to see first-hand the effects of the war on the Germans. Two of these articles were translated by Orage, using the pseudonym R.H.C.

Levy begins the series by describing a gruelling train journey from his home in Switzerland to Berlin, which was only relieved by the conversations he had with his fellow passengers. The German women, 'who are naturally given to laughing a good deal, appeared to be particularly depressed; and even the youngest of them had care-worn lines between their brows'. Each town prints its own money, which consists 'almost entirely of dirty pieces of paper, many of them ragged almost beyond recognition'. At Frankfurt, men from Mainz join the train and talk 'quite openly of a Rhenish Republic, considering it apparently an excellent solution to their problem'. Levy notes that 'my companions throughout the Rhenish provinces, like all South Germans, are for the signing of the peace. It is not so in Berlin and the East, where opinion is strongly against it, and where national sentiment - even without the dynastic bond - is likely to prove more durable'. By the time the train reaches Thuringia, the corridors and compartments are packed. It is overcrowded because there is only one train a day and, 'considering the depreciation of the value of money, travelling is still relatively cheap'. However, there is little food to be had in the station buffets where bread cannot be bought at any price. At Nuremberg Levy manages to procure a cup of *ersatz* coffee in exchange for a bar of Swiss chocolate, prompting him to muse that Lindt chocolate 'has proved to be the currency so far'. They eventually arrive at Berlin's Anhalter Bahnhof two and a half hours late. The situation there is no more encouraging. He is met by his hostess who says he must stay with her because the hotels, which charge exorbitant prices for mediocre food, are already full. There are no porters at the station and taxis are both scarce and expensive, making the tram the only feasible means of transport. Crime is rampant, he reports, and his hosts live in fear of attack, although they decline to keep firearms in the house on the grounds that 'the burglars can certainly shoot better than we'. (7 August 1919; *NA* XXV, 15, pp. 246-7)

In the second article, Levy describes a walk in the Tiergarten. The park is regarded as safer than the side streets, where attacks take place even in broad daylight. He is stopped only by women begging for bread coupons, which are more valuable than money. In the evening Levy meets a *Justizrat* who explains the difficulties facing German trade, commenting that before the war the Germans were people who kept their word, but 'war and poverty have made rascals of us all'. Levy observes that, like so many of his countrymen this German 'would hear nothing of the "atrocities" of Germany during the war, which, he said, moreover had certainly not been provoked by Germany'. Echoing the sentiments expressed in *Friedrich und die große Koalition* (1915), where Thomas Mann draws an analogy between the situation facing Frederick II in 1756 and Germany in 1914, Levy's acquaintance contends that 'it was Germany's enemies who had skilfully manoeuvred Germany into a position from which a declaration of war was the only escape; and they had thereafter exploited this purely formal gesture in order to create the myth of the "war of aggression"'. (14 August 1919; *NA* XXV, 16, p. 258)

On 21 August 1919 Levy describes the reaction in Berlin to the news from Weimar that the peace has been signed. It is unexpected news because 'up to the last the Berliners had regarded the proposed terms as quite unacceptable and were sure they would be refused'. The south and the west of Germany favoured accepting the peace terms; Berlin no longer has the power of veto in such matters. After a visit to the University, Levy notices that the students' corps still flourish, despite much talk about abolishing them. These associations were 'hotbeds of the narrowest nationalism and schools of those virtues so prized in the Germany of yesterday, "Schneidigkeit" and the fighting spirit'. In 1919 the students 'carry on just as before, with their caps and their coloured ribbons; and one sees on the cheeks of these young men fresh scars, destined, no doubt, to bear witness in the eyes of women to the courage and good breeding of the men who carry them'. He concludes wryly that 'the old Germany dies hard'. (*NA* XXV, 17, pp. 275-6)

In his final report Levy observes in every street 'wounded soldiers hobbling along, others grinding barrel organs, others, again, begging, their caps held out with a trembling hand'. On 1 July there is a transport strike in the city, although Levy remarks that 'once again it was conclusively proved to me how deep-rooted in this people is the sense of discipline and of work. Every day with unfailing conscientiousness, in spite of all the difficulties and inconveniences, in spite of the revolution - yes, even at the risk of life itself - the work of the people gets done'. Because he anticipates the strike spreading to the whole of Germany, Levy decides to return to Switzerland. In the course of a slow and difficult train journey, Levy gets into conversation with three Germans who were officers in the war. One confides that before the war he was a pacifist, and it was with a heavy heart and 'the utmost repugnance' that he helped his country fight its enemies because he considered Germany's wartime adversaries 'even better people than ourselves'. However, the peace treaty which the allies drew up for the Germans at Versailles 'has opened my eyes and shown me my mistake. They are a low rabble, far more contemptible than we are. Our duty from now on is to teach our children and our children's children to hate the French'. (*NA* XXV, 18, pp. 289-90)

Karl Marx: a political critic who 'has seldom been surpassed'

In addition to Nietzsche and the Nietzscheans, Orage devoted considerable attention to another German thinker - Karl Marx. No doubt this was inspired by 1918 marking the centenary of Marx's birth, although the articles in the *New Age* were far from eulogistic. On 4 April 1918 Orage expresses the hope that 'the reputation of Marx will not survive the war unimpaired. I can scarcely think that the German Socialists will be so proud of their Marxism in the future as they have been in the past, since it will have clearly betrayed them into one of the most shameful moral surrenders in all history. It is dangerous for a man's writings to be regarded as the "Bible" even of Socialists; and when, in addition, the Marxian Bible, unlike the other, aims at and, in a sense, achieves logical consistency, the peril of it is greater upon minds lacking the inestimable virtue of commonsense - Marx, however, was not himself a slave of his own inspiration; in other words, he was anything but a Marxian in the sense in which his followers are Marxian. He had, indeed, a very sharp word for certain of the disciples whose breed, unfortunately, has not been extinguished by it. "Amateur anarchists", he called them who "made up by rabid declarations and bloodthirsty rantings for the utter insignificance of their political existence"'. Orage is in no doubt that groups of Marx's disciples, answering perfectly to this description, are still to be found throughout Europe. (*NA* XXII, 23, p. 454)

On 16 May 1918 Orage again broaches the subject of Marx, when he attempts to distinguish the truth from the myth created by his disciples. Although he finds that Marx is not only confused, but, as an economist, 'has suffered from his disciples', Orage readily concedes that 'as a political critic he has seldom been surpassed', especially when criticising Bismarck's annexation of Alsace Lorraine and forecasting the future consequences. Orage observes that, 'though writing in London, and without our historic knowledge of the world-war, Marx might have written his manifesto to-day; but, in that case, I doubt whether he would be published in Germany, or read with much attention by Marx's followers in this country'. He is prompted to remark that the most clear and prophetic part of Marx's work is neglected by his followers, who show 'a literal reverence that transcends bibliolatry' for 'his dubious forecasts and his riddling analyses', yet for 'his most absolute and explicit political prophecies - not a word!' Orage explains that, for Germany, 1870 was 'a declared war of defence, exactly like the present

199

war'. However, no sooner 'had the ostensible motive of defence been satisfied by Sedan than the real object of German militarism began to be revealed. Unhindered by the earlier protestations of the Emperor William that Germany was at war only with Napoleon and not with France, the militarists inspired the German liberal bourgeoisie to press for annexations in the name of race and security. They dared to pretend, said Marx, that the people of the two provinces were burning to be annexed to Germany; and they, moreover, adopted without reflection the excuse of the military party that a rectification of the Imperial frontiers was a strategic necessity. Thus, concluded Marx, they insisted upon sowing in the terms of peace the seeds of new wars - the phrase is Marx's own'. (*NA* XXIII, 3, p. 41)

Psychoanalysis: 'the hopeful science of the dawning era'

Whilst Marx and Nietzsche were treated with a certain ambivalence, the pioneers of psychoanalysis were arousing increasing interest amongst contributors to the *New Age* between 1917 and 1919. The *New Age* had carried articles on the subject, mainly by the psychoanalyst M. D. Eder, as early as 1912. In 1913, A. A. Brill translated *The Interpretation of Dreams*, which was the first of Freud's works to be published in England.[71] The following year Eder's translation of *On Dreams* helped to publicise further some of Freud's ideas. Between 1919 and 1925 no fewer than thirteen works by Freud appeared in English, thus establishing his reputation in England after the war.[72]

By 1917 reviewers in the *New Age* were keen to discuss the latest works on psychoanalysis. On 11 January 1917 A. E. Randall reviews a translation by A. A. Brill of Freud's *Wit and its Relation to the Unconscious* and notes 'What Darwin did for biology, Professor Freud has done for psychology'; 'a literature of such universal interest deserves to receive translation into all the civilised languages' (*NA* XX, 11, p. 259). On 26 July 1917 there was a review of M. D. Eder's *War Shock: The Psycho-Neuroses in War; Psychology and Treatment* which reports on one hundred cases, including nineteen of shell-shock, all differing from cases in civilian practice 'mainly by the fact that the traumatic factor is of supreme importance in the causation of the trouble; the speed with which men have been taken from peaceful avocations, and plunged into the inferno of modern war, has demanded adaptations that, perhaps, few can make with complete success' (*NA* XXI, 13, p. 293). It has been argued that it was such

---

71   Samuel Hynes, *The Edwardian Turn of Mind* (London, 1968), p. 164.
72   Samuel Hynes, *A War Imagined. The First World War and English Culture* (London, 1990), p. 365.

methods outlined here for the treatment of shell-shock in the First World War that established the reputation of Freud in England.[73]

Orage himself begins to discuss psychology, albeit tentatively. In his column 'Readers and Writers' he hints at his new interest, promising as early as 8 March 1917 that 'psychological education is another of the matters I intend to devote myself to during the coming years' (*NA* XX, 19, p. 445), whilst on 21 March 1918, after an absence of two weeks from his 'Readers and Writers' column, he returns to announce that he has spent the time reading 'much of Jung and Freud' (*NA* XXII, 21, p. 417). By 19 June 1919 Orage counts himself 'among the increasing number of enthusiastic students of psychoanalysis', which he considers to be 'the hopeful science of the dawning era' (*NA* XXV, 8, p. 134). Orage's biographer, Philippe Mairet, who began contributing to the *New Age* during this period, recalls that Orage was keen on 'Freudian and kindred psychologies' and in 1919 recommended Mairet to read Jung's *Psychology of the Unconscious*.[74] Freud and Jung continued to fascinate Orage in the 1930s when he readily quoted the latest work of Jung.[75]

On 2 May 1918 Orage devotes part of his 'Readers and Writers' column to Freud. Orage argues that 'psychoanalysis is not the last word in psychological method' and desires 'a great deal more experiment'. He considers Freud's theory of dreams an 'excellent pioneer work in a field hitherto left more or less uncultivated; but it is very far from being exhaustively explanatory of the facts. Suppose it were possible to *control* dreams - in other words, to dream of what you will - would not the theory of Freud that dreams are subconscious wish-fulfilments stand in need of amendment?' However, he does not consider it utterly impossible to control dreams, arguing, somewhat vaguely, that 'sufficient experimental work has been done in this direction to prove, at any rate, that the gate of dreams is open to the intelligent will'. He finds further, and to his mind more conclusive, evidence for this argument in 'a good deal of mystical literature', especially in works by the improbably titled Vaughan the Silurist. He is pleased that writers in the *New Age* now tend towards 'philosophical discussion', for it reveals 'the existence of a general desire to re-examine the bases of thought as a preliminary to the coming work of reconstruction.' (*NA* XXIII, 1, p. 9)

Orage's reading of Freud in the context of mysticism is significant. It is this approach to Freud through mystical literature and philosophy that puts in context Orage's later interest in the Russian esoteric thinker, G. I. Gurdjieff (1874?-1949), that ultimately culminated in his resigning his editorship of the *New Age* in September 1922 and joining the Institute for Harmonious

---

73   Ibid., p. 177.
74   Philippe Mairet, op. cit., p. 79.
75   Ibid., p. 117.

Development at Avon in the forest of Fontainbleau. This dramatic shift of interest is not as contradictory as it might first appear. Orage had been fascinated by mysticism ever since his early involvement with Theosophists in Leeds.[76] As editor of the *New Age* he repeatedly recommends the *Bhagavad Gita* to his readers. There is even an inscription from this work of Indian mysticism on his tombstone, carved by Eric Gill, in the Old Hampstead Church.[77] More significantly, it can be argued that his reading of Nietzsche was a mystical, if not an occultist, one.[78] When Holbrook Jackson introduced Orage to Nietzsche by lending him what was in 1900 perhaps the only copy in Leeds of *Thus Spake Zarathustra*, Orage offered in exchange a volume of the *Bhagavad Gita*,[79] although it is unlikely that this work aroused particularly favourable comments from Jackson. The latter always retained a certain detachment from mystics and Theosophists, whom he described engagingly as 'yoga-stricken mugwumps'.[80] He even came to regret having introduced Orage to Nietzsche on the grounds that the German philosopher, after being subjected to a mystical interpretation, had unbalanced his friend's life.[81] Since it is in the period just after the First World War that psychoanalysis, and then mysticism, come to play such an important role in his life, the years 1917 to 1919 can be seen as a period of transition in Orage's thought. As with Bernard Shaw, Orage is revealing himself to be profoundly disillusioned by the First World War and searching for new values.

Between 1917 and 1919 Orage was certainly beginning to look for spiritual answers to his personal feeling of malaise. At the same time, he was exploring new avenues in economics, as he attempted to find more immediate solutions to Britain's post-war problems. This is clearly reflected in the content of the *New Age* itself: whilst before the war extensive coverage was given to literary matters, by 1919 the emphasis shifts further towards social and economic questions, with much discussion of Social Credit,[82] as articles by the movement's

---

76   Tom Steele, *Alfred Orage and The Leeds Arts Club 1893-1923* (Aldershot, 1990), p. 34ff.

77   Louise Welch, *Orage with Gurdjieff in America* (Boston, London, Melbourne, 1982), p. 173.

78   Tom Steele, op. cit., p. 53. See also David S. Thatcher, *Nietzsche in England, the Growth of a Reputation* (Toronto, 1970) and Tom Gibbons, *Rooms in the Darwin Hotel* (Nedlands, Western Australia, 1973).

79   Holbrook Jackson, *Bernard Shaw* (London, 1907), 'Prefatory Letter', p. 12.

80   Quoted by Philippe Mairet, op. cit., p. 22.

81   Tom Steele, op. cit., p. 84.

82   For a succinct explanation of 'Social Credit' see David Clark, 'Douglas', in *The New Palgrave: A Dictionary of Economics*, edited by John Eatwell, 4 vols (London, 1987), I, p. 920.

theorist C. H. Douglas (1879-1952) occupied more and more space in the periodical. Orage collaborated on these articles and perhaps his greatest achievement was to render Douglas's prose more readable.[83]

Just as he had shown a lifelong interest in mysticism, Orage had always been concerned with social and economic questions. As early as the 1890s, when he was still a schoolmaster in Leeds, he wrote two scathing attacks on the appalling living conditions of the poor in the city,[84] whilst as editor of the *New Age* he reserved a section of his journal for discussion of A. J. Penty's theories of Guild Socialism. The fusion of apparently contradictory subjects, such as Socialism and mysticism, was not unusual for the time and had its origins in the previous century. Samuel Hynes has observed that, by the end of the nineteenth century, it was quite possible for radicals, who found themselves opposing positivism, materialism, evangelism and prudery, to espouse both Socialism and mysticism, especially Theosophy.[85]

Paul Selver: Germany, 'where poetical translation has been so widely cultivated as to become traditional'

Orage's new interests did not always meet with the approval of his fellow writers. Paul Selver, who contributed to the literary section of the *New Age*, sometimes on German writers but more usually on Slavonic writers, felt increasingly alienated by the post-war *New Age*.[86] During the war Selver had joined the army, 'remaining a private from first to last',[87] until demobilisation in August 1919, although he continued to provide Orage with occasional articles throughout.

A favourite theme of Selver's during his association with the *New Age* was translation, especially mistranslation. On 4 September 1919 he takes up the theme with regard to the translation of poetry. He observes that 'in Germany, where poetical translation has been so widely cultivated as to become traditional, a recent rendering of Keats interpreted the line "Or emptied some dull opiate to drains" by assigning the last word its sanitary meaning: (*in Röhren* was the actual phrase employed)'. He finds that the only comparable examples of English trans-

---

83   According to Ezra Pound, 'Orage taught Douglas how to write'. Quoted by Wallace Martin, op. cit., p. 271.

84   See A. R. Orage, 'A Study in Mud' and 'Quixotic Energy', in *Hypnotic Leeds: Being Essays on the Social Condition of the Town*, edited by Albert T. Marles (Leeds, 1894).

85   See Samuel Hynes, *The Edwardian Turn of Mind* (London, 1968), pp. 8-9.

86   Paul Selver, op. cit., p. 71.

87   Ibid., p. 71.

lations from the German occur when the translator confuses 's' and 'f' and cites the example of a hapless translator who mistook 'greisenhaft' (senile) for 'a non-existant *greifenhaft* (griffin-like)'. He considers Shelley's *Faust* translations 'admirable', especially the prose version of the 'Prologue', and suggests that Shelley's knowledge of German was 'considerable (quite possibly superior to the overrated attainments of Coleridge)' because even the most difficult passages are 'remarkably free from error' (*NA* XXV, 19, p. 312). He returns to Coleridge as translator later that month when he looks at his translation of Schiller's *Wallenstein*, which he criticises for being too far from the original meaning (25 September 1919; *NA* XXV, 22, pp. 262-3). Mistranslation aroused interest amongst *New Age* readers as well; a letter to the editor from G. D. Brooks, for example, offers a recent mistranslation into German of H. G. Wells' *Mr. Britling sees it through*, in which 'durchsehen' instead of 'durchsetzen' is used, rendering the title 'Mr. Britling sees through it'. (18 September 1919; *NA* XXV, 21, p. 351)

Books for wartime: an increasing number of 'English heroines who married Prussian officers just before the war'

By 1917 book reviewers in the *New Age* were growing weary of anti-German fiction. Mrs Alfred Sidgwick's *Karen* prompts the reviewer to observe that 'the number of English heroines who married Prussian officers just before the war, and are now able to give a fictional representation is on the increase'. This particular heroine marries 'a better sort of German' who dies fighting a duel over her. By implication, his adversary is the type of German who would have committed atrocities in Belgium. The anonymous reviewer muses cynically that 'the Germans have failed to win the war because the genius of Karen's husband was not at the service of the General staff'. In the same article there is a review of an epistolary novel entitled *On the Edge of the War Zone* by Mildred Aldrich. The reviewer predicts disappointment for the unwary reader who expects that 'residence on the edge of the war zone, on the hill-top on the Marne enables the author to know anything about the war'. In the novel 'the nearer we get to the war, the more domestic we become; we learn that coals cost twenty-six dollars a ton, and are of poor quality' and we find 'the usual small-talk about officers billeted on her - real gentlemen, every one, like all the ranks in the French Army, so polite, so patriotic, so comme il faut, such nice, tame, pussy-footed soldiers, without an oath or a speck of dirt - just darlings, and, of course, very well connected.' (24 October 1918; *NA* XXIII, 26, p. 418)

By contrast, H. B. Swope's *Inside the German Empire in the Third Year of the War* is praised for its objectivity, based on the author's own experiences in Germany for three months in 1916 (12 July 1917; *NA* XX, 11, p. 254), and J. W. Headlam's *The German Chancellor and the Outbreak of War*, which puts the blame for the war on articles reprinted in the German press from the *Westminster Gazette*, also meets with critical approval (3 January 1918; *NA* XXII, 10, p. 196). Other wartime publications, such as Coningsby Dawson's *The Glory of the Trenches* (22 August 1918; *NA* XXIII, 17, p. 274), *The Diary of a Dead Officer: Being the Posthumous Papers of Arthur Graeme West* (15 May 1919; *NA* XXV, 3, p. 47), Sir Henry Newbolt's *Submarine and Anti-Submarine* and Boyd Cable's *Air Men of War* (*NA* XXIV, 25, p. 415), command attention. In addition, there were reviews of Karl Liebknecht's *Militarism and Anti-Militarism* (7 March 1918; *NA* XXII, 19, p. 381) and Edwyn Bevan's *German Social Democracy during the War* (10 April 1919; *NA* XXIV, 23, p. 381). Pacifist publications continued to be denounced. In his column, 'Views and Reviews', A. E. Randall slates 'the usual pacifist platitudes' contained in a posthumously-published tract by the former Fine Arts Professor at Queen's College, London, A. W. Rimington, entitled *The Conscience of Europe: The War and the Future*. (3 October 1918; *NA* XXIII, 23, pp. 369-70)

War poetry: 'bombs thrown at society'

Perhaps the most startling literary criticism was levelled at war poetry written by soldiers who had experienced the horrors of the front - the literature now most usually associated with the First World War. Stephen Maguire, who wrote an occasional column of 'Recent Verse', was highly dismissive of Siegfried Sassoon's collection *Counter-Attack and Other Poems*. Maguire argues that satire and poetry are 'almost contradictory moods'; the object of poetry is the 'creation of beauty', but satire without an object is 'meaningless'. Sassoon 'rules himself out of the realm of poetry' on two counts. First, he is 'indifferent to the creation of beauty'. Secondly, he is 'prey to the emotions which tend to satire'. His predominant emotion is hatred and 'without hatred it is probable that not more than one of these poems would have been written'. Maguire dismisses Sassoon's poems as 'bombs thrown at society', aimed at 'bringing home to civilians the horrors of war'. Maguire feels that the poet is not wholly successful in this since the reader's attention is often more preoccupied with him than the subject. To civilians, Sassoon's descriptions of death appear 'repulsive', leaving nothing to the imagination. Maguire prefers A. P. Herbert's *The Bomber Gypsy and other Poems* because, although 'more war poems', they are 'in a less violent mood than Mr Sassoon's'. (21 November 1918; *NA* XXIV, 3, p. 41)

The Music Criticism of William Atheling (Ezra Pound): 'more a secondary personality than a nom de plume'

In December 1917, Orage, who was running short of contributors, engaged Ezra Pound as resident art and music critic for the *New Age*. His art criticism appeared on alternate weeks to his music criticism; the former being written under the pen-name B. H. Dias and the latter under the pen-name William Atheling. Pound possibly took his pseudonyms more seriously than other contributors, conceiving three dimensional characters to match the names. He described William Atheling as 'more a secondary personality than a nom de plume, that is to say he had a definite appearance (baldheaded) and a definite script (crabbed with an old fashioned slant)'.[88] If Pound was not really qualified to write about Germany, his qualifications as a music critic were even more dubious. As Humphrey Carpenter observes, Pound, in his first article on 6 December 1917, describes his Atheling alter-ego as 'a musician... one who has for long watched the opera with a sort of despairing hope', yet the following week he claims that he has never attended a concert for over ten years.[89] Nor did he adopt the conventional terminology of music criticism: Brahms, for example, suggests 'a back parlour with heavy curtains, probably puce-coloured', whilst in the Kreuzer Sonata Atheling finds a passage where 'the piano jabs in, and jerks on the violin, tum, tum, ti, ump, tum, tump, ti ump...' By his own admission Pound was almost tone deaf, and showed no inclination towards modern music: in his column he never mentions Schoenberg, Ravel or Bartok, although they had all entered the London concert repertoire. When reviewing Stravinsky's *Three Pieces for String Quartet*, Atheling acknowledges Stravinsky as 'a composer of the first order' but suggests that one of the pieces should 'stop at various places where it does not' and doubts whether 'its structure is very good'.[90]

---

88   Quoted by Humphrey Carpenter, op. cit., p. 314.
89   Ibid., p. 315.
90   Quoted by Carpenter, ibid., pp. 314-15.

Chapter 6: Germany and the *New Age*: November 1919-September 1922

'Mr. Orage will shortly be leaving London in connection
with work of general and special interest. Both the
proprietorship and editorship of the *New Age* are being
transferred to Major Arthur Moore, late Royal Air Force,
and well known by a wide public as foreign correspondent of *The Times* in the Central East'.

With this small announcement on 28 September 1922 A. R. Orage handed in his
resignation as editor of the *New Age*. He predicted that his successor would
'carry on the tradition of the *New Age* in all its essentials, as well as extend and
expand them in new directions'. Orage hoped to contribute signed articles to the
journal 'from time to time: and his affectionate interest will always be with its
readers and writers' (*NA* XXXI, 22, p. 267). The editor's decision to resign was
sudden and unexpected - even to those who knew him well. The mystery was
compounded by his apparent inability to offer a satisfactory explanation. When
questioned by his secretary, Alice Marks, Orage replied that he was leaving in
order to 'find God'.[1] Indeed, Orage's decision to abandon London journalism in
favour of the esoteric teachings of G. I. Gurdjieff remains one of the most baffling
in his entire career. Even his biographer, Philippe Mairet, who is generally
sympathetic to Orage's life-long fascination with mysticism, suggests that the
editor's resignation was, at least in part, triggered by some form of emotional
crisis in the aftermath of the First World War.[2]

After the Armistice it was by no means unusual for people to
experience this sense of disorientation. For the past four years they had lived
through the conflict, with little energy for anything else. When the fighting
ended, Europe was in economic and political chaos, and those who had survived
felt the full force of 'an enormous emotional vacuum'. They had lost all sense of
direction and, faced with the task of rebuilding society, sought ways of
constructing a system different from the one that had caused the war. With old
religious and political institutions discredited, there was a renewed spiritual
hunger. Some looked to existing alternatives, such as Theosophy, whilst others
turned to new 'spiritual teachers who, though owing more to Theosophy than they
liked to admit, threatened to replace its bland generalities with something
altogether more vigorous. This new wave came once again from a vaguely

---

1   Quoted by Philippe Mairet, *A. R. Orage: A Memoir* (London, 1936), p. 88.
2   Ibid. pp. 88-9.

defined "East", but preferred the energy of militant mystical Islam to the kindly synthesis of Hinduism and Buddhism dreamt up by Madame Blavatsky'.[3] It was to this element that Gurdjieff appealed.

To the bewilderment of his colleagues at the *New Age*[4] and modern commentators alike,[5] Orage moved to Gurdjieff's Institute for Harmonious Development at Avon in the Forest of Fontainbleau. He spent a year at the Institute, studying the work of the Russian mystic who argued that knowledge was a method rather than a doctrine, to be acquired by harsh discipline and the technique of self-observation.[6] In doing this, according to one former contributor to the *New Age*, Orage joined other 'mystical Micawbers' who were waiting 'patiently for something superconscious to turn up'.[7] For the next seven years Orage lectured in the United States in order to raise funds for Gurdjieff, before returning to England in 1930.[8] He made tentative enquiries about resuming editorship of the *New Age*, which was still in circulation, although now reduced to a mere eight pages and controlled by Anglican Socialists calling themselves the Chandos Group.[9] However, when negotiations proved unfruitful, he chose instead the *New English Weekly*. Based at 38 Cursitor Street, just off Chancery Lane - in the very same office from which he had once run the *New Age* - Orage edited the *New English Weekly* from April 1932 until his death in November 1934.[10] Philippe Mairet, who had acted as assistant editor, then took over as editor of the *New English Weekly*, remaining in that position until 1949.[11]

3   Peter Washington, *Madame Blavatsky's Baboon: Theosophy and the Emergence of the Western Guru* (London, 1993), pp. 168-9.

4   See Denis Saurat, 'Visite à Gourdjieff', *La Nouvelle Revue française*, 14 (1933), pp. 686-98.

5   See Antony Alpers, *The Life of Katherine Mansfield* (London, 1980), p. 108.

6   For details of Gurdjieff's methods see Peter Washington, op. cit., pp. 239-41.

7   C. E. Bechhofer, 'The Forest Philosophers', *Century Magazine*, 118, No. 1 (May 1934), p. 26. Quoted by Peter Washington, op. cit., p. 244.

8   See John Carswell, *Lives and Letters* (London, 1978), pp. 212-13.

9   Ibid., p. 214.

10   Ibid., pp. 216-17.

11   See Philippe Mairet, *Autobiographical and other Papers*, edited by C. H. Sisson (Manchester, 1981), p. viii.

The New Age in decline: 'The Great War put an end to many things and many ideas'

By no stretch of the imagination can it be said that Orage left London on a note of triumph in 1922. The heyday of his journal was over and the last years were marked by a sense of decline and disillusionment caused by the First World War. On 1 April 1926 Orage acknowledged that 'the Great War put an end to many things and many ideas [...] We woke from the evil dream shortly after the armistice; and in the horrible light of morning we began to count our losses' ('An Editor's Progress'; *NA* XXXVIII, 1, p. 258). Indeed, the war had brought not only spiritual malaise, but economic hardship as well. By the end of 1919 the *New Age* was in a greater state of crisis than ever before. Lewis Wallace and P. T. Kenway, who had previously subsidised the periodical by generous donations, could no longer afford to do so.[12] The rising costs of producing a journal exacted their toll on Orage, who frequently had to justify to his 'dwindling body of readers'[13] the draconian measures he was being forced to take. The size and cost of the *New Age* continually troubled the editor. On 26 February 1920, for example, he notes in his 'Readers and Writers' column that the *Spectator* has gone up from 6d to 9d, whilst Chesterton's *New Witness* 'recently took the long jump of raising its price to a shilling'. The only journals to be published at the pre-war price of 6d are the *Nation, New Statesman, Saturday Review* and the *Outlook*. The *New Age*, by comparison, had to be raised from 6d to 7d in the First World War. Because costs never go down, Orage feels he has good grounds for raising the price. In 1920 he is faced with the dilemma of either raising the price further or increasing circulation by about five hundred. He predicts that the latter measure would not only keep the price down, but could increase the journal from its present sixteen pages - a cost-cutting move in the war[14] - to what Orage considers the 'natural size' of the *New Age*: twenty pages (*NA* XXVI, 17, p. 272). On 19 August 1920, with a circulation of barely two thousand per week, compared with twenty two thousand in 1908,[15] the journal was cut from sixteen to twelve pages.

This economy measure, prompted by the 'stricken state' of the *New Age*, deeply affected Orage, who, writing as R.H.C. in 'Readers and Writers',

---

12   Philippe Mairet, 'Reintroduction', *A. R. Orage: A Memoir*, second edition (New York, 1966), p. xiv.   This edition contains more information, especially about Orage's post-war interests.

13   13 July 1922; *NA* XXXI, 11, p. 125.

14   See John Carswell, op. cit., p. 144.

15   Wallace Martin, *The New Age Under Orage: Chapters in English Cultural History* (Manchester, 1967), p. 62.

recalls nostalgically that on one occasion the journal, boosted in length by a 'Feminist Symposium' - doubtless from the days of Beatrice Hastings - ran to no less than forty eight pages. The editor warns that he may be forced to cut the journal further - to eight or even four pages, although the *New Age*, he assures us, 'will fight to the last'. He is concerned not only with the financial crisis, but with the cultural desolation of post-war Europe as well. Despairingly he warns that 'the light of culture is growing dim, faith in its saving reality is hard to sustain, and I am not at all confident that the whole world is not about to be plunged into a worse than pre-medieval darkness. Against a world-movement upon this scale of grandeur, only the strongest will be able to battle successfully; in such a darkness only those who shine by their own light will continue to be visible by their own self-consciousness. We are entering a period that will winnow real from borrowed culture as the wind winnows chaff from wheat. To return to our moutons, the shrinkage of the *New Age* is at once an index and a portent: it shows how strong the wind already is, and the direction in which it is still blowing. Spring is far off.' (19 August 1920; *NA* XXVII, 16, p. 247)

Spring proved so elusive that by January 1922 valuable space in the *New Age* was occupied with advertisements for books[16] in an attempt to bring in much-needed revenue for the ailing journal. Ironically, it had been an argument over allowing advertisements in the *New Age* that prompted Holbrook Jackson to resign as joint editor in 1908. Jackson, ever the pragmatist, had wanted advertisements in the *New Age* to help fund it; Orage had refused point blank.[17] However, by the end of 1921, the *New Age* was in such a parlous state that it was to Jackson that Orage turned for advice when he decided to 'let the *back page*, and only that, for advertisements - preferably, but not absolutely, publishers. I've already got provisional orders for 8 pages during the year; and I'm wondering whether, out of your experience, you could put me on the easiest track of completing the 52 issues.'[18]

---

16   On 5 January 1922, for instance, there is a full page advertisement for the latest publications by George Allen and Unwin, including the English edition of a study of Romain Rolland by Stefan Zweig (*NA* XXX, 10, p. 124), whilst on 26 January 1922, there is an advertisement for a volume of *Selected Letters of Nietzsche*, edited by Oscar Levy and translated by A. M. Ludovici (*NA* XXX, 13, p. 172).

17   See Philippe Mairet, *A. R. Orage: A Memoir* (London, 1936), pp. 48-9.

18   Letter dated 6 December 1921, Harry Ransom Humanities Research Center, University of Texas at Austin (hereafter HRHRC), Manuscripts by and Relating to A. R. Orage.

Nevertheless, the decline of the *New Age* was not entirely due to outside circumstances. In his choice of material for the periodical after the First World War Orage was partly to blame. As the *New Age* became increasingly the organ for the editor's two great enthusiasms - economics and mysticism - readers, who had previously found sustenance from the variety of articles on politics, literature, philosophy and the arts in general, were inevitably alienated. C. H. Douglas continued to make regular appearances,[19] occasionally standing in for Orage on the political commentary 'Notes of the Week'.[20] Even when Douglas was not on hand to provide an article, Orage was keen to let his readers see what other publications were saying about Douglas and Social Credit. Thus, on 27 May 1920 'Press Cuttings' contains a whole page of articles from various journals on C. H. Douglas's *Economic Democracy*, which, along with his *Credit Power and Democracy*, was serialized in the *New Age* (*NA* XXVII, 4, p. 64). In addition, Orage himself discusses economics. On 1 December 1921 Douglas contributes a piece on 'The Question of Exports'; it is immediately followed by one on 'Current Economics' by Orage, using the pseudonym A.B.C.[21] By 4 May 1922 Orage has playfully changed his pen-name from A.B.C. to X.Y.Z. (*NA* XXXI, 1, p. 6). Only after he resigned as editor did Orage sign these articles under his own name.[22] Name playing was not new to him. In 1897, for instance, in waggish mood, he entered his name on the Leeds ward roll as Alfred O'Rage.[23] With the exception of this diversion, Orage always favoured a French pronunciation of his name, claiming Huguenot origin. However, in Fenstanton in Huntingdonshire, where he grew up and where his father was born, the name, as Bernard Shaw delighted in pointing out, was pronounced 'Orridge' to rhyme with 'porridge'.[24]

---

19 On 20 July 1922, for example, Douglas began a new series on 'The Labour Party and Social Credit' (*NA* XXXI, 12, pp. 145-6).

20 For the first three weeks in November 1919 C. H. Douglas was responsible for 'Notes of the Week' (See *NA* XXVI, 1 pp. 1-4, *NA* XXVI, 2, pp. 12-19 and *NA* XXVI, 3, pp. 33-5). Douglas took over 'Notes of the Week' again on 24 June 1920 (*NA* XXVII, 8, pp. 113-15) and on 14 April 1921 (*NA* XXVIII, 24, pp. 277-9).

21 This pseudonym, as we have seen, had been used by Orage before. See Chapter 4, p. 119, note 40 and p. 140.

22 See, for example, 5 October 1922; *NA* XXXI, 23, pp. 284-5.

23 Tom Steele, *Alfred Orage and the Leeds Arts Club 1893-1923* (Aldershot, 1990), p. 40.

24 John Carswell, op. cit., p. 16.

If the deluge of articles on economics was perplexing, it was nothing compared with the vast array of discourses on mysticism that crept into the journal between 1919 and 1922. Occasionally Orage looked to German writers for material. In August 1921, for example, he published a series of rather obscure articles on mysticism translated from the German of Volker (sic),[25] whilst on 12 January 1922 he printed the first in a series of articles entitled 'Metaphysics' by the Viennese Otto Weininger (1880-1903), adapted from his posthumously published treatise *Über die letzten Dinge* (1904) (*NA* XXX, 11, pp. 131-3). Weininger was, in fact, best known for his psycho-anthropological discourse *Geschlecht und Charakter* (1903), which asserted the intellectual superiority of man over woman and achieved a certain notoriety for its antisemitism. The fact that the author committed suicide heightened its infamy in Germany and Austria, although it was almost completely forgotten a decade later.

Perhaps even more significant in terms of the changing interests of the editor is the alteration to the subtitle of the *New Age*. Between May 1907, when Orage took over as editor, and December 1920 the *New Age* is described as 'A Socialist Review of Politics Literature and Art'. At the beginning of January 1921 it is renamed 'A Socialist Review of Religion, Science and Art. By November of that year it is called 'A Weekly Review of Politics, Literature and Art', almost a return to the original title.

M. M. Cosmoi: Regarding the war 'as an attempt at synthesis'

Between 1920 and 1921 by far the most attention was devoted to a bizarre series entitled 'World Affairs' by M. M. Cosmoi, a collaboration of A. R. Orage and Dimitri Mitrinović, 'a tall, dark bullet-headed Serbian with the lips of a Roman soldier and an erratic, soaring mind'.[26] Just before M. M. Cosmoi was unleashed, a notice in the *New Age* had expressed the wish that the column 'Foreign Affairs'[27] could be resumed, or, 'preferably "World Affairs" from a point

---

25 See 4 August 1921; *NA* XXIX, 14, pp, 159-60; 11 August 1921; *NA* XXIX, 15, pp. 171-2; 18 August 1921; *NA* XXIX, 16, pp. 183-4 and 25 August 1921; *NA* XXIX, 12, pp. 195-6.

26 Edwin Muir, *An Autobiography* (London, 1954), p. 174.

27 J. M. Kennedy, using the pseudonym S. Verdad, had been responsible for this weekly column from 1911 until his death in 1918, when Orage took over, using the same pen-name.

of view that has not hitherto been made current in practical politics.' (12 August 1920; *NA* XXVII, 15, p. 223)

It soon became apparent that foreign affairs viewed from a new angle meant approaching the subject through mysticism. On 23 September 1920, for example, M. M. Cosmoi argues that wars 'are always psychological in origin; they reveal a stress, an unresolved conflict, in the group-mind, and, finally, in the world-mind, which can find no better means of resolution into a synthesis than war'. What, then, were the stresses in Europe before the outbreak of what Cosmoi quaintly terms the 'Great Civil War'? He argues that the stresses are to be found in the 'historic circumstances surrounding and preceding the outbreak of war. Serbia versus Austria, and Germany versus France and England - these, it is plain, were the lines of conflict'. In addition, there was 'the demand of Russia to enter into European consciousness and become one with Europe'. The war was therefore 'no less than an attempt at a new and greater European synthesis'. He perceives that 'what Serbia was in relation to Austria, Germany felt herself to be in relation to France and England'. Serbia, as 'the pioneer in Europe of the Slav awakening', found herself confronted with 'a decadent, cosmopolised and increasingly de-Europeanised' Hapsburg Empire. The Austrians tried to 'stifle the life' of Serbia, a 'young nation'. Thus, 'it was in the name of a new Europe, a more completely Aryan Europe, that the heroic crusade of Serbia against Austria was undertaken'. Cosmoi contends that 'in the best minds in Germany, a similar idea had long been at work, the European "enemy" in this case being the decadent, commercialised, cosmopolised and de-Europeanised polity and culture of the dominant nations of France and England. And again, for the best minds in Germany as for those in Serbia, the war assumed the character of a heroic crusade on behalf of the New Europe, a Europe recalled to its Aryan traditions. That Serbia and Germany were not on the same side, that Germany was so blind as to fail to realise her essential spiritual unity with Serbia, was one of the most profound misunderstandings in the tragedy; and it was a German misunderstanding'. He ventures to suggest that 'had Germany understood that Serbia's challenge was the challenge of the Slav race to a higher European synthesis, the war need never have befallen Europe. Germany in spiritual unity with Serbia and Russia could have ensured the new synthesis of Europe without civil war. But the German conception of the New Europe, though Aryan in unconscious need, was purely German in conscious expression; and led its exponents to elevate Siegfried as the sole European culture-hero, to the exclusion of the other culture-heroes of the many-sided European mind. Nevertheless, it is as an attempt at synthesis that the war must be regarded; as an attempt that has so far failed.' (*NA* XXVII, 21, p. 304)

Cosmoi is convinced that the 'late European Civil War' was a 'racial crime', a 'brain-storm in the world consciousness from which only with the utmost care will the world intelligence recover'. When he reflects on the history of the conduct of the war, he acknowledges 'the depths of infamy and treachery to which the belligerent leaders on every side sank. Germany, it may be said, began it when she deliberately endeavoured to enlist a Jehad on her side and did not scruple, later, to encourage the Militarists of Japan to make trouble for the white race in Mexico and South America. But France and England and even America were not slow to descend to the same place and to employ weapons which ought to be inwardly forbidden to Aryans even when existence appears to be at stake; for a bloodthirsty and barbarous clinging to life is not Aryan morality'. This action, Cosmoi claims, has caused 'the demoralisation of spirit that undoubtedly has come over the European mind. Conscious of having committed a crime against her own best nature, and not yet courageous enough to confess it and make repentance and atonement, Europe naturally finds herself without the power to make a good resolution for the future.' (7 October 1920; *NA* XXVII, 23, pp. 237-8)

By 1921 'World Affairs' was becoming even more abstruse - probably because Orage had ceased to collaborate on the column, allowing Mitrinović free reign on M. M. Cosmoi. It was plain that Cosmoi was alienating more readers than he was enlightening. Orage's instincts as an editor finally reasserted themselves and 'World Affairs' made its final appearance on 13 October 1921.

C. H. Norman and War: 'the killing of men does not settle any question'

Despite his fascination with the direction of 'World Affairs', Orage was still interested in the work of former contributors. Amongst the established writers to return to the pages of the *New Age* was Hilaire Belloc who contributed a series of articles on 'The House of Commons' in January 1920, followed by one on 'Foreign Affairs' in September 1921. Beatrice Hastings, in the guise of Alice Morning, made her last appearance in 1920, with an article on culture in the French capital, entitled 'Something Alive in Paris?' (11 March 1920; *NA* XXVI, 19, pp. 302-3), whilst Ramiro de Maeztu contributed his final article 'East and West' on 5 August 1920 (*NA* XXVII, 14, p. 212). In addition, work by T. E. Hulme, who had written for the *New Age* before his death in the First World War, continued to attract interest. On 6 October 1921 Orage published 'Fragments', a selection of poetry from Hulme's notebook (*NA* XXIX, 23, pp. 275-6), whilst on 19 January 1922 the *New Age* carried the first in a series of 'The Notebooks of T. E. Hulme', edited by Herbert Read (*NA* XXX, 12, pp. 148-9). However, perhaps the most controversial writer to return to the *New Age* was C. H. Norman. During the First World War Norman had been one of the founding members of the No Conscription Fellowship and, as a conscientious objector, had been imprisoned for his beliefs. Before the war he had contributed regularly to the *New Age* and, as Stanhope of Chester, was the controversial predecessor   of

J. M. Kennedy as foreign affairs correspondent.[28] During the hostilities Orage, who never agreed with the pacifist argument,[29] published several articles by Norman protesting against the fighting.[30]

In his post-war series, entitled 'Suppose? Or Some Illusions about Mankind', Norman explores wasteful kinds of human activity, which he believes are usually connected with property, religion, war and militarism. He contends that 'this war has shown that war does not solve any question in reality, because mere destruction, either of your enemy or his property, only recoils upon the destroyer. The killing of men does not settle any question; it does not even solve the strength of the respective contestants, as human beings will not tolerate in these times a war that is fought to a finish in fact. The community of human suffering and the common instincts of ordinary men rise in revolt against governments and statesmen who pursue a policy of logic in murder and destruction'. He observes that the war has produced 'another curious sentiment', namely 'the mental illusion called Patriotism'. He goes on to define patriotism as 'a feeling innate in most men, convincing them that something near to them and known to them, in which all their lives have been spent, has some advantage and superiority over the rest of the world'. Those who exploited their patriotism for their own advantage during the war were, according to Norman, the Lord Chancellor who gained a legal advantage, Lloyd George who gained a political advantage, and Horatio Bottomley, the jingoistic editor of *John Bull* and inventor of the term 'Germ-huns',[31] who gained a journalistic advantage. There were no 'military, financial or naval geniuses, but a dreary lot of blunderers'. Rather surprisingly, all these wrong-doers advocated the 'wholesale suppression of patriotism throughout the Empire' by imprisoning conscientious objectors without the right of habeas corpus. Norman convincingly argues that 'patriotism, war and militarism are all waste: the first of mental energy, as there is nothing more absurd than arguing that it is finer to be an Englishman than a Frenchman or *vice versa*, or in claiming the monopoly of trade or territory or capacity for government as existing in one particular set or class of people; war, because nothing is gained by killing your opponent or stealing his property; militarism, because militarism is merely the organised expression of war and of the destructive side of patriotism.' (8 June 1922; *NA* XXXI, 6, p. 68)

---

28   See Wallace Martin, op. cit., p. 123.

29   See 20 April 1916; *NA* XVIII, 26, p. 605.

30   See, for example, 'Why I think the war should be stopped' (29 July 1915; *NA* XVII, 13, pp. 302-3).

31   Paul Fussell, *The Great War and Modern Memory* (New York and London, 1975), p. 77.

After the First World War conscientious objectors gained a more sympathetic hearing in the *New Age*, even if their action was never wholly condoned. Their treatment at the hands of the military was a particular cause for concern. At Wandsworth Detention Barracks, for example, C. H. Norman had been spat at, sworn at, force fed and strait-jacketed.[32] Bertrand Russell was so outraged to learn of Norman's maltreatment that he launched an 'Appeal on Behalf of Conscientious Objectors' (23 June 1916), which gave such gruesome details of the torture meted out to pacifists in military custody that the Wandsworth Commandant was dismissed.[33] On 22 June 1922 A. E. Randall devotes his 'Views and Reviews' column to a discussion of John W. Graham's *Conscription and Conscience*, with a preface by Clifford Allen, the President of the No Conscription Fellowship. Randall feels 'sickened by the records here quoted of the sufferings inflicted upon the conscientious objectors. They went far beyond the usual severities of our penal system, which itself is an abomination that no civilised nation could tolerate; the old delight in torture revived', and men who, 'were otherwise admirable, behaved like homicidal maniacs. On the field of battle much may be excused; the conditions are abnormal, and abnormal responses must be expected. But these barbarities were inflicted usually far from the battlefield, in the name of discipline, by men who claimed the right to govern men; and my gorge rises out at the record'. Nevertheless, Randall still believes that the conscientious objectors have only themselves to blame 'for having provoked these brutalities'. (*NA* XXXI, 8, p. 94)

Post-war Germany: 'the shadow of 1921 with its attendant bogey is here'

Alongside the more established contributors Orage welcomed less well-known writers to his periodical. Even within the constraints of a rapidly shrinking journal increasingly dominated by explorations of mysticism and economics, articles on Germany continued to arouse the interest of the editor. On 6 April 1922, for instance, Auriol Barvan investigates 'The New Germany'. He perceives that German order has been replaced with 'democracy at its worst', with the proletarian influence reigning supreme. As a result, 'instead of the proverbial cleanliness of a German town, you are somewhat astonished by the neglected appearance of the thoroughfares'. He explains that 'it is no longer 1914, or the seasons leading up to the fateful year. It is the grim present, and the shadow of 1921 with its attendant bogey is here. The gilt is off the cake, the glamour departed, and we are face to face with hard facts. The old order is swept away:

---

32 *The Collected Papers of Bertrand Russell*, Volume XIII, *Prophecy and Dissent 1914-16*, edited by Richard A. Rempel (London, 1988), p. 408.

33 Ibid., p. 410.

cafes filled not with aristocrats but Mr. "War Profiteer" and his family'. The theatres reveal 'a lowering tone and morals, a lack of public taste and artistic sense, compared to former days'. He observes with disdain that some of the nouveau-riches in the audience do not even bother to change into evening dress. To make matters worse, the housing problem in Berlin is very acute due to 'the invasion of refugees and fugitives from annexed and occupied territory', namely Alsace-Lorraine, Upper Silesia and parts of Poland formerly belonging to Prussian and Posen. There is a slump in the building trade with the high cost of materials and labour. Professional people with spare rooms in their homes find the homeless billeted upon them. There is great animosity towards the French, Barvan notes, cautioning that this bodes ominously for future conflict. However, the Germans are more concerned with re-establishing trade links, and are looking towards the United States and England, which they regard as 'a Power they can trust, owing to her sense of fair play and justice'. Faced with the immediate prospect of financial ruin, the Germans are willing to undertake the humblest jobs for meagre wages. Although there is still some militarist talk, he believes, rather oddly, that it is confined to the 'Hot Air Artist Class'. (*NA* XXX, 23, pp. 295-6)

Notes of the Week: France threatens to stir 'the ashes of the dead militarism of Germany into a possible flame'

The Treaty of Versailles, with its severe treatment of Germany,[34] continued to cast a shadow over political discussion in the *New Age*. In his column 'Notes of the Week', Orage repeatedly voices grave fears about the worsening state of Franco-German relations, as France presses for harsher measures against Germany.[35] On 26 May 1921, for example, he cautions that 'the French assumption that Germany is unchanged or can constitute any immediate danger should be instantly and explicitly challenged and denied. Not for a generation at the very least, even under the worst conceivable circumstances, is Germany likely to menace France. France's fear of Germany is altogether unworthy of France's recent victory'. The French, he observes, are seeking to make their own country secure whilst weakening Germany. By advancing this proposal, France is 'stirring the ashes of the dead militarism of Germany into a possible flame'. Orage, clearly influenced by the vocabulary of his alter-ego M. M. Cosmoi, perceives that 'apart from its economic causation, the dominant unconscious motive of the late European Civil War was the need to integrate

---

34   See William Carr, *A History of Germany 1815-1985*, third edition (London, 1987), p. 262.

35   By April 1921 Franco-German relations were at a particularly low ebb. See William Carr, ibid., p. 272.

Europe. Like its predecessors it failed, but there ought to be no doubt that the attempt will be renewed, since the integration of Europe is an indispensable condition of the integration of the world'. Although he expects that further attempts at European unification will be made, he is certain that in this task 'neither France nor Germany is called upon to play the role of hegemony; in fact, as history has conclusively proved, the dictatorial hegemony of Europe is impossible to any single nation'. Orage contends that 'such is the spiritual nature of Europe that neither Caesar nor Charlemagne, neither Napoleon nor Prussia, could impose an external uniformity upon her in the absence of the consent of all her parts. France entertains the notion still that she alone is the heir of the European tradition and that upon France *in excelsis* lies the responsibility of the integration of Europe. The day for a Europe dominated by the Roman tradition is, however, past, and equally for a Europe dominated by German or Slav or Anglo-Saxon ideas'. What is now needed, according to Orage, is 'a concept of Europe as Europe is and must become: a Europe functionally organised and only integrated by subordination of the parts to the whole. And the racial blocks, as they already exist, appear to us to indicate plainly the direction in which such a unity is to be sought'. Europe, Orage believes, is divided into three parts: 'the "Latin" block, the racial and cultural inheritors of the Roman tradition associated with Peter', then the 'Slav block', which is 'racially and culturally associated with the mystical John', and finally the 'Anglo-Teutonic block similarly associated with the humanity of Paul'. He argues that 'an integral Europe demands the specialisation of the functions of each of these groups and their co-ordination in a single spiritual organism, that of Europe as a whole. And the "foreign policies" of the respective leaders of the three groups should be directed both to this specialisation and to their simultaneous co-ordination: federations of the Latin, the Anglo-Teutonic and the Slav nations in conscious self-direction towards a European triple federation.' (*NA* XXIX, 4, p. 39)

Franco-German relations deteriorated still further in 1922 when Raymond Poincaré (1860-1934), who embodied French distrust of Germany, became Prime Minister of France.[36] He insisted that Germany pay her reparations promptly, causing a rift between the French and the British, who were keen to pursue a more lenient policy that would restore Germany, their best pre-war customer, to financial stability.[37] On 18 May 1922 Orage once more takes up the theme of France's fear of Germany. He explains that 'from every point of view that we can discover, it appears to us that France is making the wrong choice in preferring prevention to adaptation. To begin with, it is as certain as anything can be that, sooner or later, by one means or another, Germany will find her feet

---

36   Ibid., p. 262.
37   Ibid., p. 272.

again. Not only Germany herself is intent as one man upon it, but Germany's creditors all over the world demand it. Even France herself must be bankrupt unless Germany is enabled to pay her debts. Again, without anticipating so immediate a restoration of Russia as our Liberals dream of, it is likewise certain that the rehabilitation of Germany is only possible through some degree of the rehabilitation of Russian industry. In other words, Germany and Russia must in a certain sense rise together as they have fallen together'. The Treaty of Rapallo, which re-established diplomatic relations between Germany and Russia in 1922,[38] has proved that each is necessary to the other. Orage reasons that 'the politics of Europe are determined by credits in the last resort', and the 'Great Powers of Credit are on the side of the restoration of both Germany and Russia - not, of course, we hasten to add, in the interest of the credits they represent. Germany as a vast factory mortgaged to international Credit, together with Russia, a vast store of raw materials similarly mortgaged to the same international financiers, present between them a prospect too irresistible to be vetoed by France. Unless, therefore, France is prepared, as she is not, to challenge the whole financial system of the world, the disposition of credit-forces is such that Eastern Europe, including Germany, is certain to be restored at whatever cost to the future of Europe itself'. He concludes with a warning that 'the present French pacifism via the forcible subjection of Germany and Russia is as certain to bring about war as the restoration of Germany, and with only this difference that in the former case the precipitation of war will be earlier and still more disastrous for France.' (*NA* XXXI, 3, pp. 25-6)

Allied bankers 'are driving Germany upon the rocks as rapidly as possible'

At the same time as Orage criticises French policy towards Germany, he is careful to point out that Allied bankers must share some of the blame for Germany's post-war plight. He is in no doubt that 'our experienced bankers and financial experts' have done nothing but 'commit one blunder after another', instead of solving post-war problems. He argues passionately that 'in the case of Germany, it is clear that our "experts" are driving Germany upon the rocks as rapidly as possible and apparently with the deliberate intention of avoiding every other course. It is agreed, and it is essential, that Germany should pay. At the same time, it is no less agreed that of the various possible means of payment Germany shall be forbidden or made incapable of employing a single one.

---

38   Ibid., p. 272.

Germany cannot pay in gold any more than we can,[39] since America holds most of the gold of the world'. He observes shrewdly that Germany cannot pay in goods, 'since every country is erecting higher and higher tariff-walls in order to exclude German goods. Equally she cannot pay in services and the only medium of payment left her is paper-money, the value of which will speedily be reduced to zero. Yet, in spite of this commercial impasse, our experts continue to talk as if things were still normal'. With the examples of Russia and Austria before them, these experts 'still appear to think that a bankrupt country may be made solvent by reducing its ability to pay. And, what is worse, even the nations which nominally they represent - France, England and America - are suffering almost as much from the policy as their intended victims' (20 July 1922; NA XXXI, 12, p. 141). This view is in keeping with his analysis of the economic crisis at home, since by the end of the First World War Orage 'had come fully to believe that the manipulation of the currency system by the banks and the government was the real cause of the economic hardships faced by British workers'.[40]

Orage reserves particular contempt for the financial experts dealing with Austria. On 10 August 1922 he reflects that in the four years since the Armistice 'the financial condition of Austria has been going from bad to worse'. He cautions that 'it lacks nothing but a Lenin to push it over the precipice into irretrievable chaos'. Despite a large number of experts offering advice, nothing has been done to avert disaster. He contends that revolt on the lines of Lenin's Bolshevist revolution 'is no solution at all', although he acknowledges that there is little reward for 'a people that avoids the Russian solution, submits to the control of experts, and at the end finds itself as badly off as if it had handed itself over to amateurs'. He views the crisis in Austria as 'an indictment of the financial experts, none of whom, after their exemplary failure in this comparatively docile case, has hereafter the right to even an opinion upon public government.' (NA XXXI, 15, p. 177)

By the end of August 1922 Orage has lost all hope of Europe avoiding ruin. He reminds readers that 'ever since the Armistice we have been saying that Europe could not recover from a war which was caused by finance without changing her financial system. An earthquake is not a mere landslide, and the dimensions and character of the Great War ought to have convinced everybody that the world was not faced by just one of the disasters of history, but

---

39   In a study of Ezra Pound's economic education at the offices of the *New Age*, Tim Redman has demonstrated that after the First World War many people, including Orage, lost confidence in the International Gold Standard. See Tim Redman, *Ezra Pound and Italian Fascism* (Cambridge, 1991), pp. 32-40.

40   Ibid., p. 46.

by an epochal catastrophe; and that, in consequence, only something equally great on the part of mankind could possibly be expected to deal with it'. Instead of seeking the 'means of making a human effort of constructive intelligence corresponding to the blind effort of destructive stupidity, practically all our governors, together with their hordes of publicists and experts, settled down into the old grooves of thought and proceeded to treat the aftermath of an Epochal War as if it had been no more than a Napoleonic adventure. It was in vain that we pointed out that more money had been spent by Governments during the four years of the war than had been spent during the previous four centuries. The significance of an acceleration of hundreds per cent in a few short years was utterly missed, with the consequence that the precipitous downward plunge of the whole of civilisation has been treated as if it were merely one of the downs of the usual ups and downs in an otherwise stable state of things. Even at this moment, when anybody can observe for himself the appalling progress of the condition of chaos, our demented "experts" are busily engaged in repeating all the old phrases about economy, balancing budgets, getting back to the gold standard, and the rest of the ruinous lies of the dead financial system'. The only solution, according to Orage, is to be found in the system of Social Credit of C. H. Douglas. However, Douglas's 'profound and practical ideas cannot force their way against the solid block of apathy and interested stupidity which at present is opposed to them. In a very little while, unless a miracle is wrought, even they will cease to be applicable, and the world will be plunged into a darkness unrelieved by the light of its last candle. We solemnly warn our readers that the time at our disposal is now very brief. In a few months or weeks the end may come.' (31 August 1922; *NA* XXXI, 18, p. 217)

Ezra Pound: the League of Nations is 'too important an affair to be based merely on a detestation of the Hun'

Orage was not alone in his fears for post-war Europe. Ezra Pound, who continued to write for the *New Age* until 1921 when he left England 'perhaps for one year, perhaps for two, perhaps for good',[41] also explored ideas about the future structure of Europe. On 18 December 1919, in the third of a series of articles entitled 'The Revolt of Intelligence', Pound turns his attention to the concept of a League of Nations. The League of Nations, which came into being in 1920, was the subject of much discussion at the time. Bernard Shaw, for example, looked forward to seeing Europe 'provided with a new organ for supernational (sic) action' and 'an effective police' that would make disarmament

---

41   R.H.C., 'Readers and Writers', 13 January 1921; *NA* XXVIII, 13, p. 126.

feasible.[42] Inevitably, the reality failed to live up to these high expectations and Shaw was deeply disappointed to find the League of Nations 'reduced to absurdity by the fact that Russia, Germany and the United States are not in it'.[43] For his part, Pound claims to have 'no interest in any country as a nation. The league of *nations* appears to me about as safe and as inviting for the individual as does a combine of large companies for the employee. The more I see of *nations* the more I loathe them; the more I learn of civilisation the more I desire that it exist and that such scraps of it as we have should be preserved for us and for our successors'. He believes that the southern states of America 'probably had a legal right to secede in 1861', although the American Civil War was 'a great calamity of American civilisation and possibly the doom of the Anglo-Saxon race in America. The extermination of the best human stock in any district advances nothing. The decline of human liberty in the states may quite possibly date from the year of the emancipation proclamation', although he is not advocating the re-introduction of black slavery. Pound objects to 'secessions and to divisions of political units once formed'. Even in the case of Germany, he contends, 'border territory which cannot be absorbed into adjacent large countries should remain part of the German republic, *for the good of civilisation*'. In addition, he feels that Germany, 'as a particularly civilised country should be maintained against the barbarism of Russia, should contingency arise'. (*NA* XXVI, 7, pp. 106-7)

The following month Pound once more considers the idea of a League of Nations. He favours an 'International Chamber', which would be 'a larger body elected by direct vote of the people' and would sit for at least six months of the year, but would not be able to issue commands. Instead, it would have to use the power of persuasion. This is a long way removed from the League of Nations 'proposed by the "Big Four"'. Pound argues poignantly that 'an international chamber is too important an affair to be based merely on a detestation of the Hun which cannot be maintained for more than fifty or one hundred years save by artificial means. I am as ready as the next man to see the Kaiser hung, drawn and quartered, but one should not be blind to the probable duration of national loves and hates. You can be ready to torture the man who has tortured you or your brother or your friend in a German prison, but you cannot be made to extend that hate of some other man of a different district, of different features, and maintain that hate indefinitely. You cannot even shift the emotion you may feel about Tirpitz and apply it to Ebert. Hatred of Germany will, according to men's natures, endure for ten years or a lifetime, and may even descend to men's children in a certain number of cases where the hatred bred by the newspapers is flimsier stuff

---

42   Quoted by Michael Holroyd, *Bernard Shaw, Vol. III, 1918-1950. The Lure of Fantasy* (London, 1991), p. 230.
43   Quoted by Holroyd, ibid., p. 230.

than this'. Pound concedes that 'this stimulated emotion was probably necessary to win the war, but a lot of it was only "for the duration". I am not preaching a sermon of forgiveness; this is simply a recognition of human limitation'. He fears that a League of Nations backed up by force will pose a threat, chiefly because 'every local dispute may produce a world conflict. A League of Nations with the power in the hands of a small committee appointed by Governmental inner cliques in each nation is a peril'. He therefore proposes a 'League of Nations, whose sole visible being should be a large Chamber of Deputies, bearing the same relation to individual State Governments as in States where the senators are chosen directly by the people'. Such an organisation 'should be a force of international understanding, a moral force constituted in recognition of the futility of violent means.' (8 January 1920; *NA* XXVI, 10, pp. 153-4)

Janko Lavrin and the Germans: 'a race which has given to the world Goethe, Kant, Bach, Beethoven, Mozart, Wagner'

In 1920 Janko Lavrin, a Professor of Slavonic Languages, was responsible for a series on articles entitled 'Contemporary Fragments', whose scope included further investigation of the subject so popular with wartime propagandists, namely Germany and Culture. He argues plausibly that in the last few years the European nations at war 'have assumed the habit of judging their opponents not objectively, but merely by those single features which show them in the least favourable light' and are actually harmful in time of peace. This way of thinking 'paralyses the possibility of a mutual understanding and genuine co-operation between the various nations, fostering anew that racial exclusiveness, conceit, and hatred which are the best agents of a permanent disintegration of humanity'. Lavrin contends that although 'all the cruelties perpetrated by Germans during the European War will be remembered throughout history as a stain on their reputation; at the same time it would be ridiculous to condemn as merely "barbaric" a race which has given to the world Goethe, Kant, Bach, Beethoven, Mozart, Wagner, and a score of other great men, of whose works not only Germans themselves but the whole of humanity would be proud'. It would be 'equally one-sided to judge German cultural potencies merely from what we know of a pathological period', in which the Germans became 'practical maniacs'. That 'national mania', Lavrin reasons, 'was not the fault of the Germans alone, but a logical result of a general social and political pathology - in fact, the peculiar disease of the whole modern world. The fact that this disease has assumed in Germany more violent proportions than elsewhere can be easily explained by the fact that she was tempted or almost compelled by external circumstances to give, willy-nilly, a wrong, a destructive direction to all her tremendous will and energy'. The Germans 'of a century ago - the Germans of Kant, Goethe, and Schiller - seemed in truth to be one of the most promising rising races. If they

223

had not a grand and refined culture, they had at least a will to culture, perhaps a stronger conscious will to culture than any other modern nation'. However, their 'growing cultural striving' clashed with 'the growing economic and capitalistic competition of modern states, a competition which is paralysing older and more solid cultures than that of Germany'. He argues that 'shut in a relatively small territory, divided into numerous petty States, surrounded by hostile races (Slavs and French), confronted by the economic and political growth of her neighbours, Germany had but one choice - either to be strangled by her competitors or to overcome them in military and capitalistic development. From a mere instinct of physical self-preservation, Germany was soon induced to choose the second alternative, sacrificing to it her "better self" and gradually transforming all her values for its sake'. Thus, before Germany's 'cultural possibilities could reach their maturity, they had to degenerate into political factors'. Now German politics direct German culture - not vice versa. Lavrin maintains that had Germany's cultural traditions been more profound, there would have been 'an inevitable cleavage between her political and her cultural values. But as the latter were still too young and "adaptable", there resulted a bizarre co-operation between them which led modern Germans to such ruthless aggressiveness and political cynicism as to astonish her less "vital" and more "moderate" neighbours'. He considers one of the most interesting processes of modern times to be 'the gradual transformation from an aristocracy of idealistic dreamers' to one of 'aggressive "patriots" with their notorious cult of Fatherland and "mailed fist"'. It was 'amazing energy, will and organisation' that enabled the German state to rise to 'such a formidable power that it needed the coalition of two-thirds of the world to liberate Europe, as well as the German nation, from its fetters'. According to Lavrin, it is the modern German spirit that caused the German people to submit to the new German State. The Germans have 'produced types of a high individual culture, not so much out of their collective racial soul, as through their indomitable "will to culture" which always has implied eclectic "learning" and deliberate intellectual toil. Hence the conspicuous lack of what we call intuition and spontaneity in representative modern Germans, a lack of which cannot be made up even by the most clever "thinking" and philosophising'. The Germans, Lavrin believes, philosophise about things but never talk about themselves. He informs us that an 'average cultured German instinctively mistrusts everything that does not smell of the lamp, scientific toil and that "serious" *gruendlichkeit* which he erroneously takes for profundity'. Thus, the German lacks 'inner "style"'. Whilst the French spirit is reminiscent of champagne, the German spirit suggests beer and sausages. The German 'actually compromises culture itself by this very striving to become cultured "à tout prix"'. Despite his knowledge and 'what he calls "bildung"', the German remains 'something of a parvenu, indulging in intellectual self-complacency, and wavering constantly between mental servility and mental arrogance'. Thus, as a parvenu, he respects 'learned titles and "authorities'", and is impressed not by original thoughts but 'by the quantity of learned authorities' used to back up an argument. The German hero is not the Thinker, but the Professor. Lavrin is sure that 'in things intellectual, as in things culinary', the German has 'more sense for quantity than for quality'. The German is so fettered by 'authorities' that he is unable to select and reject and devotes himself entirely to some 'specialism'. He is 'an ideal investigator of scientific details, an equally ideal book-worm and walking encyclopaedia, he is, naturally, poor in creative values'. The German talent for specialisation was used by the German Empire to make him an efficient machine. Thus, as a political machine, the German is worse and more dangerous than the rest of Europe because he is unnaturally efficient. Indeed, 'knowledge and learning were mistaken for culture itself'. The war, according to Lavrin, brought the German to a crossroads where he must choose between the spirit of Bismarck or the spirit of Goethe. Since the German State and its political appetites have been checked, the Germans may now concentrate 'all their forces on real culture'. (15 April 1920; *NA* XXVI, 24, pp. 383-4)

The Nietzscheans: A. M. Ludovici, Paul V. Cohn, Oscar Levy

From 1919 onwards the *New Age* reveals a revival of interest in Nietzsche and in the work of those who had done so much to promote the German philosopher in England - Oscar Levy and his translators Paul V. Cohn and A. M. Ludovici. In addition, Janko Lavrin, who, as we have seen, explored post-war attitudes to Germany in 'Contemporary Fragments', also attempted a fresh appraisal of the philosopher so maligned by Allied propaganda during the early months of the First World War. The Nietzscheans did not always deal with subjects directly connected with Nietzsche. Paul V. Cohn, for example, translated a series from the French of A. P. La Fontaine entitled 'French Culture in England'. The articles, which had originally appeared in *L'Europe Nouvelle*, appeal for greater understanding between the English and the French.[44] A. M. Ludovici, who was demobilised in 1919, was rapidly establishing himself as an author whose interests stretched beyond Nietzsche,[45] even if his work did not always find favour with reviewers in the *New Age*.[46] Indeed, it was as a reviewer

---

44 See 6 November 1919; *NA* XXVI, 1, pp. 4-5; 13 November 1919; *NA* XXVI, 2, pp. 20-1; 20 November 1919; *NA* XXVI, 3, pp. 38-9.

45 See, for example, Ludovici's poem 'The English Flapper' (4 December 1919; *NA* XXVI, 5, p. 84).

46 A. E. Randall, in his column 'Views and Reviews', is far from enthusiastic about Ludovici's *The False Assumptions of Democracy*. See 3 December 1921; *NA* XXX, 1, pp. 10-11 and 10 November 1921; *NA* XXX, 2, p. 22.

that Ludovici achieved some of his most perceptive post-war work in the *New Age*. On 28 October 1920 he discusses the evocatively titled *War Diary of a Square Peg* by Maximilian A. Mügge, the author of *Nietzsche: His Life and Work* (1908) and the translator of *Early Greek Philosophy and Other Essays* (1911) for the Levy edition of Nietzsche's work in English. Mügge, a British subject and a gifted linguist, was born and brought up in England, and joined the army as a private in March 1916. Absurdly, he ended up in an 'Aliens' battalion. Ludovici admits he was not 'one of those who thoroughly enjoyed the war, or who firmly and obstinately believe that the war has done good' and has 'grown tired of war books'. He has only enjoyed Barbusse's *Au feu* and Sassoon's *Counter Attack*. However, he praises Mügge, whom he previously considered 'a solemn philologist', for having produced an account of his experiences as a soldier in the British army which is both amusing and accurate. He concludes that the book is 'delightfully malicious', to be read by soldier and civilian alike. (*NA* XXVII, 26, p. 369)

Oscar Levy: appealing for a 're-opening of the Nietzsche controversy in the interest of philosophical thought'

It was, predictably, Oscar Levy who petitioned Orage to have 'The Case of Nietzsche' re-opened. On 13 November 1919 the *New Age* contains a letter to the editor from Oscar Levy, still living in wartime exile in Geneva, highlighting the difficulties he is experiencing in returning to England. Levy's case was by no means exceptional. Bernard Shaw found that even contacting his Austrian-born translator Siegfried Trebitsch, who had been too old for military service and had not actually fought against England,[47] was fraught with innumerable problems.[48] Levy admits that ever since the cessation of hostilities he has felt 'a natural desire to return to my home, to have access again to my library, to converse again with my old English friends'. However, he has been told, rather surprisingly, that it may not be easy for him to return, 'not so much on account of my German citizenship, but because of my connection with Nietzsche, who, as an eminent English author informs me to-day, is "still, rightly or wrongly,

---

47   Trebitsch was forty-five in 1914. Instead of being called up, he joined Hermann Bahr, Stefan Zweig, Hugo von Hofmannsthal and Rainer Maria Rilke in working for the *Kriegsarchiv*. Siegfried Trebitsch, *Chronicle of a Life*, translated by Eithne Wilkins and Ernst Kaiser, (London, 1953), p. 225. Karl Kraus was particularly disdaindful of this organisation which he satirises as the *Kriegsfürsorgeamt*, a refuge for the literati avoiding the trenches. See *Die letzten Tage der Menschheit* (Zürich, 1945), I, 19, p. 132.

48   See Michael Holroyd, op. cit., pp. 64-5.

in official circles, held responsible for the outbreak of the war". Having applied, for some time now and in vain, for a passport - both to the Home Office and the British Consulate here - I am afraid that there may be some truth in this extraordinary statement'. He appeals to Orage and the *New Age* for 'a re-opening of the Nietzsche controversy in the interest of philosophical thought'. He contends that 'an exhaustive enquiry in what I would call "the Case of Nietzsche" is all the more necessary, as behind the present upheaval of the world there is undoubtedly going on a great war of ideas and ideals which alone can explain and even excuse our present-day bewilderment. An investigation into all those spiritual tendencies which led up to the Great War is thus required in the interest of future peace, and it should be conducted with all that fairness and impartiality which is necessarily denied to all inquiries into matters of State and politics'. He argues that 'the accusation against this philosopher seemed all the more preposterous, as he - and he alone amongst the nineteenth century philosophers - combatted all, but actually all, those pre-war ideas which have led up to the great cataclysm'. Nietzsche, Levy reminds us, opposed Socialism,[49] as well as Pan-Germanism, which flourished with the rise of the German Empire,[50] and 'never ceased to ridicule that shallow Pacifism[51] which, led by its weak attitude outside Germany, directly encouraged that country in her attack upon her neighbours.' (*NA* XXVI, 2, p. 31)

By August 1920 Oscar Levy was back in England after an absence of five years and offered the *New Age* an article entitled 'We Nietzscheans'. Levy reports that with a reprint of the complete works of Nietzsche imminent, he has been asked by the publisher, T. N. Foulis, to write a new introduction, in which he 'should prove and state as emphatically as possible that Nietzsche had neither planned the Great War, nor had ever encouraged the Germans to arbitrary attack upon their neighbours'. Levy complains that even in that 'highly distinguished organ', the *New Age*, there are disapproving reviews, admittedly 'not about that "monster" Nietzsche himself, but about his "bumptious" disciples in this country and elsewhere'. Levy regards this as 'something quite new in the history of the

---

49   One might cite *Menschliches, Allzumenschliches* where Nietzsche calls Socialism 'der phantastische jüngere Bruder des fast abgelebten Despotismus, den er beerben will'. See Friedrich Nietzsche, *Werke*, I, p. 683.

50   In *Zur Genealogie der Moral*, for example, Nietzsche criticises 'die nationale Einklemmung und Eitelkeit, das starke, aber enge Prinzip «Deutschland, Deutschland über alles»'. *Werke*, II, p. 896.

51   We might cite *Zur Genealogie der Moral* where Nietzsche depicts pacifism, along with democracy, the campaign for female equality and compassionate religion, as a symptom of life in decline, as a manifestation of weak vitality. Ibid., pp. 892-3.

Nietzsche propaganda in England'. He discerns three stages in the campaign against the German philosopher. The first, between 1897 and 1907, was characterised by the 'dead silence' which greeted Nietzsche in England. The second came in the form of wartime anti-Nietzsche propaganda which made the philosopher a household name in England. In the third stage Nietzsche has been appreciated, or, at least, 'has been swallowed (though by no means digested) by the intelligentsia', but now, 'we, the Nietzscheans, are accused of being the unbalanced and unworthy disciples of a great and dignified master'. Although Levy concedes that the war had political causes, he is quite certain that ideas also contributed to it. The fact that Nietzsche 'vehemently combatted' these ideas proves to Levy that the German philosopher 'cannot possibly have been one of the intellectual authors of the war'. In the first place, Levy reminds us, Nietzsche combatted 'nationalism, with its moral haughtiness and consequent aggressive attitude towards the foreigner'.[52] Secondly, in an odd pairing, Nietzsche, opposed Socialism, 'with its ignorance of foreign affairs and its blind trust in the leading bourgeoisie'. Finally, he attacked pacifism, 'with its romantic faith in the neighbours' goodness and its wild hatred when that faith was proved to be misplaced'. (5 August 1920; NA XXVII, 14, p. 217)

 Even when Oscar Levy returned to England he did not escape the prying eye of the authorities. On 15 September 1921 Orage published a letter from Levy remarking on the anomaly in the Alien Restriction (Amendment Act, 1919, Section 10, 1), whereby the Home Office is empowered to extradite Levy, who has lived in England 'with only one interruption since 1894', along with his wife who is a German citizen, yet their only child, their twelve year-old daughter, is allowed to remain (NA XXIX, 20, p. 240). This 'disgraceful Aliens Act', as Bernard Shaw called it, also proved an obstacle to a proposed visit to England from Siegfried Trebitsch in the early 1920s. Trebitsch could not count on his visa alone and had to appeal to Shaw who, as a British citizen, provided an authorative letter to disarm 'the austere passport control officials' at Dover.[53]

---

52 We might cite, for example, *Ecce Homo* where Nietzsche accuses the Germans of having fostered nationalism and having on their conscience 'diese *kulturwidrigste* Krankheit und Unvernunft, die es gibt, den Nationalismus, diese *névrose nationale*, an der Europa krank ist, diese Verewigung der Kleinstaaterei Europas, der *kleinen* Politik'. *Werke*, II, p. 1148.

53 Quoted by Michael Holroyd, op. cit., p. 70.

Nietzsche: not guilty of causing 'the most senseless and idiotic war ever recorded among the monumental follies of humanity'

Levy certainly succeeded in re-opening the debate on Nietzsche. In a letter to the editor, Georg Pitt-Rivers claims that Nietzsche and Treitschke are still being linked with war, although Bolshevism is now being linked with Prussianism and Nietzsche. He recommends reading 'so thorough and irreproachable' a writer as 'Professor' J. A. Cramb,[54] the author of *Germany and England* (1913). He reminds readers that Cramb wrote that 'Treitschke was bitterly and irreconcilably prejudiced against the creator of Zarathustra from the very beginning of the former's career... He even quarrelled with Overbeck because of the latter's sympathy with his young colleague at Basle' (22 January 1920; *NA* XXVI, 12, p. 195). The following month George Pitt Rivers argues that although Nietzsche said 'A good war justifies any cause', we should remember that the converse is '*no* cause justifies a bad war' and the First World War was not 'a good war'. Indeed, it was 'the stupidest, the most senseless and idiotic war ever recorded among the monumental follies of humanity. A war *no* cause could justify, for it was a war in which the two finest races in Europe engaged for the mutual extermination of their best stock, to leave Europe anaemic and bled white of all that was noble and healthy.' (12 February 1920; *NA* XXVI, 15, p. 241)

Post-war fascination with Nietzsche was not confined to England. In his column 'Our Generation', Edwin Muir draws attention to the recent surge of popularity which Nietzsche was enjoying in France. He reflects that 'considering how bitter sentiment among intellectuals in France has been towards Germany, one may read more than usual significance into this, and see in the fact of Nietzsche's recognition in the country in Europe by accident most hostile to him the presage of his approaching recognition by all Europe as modern Europe's most significant spiritual event.' (14 July 1921; *NA* XXIX, 11, p. 125)

On 4 March 1920 Hermann George Scheffauer, an American-born German living in Berlin, condemns the *New Age* for publishing a truncated and misleading version of his article 'Germany's New Sturm und Drang'. In this matter he has some justification, since when the *New Age* published the article Scheffauer's attempts to argue that 'there is still an appeal in culture to a Germany situated as Germany is to-day', Orage, through his alter ego R.H.C., repeatedly intervenes with comments on Scheffauer's argument, so that the piece is

---

54   Cramb, who had taken a classics degree at Glasgow University, was a self-styled professor on the periphery of the academic world. See Stuart Wallace, *War and the Image of Germany. British Academics 1914-1918* (Edinburgh, 1988), p. 68.

unconvincing.[55]   In his letter of complaint Scheffauer criticises Orage for suggesting that Nietzsche is no longer read in Germany. It is, he argues, 'only an English fiction which is dead - that false imperialistic interpretation of Nietzsche which the English invented and attributed to the Germans. But it is not true in relation to what is sound and ascendant in the philosophy of Nietzsche. That new and popular editions of Nietzsche are appearing, that Nietzschean reviews are published and Nietzschean societies founded, seem to be dromedaries of fact at which R.H.C. does not strain'.   R.H.C. has suggested that no-one heeded Nietzsche in 1918. However, Scheffauer counters, 'history ought to tell my critic that prophets of culture, especially anti-national prophets, are seldom listened to after victorious wars of conquest in the lands of victors - that only defeat brings introspection and a revival and revaluation of spiritual values.' (*NA* XXVI, 18, p. 294)

A. R. Orage: Nietzsche 'purged of his colossal errors by the Great War' has 'a considerable future'

Orage's attitude towards Nietzsche and the Nietzscheans remained ambivalent. He could not wholly espouse Levy's argument. In his column 'Readers and Writers' Orage argues that the 'English mind is easily "put off" a subject, and particularly easily off a subject as uncongenial as Nietzsche; and it has been shown, I believe, to remain in this state for a century or more'. He is convinced that 'having the plausible excuse for being "off" Nietzsche which the war provided, the English intellectual classes - note that I do not say the intellectual English classes, for there are none - will continue to neglect Nietzsche until he has really been superseded, as I believe he will in all probability be before very long'. In his opinion, psychoanalysis 'has taken a good deal of Nietzsche in its stride; and it is quite possible that the re-reading of Indian philosophy in the light of psychoanalysis (of which, by the way, we have only as yet the ABC) will gather up most of the remainder'. If Nietzsche is ever read again in England, his work will be approached in an entirely different light to that previously attempted by commentators. He concedes only that there are some 'fragments' worth preserving, 'since indubitably they will be the fragments of a giant thought'. The 'Nietzsche of the future', he predicts, 'may be contained in a very small volume, chiefly composed of aphorisms. He aimed, he said, at saying in a sentence what other writers say in a book: and he characteristically added that he aimed at saying in a sentence what other writers did *not* say in a book. And in my judgement he very often succeeded. These successes are his real contribution to

---

55   The original article, which appeared on 22 January 1920, replaced 'Notes of the Week' as the opening item. See *NA* XXVI, 12, pp. 181-2.

his own immortality, and they will, I think, ensure it'. Orage ventures to suggest that Oscar Levy might prepare a volume on these lines because he feels that, whilst 'it may be the case that Nietzsche will be read in his entirety again, I very much doubt it'. He questions Levy's assertion that Nietzsche is being read as never before in Germany. Nietzsche, Orage contends, was above all 'a great culture-hero; as a critic of art he has been surpassed by no man. But is there any appeal in culture to a Germany situated as Germany is to-day? I am here only as a literary causeur. With the dinosaurs and other monsters of international politics I cannot be supposed to be on familiar terms. My opinion, nevertheless, based upon my own material, is that Germany is most unlikely to resume the pursuit of culture where she interrupted it after 1870, or, indeed, to pursue culture at all. And the reason for my opinion is that Russia is too close at hand, too accessible and, above all, too tempting to German cupidity. Think what the proximity to Germany - to a Germany headed off from the Western world - of a commercially succulent country like Russia really means. Germans are human, even if they are not sub-human; and the temptation of an El Dorado at their doors will prove, I fear, to be more seductive than the cry from the muezzin to come to culture, come to spiritual conquests will be met by the big bagmen calling them, on the other side, to commercial conquests. Who can doubt which appeal will be the stronger? Germany refused to attend to Nietzsche after 1870 when he spoke to them as one alive; they are less likely to listen to a voice from the dead after 1918.' (18 December 1919; *NA* XXVI, 7, pp. 109-10)

Nevertheless, the following year Orage is slightly more charitable. On 2 September 1920 he observes that Nietzsche, once 'purged of his colossal errors by the Great War, has still a considerable future; but I must remark that, in my friendly judgement, his disciples, and particularly Dr. Oscar Levy, are delaying his renaissance' (*NA* XXVII, 18, p. 271). No doubt Levy felt he was far from delaying Nietzsche's renaissance as he devoted most of his time to trying to revive interest in the controversial philosopher. In addition to writing articles to periodicals such as the *New Age* and the *Times Literary Supplement*, Levy also edited a selection of Nietzsche's letters, which appeared in 1922, and presided over a new edition of the complete works, which was published in 1924.[56]

Nietzsche 'was only a battle trumpet, and the battlefield lies in the Mahabharata'

Whilst Oscar Levy's attempts to revive interest in Nietzsche were treated with caution, writers seeking to approach the German philosopher from a new angle - either in the context of Indian philosophy or even psychoanalysis,

---

56   See Gertrud von Petzhold, 'Nietzsche in englisch-amerikanischer Beurteil-ung bis zum Ausgang des Weltkrieges', *Anglia*, 53 (1929), p. 164.

were greeted with enthusiasm by Orage. After the First World War it was not unusual for his correspondents to draw a direct parallel between Eastern mysticism and Nietzsche. On 23 June 1921, for example, M. M. Cosmoi argues that Nietzsche, 'the author of the scripture of the Superman', was also 'a prophet of the Seraphimic or Seraphic dispensation of the world, and he was the prophet of the new Aryandom; he was a Teuton by birth, and a Slav by descent;[57] a European in character, however, and a Superman and a Seraphic spirit in his goodness'. He argues that 'only a new dispensation altogether, only a motive of a New Æon can lead Europe and the world into transcendence of Solovyov's synthesis. Nietzsche's will was aflame and fierce enough to give an Aryan and Seraphimic impulse to Europe; Blavatsky's cosmic awareness was Christian and real enough to formulate the concept of Universal Humanity.' (*NA* XXIX, 8, p. 87)

On 13 May 1920 Orage published an article entitled 'Nietzsche and the Provincials' by J. A. M. Alcock, a practising psychoanalyst who contributed pieces on the subject almost every week between 1920 and 1922.[58] In a recent discussion of Pfister, Alcock had argued that there was 'more to be discovered in the *Mahabharata* than in Nietzsche'. He reports that certain critics have objected to his argument on the grounds that the *Mahabharata* is 'unattractive to the modern mind, and doubted the correctness of throwing over Nietzsche on the grounds that he was a modern, had his finger on the pulse of Europe, and was intuitively applying a method similar to psychoanalysis to remedy the European sickness'. Alcock admits that he 'must plead guilty to having classed together Nietzsche and the Nietzscheans, which was not prudent, for what do they know of Nietzsche who only Nietzscheans know. And I confess that when I wrote the offending sentence it was not Nietzsche himself who was uppermost in my mind'. He recognises that 'psychoanalysts have by no means been unmindful of Nietzsche'. Jung's *Psychology of the Unconscious* contains 'a whole string of quotations from Nietzsche', whilst in his *Analytical Psychology*, Jung 'very clearly shows how Nietzsche was a half-man and how full man is Nietzsche plus Wagner!' Although Nietzsche aimed to live by instinct, he really lived by just one, namely 'the will to power. That other instinct, love, stayed in his unconscious, as the toad he could not swallow, a piece of "primordial matter" that the *Mahabharata* says must be transcended, transmuted. This is shown by Jung, who goes on to decide that Nietzsche actually lived "beyond instinct", which height "could only be manufactured by means of most careful diet, choice climate, and, above all, by many opiates"'. In addition, Jung said of Nietzsche that 'he spoke of yea-saying,

---

57   Nietzsche's own self-stylisation was not as a Slav, but as a Polish aristocrat. Letter to Heinrich von Stein, early December 1882, in *Werke*, III, p. 1195.
58   Wallace Martin, op. cit., p. 274.

but lived the nay'. Alcock believes that for Nietzsche, energy is not 'eternal delight', as it was for 'that other Dionysian, Blake', but 'eternal war, conflict, and it is *that* which constitutes the snare to his followers, and made me speak of him as a by-path; in and by himself and followed blindly'. Whilst Nietzsche is 'a path that has been explored', the *Mahabharata* 'awaits exploration'. Alcock maintains that a 'true Nietzschean' should not find the *Mahabharata* unattractive. Jung emphasised 'one of Nietzsche's positive aspects, that he lived a life of "rare consistency". Now, what is one of the most salient points in the *Mahabharata* but the making and fulfilling of vows? What was Nietzsche's other positive aspect? A transcending of good and evil, a transvaluation of values, the concept of the superman'. The *Mahabharata*, Alcock contends, 'embodies Nietzsche's concept and all the rest. Nietzsche was in touch with the unconscious, but only partially. He was half-harmonised, but there was a "toad" in the path, a block in the libido. The *Mahabharata* is pure unconscious, and there are no free toads there, but, on the contrary, many ways of dealing with them. It is a fountain of delight, a garden of divinity. It is health to the sick and nectar to the healthy'. According to Alcock, 'a transvaluation of values in psychological language is the attainment of another state of consciousness'. Only in India can we find reliable and detailed instructions for such attainment. These instructions are to found in India's 'most easily accessible and most universal writing', the *Mahabharata*. It is only burking the question to call it unattractive to moderns, and to say that it is not applicable to modern conditions. The unconscious knows better than this, for Eastern symbols are appearing in dreams, and Europe after her war is undergoing a change of life to contemplation, as opposed to her previous absorption of interest in the world without. And, moreover, "conditions" in the unconscious are neither modern nor ancient, but universal. Now, where else are we to turn except to where the unconscious is most plain?' Nietzsche, Alcock concludes, pointed the way, but 'he was only a battle trumpet, and the battlefield lies in the *Mahabharata*.' (*NA* XXVII, 2, pp. 28-9)

Distinguishing 'Nietzscheanism from real Nietzsche'

Between November 1921 and July 1922 Orage ran a series of articles entitled 'Nietzsche Revisted' by Janko Lavrin, who was already familiar to *New Age* readers as the author of 'Contemporary Fragments'.[59] In the first of these pieces, on 10 November 1921, Lavrin scrutinises 'Nietzsche and the Nietzscheans'. He observes perceptively that 'it would be difficult to point out another philosopher or thinker of the nineteenth century whose vogue and fate could be compared with those of Nietzsche. Entirely ignored until the end of his literary

---

59   See pp. 223-5 for a discussion of this series.

activities, he suddenly became the slogan and standard of radical "modernism", he was proclaimed - almost in a night - the apostle of a new culture, and soon after that the gospel of his Zarathustra degenerated into fashion, breeding adepts and interpreters all over the world. In a few years his name and doctrine permeated so deeply the whole of modern culture that in whatever direction we go we are almost sure to find at least some reference to Nietzsche'. What Lavrin terms the 'sensational influence of a single man on the current thought of Europe, on modern art and literature', presents 'a spectacle which is all the more strange because of the fact that Nietzsche's enormous popularity was largely due to detached single aspects of his writings, rather than to synthetic comprehension of his work and personality. To many, Nietzsche was a surprising discovery because his philosophy was not a dry logical "system" but something more alive: an intimate psychological document - the history of a personal Golgotha up to the very moment of self-crucifixion. His arguments were fascinating for the very reason that they were not stereo-typed arguments of an "objective" and cold arm-chair philosopher, but arguments of temperament, of passion, of blood - of personality, in short. Lavrin identifies 'Nietzsche's exaggerated and passionate subjectivism' as the reason for his books appearing to have 'an objective significance and value', thus making Nietzsche himself a kind of symbolic figure.

A further reason for the fascination with Nietzsche is the 'highly artistic form of his writings'. Lavrin concedes that 'we often discover in them a curious mental "baroque", grandiloquent solemnity, and an unconscious German tendency to overwhelm us by the "colossal"'. However, all these defects 'are more than counterbalanced by his extreme pliability, originality of metaphors and maliciousness of expression. It is the lucky combination of his incredible feminine sensitiveness with his masculinity of expression and form that gives to his books a kind of intriguing charm even when we reject their content'. As a Slav, Nietzsche was 'the greatest musician of the German language, making that rather clumsy instrument dance and sing as no-one before him'. Lavrin argues that Nietzsche 'came with his gospel of new values just in a time of complete cultural, moral and intellectual disorientation and confusion, denouncing with a divine ruthlessness all the foundations of modern life, modern culture and modern man'.

Nevertheless, there is also a darker side to Nietzsche's influence, Lavrin informs us. The 'ironical fate of Nietzsche' was that 'his "gospel" was first taken up just by those against whom it was mainly directed - by modern decadents, half-cultured dilettanti and intellectual snobs. Our degenerate raffinés acclaimed him as a new kind of mental drug with which they intoxicated themselves that they might forget - beneath the pose of "supermen" - their nothingness and impotence, adapting at the same time Nietzsche's super-moral (sic) "beyond good and evil" to their own immoral slogans'. Those who were 'stronger and more cunning deliberately mistook Nietzsche's "will to power" and remade it in such a way as to justify by it that system of individual, political or social violence which they found necessary. In this respect some of the official German imperialists and the representatives of that zoological nationalism which was one of the causes of the European war excelled. Many so-called free-thinkers again embraced Nietzsche's atheism, forgetting that his atheism was far from that of an "enlightened free-thinker" as a popular penny pamphlet about the non-existence of God from the Luciferic *Thus Spake Zarathustra'*.

Lavrin, like Orage, contends that as with so many thinkers, Nietzsche has been ruined by his apostles. Even his true admirers distort his thought and just see what they choose to see. It was an 'intellectual mob' that created Nietzscheanism. However, like all fashions, Nietzsche 'had his "season" after which he was somewhat neglected'. Nevertheless, 'now that the whirl of dust and incense stirred up round his doctrine has passed away it would be perhaps good to consider it again - not through his exponents, but through Nietzsche himself. By finding out the psychological roots of his "philosophy" we may perhaps be able to see more deeply into its essence and distinguish, moreover, Nietzscheanism from real Nietzsche; for most of Nietzsche's doctrine is perhaps nothing but a grandiose mask of Nietzsche himself - more, a shelter in which he took refuge from himself'. Thus, according to Lavrin, the problem of Nietzsche 'as the representative of modern consciousness is of far greater interest than that of Nietzsche as mere "philosopher"'. Questions arise as to 'what is Nietzsche's place in modern life, what is really tragic and vital in him from the standpoint of our spiritual needs and crisis and what can our post-war period learn from his dilemma, his striving and his failure.' (*NA* XXX, 2, pp. 21-2)

Psychoanalysis and the New Age: seeking 'a more profound analysis and synthesis of human psychology'

In addition to a revival of interest in Nietzsche, there was much discussion of the work of German psychoanalysts in the *New Age*. Before the First World War Orage recognised the potential of the subject and encouraged M. D. Eder, a pioneer in the field, to explain the latest theories in the *New Age*. He also invited contributions on psychoanalysis from A. E. Randall and M. B. Oxon, alias Lewis Wallace, the banker who, with Bernard Shaw, had provided the financial backing for the *New Age*. By 1918 much more literature on psychoanalysis was available in English. Whilst Orage could never 'have been rightly called a "believer" in psychoanalysis',[60] he nevertheless grasped its significance. As early as 31 January 1918 he perceived that 'of all the new sciences, psychoanalysis is the most inviting' and 'the first results, as is only

---

60   Philippe Mairet, op. cit., p. 79.

natural, are mainly therapeutic; but obviously the method and conclusions of psychoanalysis will prove to be applicable to education, history, religion, and to statesmanship in the very widest sense' (*NA* XXII, 14, p. 271). The following year Orage traces a direct link between psychoanalysis and mysticism. In his literary column 'Readers and Writers' he proudly informs his readers that the future of the *New Age* is 'the future of vital thought in this country; vital thought, that is to say, as expressed in the writing of people willing to write for love'. The journal gathers 'vital thought' to carry its readers forward in two directions. First, 'in the direction of a more radical and simple analysis and synthesis of modern industrial society', and, secondly, 'in the direction of a more profound analysis and synthesis of human psychology'. C. H. Douglas has played a vital role in the first objective. In the second, Orage explains, 'no reader, from the earliest volume to the latest can have missed the recurrence in the *New Age* of, let us call it, a "mystical" note, indicative of a constant search for a profounder psychology than is, I believe, to be found elsewhere in contemporary journalism. I have no doubt that many of such articles have appeared to be "moonshine"; certainly lit by a light that never was upon sea or land. But, at least, their strain has been constant; and I think I may safely say that in modern psychoanalysis it is likely to find a further expression than ever before in the secular West. He feels that he risks 'little in predicting that, side by side with the more simple analysis of society, our future writers will unfold a more profound analysis of man'. (6 November 1919; *NA* XXVI, 1, pp. 12-13)

In his quest for a more profound analysis of man, Orage was concerned not only with taking a person's psyche to pieces, but with the more difficult task of putting it back together again. He often spoke of Freud as 'the great analyst of the age', and called for him to be succeeded by 'a great synthetist'.[61] With this in mind, practising analysts, such as M. D. Eder, Maurice Nicoll and James Young, helped Orage form a group to consider methods of psychosynthesis in psychoanalysis.[62] They were joined by Havelock Ellis, and, occasionally, by Dmitri Mitrinović. The presence of the author of 'World Affairs' is significant in that it reflects the tendency of the group towards esoteric teaching in its search for a psychosynthetist that would ultimately culminate in the introduction of Gurdjieff into their circle. In the *New Age* Orage both re-commended works by Freud, Jung and Ernest Jones, and invited contributions from practising psychoanalysts. His most regular correspondent on the subject

---

61   Quoted by Antony Alpers, op. cit., p. 368.
62   Philippe Mairet, 'Reintroduction', *A. R. Orage: A Memoir*, second edition (New York, 1966), p. xiv.

was J. A. M. Alcock, who, as we already have seen, was responsible for a discussion of Nietzsche in the context of Indian mysticism.[63]

On 8 January 1920 Alcock devotes his review article to a discussion of E. B. Holt's *The Freudian Wish*, Freud's *The Interpretation of Dreams*, *Psychopathology of Everyday Life*, *Wit and its Relation to the Unconscious*, *Three Contributions to the Sexual Theory*, M. K. Bradbury's *Analytical Psychology*, Maurice Nicoll's *Dream Psychology* and Ernest Jones' *Papers on Psychoanalysis*. Alcock believes that it will 'soon become, if it is not so already, the fashion to decry Freud' and 'the more advanced psychoanalysts are claiming to have transcended him'. Freud's pupil Alfred Adler (1870-1937) broke with Freud in 1911; Carl Gustav Jung (1875-1961), who was influenced by Freud, argued with his mentor in 1912. Both Adler and Jung rejected Freud's view that sex was the sole determinant of action. Alcock aims to forestall the 'fashion to decry Freud' by discussing Freud and evaluating his most important works, which he considers to be *Dream Interpretation*, *Psychopathology of Everyday Life* and *Wit and its relation to the Unconscious* (*NA* XXVI, 10, p. 160). Alcock is in no doubt that Freud occupies 'a most definite place in psychoanalysis, and that place is on the first rung of the ladder of psychological development - the freeing of the libido from infantile sexual complexes.' (14 October 1920; *NA* XXVII, 24, p. 345)

On 29 January 1920 Alcock attempts to highlight the differences between the theories of Freud and those of Adler. He points out that Jung distinguishes between the Adlerian, the introvert, and the Freudian, the extrovert. The Adlerian is 'the man of forethought', whilst the Freudian is 'the emotionalist, the expansive, at ease in every social situation'. He explains that they are 'Apollo and Dionysus, reason and desire; or, if the reader will, they may be symbolised as Brahmana and Kshatriya, student and warrior'. Alcock reminds us that in order to illustrate further this dichotomy Jung cites Nietzsche and Wagner. However, 'for domestic consumption', Alcock prefers to consider the English and the Irish. He contends that 'The Englishman is primarily an introvert in the sense that his emotions are crude and explosive, and his actions quite as deliberate as they have any need to be. The Irish do not, as a mass, think. They are fluent and adaptable, and *float* easily; but they do this by a feeling for life, not according to plan. They live by reaction, and need no preliminary planning for themselves through circumstance'. According to Jung 'the extrovert is Freudian', and 'the extrovert is the one to develop hysterical symptoms'. Alcock observes that 'a hysterical symptom is a protection par excellence. It is certainly produced by feeling, but behind the feeling there is just as certainly the will to self-preservation, and, in this sense, the extrovert is an Adlerian'. Both Freud and Adler 'deal essentially

---

63   See pp. 232-3.

with instincts so far as they are consciously aware'. Alcock ventures to suggest that the 'extrovert and introvert are consciously Freudian and Adlerian, yet in their under aspects in the personal sides of their unconscious, they are actually Adlerian and Freudian'. Alcock calls for a mixture of Adlerian and Freudian methods to cure patients on the grounds that 'we all in actuality consist of a syndrome of the two archetypes in varying proportions.' (*NA* XXVI, 13, pp. 207-8)

On 12 February 1920 Alcock turns his attention to Jung's *Psychology of the Unconscious*. He observes that Jung 'works with his whole soul, and not by reason only, nor by emotion only' and is the first psychologist to 'show that it is not possible to accept an entirely sexual basis for neurosis'. Jung argues that there are biological impulses in man that are not sexual, 'though they may appear in sexual clothing'. The libido is 'energy, the driving force of life'. Alcock explains that 'it will be sufficient if we say here that according to our individual psychology, the expressions of love or inspiration will be found to be identical with what Jung wishes to imply when he speaks of libido'. This can be linked with the concept of the 'Freudian wish', which, in turn, 'becomes the Theosophist's "etheric membrane"'. To the Theosophist this is 'the urge to be, to grow, to create. And this impulse passes through and beyond sexuality, so that in *Psychology of the Unconscious* we find a clear demonstration of "desexualised" libido.' (*NA* XXVI, 15, pp. 235-6)

Treatment for War Shock: Psychoanalysis 'is frequently the last rope one can fling a man'

Alongside the theories of psychoanalysis came explanations of its practical application to shell-shock victims from the war. On 1 April 1920 J. A. M. Alcock explores 'War Shock', the problem of war neuroses, with over thirty thousand cases in Great Britain, 'of whom perhaps a few thousands are receiving any respectable treatment'. Although several books on the subject have appeared, only a handful are of any value, namely Maurice Nicoll's *Dream Psychology* and Ernest Jones' *Papers on Psychoanalysis*. They deal respectively with 'the two "root complexes", or initial entanglements of the human libido, the mother and the ego. Trouble starts with difficulty in adaptation to the circumstance of war. The difficulty is due to conflict, which is a clashing of factors in the patient's psychological composition, and is determined by some external circumstance, either shell-fire, or being ruined, blown up or buried, or, perhaps, the preliminary army training. And fear of present circumstance wakes memories of, and desire for, easier circumstance. Speaking rather roughly, we may note two not unusual conflicts': between 'desire to run away and desire to "stick it out"', between 'patriotic desire to slay the country's enemies and gentle desire to do nothing so vile as to slay anyone'. We may also note that 'it is a conflict between desires. It is not a repression, so much as a splitting, of desire, its exact nature being determined by individual psychology'. According to Alcock, when 'this split or fracture has formed', the first thing that happens is 'an attempt at self-cure. This is where repression comes into play. Just as a boil in the skin may become "blind" and subside without suppurating, because of the local protective reaction of the body, so the psyche may overlay its split and consciousness. But just as the blind boil leaves a trace of hardening in the skin, so the psychic fracture leaves, as it were, a knot, in what I would call the pre-conscious rather than the unconscious, round which emotional-intellectual associations, karma, begin to form. The actual occasion of the split is barred from consciousness, *but* it is still in the pre-conscious of that primal occasion, then there is an emotional-intellectual reaction that he cannot understand. And should this happen often enough, an undercurrent of regression is started, and that drags him into a condition of neurosis'. What is needed is 'a free association of ideas round the cause in consciousness of neurosis' to arrive at 'the buried malformation' that has brought about the neurosis. (*NA* XXVI, 22, pp. 253-4)

On 29 April 1920 Alcock devotes his column to a review of M. D. Eder's *War Shock*. Eder had been in charge of a psycho-neurological department during the First World War. His book deals with the first hundred cases of war neurosis that he treated, and in it he claims to have cured eighty cases. Alcock comments that 'we should pray that the army will use it as a handbook of psychiatry, when the occasion again arises'. Eder treated most cases with hypnosis and suggestion. Alcock recalls that before the war 'psychological medicine was an exceedingly tiny seedling in this country'; even in 1920 it is not 'an excessively large plant'. As a result 'war neuroses came as a surprise'. In a bitter indictment of the lack of facilities to cope with such cases, Alcock reflects that 'there was no one treatment for them, and the country is in consequence now full of pensioners in various types of neuroticism. To-day there is no war, and what is worse, the country is at a standstill. This is bad for the neurotic, for there is no fixed, objective duty like a war, that he can buckle down to again. In point of fact, he cannot even be sure of finding the most ordinary job of work. For if he is rash enough to mention the word "shell-shock", it means that the majority of people will refuse him employment outright. And if he is given training in a trade, he is apt to have difficulties with the Unions'. Eder does not want his patients discharged until they are fit again, although this advice has not been heeded by the army, which, in Alcock's view, is 'a gross mistake'. Psychoanalysis for war shock, he observes, 'is frequently the last rope one can fling a man' since it is not the form of treatment automatically prescribed. However, Eder shows 'beyond question that the best treatment for simple war-shock is hypnotic suggestion based upon a preparatory psychoanalytic examination.' (*NA* XXVI, 26, pp. 419-20)

A. E. Randall: 'Psychologically, we were not prepared for war; psychologically, we are not prepared for peace'

In his column 'Views and Reviews' A. E. Randall also reveals an interest in the impact of the First World War on human consciousness. On 13 May 1920, for example, he turns his attention to 'A Psychologist at War', with a discussion of Henry de Man's *The Re-making of a Mind*. Randall notes that 'a flood of post-war literature and exhortation' has not produced 'any considerable works in the English tongue. It is impossible that such a crisis could pass without producing lasting effects, but our literature, at least, gives small indication of them'. He reflects perceptively that 'the war came as a surprise to us; we reacted to it impulsively; but the removal of that focus of emotion, and the absence of any large, articulated, political ideas, has resulted in the confused cynicism that is the burden of most of our books. The simple truth that, to learn anything by an experience, one must be prepared for it, discounts the rather windy idealism of those who imagined that the war would clear the ground on which they could rebuild civilisation to their heart's desire. Psychologically, we were not prepared for war; psychologically, we are not prepared for peace; and the history of England since the Armistice suggests that the high tide of national emotion has ebbed, leaving a new and more efficient family of limpets clinging to our Rock of Ages'. (*NA* XXVII, 2, p. 29)

On 18 May 1922 Randall welcomes the attempt by Freud to provide a much-needed 'authorative introduction to the study of psychoanalysis'. *Introductory Lectures on Psychoanalysis*, translated by Joan Riviere, is a collection of three courses of lectures given by Freud at Vienna University between 1915 and 1917. Randall praises Freud as a lecturer for 'his lucidity, his patience, his schematical progress; his incidental tackling and masterly handling of the current polemics of the subject', which 'take us back to the great days of the evolution controversy' (*NA* XXXI, 3, pp. 33-4). The following week Randall continues his discussion of this work, observing that psychoanalysis is a medicine for the rich. Some analysts have yielded to 'the temptation to substitute priest-craft for psychoanalysis'. Nevertheless, the rich 'are fair game for everybody, and, after all, they waste no more on a course of psychoanalysis than they would spend on a motor-car - not so much, in fact'. The danger therefore is not to the rich, but to the doctor because 'until doctors have no pecuniary interest in their patients, that danger cannot be eliminated'. Randall contends that it is no more possible to believe that psychoanalysts 'are all Freuds than it is that all Christians are Christs, or all Nietzscheans Nietzsches.' (25 May 1922; *NA* XXXI, 4, p, 47)

By 1922 the market was saturated with works on psychoanalysis. The subject was being discussed not only in the *New Age* but in contemporary journals as well. The situation was best summed up on 23 April 1923 by Raymond Mortimer in the *New Statesman*, when he observed 'we are all psychoanalysts now. That is to say it is as difficult for an educated person to neglect the theories of Freud and his rivals as it would have been for his father to ignore the equally disconcerting discoveries of Darwin'.[64] However, with the profusion of literature on psychoanalysis, Orage soon began to express reservations about the subject. On 24 February 1921 he notes that a recent American bibliography of works on Guild Socialism ran to four pages of close type. He confesses that he was 'horrified', commenting 'so much said and so little done; in the beginning was the word, and at the end also, nothing but words!' He wonders whether 'the same unhappy fate' awaits every new idea and asks 'Must all our little Babes in the Wood be buried in leaves?' He perceives that this 'is certainly the danger of psychoanalysis. Only a few years ago I could encourage young students of psychoanalysis by observing that they might still hope to cover the whole of the literature on the subject; it had not got beyond a six months' reading. To-day I am depressed by the dead mass and weight of it. Literally hundreds, if not thousands of books have now been published on the subject; and a skilled guide is necessary to enable one to pick one's way through it. Even then I doubt whether the journey is as profitable as it was to read Freud and Jung alone, and afterwards to *think* about it. For it can safely be remarked of psychoanalysis, as of Guild Socialism, that the earlier expositions left nothing to be filled up but the blanks. The later material is a radial but not a radical development of the primitive.' (*NA* XXVIII, 17, p. 201)

'Readers and Writers': 'Bleeders and Blighters'

After the First World War Orage, as R.H.C., continued to contribute to 'Readers and Writers' and published a collection of his essays from that literary column.[65] However, by the summer of 1921 Orage, allowing himself 'no respite from the hard labor (sic) of his weekly editorials on Social Credit', was spending 'much time gazing into the abyss of the unconscious with his psychoanalytic group' and 'ceased to produce articles of the kind in which he had always found pleasure and relaxation'.[66] 'Readers and Writers' was the main casualty of these trying circumstances and Orage left it in the hands of a variety of younger writers. In addition to Paul Selver, who had written the column before the war, Herbert

---

64   28 April 1923, p. 82. Quoted by Samuel Hynes, *A War Imagined: The First World War and English Culture* (London, 1990), p. 366.

65   The anthology *Readers and Writers* was published in 1922 under Orage's own name rather than the pseudonym R.H.C. Plans for 'at least three further volumes' to follow never came to fruition. See 27 October 1921; *NA* XXIX, 26, p. 308.

66   Philippe Mairet, 'Reintroduction', op. cit., p. xix.

Read (1893-1968), Edith Sitwell (1887-1964) and C. E. Bechhofer (1894-1949) took turns at 'Readers and Writers'. It was Bechhofer[67] who, as an anarchic, 'fattish, red-faced youth' of 'about eighteen',[68] dubbed Orage's prized literary column 'Bleeders and Blighters'.[69]

A rather less irreverent contributor to 'Readers and Writers' was Edith Sitwell, whose poetry had already appeared in the *New Age*. She was brought to the column by Edwin Muir, who had criticised the poetry of Sacheverell and Osbert Sitwell. The Sitwells duly arrived in Orage's office, threatening legal action. The matter was resolved amicably when Orage invited Edith to write for the *New Age*.[70] In her hands 'Readers and Writers', perhaps understandably, devotes increasing attention to poetry. On 27 July 1922, for example, she recognises Isaac Rosenberg and Wilfrid Owen as 'two great poets killed in the war' (*NA* XXXI, 14, p. 161). Previously columnists had shown little enthusiasm for war poetry. Stephen Maguire, who wrote an occasional column of 'Recent Verse', had been highly disapproving of Siegfried Sassoon's collection *Counter-Attack and Other Poems* when he dismissed Sassoon's verse as 'bombs thrown at society', whose dubious aim lay in 'bringing home to civilians the horrors of war'. (21 November 1918; *NA* XXIV, 3, p. 41)

Paul Selver: 'it is certain that there are now more Englishmen capable of ordering their lunch in German'

On 10 June 1920 Paul Selver returned to the 'Readers and Writers' column for the first time in over five years. In the First World War he had been in the army and became a civilian again in August 1919.[71] He marks his return to regular journalism by taking up the question he last posed on 3 September 1914, namely: the negative effect of war on the position of German language and literature in England. He remarks that 'it is certain that there are now more Englishmen capable of ordering their lunch in German than when I made that conjecture; and German literature is not doing badly either'. He notes that for several months the *Times Literary Supplement* has devoted 'more attention to German books than it was ever known to do in the brave days of old' and has produced intelligent reviews, as is exemplified by a recent critique of one of

---

67   Despite his German-sounding name, Bechhofer was, in fact, of part Welsh, part Russian descent. See 'Rural Walks', 15 July 1920; *NA* XXVII, 11, p. 171.
68   Paul Selver, *Orage and the New Age Circle* (London, 1959), p. 29.
69   Ibid., p. 50.
70   Wallace Martin, op. cit., p. 282.
71   Paul Selver, op. cit., p. 7.

Schnitzler's latest tales, *Casanovas Heimfahrt*. In addition, Selver welcomes the appearance of *Theodor Fontane: A Critical Study* by Kenneth Hayens, a lecturer in German at Dundee University, although he regrets that the British public is 'still waiting for an adequate manual of the mere rudiments of modern German literature'. Although Hayens' work is 'a detailed critical study', Selver finds his approach somewhat laborious. He favours instead Albert Soergel's briefer appraisal of Fontane in *Dichtung und Dichter der Zeit*, which manages to convey 'more information than the whole of Hayens'. Selver commends Fontane's English impressions,[72] reminding readers that Fischer reissued a selection in Berlin in 1915, entitled, in Selver's English translation, *The English Character, To-Day as Yesterday*, and 'superimposed with the following twaddle: "Since our enemy's name is England and nothing is more urgent for us than to know our opponent, it was a stroke of luck that we were able to turn up the *Summer in London* by Theodor Fontane, who seventy years ago, in spite of all admiration, expressed his foreboding of the twilight of the gods, which would come upon the whole empire'. Sensitive as he is to the excesses of chauvinism, Selver himself is not wholly free from blame on this count. In the same article, he goes on to make the sweeping observation that France lost nearly four hundred poets in the war, including Apollinaire, whereas Germany 'probably had less to lose than this'. He regards only the death of Richard Dehmel on 8 February 1920 as 'a loss to more than Germany'. According to Selver, 'the only other Germans since Heine' who can be ranked with Dehmel are Detlev von Liliencron (1844-1909), Rainer Maria Rilke (1875-1926) and Stefan Georg (1869-1933). Selver considers much of Dehmel's work to be 'the tortuous product of sexual obsession, and although it would be doubly unfair to call him the D. H. Lawrence of Germany, the comparison will serve as a sign-post. There is, at least, a cragginess of language that the two have in common which, in the case of Dehmel, sometimes attains immensity. Yet he could also achieve the delicate lyricism of his famous *Helle Nacht*, a translation from Verlaine. This exquisite piece, which has run the gauntlet of the anthologists and emerged unimpaired from the ordeal, shows that the German language can be effectively employed for other purposes than text-books on thermo-dynamics.' (*NA* XXVII, 6, pp. 89-90)

---

72   Fontane (1819-98) visited Britain on three occasions between 1844 and 1859. In addition to articles and diaries, he recorded his impressions, which were not wholly favourable, as *Ein Sommer in London* and *Jenseits der Tweed* (1860), which appeared in one volume as *Aus England und Schottland* in 1900. See D. Barlow, 'Fontane's English Journeys', *German Life and Letters*, 6 (1953), pp. 169-77. See also Friedrich Schönemann, 'Theodor Fontane und England', *PMLA*, 30 (1915), pp. 658-71.

In addition to literary criticism, Selver contributed a series of articles entitled 'On the Translation of Poetry'. In the first in this series he discusses Shakespeare in translation and singles out for praise the work by Tieck and Schlegel, which 'represents the most successful attempt to reproduce Shakespeare in another language' (20 November 1919; *NA* XXVI, 3, p. 44). On 18 March 1920 Selver turns his attention to a more recent German edition of Shakespeare, which still relies on Schlegel and the revised Tieck translation. Edited by Friedrich Gundolf, this new edition was begun in 1908, but halted in 1914. The tenth and final volume did not appear until 1918. Selver is prompted to speculate whether the German translations of Shakespeare have made Shakespeare more popular in Germany than in England. In order to redress the balance he suggests translating the German version into English and thus reviving interest in Shakespeare at home. (18 March 1920; *NA* XXVI, 20, p. 324)

After the First World War Selver could not disguise his disappointment with the changes at the *New Age*. It had 'already become the organ of the Douglas Credit Scheme, on which Orage expended more energy than he could afford. He was now within a year or two of fifty, and although he seemed to have changed little from the Orage whom I had first seen in May 1911, he admitted to me that he was feeling the strain of the millions of words he had to put to paper during his editorship of the *New Age*'.[73] Selver particularly disliked the influence of Douglas, Ouspensky and Gurdjieff.[74] When Orage left London, Selver stopped contributing to the *New Age*, which he found lacking in inspiration.[75]

Herbert Read and German literature: Goethe's work is 'literary lumber among which the modern reader must proceed warily'

In 1921 Herbert Read took over 'Readers and Writers', although very much under the editor's guidance.[76] The *New Age* was the first publication in which his work appeared between 1916 and 1920. Read had been a member of the Leeds Arts Club in his youth, where, even after Orage had left the city, 'he was a name and a legend'.[77] As an army officer in the First World War Read had taken a copy of the *New Age* into the officers' club. A junior subaltern found it, leafed through it, 'the colour deepened in his florid face', and demanded 'who

---

73   Paul Selver, op. cit., p. 71.
74   Ibid., p. 78.
75   Ibid., p. 73.
76   See Wallace Martin, op. cit., pp. 52-6.
77   Herbert Read, *New English Weekly. A. R. Orage Memorial Number*, VI, 5 (15 November 1934), p. 112.

brought this bloody rag into the mess?'.[78] Thereafter he read the *Tatler* in public and the *New Age* in private. Read became more and more alienated by the 'increasingly staid' *New Age*,[79] but nevertheless offered a war story to Orage in February 1920. Orage rejected it as 'dull in every sense' and reflected 'it is not my place, of course to offer you advice, but if I did, it would be to urge you to forget the war and its experiences in *their detail*, and to bring into consciousness what your *unconscious* thought of it all! What did your *soul* learn in the Great War?'.[80] Despite this rejection, Orage continued to hold Read in high esteem. When he decided to resign as editor, he wrote to Read asking whether he might 'feel disposed to "edit" the N.A. for a year for a couple of guineas a week? Your duties would really be rather small, because practically everything would be arranged'.[81] However, Read declined the offer.

As a columnist Read reveals a keen interest in German literature. On 15 September 1921, for instance, he proposes calling the next intellectual movement 'New Humanism', based on that which 'had its brief life in the latter third of the eighteenth century: that humanism typified in the clear, harmonious intellect of Lessing'. Read argues that this new humanism 'should have found its complete exponent in Goethe, but the unlucky star of modern Europe had already risen in Rousseau, and Goethe fell a victim to its malignity. Goethe is a split genius, a battered torso. It is not difficult to distinguish the good and the bad, the present and the missing in his work. The conjunction of opposites is always there - in *Wilhelm Meister* no less than in *Faust*, in his romantic classicism no less than in his classical romanticism. And all the same he does fulfil Pascal's definition of a genius, which is to contain in oneself opposite extremes and to occupy all the space between them: as Pascal himself did. Goethe is nothing but extremes, and the volume of his work appears to me as no more than literary lumber among which the modern reader must proceed warily to discover the value that does undoubtedly exist there.' (*NA* XXIX, 20, p. 236)

Read was far from insular when discussing contemporary literature. On 6 October 1921, for example, he hopes to see an English translation of Georg Lukács' *Die Theorie des Romans* (1920) (*NA* XXIX, 23, p. 273), whilst on 15 December 1921 he castigates English critics for being 'curiously silent' about Romain Rolland. He notes the recent appearance in English of Stefan Zweig's 'comprehensive study', entitled *Romain Rolland: the Man and his Work*. However, he criticises Zweig for not offering enough analysis of Rolland's

---

78   Quoted by James King, *The Last Modern. A Life of Herbert Read* (London, 1990), p. 39.
79   Quoted by James King, ibid., pp. 69-70.
80   Letter dated 9 February 1920. Quoted by Wallace Martin, op. cit., p. 280.
81   Quoted by John Carswell, op. cit., p. 186.

emotions in wartime. Zweig is more successful with exposition and description. He is wrong to compare Rolland with Goethe because the latter 'had his weak moments', whereas Rolland 'never had his strong ones' (*NA* XXX, 7, p. 81). On 29 December 1921 Read hails a new work on Nietzsche by a French university professor, Charles Andler. *Nietzsche, sa vie et sa pensée*, already running to two volumes, with a further four proposed, is likely to be at the forefront of commentaries on the German philosopher. The first volume examines the forerunners of Nietzsche - Goethe, Schiller, Hölderlin, Kleist, Fichte and Schopenhauer, the French moralists Montaigne, Pascal, La Rochefoucauld, Fontenelle, Chamfort and Stendhal, as well as Burkhardt and Emerson. The second volume ranks as 'a brilliant piece of biography', describing Nietzsche's youth to his break with Wagner (*NA* XXX, 9, p. 103).

Edwin Muir: 'our values before the war and our values now are so different'

Edwin Muir (1887-1959) usually wrote for the *New Age* under the more English-sounding pseudonym Edward Moore. His first published work had appeared in the journal in 1913. As Edward Moore he was responsible for the series 'We Moderns', 'New Values' and 'Our Generation'. A series entitled 'Epistles to the Provincials' by Hengist has also been identified as the work of Muir.[82] By the 1920s work under his real name occasionally appeared.[83] He moved from Glasgow to London at the end of 1919, and, at Orage's invitation, became the Assistant Editor of the *New Age* in January 1920.[84] Orage had hoped to train Muir to write 'Notes of the Week', although this did not succeed and Muir continued to write on subjects of a more literary nature. During this time Muir was experiencing emotional difficulties: between 1917 and 1921 he published no poetry. Orage arranged for him to undergo a course of psychoanalysis, provided free of charge by Dr. Maurice Nicoll, who was a friend of Orage.[85]

Muir's series 'Our Generation' was a sort of literary causerie in the manner of Orage's 'Readers and Writers' and A. E. Randall's 'Views and Reviews'. It often reflects Muir's growing interest in German literature and thought. On 18 November 1920, Muir responds to a reply to the Oxford Manifesto by ten German university professors who are members of the Reichstag. They believe they are 'speaking in the name of German science' and hope that scientific work will contribute to universal harmony. Muir observes that 'for Germans - or even for a

---

82   Wallace Martin, op. cit., p. 279.
83   See, for example, the poem *Ballad of Eternal Life* by Edwin Muir (6 July 1922; *NA* XXXI, 10, p. 121).
84   Wallace Martin, op. cit., p. 279.
85   Edwin Muir, *An Autobiography* (London, 1957), p. 156.

few Germans - to resolve in their agony, which is not tempered by pity of any nation in the world, that they will set themselves to work whose object it is to benefit not themselves merely but the world, is not, in their present condition, a commonplace action but one of those strokes of higher nature which in a work of the imagination would fill us with delighted astonishment. The Press, which is without imagination or even human feeling, will, no doubt, point out triumphantly, that while over fifty professors signed the Oxford Manifesto only ten have replied to it. But how much more effort it must take in a disgraced nation to be magnanimous than in a victorious one! Human nature is so constituted that the greater offence a man commits, and the more need, therefore, there is for repentance, the more difficult it is to repent. This we should recognise before we say that the response to the Oxford Manifesto is disappointing.' (*NA* XXVIII, 3, p. 29)

On 4 May 1922 Muir devotes his column to a recent much-discussed interview with the German foreign minister, Walter Rathenau, in the *Manchester Guardian*. Dr. Rathenau, Muir argues, warrants our attention because he is 'so much more than a foreign minister'. He is 'conscious of psychological entities as distinct from actual political necessities'. Muir quotes Rathenau's speech, in which he argues that '"Everyone is talking of peace as if it existed in Europe. Peace is something more than the absence of shooting. The cannon are in their bastions. You may walk from the Rhine to the Vistula and not hear a shot fired nowadays. Yet peace does not exist. Peace means something positive, not merely negative"'. Muir comments aptly that 'our values before the war and our values now are so different that we cannot find any meeting point between them even in the extremes. To realise this is, in a sense, the beginning of sanity. The European nations in the first year or two of the war fought as normally peaceable communities. They are now struggling for peace as if they were infatuated with war, without knowing that their values are a legacy left behind them by the war in which they were born. A state of mind once it is created is not easily destroyed. It is unconscious of itself and it can only be changed unconsciously, by a great shock, or consciously, by our seeing it in its true form'. Muir perceives that 'psychological conviction' is absent from 'the present state of peace, making it profitless and illusory'. He argues that 'we do not believe, and more important still, we do not feel, that anything is settled, or that there is one little square yard of stability on which the prosperity of a generation can be built. Peace is that state in which men normally have confidence, in which they can approach problems with the belief that they are solvable, and in which it is almost inconceivable, a subversion of natural laws, that practical affairs cannot be efficiently managed. Now the psychological attitude of almost all men is at present the very opposite of this. The inability to do things well is accepted almost as the rule, while problems are *ipso facto* regarded *en bloc* as things incapable of solution. And that being so they are hardly regarded, and it is considered an academic thing merely to be concerned with them and to discover solutions.' (*NA* XXXI, 1, p. 4)

Rathenau's views were followed with some interest in the *New Age*. On 19 January 1922, for example, there was a review of his highly pessimistic vision of Germany, *The New Society*, in which he predicts that Socialism will take control. Nevertheless, as the reviewer points out, the author offers some hope by arguing that 'Germany must forego material ambitions in order to fulfil her world task of culture - *Bildung*, not *Kultur*, a word which Germany ought to prohibit by law for thirty years to come'. The reviewer greets this ideal with cynicism on the grounds that 'intellectual training will not take the place of leisure and freedom; and Herr Rathenau's Work-State, in however heroic mood conceived, is an unimaginable basis for a new culture.' (*NA* XXX, 12, p. 154)

On 10 August 1922 Edwin Muir refers to a recent article on England in *Berliner Tageblatt*, attacking its American author, Arthur Kerr, for saying nothing new (*NA* XXXI, 15, p. 180). This would suggest that at this stage Muir was able to read German. His assimilation of the language was rapid by any standard. When he first arrived at the *New Age* he knew no German and first read Nietzsche in Oscar Levy's English translation.[86] Despite this inauspicious beginning, he would, with his wife Willa, subsequently play an important role in Anglo-German literary relations by translating Kafka into English.[87] In the summer of 1921 the Muirs left England for Prague, stopping off in Hamburg where they 'knew only a few words of German'.[88] In Prague, perhaps encouraged by his colleague from the *New Age* Paul Selver, he began to learn Czech. However, in March 1922 the Muirs moved to Dresden and concentrated on German. By 1923 they were reading Hugo von Hofmannsthal. Between 1924 and 1925 they translated work by Gerhart Hauptmann: his plays *Winterballade* (1917), *Der weiße Heiland* (1920) and *Indipohdi* (1921) and his novel *Die Insel der großen Mutter* (1924). In 1926 they translated Lion Feuchtwanger's *Jud Süß* (1925). At about this time Muir read an article on Kafka, became interested and bought the novels.[89] In 1927 sales of *Jew Süß* were high enough to convince the publisher, Secker, to risk publishing the Muirs' Kafka translations.[90]

On 14 September 1922 Muir explains that in Munich recently there was instituted an association, which may 'be of some account for the culture of Europe'. It is composed of those who say that the writings of Nietzsche have had

---

86   Ibid., p. 182.
87   See Elgin W. Mellown, 'The Development of Criticism: Edwin Muir and Franz Kafka', *Comparative Literature*, 16 (1964), p. 320.
88   Edwin Muir, op. cit., p. 126.
89   Elgin W. Mellown, op. cit., pp. 311-12.
90   Ibid., p. 315.

an effect on both their minds and their lives. The chief members of this Munich group are Thomas Mann, 'the talented novelist', and Hugo von Hofmannsthal, 'a man of genius and a poet for whom we have no peer at present in England'. In the same article Muir also discusses Major C. P. Isaac's *Germany in the Throes.* The author paints a picture of high prices and hard work in Germany where twenty marks are worth only one penny. A newspaper costs three marks. A tram fare has soared from five to eight marks. Goods are more valuable than money. Only the American dollar has any purchasing power. As a result Germans have renamed America 'Dollarika'. Muir comments: '*Das Leben wird jetzt sehr knapp.* Living is getting very difficult.' (*NA* XXXI, 20, pp. 244-5)

The New Spirit in Germany: 'Those three considerable writers, Hans Vaihinger, Hermann Graf Keyserling and Oswald Spengler are in the sun'

When looking towards modern German literature writers in the *New Age* started to explore the work of Hermann Graf Keyserling (1880-1946), Oswald Spengler (1880-1936) and Hans Vaihinger (1852-1933). Since all three writers were indebted to Eastern philosophy, it was perhaps inevitable that Orage, with his post-war leaning towards mysticism and tendency to interpret the work of Nietzsche and psychoanalysts in relation to the *Mahabharata*, should promote *Das Reisetagebuch eines Philosophen*, *Der Untergang des Abendlandes* and *Die Philosophie des Als Ob.* In his *Das Reisetagebuch eines Philosophen*, with its account of the author's travels in India and his rejection of western rationalism in favour of eastern philosophy and intuition, Keyserling observes that in India logic has never assumed the role of providing ultimate answers; that has been left to mystic intuition. Logic has 'either systemised facts, or speculated further on given facts, or analysed what has been discovered in minute detail'. He cautions westerners against reproaching the Indians for never having produced a Parmenides or a Hegel. He perceives that 'the Indians do not equal the Europeans in keenness in logic; it would certainly not be difficult for them to construct similar world systems. They did not do it because, as metaphysicians, they were too profound for this: they knew that logical intellect does not penetrate to the roots; they have never been rationalists. This is then one of the great examples that the Indian people have set the world: that talent for reason does not necessarily bring about rationalism; that a maximum amount of logical astuteness does not necessarily destroy objectiveness.'[91] Spengler, in his depiction of the

---

91   Hermann Graf Keyserling, *Das Reisetagebuch eines Philosophen*, 2 vols (Darmstadt, 1920), I, pp. 115-16.

decline of the Western world, is equally suspicious of the tendency of those in the west to prize their culture at the expense of that in the east.[92]

As early as 1920, a contributor using the pen-name E. M. - possibly Edwin Muir - observes that the first volume of Spengler's *Der Untergang des Abendlandes* (1918)[93] is 'a meretricious work' to those 'who are eternal Europeans'. E. M., who nevertheless admires Spengler, commends instead *Preußentum und Sozialismus*, which has sold over fifty thousand copies in Germany. In this work Spengler attributes Socialism to roots other than Marx, who, according to E. M., is, at best, 'the step-father of Socialism'. Spengler's style can be likened to that of Nietzsche, in that it is 'great but one-sided'. (22 July 1922; *NA* XXXI, 12, pp. 146-7)

The editor of the *New Age* was quick to grasp the significance of the way German thought was developng. On 7 April 1921 Orage admits that he has not yet read Spengler's *Decline of the West* and Keyserling's *Diary of Travel*, but, according to the reports of his friends who have read these works, they are 'of epoch-making importance from their originality of thought and tragedy of outlook'. In his *Der Untergang des Abendlandes* Spengler, according to Orage, 'foresees the approaching end of Western civilisation and regards it as being inevitable. That a German should have this opinion is not a matter of surprise; but I am astonished at the number of non-Germans who share it' (*NA* XXVIII, 23, pp. 272-3). The non-Germans to whom Orage refers must have been able to read German since the first volume of Spengler's *Der Untergang des Abendlandes* was not translated into English until 1926, the second in 1929.[94] Keyserling, the first cousin once removed of the novelist Eduard Graf Keyserling (1855-1918), had expected to see his *Das Reisetagebuch eines Philosophen*, which was based on his tour of the East between 1911 and 1912, published in the autumn of 1914. However, as with the Spengler, because of the outbreak of the First World War, it was not published in Germany until 1919,[95] and first appeared in English in 1925. Vaihinger's *Die Philosophie des Als Ob*, which was written between 1876 and 1878, and published in 1911, was translated into English in 1924 by C. K. Ogden, the editor of the *Cambridge Magazine*.

---

92   Oswald Spengler, *Der Untergang des Abendlandes*, 2 vols (Munich, 1923), I, p. 20.

93   The second volume appeared in 1922. The first volume was already complete in 1913/14.

94   Horst Oppel, *Englisch-deutsche Literaturbeziehungen*, 2 vols (Berlin, 1971), II, p. 93.

95   See Hermann Graf Keyserling's account in *Die Philosophie der Gegenwart in Selbstdarstellungen*, edited by Raymund Schmidt, 4 vols (Leipzig, 1923), IV, p. 114.

However, it was not Orage but Huntley Carter who did most to promote Vaihinger, Spengler and Keyserling in the *New Age*. Before the First World War he had reported on the theatre in various European capitals. In the series after the war, Carter was sent to observe at first hand the 'New Spirit in Germany'. This series of articles, although dealing mainly with cultural developments, could not help but reflect the post-war economic crisis which confronted the traveller in Germany. On 15 July 1920, for instance, Carter reports that his first impression of Cologne was the shortage of food, with hunger and disease constant problems. Crime has become the only solution, with the result that a 'wave of immorality' is sweeping Central Europe. He informs readers that 'the shortage of food and the fear of starvation has simply let loose the very worst criminal instincts of the entire German-Austrian nation'. He is in no doubt that 'a great nation was driven by the reverses of war into the lower stages of immoral conduct. By immoral conduct I mean conduct that destroys the spiritual life of human beings. The story is one of bitter struggle to avert and overcome a food catastrophe'. Vital food was scarce after 1915 and rations were insufficient, therefore 'all sorts of illegal means were adopted to supplement the Government allowance'. In addition, there was what he terms 'sexual immorality' when women, 'even the most cultured and refined, became so devitalised by undernourishment that they seemed to lose all control of their moral faculties'. As a result, there was an outbreak of 'abnormal lust' which 'manifested itself perhaps more markedly in the districts occupied by the Allies. With the coming of our full-blooded, lusty, and vigorous soldiers, possessing vital attractions, that the half-starved German men lacked, women set out in body to trap them, as though under the belief that sexual relations with these soldiers was necessary to restore their own devitalised bodies'. Despite this sorry state of affairs, Carter is convinced that the German people are 'accessible to the emotional impulse of the new idealism which has recently made its appearance in economics, philosophy, and industry, and is strongly manifested in the new forms of art and drama'. He has been assured by a large German publisher that 'there is a demand for solid books' such as Vaihinger's *Die Philosophie des Als Ob* and Spengler's *Der Untergang des Abendlandes. (NA* XXVII, 11, pp. 155-6)

In a letter to the editor the following week Carter elaborates further on the state of philosophy in post-war Germany. Because the German people are in despair, they feel alienated by 'German philosophic speculation, notorious throughout the world for its depth and solidity'. At the same time, he is aware that 'philosophical thought is taking the direction of the general emotional impulse exhibited by the German people'. This contributes to 'the present desire for justice, the desire for ultimate peace. In short, it is inspired by the anti-militaristic spirit', which, he claims, predominates in post-war Germany. Carter perceives that the most obvious change in contemporary German philosophy is 'its break with political influences, and its search for an idealism uncoloured by

Germanism'. In future it will refuse to be 'the handmaiden of aggressive and world-annexing politics. At any rate, Fichtean and Hegelian and the worst side of the Nietzschean political thought and philosophy have lately been walking the plank, and many persons will share our feelings of relief when they go overboard altogether'. Instead, it is 'those three considerable writers', Hans Vaihinger, Hermann Graf Keyserling and Oswald Spengler, who are 'in the sun'. Of those writers Keyserling's *Das Reisetagebuch eines Philosophen* and Spengler's *Der Untergang des Abendlandes* are finding most favour amongst the Germans. (22 July 1920; *NA* XXVII, 12, p. 191)

Two years later Carter is delighted to report that 'a miraculous change has taken place in the mind of the civilised world most deeply punished by the war'. He argues that the 'German people are well equipped to perform the miracle of emerging from the fiery furnace of seven years' unparalleled horrible experience, transfigured bodily and mentally, clothed in a new thought, new action, new language, a new illumination, and capable, if no other nation is ready to do so, of re-uniting Europe in a spiritual and moral harmony, capable indeed of promoting spiritual self-determination not based on separation and isolation, but on unison - a unison without which the world is likely to be ruined beyond all conjecture'. According to Carter, 'present-day Germany is the spiritual heir of Kant, Goethe and Beethoven. It is the secular heir of a long line of thinkers and doers who came after these three, who were bewitched by false materialistic doctrines, and who gradually changed and debased the whole character of the noble structure of practical philosophy, which the three upheld. To the world of Kant, Goethe and Beethoven, the German people really belong. They are seeking to regain their understanding of it and to re-enter it'. Carter likens the Germans to 'lost sheep who have strayed from the fold of humanist traditions and become lost in a world of false realities, materialistic, mechanistic, militaristic, mammonistic and altogether venal. Surrounded by these things they have made a false interpretation of life, mind, morals and society'. Nevertheless, the Germans have also 'preserved the moral principle and the moral purpose inherited from their spiritual ancestors, which by the aid of a new and powerful influence have made it possible for them to survive a crisis so full of terror and disaster, and to maintain a temper which has displayed no sign of undignified resentment'. Carter perceives that 'these two great currents of thought and energy were actually the re-civilising factors which were preparing to sweep over not only Germany and Europe, but the civilised world'. They issued in 'neo-Vitalism or Activism', which 'together with a certain occult influence coming from the East, provided a stimulus to the soul-moving discontent of the civilised peoples'. In this way Germany was 'revitalised and rehumanised, whilst gaining spiritual unity'. Carter points out that 'the great task of the "new world makers" at Versailles should have been to promote this spiritual unity, to build a new synthesis, and not aim at its destruction, and the manufacture of a shoddy imitation of the old Europe through a not very subtle process of political disintegration'. Before the First World War there were no less than three Germanies. The first two were 'merely false guides masked under the forms of just administration and self-protection for the purpose of leading the German people to the servile, humiliating complaisance of a courtier'. The third Germany was 'the re-initiator of Vitalism which was springing up everywhere to oppose obsolete politics and militarism, which in the name of a self-conscious and self-seeking nationalism did not scruple to prostitute the dignity of the German people and so betray their most sacred offices'. Carter argues that 'the fact of the pre-war growth and development of neo-Vitalism - that is, an element made up of eighteenth century idealism, modern science and Eastern philosophy - in Germany, and the persistence of the moral spirit in the German people must be kept well in mind in order to understand the change in Germany during the war and since. For it is due to these great and powerful influences operating largely through adversity on a proud and highly sensitive people that a moral, intellectual and cultural awakening took place during the war in spite of the fact that the German people seemed to be reduced by overwhelming disaster to a condition of hopeless servitude'. Carter finds proof of a 'neo-Kantian philosophic trend' in the great popularity of three books: Vaihinger's *Die Philosophie des Als Ob*, Spengler's *Der Untergang des Abendlandes* and Keyserling's *Das Reisetagebuch eines Philosophen*. These works form 'a philosophical trilogy'. Vaihinger aims to 'prove that all thinking is fiction', whilst Spengler 'handles the hypothesis that the form of thinking called culture is ephemeral' and Keyserling 'handles the unity of thinking and doing on Eastern lines as the only path to salvation for Western peoples'. These works, Carter notices, have run into several editions, with Vaihinger enjoying most popularity, whilst Spengler has 'fallen behind a little'. However, despite the success of *Die Philosophie des Als Ob* in Germany, where it was already running to a fourth edition by 1920, English publishers have shown no interest in Vaihinger. (15 June 1922; *NA* XXXI, 7, pp. 81-2)

German Art: 'some very good things indeed are emerging under the banner of Expressionism'

Carter did not confine his observations to literature and philosophy. On 29 July 1920, for example, he turns his attention to art in Germany. He observes that poets, architects and painters have 'no longer got their eyes fixed intently on sterile technical experiment and intellectual formulae, but are glancing towards the human aspects of life with a real desire to penetrate and express their mysteries'. In Berlin he has seen an exhibition by the group calling itself 'Der Sturm', whilst elsewhere in Germany he has come across 'a movement called Dadaism', which he first saw in Cologne. According to Carter, Dada paintings are 'a wild development of the most extreme of the pre-war Futurist pictures'. He reports that there is 'much yelling and roaring and squeaking among the Dadaists', which he attributes to 'youthful exuberance'. He is more impressed by Kurt Schwitters (1887-1948) of the 'Sturm' group for his *Merzplastiks*, the theatre architecture of Bruno Taut and the commercial architecture of Eric Mendelsohn. He observes that Kandinsky is also influencing a new generation and that there is much talk of 'Expressionismus' as 'the natural culmination of Impressionismus'. He seeks to 'assure intelligent persons in England' that 'some very good things indeed are emerging under the banner of Expressionism, both in the studio and the theatre'. In addition, he commends Paul Klee (1879-1940), whose work he has seen in Munich, and predicts that the satirical drawings and paintings of Georg Grosz (1893-1959), one of the founders of Dada in Berlin, will be well worth watching. (*NA* XXVII, 14, pp. 197-8)

The German Theatre in Wartime: 'Hymns of Hate and spy plays were not a prominent feature'

Carter's excitement about post-war German culture extended to the theatre as well. He finds much to admire there and contends that not only did the German theatre maintain the best traditions during the war, but 'it emerged in a condition that permitted the immediate pursuit of advance'. Even in the First World War the Germans put on fine plays, including works by Shakespeare. At the same time, there was a marked erotic tendency during the war, or, as Carter observes, 'Wedekind's sexual filth was a great financial success'. Even a more commercial venture like Max Reinhardt's Theatre put on 'the excessively erotic *Box of Pandora*' some three hundred times. During the first two months of the war the German theatre, according to Carter, 'lost its balance under a strong wave of patriotism', but then recovered. From that stage onwards two sorts of play were staged. First, there were serious plays in state theatres. Secondly, there were lighter, more erotic plays at privately owned theatres, which in 1920 boast 'sensational naked dancers'. Carter is convinced that 'on the whole, the German war-time theatre was a much better affair than our own. It kept its head. It did not exhibit the bitterness and insane animosity of the English theatre. Hymns of Hate and spy plays were not a prominent feature. International authors were not banned, and plays by Molière, Shakespeare and Bernard Shaw were frequently presented without causing a nation-wide riot'. The theatre in Germany, Carter is pleased to report, has maintained its high standards since the Armistice as well. He notes that the German Revolution inspired some writers who were engaged in it. In this respect he praises Walter Hasenclever (1890-1940) and observes that theatres for revolutionary plays, such as the Tribune in Berlin, are 'springing up no doubt to encourage the present strong leaning towards anti-military plays'. (5 August 1920; *NA* XXVII, 14, pp. 212-13)

Attempts to bring the latest innovations in German theatre to the English stage did not always meet with total success, in spite of the best efforts of the former drama critic of the *New Age*, Ashley Dukes. During the First World War Dukes had fought on the Western front, but felt no desire to write about his experiences.[96] Instead, whilst on leave in Cologne in 1919, he took the opportunity to investigate the latest movements in German theatre.[97] He was greatly impressed by Kaiser's *Von Morgens bis Mitternachts* (1916), which he described as 'the most characteristic prose work the expressionists had produced, and so the best to translate for the English speaking stage'.[98] Dukes' aim to bring German avant-garde theatre to English audiences was far from easy given the anti-German sentiment in post-war England and 'the general hostility to all forms of modernism, German or otherwise'.[99] In the *New Age* A. E. Randall, writing under the pen-name John Francis Hope, watched the import of modern German drama with interest, but no great enthusiasm. On 8 April 1920, for instance, Randall discusses a recent production at the Lyric, Hammersmith of Dukes' translation of Kaiser's *From Morn to Midnight*. Randall attacks Dukes the translator on the grounds that in Dukes' hands the play becomes 'a platitudinous literary exercise which has practically no sense of the theatre'. The cast, which includes Edith Evans,[100] fares little better, possibly, Randall concedes, because the text itself is not inspiring. Kaiser, he argues, 'seems to want dramatic effect without writing for it'. Although the author sought economy of words, he 'chose the wrong ones, and the dialogue lacked point, wit, and beauty' (*NA* XXVI, 23, pp. 367-8). However, Randall was not entirely prejudiced against Ashley Dukes. On 20 January 1921 he attacks Storm Jameson's *Modern Drama in Europe* for failing to mention Ashley Dukes who had written *European Dramatists*, based on his articles in the *New Age* ten years previously. (*NA* XXVIII, 12, p. 141)

In the course of 1921 Randall reviews two productions of Wilhelm von Scholz's play *The Race with the Shadow*. At this time in Germany Wilhelm von Scholz (1874-1969) was enjoying great success with his play *Der Wettlauf mit dem Schatten* (1921). On 10 November 1921 Randall discusses a

---

96   Ashley Dukes, *The Scene is Changed* (London, 1942), p. 46.

97   Ibid., p. 51.

98   Ibid., p. 54.

99   J. M. Ritchie, 'Ashley Dukes and the German Theatre between the Wars', in *Affinities. Essays in German and English Literature*, edited by R. W. Last (London, 1971), p. 100.

100   According to Ashley Dukes, Edith Evans was one of the few members of the cast not to withdraw from this 'enemy' German play. Op. cit., p. 63.

performance by the Everyman Theatre, Hampstead. Although the *Daily Herald,* *Daily News* and *The Times* all present a 'John Bullish' reaction by being 'distressed' by the play, Randall counters that there is nothing like it in London. He observes that 'perhaps if we accept the *Race with the Shadow* as part payment of the German indemnity, it may have significance for the *Times* leader writers; it certainly seems to have none for its dramatic critic'. English critics 'object to soul-searching, particularly at a crisis in history. Whatever happens, we must keep reality out of the theatre as we keep it out of politics, we must deal only with effects, never with causes - the penalty being that unless we do we shall have to become masters of our fate'. However, the critics overlook the fact that 'the play puts forward a new theory of artistic creation, and not a Freudian one'. Now we have 'the artist as Recording Angel, the unconscious instrument by which the things that are hidden shall be revealed'. He concedes that 'this, of course, is not the sort of play we are accustomed to', *The Times* calls it 'distressing', the *Daily News* 'pretentious', whilst the *Daily Herald* complains that 'it was made in Germany'. Randall, by contrast, praises it for being 'the most significant and powerful play that I have seen in my life', even though it is a far from perfect with clumsy language. Nevertheless, it 'links up genius with cognition, feeling and willing, and makes the man responsible for his Daemon' (*NA* XXX, 2, pp. 20-1). Earlier that year Randall had already praised the Everyman Theatre, Hampstead for 'the most vital dramatic enterprise in London' when it performed Granville-Barker's version of Schnitzler's *A Farewell Supper.* (30 June 1921; *NA* XXIX, 9, p. 103)

Bernard Shaw: 'Brawling in the Theatre'

Whenever the *New Age* was short of contributors, Orage could always rely on Bernard Shaw to provide material - free of charge. In 1908 alone Shaw estimated that he had donated articles to the value of £1000 to the journal.[101] He held Orage in such high esteem that he provided over two dozen articles until Orage's resignation.[102] Shaw's last contribution, an amusing piece entitled 'Brawling in the Theatre', appeared on 13 January 1921. In the article he criticises what he considers the post-war phenomenon of audiences clapping and slowing down the pace of the play and the actors on stage. For Shaw the 'real culprits' are the playgoers themselves. He contends that audiences 'have been educated quite easily to listen to Wagner's music-dramas without uttering a sound from the first chord of the act until the last, though they had been accustomed to

---

101 Michael Holroyd, *Bernard Shaw II, Vol. II, 1898-1918. The Pursuit of Power* (London, 1989), p. 191.
102 Ibid., p. 192.

uproarious encoring, and to making dead bodies rise and bow, to calling prisoners out of their dungeons into the castle yard to smirk acknowledgements for "Ah, che la morte". If they cannot always repress a chuckle, they can at least refrain from a heehaw'. If playgoers will not comply with his demands, Shaw threatens to write unfunny plays and not amuse his audiences. (*NA* XXVIII, 11, p. 129)

Books for Peacetime

Books about the war continued to appear between 1919 and 1922, as the review columns of the *New Age* reveal. Books reviewed in the *New Age* included *U-Boat 202: the War Diary of a German Submarine*, translated from the German of Lieutenant Commander Freiherr von Spieyel by Captain Barry Domville R. N. This work is deemed interesting because it shows the contrast 'between the spirit of the German and the English submarine commanders'. In the same article there is a review of Coningsby Dawson's *Living Bayonets*, an anthology of letters to the author's family. It contains absurd moments such as when Dawson discovers that God is on the side of the Allies, 'just as Mr. Bottomley did'. Indeed, Dawson's letters sound 'like a speech of the Prime Minister' in that they are full of propaganda and bombast (11 December 1919; *NA* XXVI, 6, pp. 98-9). On 13 May 1920 there is a review of G. F. Nicolai's *The Biology of War*, translated by Constance and Julian Grande. The author, a former professor of physiology at Berlin University, had been imprisoned for protesting against the violation of Belgian neutrality. He condemns 'in the frankest terms German ideas, German militarism and Germany's role in the war'. However, the treatment meets with disapproval. Nicolai displays 'learning astonishing and truly German', but rarely says anything of interest. The reviewer regrets that 'in the worst German tradition he insists on tracing everything as far back as he can go' and on supporting his argument 'with a cloud of authorities.' (*NA* XXVII, 2, p. 30)

Music: 'it is sheer pig-headed stupidity to pretend that there are no other song-writers than Brahms, Schumann and Schubert'

On 13 November 1919 Ezra Pound's alter ego, William Atheling, launches a bizarre attack on the predominance of German lieder in the concert repertoire. He contends that 'it is sheer pig-headed stupidity to pretend that there are no other song-writers than Brahms, Schumann and Schubert; it is quite possible to fill programmes without German music. Indeed, it is 'rank bad art' to play German music and sing the lyrics in English translations which 'have no relation to the melody or the spirit' of the original German. In the case of Brahms, 'the lieder words are in nine cases out of ten such muck that *any* translation would be insupportable, and it is only by reason of the audience *not* understanding the German that they are able to enjoy the singing'. He is in no doubt that what he calls 'the slop of Victorian ballads is due in large part to these German lieder. People imitating the translations of ninth-rate Deutsch zendimendalisch gedichte (sic), adding two quarts of dish-water and removing the weight of the originals, produced the Chappel standardised English song. If singers want these tunes they might, at least, since German is still taboo, sing them in Russian or Yiddish.' (*NA* XXVI, 2, p. 28)

Conclusion: Germany and the *New Age*:
'our wretched German cousins'

From humble beginnings A. R. Orage rose to become an influential figure in literary circles, respected and accepted by members of the intelligentsia. Although possibly not quite the first rate writer and intellectual he aspired to be - his prose style in his *New Age* articles is at times extremely heavy and his constantly changing ideas do not always withstand rigorous scrutiny - his real talent lay in encouraging young, more talented writers by offering constructive criticism and taking the risk of publishing their work. Katherine Mansfield, for example, not only owed her first appearance in print to Orage, but also maintained that he taught her how to write.[1] To more established writers Orage offered a chance to enter into controversial debates with their contemporaries in the pages of the *New Age*, where he allowed them free reign to say what they liked. Thus, he made his periodical a platform for new and provocative thought. At the same time, he allowed his journal to reflect his own changing enthusiasms and concerns as he developed, although throughout he betrays a constant interest in German life and literature. As the editor of the *New Age*, encouraging discussion of issues relating to Germany, Orage acted as an intermediary in Anglo-German cultural relations. Through the articles he published he attempted to present to his readers a balanced view of Wilhelmine Germany.

Given the multiplicity of contributors to the *New Age*, many of them expressing conflicting opinions, it may perhaps appear doubtful whether any single attitude towards Germany can be traced. However, if we consider the themes that recur in the periodical, we may come closer to understanding the perception of Germany of Orage and his circle. In its approach to German politics, literature, art, music and philosophy it betrays none of the Germanophobic outpourings that were the norm during the First World War. Although never the sole work of one man in the way that *Die Fackel* of Karl Kraus or *Die Aktion* of Franz Pfemfert were, it did perhaps share some of the radicalism of contemporary publications in Vienna and Berlin, even if it did not espouse the pacifism of these journals. Indeed, only in Germany would Orage have been 'a pioneer of pacifism in the world'.[2] Pacifists in England 'outrage the proprieties of language when they refer to war as murder'.[3] Whilst Orage was prepared to publish denunciations of the war by the conscientious objector C. H. Norman, he

---

1   Philippe Mairet, *A. R. Orage: A Memoir* (London, 1936), p. 59.
2   16 March 1916; *NA* XVIII, 20, p. 461.
3   20 April 1916; *NA* XVIII, 25, p. 581.

always allowed A. E. Randall plenty of opportunities to counter with the anti-pacifist argument.

Generally, contributors to the *New Age* favoured some form of armament. As early as 1907 Cecil Chesterton argues that 'one need not be a Jingo to recognise that so long as nations exist they must be prepared to resist by force if necessary the wanton aggression of other nations'.[4] Orage also advocates a defence system, but before 1914 he never perceives Germany as a threat. He claims that 'There neither is, was, nor will be any real German peril to England; but an artificial one is always there to be created'.[5] He fears not German invasion, but the 'triumphant capitalist'.[6]

The *New Age* circle was far from chauvinistic. Perhaps the most outspoken critic of wartime attitudes was Beatrice Hastings. At the outbreak of war she wrote from Paris that she felt there was 'no possibility of suddenly hating my German friends'.[7] She has 'never said anything very bad of Germans, even when their airmen came bombarding Paris; honestly, I couldn't, knowing only nice ones in England, whose worst fault was a confidence in our ideals of liberty which verged on the scandalous'.[8]

It is not until August 1914 that Orage joins in the jingoistic outpourings of his countrymen, when he calls Germany 'the least civilised of the four Western Powers',[9] and suggests that the Allies face an 'untamed, snapping, barking brute' as they confront the 'nakedness of the Teuton'.[10] However, he cautions against an alliance with Russia at a time when England and France are ranged against 'a Germany of which we are the natural and predestined allies'.[11] He concedes that Germany's aim to be ranked as a world power is 'legitimate and necessary to her', even if her methods are 'tragically mistaken'. It is not the act of madmen but of reasonable, fallible creatures - much as we are'.[12] During the height of the hostilities he opposes vilification of Germany on the grounds that 'Germans are men even if they are possessed by a collective madness; and we are to assure them that when their fit is over we shall treat them again as men rather than as madmen'. He believes that the 'people of Germany' are 'much the same as ourselves'. Indeed, 'our wretched German cousins' have become 'temporarily

---

4   2 May 1907; *NA* I, 1, p. 2.
5   13 January 1910; *NA* VI, 11, p. 243.
6   14 November 1912; *NA* XII, 2, p. 27.
7   13 August 1914; *NA* XV, 15, p. 350.
8   17 January 1918; *NA* XXII, 12, p. 227.
9   13 August 1914; *NA* XV, 15, p. 348.
10   20 August 1914; *NA* XV, 16, p. 362.
11   13 August 1914; *NA* XV, 15, pp. 337-8.
12   'The Case for Germany', 9 March 1916; *NA* XVIII, 19, pp. 438-9.

bestial and insane' only under the provocation of popular fear and Prussian ambition'.[13]

Orage's tolerant attitude towards the Germans is shared by both Ezra Pound and Janko Lavrin. Pound, who began his career in journalism at the *New Age*, contributed some highly perceptive pieces on Germany. In 1920 he confesses that he is 'as ready as the next man to see the Kaiser hung, drawn and quartered', but recognises the transience of 'national loves and hates'. He contends that 'You can be ready to torture the man who has tortured you or your brother or your friend in a German prison, but you cannot be made to extend that hate to some other man of a different district, of different features, and maintain that hate indefinitely'.[14] Janko Lavrin also favours reconciliation on the grounds that 'it would be ridiculous to condemn as merely "barbaric" a race which has given the world Goethe, Kant, Bach, Beethoven, Mozart, Wagner, and a score of other great men, of whose works not only Germans themselves but the whole of humanity would be proud'. Germany is 'something of a parvenu', respecting 'learned titles', and is impressed not by original thoughts but 'by the quantity of learned authorities' used to back up an argument. Lavrin suggests that 'in things intellectual, as in things culinary', the German has 'more sense for quantity than for quality'. The Germans mistook 'knowledge and learning' for 'culture itself' but, once the war is over, they may concentrate on real culture.[15]

Only J. M. Kennedy, writing under the pen-name S. Verdad, challenges the faith in Germany expressed by Orage and some of his contributors. In 1910 Kennedy argues that his own experience of Germany within the last few years has proved to him that nothing would be more popular throughout the German Empire than a war with England'.[16] He disapproves of modern Germany, preferring instead the early nineteenth century *Allemagne* of Madame de Staël. Germany was 'a land where the inhabitants were lost in the clouds of abstract idealistic, romantic thought, a land whence no "practical" proposal ever emanated'. The German was 'an amiable sort of clumsy animal' whom the English, a 'thoroughly practical people', could not take seriously.[17] He is convinced that the modern German spirit is so 'thoroughly anti-cultural, anti-poetic, anti-philosophic' that it is inconceivable that it will ever again produce writers of the calibre of Heine or Goethe. According to Kennedy, Wilhelmine

---

13   3 May 1917; *NA* XXI, 1, pp. 1-2.
14   8 January 1920; *NA* XXVI, 10, pp. 153-4.
15   15 April 1920; *NA* XXVI, 24, pp. 383-4.
16   See 12 May 1910; *NA* VII, 2, p. 27.
17   See 13 April 1911; *NA* VIII, 24, p. 555.

Germany is 'too materialistic, too Imperialistic, too modern'.[18] He prefers the Austrians, Bavarians and Southern Germans - 'a peaceful people'.[19]

It is Prussia, rather than Germany, which is criticised in the *New Age*. Orage is sure that 'Prussia alone is responsible for the war'. The Allies must therefore defend Europe and the world against the domination of the Prussians who go about 'with *kultur* in one hand and a bomb in the other'.[20] At the same time Orage is careful to avoid the worst excesses of some of his contemporaries. In an attack on the bellicosity of G. K. Chesterton's *New Witness*, for example, he warns 'it is useless to merely vilify the Prussians' or 'to declare that they must be exterminated like rats before peace can reign'.[21]

Since Prussia is perceived as the true enemy, Orage is dismayed to find England transformed by the war into a state run on Prussian lines. The real war criminals he identifies not as the Germans but 'our capitalist and governing classes', who, 'as the price for destroying Prussianism abroad, are insisting upon establishing Prussianism at home'.[22] The negotiations at Versailles only prove to him that 'the jackboot we have taken off the German people is now on the other leg'.[23] Four years earlier both Orage and Kennedy had accused Lloyd George of threatening England with Prussianism when he came out in favour of conscription. Kennedy brands him 'the Welsh champion of Prussianism in the Cabinet' for lending support to that 'essential feature of the Prussian system'.[24] Orage favours 'voluntaryism' (sic) rather than conscription, or compulsion as it was invariably called by contributors to the *New Age*. He seeks only the 'conscription of wealth' to pay for the war.[25]

Opinion was divided amongst contributors as to which thinkers had influenced German policy. Kennedy could not blame General Friedrich von Bernhardi, the author of *Deutschland und der nächste Krieg*, for the war. In 1912 Kennedy regretted that more Englishmen had not paid taken notice of 'authoritative Germans' such as Bernhardi, who had been 'writing and speaking about the inevitable struggle with England'. He admires the German general for stressing the 'evil effects of pacifism on the average State' and for asserting that it is the 'sacred right' of a nation to 'explain itself by force of arms'.[26]

---

18   28 September 1911; *NA* IX, 27, p. 510.
19   1 October 1914; *NA* XV, 22, pp. 515-16.
20   28 February 1918; *NA* XXII, 18, pp. 341-4.
21   1 November 1917; *NA* XXII, 1, p. 4.
22   17 May 1917; *NA* XXI, 3, p. 51.
23   15 May 1919; *NA* XXV, 3, pp. 33-4.
24   30 September 1915; *NA* XVII, 22, pp. 519-20.
25   4 May 1916; *NA* XIX, 1, p. 5.
26   4 April 1912; *NA* X, 23, p. 533.

The Spanish writer Ramiro de Maeztu was unable to apportion blame for the war to any thinker in particular, tracing instead the cause to a flaw in the German national character. He denies that Treitschke's historical writings were as influential as J. A. Cramb supposed in *Germany and England*. Nietzsche's sole influence on the Germans was 'teaching them how to write beautifully'. Bernhardi was 'only one of hundreds of officers who have used their pen to extol the importance of their trade'. According to de Maeztu, it was not a militarist philosophy which made the German people 'the passive tool of a military caste', but 'the radical pacifism of the German people, its incredible docility, and above all, the mania for abstractions of its intellectual classes, which has withdrawn them from any kind of any political action'.[27]

Orage was far from agreeing with his colleagues. He absolved neither Bernhardi nor the professor of Prussian history, Heinrich von Treitschke, from war guilt, contending that 'the utterances of General von Bernhardi and Dr. von Treitschke are very far from being the exaggerated opinions of specialists; the whimsical beliefs of eccentric people whose views may be disregarded'. He alleges that, contrary to popular opinion, Bernhardi was inspired not by Nietzsche but by Houston Stewart Chamberlain. The 'Treitschke-Bernhardi school includes every German professor, every German journalist, every pamphleteer, every poet, every dramatist, every scholar'.[28] Writing under the pseudonym G. D., Orage accords some of the blame to Carlyle. He reasons that Carlyle wrote a biography glorifying Frederick II, the 'fountain head of Prussian jack-bootery', which is respected in all German universities. The only Englishman to merit the admiration of Treitschke was Carlyle, thus proving to Orage that Carlyle 'had undoubtedly more to do with the cause of the present war than Nietzsche'.[29]

German Culture: from 'the period before the Fall' to the post-war era

Orage encouraged his contributors to take an interest in German literature, art, music and thought before, during and after the First World War. In 1910, for example, he published the short stories of the then unknown Katherine Mansfield now contained in the collection *In a German Pension*. Based on her experiences as a guest in a Bavarian boarding house, Mansfield's depiction of the Germans is not always sympathetic, but offers a first-hand insight into life and attitudes in Germany before the First World War.

Curiosity about Germany and its culture was not diminished by the war. In the post-war period some of Orage's more established contributors, such

---

27   4 March 1915; *NA* XVI, 18, p. 481.
28   15 October 1915; *NA* XV, 24, p. 573.
29   18 March 1915; *NA* XVI, 20, pp. 534-6.

as Huntley Carter, as well as members of the younger generation of writers, such as Herbert Read and Edwin Muir, discussed the latest developments in German literature.   Muir, for example, commends Thomas Mann and Hugo von Hofmannsthal and joins Huntley Carter and Orage in recognising Hans Vaihinger's *Die Philosophie des Als Ob*, Hermann Graf Keyserling's *Das Reisetagebuch eines Philosophen* and Oswald Spengler's *Der Untergang des Abendlandes.*

The *New Age* accorded considerable attention to the German theatre both before and after the First World War, with Huntley Carter contributing a large number of articles on the subject based on his own observations as he travelled throughout Europe. From spring 1911 onwards he depicts Germany as a centre for theatrical innovation, although he disapproves of 'hyper-modern perversities and atrocities' such as Wedekind's *Frühlings Erwachen* and Shaw's *Mrs Warren's Profession.*[30]   During a visit to Germany in 1920 he is still favourably impressed by the German theatre, admiring both its productions of Shakespeare and of modern writers such as Walter Hasenclever. When he turns his attention to art he finds much to praise: amongst the German post-war innovators are Kurt Schwitters, Bruno Taut, Eric Mendelsohn, Wassily Kandinsky, Paul Klee and Georg Grosz.

Carter's reports on the German theatre were originally prompted by the articles of the critic and translator Ashley Dukes who, at Orage's instigation,[31] had introduced modern German dramatists to readers of the *New Age*. In the course of 1910 he had discussed plays by August Strindberg, Hugo von Hofmannsthal, Gerhart Hauptmann, Hermann Sudermann, Frank Wedekind, Ludwig Thoma and Arthur Schnitzler, whom he singled out for particular praise.

Contemporary German writers always fascinated Paul Selver who, in his articles for Orage's literary column 'Readers and Writers', never tried to disguise his 'wholly romantic' attitude to Germany.[32]   Between 1913 and 1915 he discussed Hermann Bahr, Arno Holz, Karl Bleibtreu, Georg Hermann, Schnitzler's stories and Thomas Mann's *Buddenbrooks*. He reacted sharply against the deluge of anti-German propaganda that accompanied the outbreak of war and confessed that he was 'heartily sick of the yelp, yelp, yelp about Huns'.[33] At the same time he relished the absurd translations that the hostilities prompted. Thus, as the Germans try to expunge all enemy words from their vocabulary, they must change Notre Dame to 'Unsere liebe Frau', whilst a dinner jacket, hitherto

---

30   27 July 1911; *NA IX*, 13, pp. 293-4.
31   Ashley Dukes, *The Scene is Changed* (London, 1942), p. 32.
32   Paul Selver, *Orage and the New Age Circle* (London, 1959), p. 55.
33   8 October 1914; *NA XV*, 23, p. 555.

called a 'Smoking' in German, must be 'variously metamorphosed into Rauchjackett, Abendsakko, Frackjacke, Halbfrack, kleiner Frack!'[34]

Selver's interest in German literature is shared by Orage who praises Lichtenberg's aphorisms, commends Schopenhauer whom he regards as 'more English than German', hails Chamisso's *Peter Schlemihl: The Shadowless Man* and Lessing's *Laokoon* as 'a fine example of German criticism in the period before the Fall', and suggests that readers 'skip Hegel' in favour of Kant.[35] After the First World War the *New Age* devoted much attention to the work of Freud and Jung, with Orage again taking a keen personal interest in the subject.[36]

Orage and Nietzsche: 'A little Nietzsche is a dangerous thing'

Arguably the most striking aspect of the *New Age* is the predominance of Nietzsche. It has been estimated that between 1907 and 1913 Orage published no fewer than eighty items relating to the German philosopher, who held enormous appeal for early twentieth century intellectuals.[37] The influence of Nietzsche on Orage can be traced from the latter's early attempts to 'reduce Leeds to Nietzscheism'[38] at the Leeds Arts Club, where he developed 'supermania',[39] to his conclusion that 'Dionysos and Leeds would not mix',[40] and decision to leave for London. There, as editor of the *New Age*, he continued to champion Nietzsche, arguing that the German philosopher 'will always appeal to the Latin more than the Teutonic temperament,'[41] and remonstrating with the first publishers of Nietzsche in English for having priced the philosopher out of the reach of ordinary people.[42]

---

34   1 April 1915; *NA* XVI, 22, p. 589.

35   See *NA* XIII, 6, p. 145, *NA* XVI, 26, p. 695, *NA* XVII, 20, p. 477 and *NA* XVII, 4, p. 85.

36   He hails psychoanalysis as 'the hopeful science of the dawning era'. See 19 June 1919; *NA* XXV, 8, p. 134.

37   John Carey, *The Intellectuals and the Masses: Pride and Prejudice among the Literary Intelligentsia, 1880-1939* (London, 1992), p. 4.

38   Holbrook Jackson. Quoted by Patrick Bridgwater, 'English Writers and Nietzsche', *Nietzsche: Imagery and Thought*, edited by Malcolm Pasley (London, 1978), p. 225.

39   Holbrook Jackson, *New English Weekly. A. R. Orage Memorial Number*, VI, 5 (15 November 1934), p. 114

40   Quoted by Tom Steele, 'The Leeds Art Club: A Provincial Avant-Garde?', *Literature and History*, 14, 1 (Spring 1988), p. 98.

41   17 October 1907; *NA* I, 25, p. 398.

42   20 June 1908; *NA* III, 8, p. 153.

Despite this early enthusiasm for promoting Nietzsche, Orage was quicker than most to seize upon the philosopher's shortcomings. As early as 11 March 1909 Orage distinguishes between Nietzsche the political philosopher and Nietzsche the poet, contending that 'Nietzsche as a poet learned more than Nietzsche as a thinker could ever express. His doctrine, besides, is vulgarly Imperialist. Nietzsche was the German Eagle!'[43] He went on to describe Nietzsche as 'The Lyrical Bismarck', as 'Bismarck's intellectual executor, Bismarck's justification', and identified 'the essentially Prussian, and Imperial-Prussian, character of his speculations'.[44]

Orage was very much alone in his views and was not always in agreement with the Nietzscheans, Oscar Levy, A. M. Ludovici and J. M. Kennedy, who all contributed to the New Age, although Ludovici later praised Orage's perceptive reading of Nietzsche.[45] Orage attacks the Nietzscheans as 'parasites on the weaknesses of Nietzsche, parasites on his weaknesses and mistakes', which Orage considers to be his theories of a new aristocracy and the superman. Nietzsche is 'only at his best when he is demonstrating that man is a caged animal, and is seen beating his head against the bars'. As a 'preacher of human discontent', Nietzsche 'is comparable with Job', but as a reformer, Nietzsche 'is ridiculous'.[46] He is a nihilist 'who destroys with no notions of what is to take its place'.[47]

However, despite his reservations, Orage was swift to defend the philosopher against any suggestion of having inspired German military policy in 1914. Although Nietzsche anticipated a conflict on the scale of the First World War, it was 'for a remote future'. Nietzsche was 'a European who sought to abolish national distinctions within Europe', but Prussia seeks uniformity by spreading Prussian ideas in Europe. He would therefore have condemned Prussia's war.[48] Orage believes that the question as to whether Nietzsche influenced German wartime strategy must be 'left open; for there is as much evidence for the one view as for the other'. He finds that Nietzsche's work is full of ambiguities because Nietzsche, 'not being a man of action', was never 'compelled to make up his mind upon any point': he 'could afford (or he allowed himself) to express contradictory judgements upon almost every problem that occurred to him'. Indeed, there is 'too much praise of force in Nietzsche to permit us to doubt that if the unity of Europe had been achieved by force he would have

---

43   NA IV, 20, p. 399.
44   27 January 1910; NA VI, 13, p. 304.
45   See 14 November 1918; NA XXIII, 3, p. 41.
46   1 December 1910; NA VIII, 5, p. 107.
47   22 August 1912; NA XI, 17, p. 398.
48   27 August 1914; NA XV, 17, p. 396.

repudiated it'. Thus, in 1917, a 'Lyrical Bismarck' still 'best defines Nietzsche in relation to Germany'.[49] Before the war the Germans 'swallowed his praise and ignored his warnings'. He is 'only a blessing outside Germany' and 'more of a danger than a saviour' in his own country, since, according to Orage, his vocabulary is 'for the most part militarist'.[50] In 1919 Orage predicts that Nietzsche will be superseded 'before very long', probably by psychoanalysis and Indian philosophy. Whilst some 'fragments' may be worth preserving, the 'Nietzsche of the future may be contained in a very small volume', comprising mainly aphorisms. He doubts if the German will be read in his entirety again and sees little appeal to the post-war generation on the grounds that 'Germany refused to attend to Nietzsche after 1870 when he spoke to them as one alive; they are less likely to listen to a voice from the dead after 1918'.[51]

Perhaps Orage's most valuable contribution to Anglo-German literary relations was his indefatigable promotion of Nietzsche to an English audience. This lies not only in his wholehearted admiration for the philosopher, expressed both at the Leeds Arts Club and in his books *Nietzsche: the Dionysian Spirit of the Age* (1906) and *Nietzsche in Outline and Aphorism* (1907), but also in his defence of Nietzsche against the more outrageous claims of wartime propagandists and in his criticism of Nietzsche and the Nietzscheans. In view of the pitfalls into which both the devotee and the opponent of Nietzsche may tumble, as highlighted by Orage, it might be fitting to conclude with his own epigram on the subject:

'Drink deep or taste not the Nietzschean spring
A little Nietzsche is a dangerous thing'.[52]

49   14 June 1917; *NA* XX, 7, p. 158.
50   4 September 1919; *NA* XXV, 19, p. 310.
51   18 December 1919; *NA* XXVI, 7, pp. 109-10.
52   20 August 1914; *NA* XV, 17, p. 396.

THE
NEW AGE

A WEEKLY REVIEW OF POLITICS, LITERATURE, AND ART.

No. 1286] New Series. Vol. XXI. No. 1. THURSDAY, MAY 3, 1917. [Registered at G.P.O. as a Newspaper.] SIXPENCE

CONTENTS.

	PAGE
NOTES OF THE WEEK	1
FOREIGN AFFAIRS. By S. Verdad . . .	4
TOWARDS NATIONAL GUILDS. By National Guildsmen	5
THE COLLECTED PAPERS OF ANTHONY FARLEY. Edited by S. G. H.	6
EDUCATION FOR LIBERTY. By Kenneth Richmond	8
NOTES ON SLAVONIC AND OTHER NAMES. By P. Selver	9
THE FAILURE OF THE NATIONAL CHURCH. By a Trade Unionist	10
READERS AND WRITERS. By R. H. C. . .	12
TWO TUPPENNY ONES, PLEASE. By Katherine Mansfield	13
WE MODERNS. By Edward Moore . . .	14

	PAGE
INTERVIEWS : V.—MR. JACOB EPSTEIN. By C. E. Bechhofer	15
A DEFENCE OF TAILORS. By Dikran Kouyoumdjian	16
AN INDUSTRIAL SYMPOSIUM. Conducted by Huntly Carter	17
(62) Professor T. A. Smiddy.	
IN THE BARBER'S SALOON. By Anton Tchehov. (Translated by P. Selver)	19
REVIEWS	20
PASTICHE. By W. M. H., H. F. . . .	21
LETTERS TO THE EDITOR from E. T., A Soldier, George Raffalovich, Frederick H. Evans, Meredith Starr, F. F. Fowell, Harry W. Leggett	22
MEMORANDA (from last week's NEW AGE) . .	23
PRESS CUTTINGS	24

NOTES OF THE WEEK.

WE are glad to see that the "Times Literary Supplement" supports our view of Germany, for the "Times" is not likely to be accused of writing with the hidden hand. We are to remember, says our authority, that Germans are men even if they are men possessed by a collective madness; and we are to assure them that when their fit is over we shall treat them again as men rather than as madmen. This view, besides being obviously wise—for the alternative, as we have pointed out before, is a war of extermination—has ample immediate evidence, and evidence, too, which accumulates from day to day. The strikes in Germany to which attention was drawn last week have multiplied instead of diminished under the threat of General Gröner that he would treat the "traitors" without mercy; and the appeals of the profiteers for more profits have redoubled with the prospect of the complete loss of their American shipping. But are not profiteering and threats against strikers common in England? Precisely the same code-book of official language appears to be in use in the two countries. It follows, therefore, that the people of Germany are much the same as ourselves with only, perhaps, these differences in our favour : that we are somewhat less of a mere population and more of a people; and that we can be driven to a rebellion. How soon, however, we may be deprived of these distinctions nobody can say; but when they are gone our superiority will have gone with them.

* * *

America's entry into the war will in all probability shorten the war—confining it, let us hope, to the harvest of this year—but in all certainty it will bestow upon us another boon, the boon of ensuring peace when once peace is re-established. The obligation we shall thereby have put ourselves under to America need not be onerous or humiliating unless we choose to make it so. America's present attitude towards England is inevitably, it is true, a little suspicious, as the "Times' " Washington Correspondent has been careful to point out; and it threatens at any moment, with much justification, to become a little patronising ; but all this

atmosphere of faint distrust and positive tendency to regard us with pathos can be dissipated if we adopt the right means. What are they? Put somewhat crudely they are that England should behave both in the war itself and in the political problems arising out of and connected with the war like a great gentleman. America, it must never be forgotten, is in the position of a nouveau riche among nations, but of a nouveau riche aware of and fully entitled to a splendid future. What America, therefore, demands of England is ideals; and it is with practical idealism, above everything else, that we must repay America for her help unless we are to lose prestige by it. For this reason, if for no other, we were delighted to see the passage in the official Admiralty report which counted ourselves fortunate in being able to save the lives of German officers and men in the recent sea-fight ; and no less were we charmed by the courtesy of the Vice-Admiral of the Dover patrol in sending a wreath inscribed "To a brave enemy" to the burial of the German dead. Such acts are both English in spirit and American in aspiration. That Lord Beresford and others of his sort should regard such actions as exhibiting "maudlin sentimentality" and "shoddy chivalry" is nothing against them. Lord Beresford has always played in melodrama rather than in tragedy ; and nature has cast him for a comic role.

* * *

No less, and for much the same reasons, are we glad to see that the adoption by the Government of the policy of Reprisals has aroused protests in many quarters. If not published, however, merely for export, they ought to put an end to the policy before it is any further pursued. Wreaking vengeance on the innocent is not, in any event, likely to be effective, for the simple reason that it assumes in the enemy a disposition of mind which the original act has already disproved ; and upon every other ground that can be taken Reprisals can be shown to be definitely wrong. By reprising upon illegitimate acts on the part of the enemy not only do we descend to his level (thereby robbing ourselves of the inestimable advantage of moral superiority) ; not only do we by implication declare that rule and order are no match for anarchism (thereby abandoning our claim to be re-establishing

1 Front cover of the *New Age*

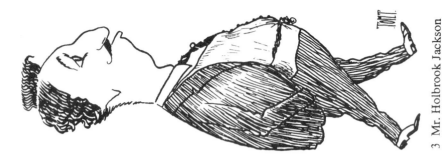

3 Mr. Holbrook Jackson

2 Mr. Bernard Shaw

5 Mr. Cecil Chesterton

4 Mr. G. K. Chesterton

271

7 Mr. H. G. Wells

6 Mr. Arnold Bennett

9 Mr. Ezra Pound

8 Mr. Hilaire Belloc

11 Mr. J. M. Kennedy

10 Mr. C. H. Norman

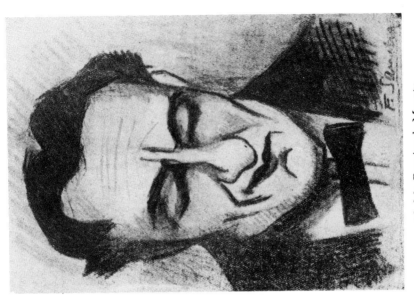

13 Mr. Ramiro de Maeztu

12 Mrs. Beatrice Hastings

275

Appendix 1: Poems by Nietzsche in Translation

The verse translations by E.M. that appeared in the *New Age* may be compared with the original poems, all contained in Nietzsche, *Gedichte aus den Werken und Aufzeichnungen der Jahre 1882-1888*, in *Gesammelte Werke*, edited by Richard Oehler, Max Oehler and Friedrich Chr. Würzbach, 23 vols (Munich, 1927), XX, pp. 155-235, and the first English translations by John Gray, in *A Genealogy of Morals. Poems by Friedrich Nietzsche*, edited by Alexander Tille (London, 1899), pp. 262-85.

Among Enemies (From a Gypsy Proverb)

There's the gallows, here's the halter
And the red-beard hangman, see!
Round me, crowds with poisonous glances -
    But it's nothing new to me!
This I learned from myriad ventures,
    Laughing in your face I cry -
What's the use of you to hang me?
Kill me? Why, I cannot die!

You're the beggars, for you envy
    What your life has never won.
True, I suffer, yes, I suffer,
    Ah, but you! you're dead and done!
After myriad deadly ventures
    Light and cloud and breath am I -
What's the use of you to hang me?
    Kill me? Why. I cannot die!
    (5 September 1907; *NA* I, 19, p. 301)

A Last Desire

Even so to die
As once I saw *him* die -
My friend, who like a God
Cast lightning glances into my shadowy youth,
Wanton and profound,
A dancer in the battle.

Among the warriors the gladdest,
Among the conquerors the saddest,
Building upon this fate another fate,
Hard, looking forward and backward:
Shuddering, *because* he conquered,
Exulting, that in conquering he died.

And as he died, commanding,
Commanding that we should *annihilate*...

Even so to die,
As once I saw him die,
Conquering, annihilating...
    (12 September 1907; *NA* I, 20, p. 311)

The Fire Signal

Here, between the seas the island grew,
Sheer towers in air an altar stone:
Here Zarathustra, under the black sky,
Lights for himself a beacon fire,
A burning question mark for such as have an answer

This flame with gray-white belly
To the cold distance shoots its greedy tongue,
Toward ever cleaner heights it twists its neck -
A snake reared upright with impatience;
This mark I set in place before me.

This flame is my soul itself:
Toward new distances insatiably
Upward, upward burns the wavering fire.
Why fled Zarathustra from beasts and men?
Why parted he sheer from all hands secure?
Six lonelinesses he knows already -
But for him the sea's self was not lonely enough,
The isle bade him mount, on the cliff he is grown to a flame,
After the seventh loneliness now
Searching he flings his hook over his head.

Oh battered sailors! Wrecks of ancient stars!
Ye seas of the Future! Heavens unexplored!
After all things lonely now I fling my hook:
Give answer to the impatience of the flame,
For me, the fisherman on the mountain cliff,
Capture my seventh, last loneliness...
(26 September 1907; *NA* I, 22, p. 342)

Fame and Eternity

Hush!
Of great things - (great things I behold) -
We should be silent
Or else speak greatly:
Speak greatly, oh ecstasy of my wisdom!

I gaze aloft -
There seas of light are rolling,
Oh night, oh stillness, oh sound that is silent as death!
I behold a sign,
Far off, how far!
Slowly there sinks, twinkling before me, the
shape of a star.

Star, of all Being most high,
Table of the eternal imagery,
Comest thou to me?
Thy speechless beauty,
Which hath beheld -
Shrinketh it not before my gaze?

Shield of Necessity!
Table of the eternal imagery! -
But thou knowest it now:
What all men hate,
What alone I love,
That thou *art* eternal,
That thou *art* of necessity!
For at Necessity alone
My love is kindled into eternity.

Shield of Necessity!
Star, of all Being most high!
That no wish can attain,
No Nay can stain,
Everlasting Yea am I,
For I love thee, O Eternity!
   (17 October 1907; *NA* I, 25, p. 391)

Fragments and Parables I

These are the songs of Zarathustra, which he sang to himself that he might endure his last loneliness.

(3)

I am at home on high places,
After high places I have no longing.
I do not lift up my eyes:
I am one that looks downwards,
One that must bless -
All they that bless look downwards.

(5)

All things I gave away,
All my goods and my gear;
I have nothing left to me now
But this great Hope of mine.

(7)

My happiness to come!
What is now my happiness
Casts a shadow in the light of it!

(12)

Dust of shattered stars:
Out of this dust I built a world.

(13)

Not that you overthrew idols:
That you overthrew the idol-worshipper within you,
In this your courage lay.

(14)

There they stand,
The heavy cats of granite,
The values of the old days:
Alas! how will you overthrow these?...
Scratching cats
With muffled paws,
There they sit
And look - poison!

(67)

Cast your burden into the deep!
Oh man, forget! Oh man, forget!
Divine is the art of forgetting.
Do you want to be at home on high places?
Cast your burden into the sea!
Here is the sea, cast your Self into the sea:
Divine is the art of forgetting!
(14 November 1907; *NA* II, 3, p. 50)

Appendix 2: Goethe in Translation

Robert Levy's translation of Goethe may be compared with the original, contained in Goethe, *Gedichte und Epen*, in *Goethes Werke*, edited and revised by Erich Trunz, fifth edition, 14 vols (Hamburg, 1960), I, pp. 273-6.

The God and the Harlot

> Thrice and thrice again M'hadeva
> Comes to Earth, whose Lord he is,
> Taking flesh that he may throughly
> Know our joys and miseries.
> Here he stoops to dwell and suffer
> All things human, human-wise:
> Who could mete out wrath or pardon
> Man must see through mortal eyes.
> In the city he sojurns awhile, the Most Holy;
> He spies out the great, he takes thought on the lowly,
> Departing ere sunset has paled from the skies.

> Comes he where the last low houses
> Lie without the city gates;
> There, with painted cheeks, is waiting
> One, a fair unfortunate.
> 'Greeting, child!' 'Thine handmaid thanks thee
> Gladlier than thou wottest of!'
> 'Nay, who art thou?' 'Lord, a harlot,
> And this house the house of love.'
> And hasting, she clashes the cymbals, advancing
> Bewildering sweet in the whirl of her dancing,
> And gives him a blossom in token of love.

> Coaxing him to cross the threshold,
> Blithesomely she draws him in:
> 'Come, fair stranger, thou shalt help me
> Light the little lamp within.
> Thou art wearied? I'll refresh thee!
> Or thy feet are sore, perchance?
> Thine be all that thou shalt ask me -
> Rest, or jest or dalliance.'
> She busily tends his feigned hurt: he disdains not

Her minist'ring - even her harlotry stains not
The heart he perceives in her touch and her glance.

All mean service he lays on her;
She but joys the more for this;
So by soft degrees grows nature
What had erst been artifice.
Not in vain the petals scatter,
So at last the fruit be whole;
Love is near, when meek obedience
Fills, unquestioning, the soul.
But even yet hardlier seeking to prove her,
The Lord of the Uttermost chooseth to move her
To ecstasy, terror and infinite dole.

So the painted cheeks he kisses,
And she knows the might of love,
For the first time falls a-weeping
At the cruel bliss thereof:
Sinking, not for lust before him,
Nor for wage of harlotry -
Nay, the lissome limbs refuse her
Their bewonted ministry!
And all the while Night has been furtively spinning
A veil for the couch wherunto they are winning,
To screen from the stars the delights yet to be.

Sleep falls late upon their dalliance;
Waking after little rest,
By her heart she finds him lying
Dead, her well-beloved guest.
With a cry she yearns above him,
But she cannot waken him...
Soon they bear him to the burning
Naked, cold and stark of limb.
She hears the priests' death-chant, and frenzy comes
        o'er her:
She raves and runs headlong; folk scatter before her:
'Who art thou that strivest? What wilt thou with
        him?'

'Give me back my man, my husband -
I'll not yield him to the grave!
Would ye burn and bring to ashes
Limbs so godlike, young and brave?'
Down she flings her by the litter,
Shrieking to the Infinite:
'Mine he was! He knew none other!
He was mine for one sweet night!'
The priests sing: 'We carry the old to the burning,
Whose blood hath grown chill in the days of their yearning;
The young, whom Death took ere they wist of his
      might.

'Hear thy priests: thou wert not wedded,
Gavest him no wifely vow;
Nay, thou livest as a harlot,
Naught of duty owest thou.
What shall cleave to him that goeth
Where the silent dead abide?
This the duty and the glory
Of a wife, and none beside.
Ho, trumpets, awake ye the gods from their sleeping!
Ye Holy Ones, take, in quick flame, to your keeping
This youth, this day-flow'r that hath withered and
      died!'

Priestly, pitiless, they double
All the woe she suffereth,
Till, with hungry arms, she flings her
Prone upon the burning death.
But the youth, reclothed in Godhead,
From the ravening flames doth rise,
And in folding arms upbeareth
His beloved to the skies.
The Gods, the immortals, have joy in relenting
Toward children unfortunate, lost but repenting,
And bear them in fiery arms to the skies.
     (6 January 1910; *NA* VI, 10, p. 235)

Bibliography

PRIMARY SOURCES

Newspapers and Journals

Die Fackel, 5 June 1908

The *Manchester Guardian*, 7 November 1934

The *New Age*, 1907-26

The *New English Weekly. A. R. Orage Memorial Number*, 15 November 1934

The *New Witness, 1917*

The Times, 7 November 1934

Published Works

Orage, A. R.,
  Consciousness: Animal, Human and Superhuman (London, 1907)
  Nietzsche: the Dionysian Spirit of the Age (London, 1906)
  Nietzsche in Outline and Aphorism (London, 1907)
  Readers and Writers by R.H.C. 1917-1921 (London, 1922)
  'A Study in Mud' and 'Quixotic Energy', in *Hypnotic Leeds: Being Essays on the Social Condition of the Town*, edited by Albert T. Marles (Leeds, 1894), pp. 17-20 and pp. 43-7

Unpublished Works

Harry Ransom Humanities Research Center, The University of Texas at Austin, Manuscripts by and Relating to A. R. Orage:

Orage, A. R.,
  46 Letters, 3 Postcards, to Holbrook Jackson (1900-34)
  'The Philosopher (On Shaw)', (unpublished manuscript, N. D.)

Jean Orage,
Letter to Holbrook Jackson (N. D.)

SECONDARY SOURCES

Alpers, Antony,
The Life of Katherine Mansfield (London, 1980)

Archer, William,
'Fighting a Philosophy', *Oxford Pamphlets* (November, 1915)
501 Gems of German Thought (London, 1916)

Aschenheim, Steven E.,
The Nietzsche Legacy in Germany 1890-1990 (Berkley, 1992)

Barker, Ernest,
'Nietzsche and Treitschke. The Worship of Power in Modern Germany',
Oxford Pamphlets (1914)

Barlow, D,
'Fontane's English Journeys', *German Life and Letters*, 6 (1953), pp. 169-77

Benn, Gottfried,
Ithaka, in *Gesammelte Werke*, edited by Dieter Wellershoff, 8 vols
(Wiesbaden, 1968), VI
Wie Miß Cavell erschossen wurde, in *Gesammelte Werke*, edited by Dieter
Wellershoff, 8 vols (Wiesbaden, 1968), IV

Bergonzi, Bernard,
'Before 1914: Writers and the Threat of War', *Critical Quarterly*, 6 (Summer
1964), pp. 126-34
Heroes' Twilight: A Study of Literature of the Great War (London, 1965)

Bernhardi, Friedrich von,
Deutschland und der nächste Krieg (Stuttgart and Berlin, 1912)

Blaicher, Günther,
Das Deutschlandbild in der englischen Literatur (Darmstadt, 1992)

Blatchford, Robert,
Germany and England: The War that was foretold (London, 1914)

Bridgwater, Patrick,
'English Writers and Nietzsche', in Nietzsche: Imagery and Thought, edited by Malcolm Pasley (London, 1978), pp. 220-59
Nietzsche in Anglosaxony (Leicester, 1972)
'Three English Poets in Expressionist Berlin', German Life and Letters, 45, No. 4 (October 1992), pp. 301-22

Buitenhuis, Peter,
The Great War of Words. Literature as Propaganda 1914 and After (London, 1989)

Butter, P. H.,
Edwin Muir: Man and Poet (London, 1966)

Carey, John,
The Intellectuals and the Masses: Pride and Prejudice among the Literary Intelligentsia, 1880-1939 (London, 1992)

Carpenter, Humphrey,
A Serious Character: The Life of Ezra Pound (London, 1988)

Carr, William,
A History of Germany 1815-1985, third edition (London, 1987)

Carswell, John,
Lives and Letters (London, 1978)

Ceadel, Martin,
Pacifism in Britain 1914-1945: The Defining of a Faith (Oxford, 1980)

Chesney,
The Battle of Dorking: Reminiscences of a Volunteer, in Blackwood's Edinburgh Magazine, 109, No. 667 (May, 1871), pp. 539-71

Chesterton, Cecil,
The Prussian Hath Said in his Heart (London, 1914)

Chesterton, G. K.,
The Barbarism of Berlin (London, 1914)
The Crimes of England (London, 1915)
George Bernard Shaw (London, 1909)
The Innocence of Father Brown (London, 1911)
The Man who was Thursday (London, 1908)
The Secret of Father Brown (London, 1927)

Childers, Erskine,
The Riddle of the Sands (London, 1903)

Clark, David,
'Douglas', in *The New Palgrave: a dictionary of economics*, edited by John
Eatwell, 4 vols (London, 1987), I, p. 503
'Monetary Cranks', in *The New Palgrave: a dictionary of economics*, edited
by John Eatwell, 4 vols (London, 1987), III, pp. 501-2

Coates, John D.,
Chesterton and the Edwardian Cultural Crisis (Hull, 1984)

Cockburn, Claud,
Bestseller: The Books that Everyone Read 1900-1939 (London, 1972)

Cockett, Richard,
David Astor and the Observer (London, 1991)

Cole, Michael,
'A Profounder Didacticism: Ruskin, Orage and Pound's Reception of Social
Credit', *Paideuma*, 17, No. 1 (Spring 1988), pp. 7-28

Collingwood, R. G.,
The Idea of Nature (London, 1945)

Corrin, Jay P.,
G. K. Chesterton and Hilaire Belloc: The Battle Against Modernity
(London, 1981)

Cumberland, Gerald,
Set Down in Malice. A Book of Reminiscences (London, 1918)

Dodds, E. R.,
The Ancient Concept of Progress and other Essays on Greek Literature and Belief (Oxford, 1973)

Dose, Gerd,
'The Soul of Germany. Bemerkungen zum anglo-amerikanischen Deutschlandbild vor und zu Beginn des Ersten Weltkrieges', in *Images of Germany*, edited by Hans Jürgen Diller (Heidelberg, 1986), pp. 21-55

Dukes, Ashley,
The Scene has Changed (London, 1942)

Elwell-Sutton, A. S.,
Humanity versus Un-humanity. A Criticism of the German Idea in its Political and Philosophical Development (London, 1916)

Ffinch, Michael,
G. K. Chesterton: A Biography (London, 1986)

Field, Geoffrey G.,
Evangelist of Race: The Germanic Vision of Houston Stewart Chamberlain (New York, 1981)

Figgis, John Neville,
The Will to Freedom (Port Washington, New York, 1969)

Fischer, Fritz,
Griff nach der Weltmacht (Düsseldorf, 1961)
Krieg der Illusionen (Düsseldorf, 1969)

Fontane, Theodor,
Aus England und Schottland, in *Sämtliche Werke*, edited by Charlotte Jolles, second edition, 28 vols (Munich, 1971), XVII

Ford, Ford Madox,
The Good Soldier. A Tale of Passion (London, 1915)
Parade's End (London, 1924-8)

Forster, E. M.,
Howards End (London, 1986; Penguin edition)

Fussell, Paul,
The Great War and Modern Memory (New York and London, 1975)

Gawthorpe, Mary,
Up the Hill to Holloway (Maine, 1962)

Gibbons, Tom,
Rooms in the Darwin Hotel (Nedlands, Western Australia, 1973)

Goethe, J. W. von,
Gedichte und Epen, in *Goethes Werke*, edited and revised by Erich Trunz, fifth edition, 14 vols (Hamburg, 1960), I

Grundlehner, Philip,
The Poetry of Friedrich Nietzsche (Oxford, 1986)

Halliday, John D.,
Karl Kraus, Franz Pfemfert and the First World War: A Comparative Study of 'Die Fackel' and 'Die Aktion' between 1911 and 1928 (Passau, 1986)

Haste, Cate,
Keep the Home Fires Burning. Propaganda in the First World War (London, 1977)

Hastings, Beatrice,
The Old 'New Age'. Orage - and others (London, 1936)

Hinton Thomas, R.,
Nietzsche in German Politics and Society 1890-1918 (Manchester, 1983)

Holroyd, Michael,
Bernard Shaw, 4 vols (London, 1988-92)

Hügel, Friedrich von,
The German Soul in its attitude towards Ethics and Christianity, the State and War (London, 1916)

Humble, M. E.,
'The Breakdown of a consensus: British Writers and Anglo-German Relations 1900-1920', *Journal of European Studies* (March 1977), pp. 41-68

'Early British Interest in Nietzsche', *German Life and Letters*, 24 (1971), pp. 327-35

Hyams, Edward,
  The New Statesman: The History of the First Fifty Years 1913-1963 (London, 1963)

Hynes, Samuel,
  Edwardian Occasions: Essays on English Writing in the Early Twentieth Century (London, 1972)
  The Edwardian Turn of Mind (London, 1968)
  A War Imagined: The First World War and English Culture (London, 1990)

Jackson, Holbrook,
  'Personal Recollections', *The Windmill* (1948), pp. 41-50
  Bernard Shaw (London, 1907)

Joll, James,
  'The English, Friedrich Nietzsche and the First World War', in *Deutschland in der Weltpolitik des 19. und 20. Jahrhunderts*, edited by Imanuel Geiss and Bernd Jürgen Wendt (Düsseldorf, 1973), pp. 287-305

Keyserling, Hermann Graf,
  Das Reisetagebuch eines Philosophen, 2 vols (Darmstadt, 1920)

Kilty, Margaret M,
  'Ramiro de Maeztu: Journalist and Idealist' (unpublished MA dissertation, University of Leeds, 1962)

King, James,
  The Last Modern. A Life of Herbert Read (London, 1990)

Kirkpatric, B. J.,
  A Bibliography of Katherine Mansfield (Oxford, 1989)

Koester, Eckart,
  Literatur und Weltkriegsideologie (Kronberg, 1977)

Nozick, Martin,
'An Examination of Ramiro de Maeztu', *PMLA*, 69, No. 2 (1954), pp. 719-40

Oppel, Horst,
Englisch-deutsche Literaturbeziehungen, 2 vols (Berlin, 1971)

Petzhold, Gertrud von,
'Nietzsche in englisch-amerikanischer Beurteilung bis zum Ausgang des Weltkrieges', *Anglia*, 53 (1929), pp. 134-218

Read, Herbert and Denis Saurat,
A. R. Orage: Selected Essays and Critical Writings (London, 1935)

Reckitt, Maurice,
As it Happened. An Autobiography (London, 1941)

Redman, Tim,
Ezra Pound and Italian Fascism (Cambridge, 1991)

Reed, T. J.,
Thomas Mann. The Uses of Tradition (Oxford, 1974)

Rempel, Richard A., ed.,
The Collected Papers of Bertrand Russell, Volume XIII, *Prophecy and Dissent 1914-16* (London, 1988)

Ritchie, J. M.,
'Ashley Dukes and the German Theatre Between the Wars', in *Affinities. Essays in German and English Literature*, edited by R. W. Last (London, 1971), pp. 97-109

Rolland, Romain,
Au-dessus de la mêlée (Paris, 1916)

Sanders, M. L. and Philip M. Taylor,
British Propaganda during the First World War, 1914-18 (London, 1982)

Saurat, Denis,
'Visite à Gourdjieff', *La Nouvelle Revue française*, 41 (1933), pp. 686-98

Schmidt, Raymund, ed.,
   Die Philosophie der Gegenwart in Selbstdarstellungen, 4 vols (Leipzig, 1923)

Schönemann, Friedrich,
   'Theodor Fontane in England', *PMLA*, 30 (1915), pp. 658-71

Schröter, Klaus,
   'Chauvinsim and its Tradition: German Writers at the Outbreak of the First World War', *The Germanic Review*, 43 (1968), pp. 120-36

Selver, Paul,
   Orage and the New Age Circle (London, 1959)

Sessa, Anne Dzamba,
   Richard Wagner and the English (New Jersey, 1978)

Sewell, Brocard,
   Cecil Chesterton (Whitefriars, Faversham, Kent 1975)

Shaw, Bernard,
   Dramatische Werke (Autorisierte Übertragung von Siegfried Trebitsch), 5 vols (Berlin, 1921)
   Translations and Tomfooleries (London, 1926)
   'Was ich der deutschen Kultur verdanke', *Die Neue Rundschau*, XXII (Berlin, 1911), pp. 335-49
   What I really wrote about the war (London, 1931)

Spengler, Oswald,
   Der Untergang des Abendlandes, 2 vols (Munich, 1923)

Steele, Tom,
   Alfred Orage and The Leeds Arts Club 1893-1923 (Aldershot, 1990)
   'From Gentleman to Superman. Alfred Orage and Aristocratic Socialism', in *The Imagined Past: History and Nostalgia*, edited by Christopher Shaw and Malcolm Chase (Manchester, 1989), pp. 112-27
   'The Leeds Art Club: A Provincial Avant-Garde?', *Literature and History*, 14, No. 1 (1988), pp. 91-109
   'Nietzschifying Leeds. The Oraging of the Leeds Art Club' (unpublished paper presented to Leeds City Reference Library, N. D.)

Stock, Noel,
   The Life of Ezra Pound (London, 1970)

Taylor, A. J. P.,
   The First World War (London, 1963)

Thatcher, David S.,
   Nietzsche in England, the Growth of a Reputation (Toronto, 1970)

Toller, Ernst,
   Eine Jugend in Deutschland, in *Gesammelte Weke*, edited by Wolfgang
   Frühwald and John M. Spalek, 6 vols (Appl., Wemdin, 1978), IV

Tomalin, Claire,
   Katherine Mansfield. A Secret Life (London, 1987)

Trebitsch, Siegfried,
   Chronicle of a Life, translated by Eithne Wilkins and Ernst Kaiser (London,
   1953)

Turner, L. F. C.,
   Origins of the First World War (London, 1970)

Tymms, Edward,
   Karl Kraus: Apocalyptic Satirist (London, 1986)

Vaihinger, Hans,
   Die Philosophie des Als Ob (Leipzig, 1918)

Villers, Jean-Pierre de,
   Le premier manifeste du futurisme (Ottowa, 1986)

Wallace, Stuart,
   War and the Image of Germany. British Academics 1914-1918 (Edinburgh,
   1988)

Washington, Peter,
   *Madame Blavatsky's Baboon: Theosophy and the Emergence of the
   Western Guru* (London, 1993)

Wearing, J. P.,
The London Stage 1900-1909: A Calendar of Plays and Players, 2 vols
(London, 1981)

Wehler, Hans-Ulrich,
Das deutsche Kaiserreich 1871-1918, third edition (Göttingen, 1980)

Welch, Louise,
Orage with Gurdjieff in America (Boston, London, Melbourne and Henley,
1982)

Wells, H. G.,
Mr Britling sees it through (London, 1916)
The War in the Air (London, 1914)

Willett, John,
The Theatre of Erwin Piscator (London, 1978)

Wilson, Colin,
The Outsider (London, 1956)

Winkgens, Meinhard,
'Die Funktionalisierung des Deutschlandbildes und seiner Konnotationen
einer idealistischen Kultur in E. M. Forster's *Howards End*', in *Images of
Germany*, edited by Hans Jürgen Diller (Heidelberg, 1986), pp. 113-42

Woods, Oliver and James Bishop,
The Story of the Times (London, 1983)

Young, Harry F.,
*Maximilian Harden. Censor Germaniae. Ein Publizist im Widerstreit 1892
bis 1927* (Münster, 1927)

Harald Husemann

As Others See Us
Anglo-German Perceptions

Frankfurt/M., Berlin, Bern, New York, Paris, Wien, 1994. 151 pp., 4 fig.
ISBN 3-631-46677-3   pb. DM 53.--*

This collection of articles shows that some media products ought to carry a mental health warning: Some school books still contain simplistic presentations of England and Germany. English and German journalists admit that the entertainment value of their articles sometimes takes precedence over impartial reporting. English children's books may contain a reasonable mixture of good and bad Germans but some wartime films needed more sinister types for propaganda. "Made in Germany" originated in English legislation as a label against German competition but became a German marketing tool. A minister in Margaret Thatcher's cabinet made unprintable remarks about Germany. When they were printed, the Ridley Affair proved to be the beginning of the downfall of Britain's controversial Prime Minister. **Contents:** The image of England and Germany in schoolbooks, fiction, film, television and advertising · The press sometimes puts entertainment above impartial reporting · When a British Cabinet Minister's views on Germany proved too entertaining the Ridley Affair and Margaret Thatcher's downfall ensued

Peter Lang **Europäischer Verlag der Wissenschaften**
Frankfurt a.M. • Berlin • Bern • New York • Paris • Wien
Auslieferung: Verlag Peter Lang AG, Jupiterstr. 15, CH-3000 Bern 15
Telefon (004131) 9402121, Telefax (004131) 9402131
- Preisänderungen vorbehalten - *inklusive Mehrwertsteuer